SAP
Personnel Administration and Recruitment
Technical Reference and Learning Guide

SECOND EDITION

P. K. AGRAWAL

Formerly Program Manager
Tata Technologies Limited
Pune

PHI Learning Private Limited

New Delhi–110001

2011

₹ 550.00

SAP HR PERSONNEL ADMINISTRATION AND RECRUITMENT: Technical Reference and Learning Guide, Second Edition
P.K. Agrawal

Warning and Disclaimer
While every precaution has been taken in the preparation of this book, the author and the publisher do not guarantee the accuracy, adequacy, or completeness of any information contained in this book. Neither is any liability assumed by the author and the publisher for any damages or loss to your data or your equipment resulting directly or indirectly from the use of the information or instructions contained herein.

Trademark Acknowledgements
SAP, SAPconnect, SAPNet, SAPoffice, SAPscript, ABAP, Basis, ECC are registered or unregistered trademark of SAP AG.

All product and service names mentioned in this book are registered or unregistered trademarks or service marks of their respective companies. Use of any product or service name in this book should not be regarded as affecting the validity of any trademark or service mark.

ISBN-978-81-203-4223-1

The export rights of this book are vested solely with the publisher.

Second Printing (Second Edition)   ...   .   **January, 2011**

Published by Asoke K. Ghosh, PHI Learning Private Limited, M-97, Connaught Circus, New Delhi-110001 and Printed by Raj Press, New Delhi-110012.

This book is dedicated to
SAP consultants and users
who deserve to understand SAP much better

Table of Contents

Each chapter is rated for its importance and relevance for functional consultants (FC), users (US), business process owners (PO) and senior managers (SM). In MR you can keep your own rating and in UL, your understanding level.

SAP Menu

Sequence number	SAP Menu (ECC 6.0)	Where covered	Why not covered
	🗁 SAP menu		
1	▷ 🗀 Office		Not PA
2	▷ 🗀 Cross-Application Components		Not PA
3	▷ 🗀 Collaboration Projects		Not PA
4	▷ 🗀 Logistics		Not PA
5	▷ 🗀 Accounting		Not PA
6	▽ 🗁 Human Resources		
6.1	◈ PPMDT - Manager's Desktop		Not PA
6.2	▽ 🗁 Personnel Management		
6.2.1	▽ 🗁 Administration		
6.2.1.1	▽ 🗁 HR Master Data		
6.2.1.1.1	◈ PA40 - Personnel Actions	3.1	
6.2.1.1.2	◈ PA30 - Maintain	1.2	
6.2.1.1.3	◈ PA20 - Display	1.2	
6.2.1.1.4	◈ PA10 - Personnel File	3.1	
6.2.1.1.5	◈ PA70 - Fast Entry	1.1	
6.2.1.1.6	◈ PA42 - Fast entry: Actions	3.1	
6.2.1.2	▽ 🗁 Info System		
6.2.1.2.1	▽ 🗁 Reports		
6.2.1.2.1.1	▽ 🗁 Employee		
6.2.1.2.1.1.1	◈ S_PH0_48000450 - Date Monitori	11.1.6	
6.2.1.2.1.1.2	◈ S_PH9_46000216 - Service Anniv	28.1.2	
6.2.1.2.1.1.3	◈ S_PH9_46000225 - Powers of Att	17.1.6	
6.2.1.2.1.1.4	◈ S_PH9_46000224 - Education an	13.1.6	
6.2.1.2.1.1.5	◈ S_PH9_46000223 - EEs Entered	3.2.7	
6.2.1.2.1.1.6	◈ S_PH9_46000222 - Family Memb	12.1.7	
6.2.1.2.1.1.7	◈ S_PH9_46000221 - Birthday List	5.1.6	
6.2.1.2.1.1.8	◈ S_PH9_46000220 - Vehicle Searc	18.1.7	
6.2.1.2.1.1.9	◈ S_AHR_61016354 - Telephone D	18.1.7	
6.2.1.2.1.1.10	◈ S_AHR_61016356 - Time Spent ir	30.1.8	
6.2.1.2.1.1.11	◈ S_AHR_61016357 - Defaults for F	30.1.8	
6.2.1.2.1.1.12	◈ S_AHR_61016358 - Reference Pe	51.13.6	
6.2.1.2.1.1.13	◈ S_AHR_61016360 - HR Master D:	3.2.7	
6.2.1.2.1.1.14	◈ S_AHR_61016362 - Flexible Emp	3.2.7	
6.2.1.2.1.1.15	◈ S_AHR_61016369 - Employee Lis	3.2.7	
6.2.1.2.1.1.16	◈ S_AHR_61016370 - List of Matern		TM
5.2.1.2.1.1.17	◈ S_AHR_61016359 - Severely Cha		Deleted

Sequence number	SAP Menu (ECC 6.0)	Where covered	Why not covered
6.2.1.2.1.2	▽ 🗀 Organizational Entity		
6.2.1.2.1.2.1	◈ S_L9C_94000095 - Headcount Changes	4.1.7	
6.2.1.2.1.2.2	◈ S_AHR_61016373 - Headcount Development	4.1.7	
6.2.1.2.1.2.3	◈ S_AHR_61016374 - Nationalities	5.1.6	
6.2.1.2.1.2.4	◈ S_AHR_61016376 - Salary According to Senic	30.1.8	
6.2.1.2.1.2.5	◈ S_AHR_61016378 - Assignment to Wage Lev	30.1.8	
6.2.1.2.1.2.6	▽ 🗀 Age/Gender		
6.2.1.2.1.2.6.1	◈ S_PH9_46000218 - Statistics: Gender Sor	5.1.6	
6.2.1.2.1.2.6.2	◈ S_PH9_46000217 - Statistics: Gender Sor	28.1.2	
6.2.1.2.1.3	▽ 🗀 Documents		
6.2.1.2.1.3.1	▽ 🗀 Infotype Change		
6.2.1.2.1.3.1.1	◈ S_AHR_61016380 - Logged Changes in I	44.1.7	
6.2.1.2.1.3.2	▽ 🗀 Report Start		
6.2.1.2.1.3.2.1	◈ S_AHR_61016381 - Log of Report Starts	44.4.6	
6.2.1.2.1.4	▷ 🗀 Administration US		CS
6.2.1.2.1.5	▷ 🗀 Administration Canada		CS
6.2.1.2.1.6	▷ 🗀 Administration Taiwan		CS
6.2.1.2.1.7	▷ 🗀 Administration Japan		CS
6.2.1.2.1.8	▷ 🗀 Administration Malaysia		CS
6.2.1.2.1.9	▷ 🗀 Administration Brazil		CS
6.2.1.2.1.10	▷ 🗀 Administration Public Sector France		CS
6.2.1.2.1.11	▷ 🗀 Administration Public Sector Great Britain		CS
6.2.1.2.1.12	▷ 🗀 Administration Public Sector Belgium		CS
6.2.1.2.2	◈ S_PH0_48000510 - Ad Hoc Query	47.1	
6.2.1.3	▽ 🗀 Tools		
6.2.1.3.1	◈ HRRSM00FBA - External Human Resources Master [		OoS
6.2.1.4	▽ 🗀 Settings		
6.2.1.4.1	▽ 🗀 Current Settings		
6.2.1.4.1.1	◈ S_AHR_61011474 - Define Organizational Units	4.20.1	
6.2.1.4.1.2	◈ S_AHR_61011490 - Define Positions	4.16.1	
6.2.1.4.1.3	◈ S_AHR_61011475 - Define Jobs	4.19.1	
6.2.1.4.1.4	◈ S_AHR_61011491 - Define Jobs (USA)		CS
6.2.1.4.1.5	◈ S_AHR_61011476 - Define Jobs (Canada)		CS
6.2.1.4.1.6	◈ S_AHR_61011132 - Define school information (JF	13.6	
6.2.1.4.1.7	◈ S_AHR_61011133 - Define faculty information (JF	13.8	
6.2.1.4.1.8	◈ S_AHR_61010818 - Assign residence tax collecto		CS
6.2.1.4.1.9	◈ S_L7D_24000324 - Define Shukko Partners		CS

Sequence number	SAP Menu (ECC 6.0)	Where covered	Why not covered
6.2.2	▽ 🗁 Recruitment		
6.2.2.1	▽ 🗁 Appl.master data		
6.2.2.1.1	🔗 PB10 - Initial data entry	52.8	
6.2.2.1.2	🔗 PB40 - Applicant actions	52.13.3	
6.2.2.1.3	🔗 PB30 - Maintain	52.13.2	
6.2.2.1.4	🔗 PB20 - Display	52.13.2	
6.2.2.1.5	🔗 PU90 - Delete	52.23	
6.2.2.1.6	▽ 🗁 Bulk processing		
6.2.2.1.6.1	🔗 PBA1 - Applicants by name	52.16.4	
6.2.2.1.6.2	🔗 PBA2 - Application	52.16.5	
6.2.2.1.6.3	🔗 PBA4 - Receipt of application	52.16.4	
6.2.2.1.6.4	🔗 PBAC - Applicant statistics	52.18	
6.2.2.1.6.5	🔗 PBA3 - Vacancy Assignments	52.16.6	
6.2.2.1.6.6	🔗 PBAB - Maintain Vacancy Assignments	52.16.6	
6.2.2.2	▽ 🗁 Applicant activity		
6.2.2.2.1	🔗 PB60 - Maintain	52.14.2	
6.2.2.2.2	🔗 PB50 - Display	52.14.2	
6.2.2.2.3	🔗 PBA9 - Planned activities	52.14.6	
6.2.2.2.4	🔗 PBAL - Bulk processing	52.14.5	
6.2.2.2.5	▽ 🗁 Print letters		
6.2.2.2.5.1	🔗 PBAT - Execute	52.15	
6.2.2.2.5.2	🔗 PBAK - Print labels	52.15	
6.2.2.2.5.3	🔗 PBA6 - Complete activities	52.15	
6.2.2.2.6	▽ 🗁 Transfer applicant data		
6.2.2.2.6.1	🔗 PBA7 - Execute	52.20	
6.2.2.2.6.2	🔗 PBA8 - Complete activities	52.20	
6.2.2.3	▽ 🗁 Selection procedure		
6.2.2.3.1	▽ 🗁 Applicant pool		
6.2.2.3.1.1	🔗 PBAE - List	52.5.1	
6.2.2.3.1.2	▽ 🗁 Via qualifications		
6.2.2.3.1.2.1	🔗 PBAP - Internal applicants	52.5.2	
6.2.2.3.1.2.2	🔗 PBAQ - External applicants	52.5.2	
6.2.2.3.1.2.3	🔗 PBAI - All applicants	52.5.2	
6.2.2.3.1.3	🔗 PBAG - Via positions	52.5.2	
6.2.2.3.2	🔗 PBAH - Decision	52.16.6	
6.2.2.3.3	🔗 PBAF - Administration	52.16.6	

Sequence number	SAP Menu (ECC 6.0)	Where covered	Why not covered
6.2.2.4	▽ 🗀 Advertising		
6.2.2.4.1	▽ 🗀 Vacancy		
6.2.2.4.1.1	◈ PBAY - Maintain	52.4	
6.2.2.4.1.2	◈ PBAZ - Display	52.4	
6.2.2.4.1.3	◈ PB80 - Evaluate	52.18	
6.2.2.4.2	▽ 🗀 Advertisement		
6.2.2.4.2.1	◈ PBAW - Maintain	52.6.3	
6.2.2.4.2.2	◈ PBAX - Display	52.6.3	
6.2.2.4.2.3	◈ PBA0 - Evaluate	52.6.2	
6.2.2.4.3	▽ 🗀 Recruitment instrum.		
6.2.2.4.3.1	◈ PBAV - Display	52.6.1	
6.2.2.4.3.2	◈ PBAA - Evaluate	52.6.2	
6.2.2.5	▽ 🗀 Info System		
6.2.2.5.1	▽ 🗀 Reports		
6.2.2.5.1.1	▽ 🗀 Applicants		
6.2.2.5.1.1.1	◈ S_AHR_61015508 - Variable Applicant List	52.22.2	
6.2.2.5.1.1.2	◈ S_AHR_61015509 - Applicants by Name	52.16.4	
6.2.2.5.1.1.3	◈ S_AHR_61015510 - Applicants by Action	52.16.4	
6.2.2.5.1.1.4	◈ S_AHR_61015511 - Applicants' Education an	52.5.3	
6.2.2.5.1.1.5	◈ S_AHR_61015512 - Applications	52.16.5	
6.2.2.5.1.1.6	◈ S_AHR_61015513 - Applicant Statistics	52.18	
6.2.2.5.1.1.7	◈ S_AHR_61015514 - Planned Activities	52.14.6	
6.2.2.5.1.2	▽ 🗀 Vacancy		
6.2.2.5.1.2.1	◈ S_AHR_61015515 - Vacancy Assignments	52.16.6	
6.2.2.5.1.2.2	◈ S_AHR_61015516 - Vacancies	52.18	
6.2.2.5.1.3	▽ 🗀 Advertisement		
6.2.2.5.1.3.1	◈ S_AHR_61015517 - Job Advertisements	52.6.2	
6.2.2.5.1.3.2	◈ S_AHR_61015518 - Recruitment Instruments	52.6.2	
6.2.2.5.2	◈ S_PH0_48000512 - Ad Hoc Query	52.22.1	

SAP Customizing Implementation Guide

Sequence number	SAP Customizing Implementation Guide (ECC 6.0)	Where covered	Why not covered
29.4.5.12.1.5	Define personnel subarea grouping for prima	4.5	
29.4.5.12.1.6	Define Wage Type Permissibility for each PS	29.6	
29.4.5.12.2	Define number range interval for check replacem		
29.4.5.13	Vacation Allowance		OoS
29.4.5.14	Holiday Bonus		OoS
29.4.5.15	Commuter Allowance / Route Management		OoS
29.4.5.16	Overseas Salary		CSI 0560
29.4.5.17	Employee Remuneration Information		TM
29.4.5.18	Leave Compensation		TM
29.4.5.19	Standard Wage Maintenance		CSI 0052
29.4.5.20	Seniority		CS
29.4.5.21	External Transfers		
29.4.5.21.1	Wage Types		
29.4.5.21.1.1	Create wage type catalog	29.1.1	
29.4.5.21.1.2	Check wage type group 'External Bank Trans'	29.7	
29.4.5.21.1.3	Check Wage Type Catalog		
29.4.5.21.1.3.1	Check wage type text	29.3	
29.4.5.21.1.3.2	Check entry permissibility per infotype	29.4	
29.4.5.21.1.3.3	Define Wage Type Permissibility for each	29.6	
29.4.5.21.1.3.4	Check wage type characteristics	29.2	
29.4.5.21.1.4	Define employee subgroup grouping for prim	4.9	
29.4.5.21.1.5	Define personnel subarea grouping for prima	4.5	
29.4.5.21.2	Define payee key	37.4	
29.4.5.21.3	Define payee key		CS
29.4.5.21.4	Define permissibility of payee key	37.5	
29.4.5.21.5	External Transfers (Russia)		CS
29.4.5.22	Insurance		
29.4.5.22.1	Create insurance types	21.2	
29.4.5.22.2	Create insurance companies	21.3	
29.4.5.23	Membership Fees		
29.4.5.23.1	Define types	37.2	
29.4.5.23.2	Define Default for Membership Fees	37.3	
29.4.5.23.3	Define union's function	37.6	
29.4.5.23.4	Wage Types		
29.4.5.23.4.1	Create wage type catalog	29.1.1	
29.4.5.23.4.2	Check wage type group 'Membership Fees'	29.7	
29.4.5.23.4.3	Check Wage Type Catalog		
29.4.5.23.4.3.1	Check wage type text	29.3	
29.4.5.23.4.3.2	Check entry permissibility per infotype	29.4	

Reasons for 'why not covered'

Code	Reason
Appraisal	Appraisal module is out of scope of this book.
CM	Compensation Management module is out of scope of this book.
CS	Country specific functionality is out of scope of this book.
CSI	Country specific infotypes are out of scope of this book. Infotype number is given after the word CSI.
Deleted	This report has been deleted by SAP.
ESS	Employee Self Service is out of scope of this book.
FI	These configurations are done by the FI consultant.
Not PA	These modules are not Personnel Administration.
Obsolete	These functionalities are obsolete. They are replaced by other functionalities.
OM	Integration with Business Partners is covered in the book on Organizational Management.
OoS	These nodes are out of scope of this book.
Payroll	Payroll module is out of scope of this book.
TM	Time management module is out of scope of this book.

Preface

If you are a consultant or user of SAP HR Personnel Administration or Recruitment, and at some point you did not know what the values in a particular field meant, or what would be the impact of selecting a particular value, this book is for you. If you did not know whether a certain functionality was supported by SAP, this book is for you. This book is also for you, if you did not know why your system was behaving in a certain way.

This book has evolved from the difficulty that each one of us experiences in 'Managing SAP'. As I constantly struggled, trying to understand the concepts of SAP and explore their linkages with other concepts, I found memory to be a major handicap. So I started taking notes. Before long, I could not find what I had written. Then I started reorganizing my notes. And finally I started feeling more comfortable. I knew where to write when I learnt something new, and I could find things I was looking for.

The notes improved continuously, and then came the desire to share them with others. Hence this book. While writing this book, I have tried to be as clear, crisp and comprehensive as possible.

This book is also meant for users of SAP, business process owners and senior managers of companies, who have implemented, or are in the process of implementation, or are planning to implement, or are evaluating SAP HR Personnel Administration or Recruitment. Their need to understand the subject is not as comprehensive as that of functional consultants. How all these category of readers should use this book is described below.

How to use this book

There are two ways in which you can use this book. You can use it as a learning guide, and you can use it as a technical reference. When you use this book as a learning guide, you have to cover it in several iterations. Each iteration is designed to enhance your knowledge and prepare you for the next iteration.

In terms of job roles one can classify the readers as senior managers, business process owners, users, and functional consultants. Senior managers need to know only the important concepts, and what SAP can do for them. BPOs need to know more of SAP concepts and should have a good idea of how to perform different tasks in SAP. Users need to have a thorough understanding of different tasks they have to perform in SAP and concepts underlying them. Functional consultants need to know everything, or at least everything important.

In the table of contents, each topic is classified in terms of relevance and importance for each category of readers. Each topic is given A, B, C, or X rating for each category of readers. During each iteration, you can decide the role and importance level you intend to cover. You can select the role you are going to refer to in an iteration, based on your job role, but that is not essential. For example, if you are going to be a user of SAP, but do not know anything about SAP, you may select senior manager role in your first iteration. Having learnt important concepts, you may select BPO role in the next iteration. Finally you may select user role. Also, once you become a proficient user, you may go through the book from the perspective of a functional consultant.

In the table of contents, I have left two blank columns. Although I have given an importance rating to each topic, you can decide the importance based on your requirements. For example, if you are not implementing challenge, or corporate functions, or company instructions, you may mark them as not relevant for you. Similarly, you can decide the importance rating. There is nothing sacrosanct about the rating given by me. You may note this rating in the blank column 'MR', meaning my rating. As you read a topic, you will achieve a level of understanding. You can record it in the column 'UL', meaning understanding level. You may use A/B/C/X, or any other rating scale. After you complete an iteration, these columns will help you decide, which topics to revisit.

When you are reading this book, you will need to work on the system. When you are reading only the important concepts as senior manager, it may be possible to read the book without hands-on experience. However, as you go deeper and deeper, working on the system will become more and more necessary.

If you are using this book as a technical reference, apart from the table of contents and index, you can also locate the relevant material by using 'SAP Menu (ECC 6.0)' and 'SAP Customizing Implementation Guide (ECC 6.0)'. Expanded trees of both the SAP menu and the SAP Customizing Implementation Guide are given after the table of contents. Once you find the node in these structures, you will be guided to the relevant chapter. If that node is not covered in the book, that is also mentioned along with the reason for not covering it. In such cases you have to look for information elsewhere; this book will not help you.

You can also use the structure of this book to keep your discoveries in an organized way. You can maintain a Word or Excel document where you record your discoveries either with reference to page numbers or with reference to chapter numbers. You can also share your discoveries with me (agrawal.prem@gmail.com) and help make this book even more useful in future editions.

You can also use the structure of this book for guiding your discussion with the users and recording their input. That document will finally become the configuration-cum-user manual.

Acknowledgements

I am deeply indebted to my employer, my colleagues (particularly Sreedhar Raju, Milind Deval, and Anand Dhodapkar), and my family, who contributed in different ways to make this book possible. I express my sincere gratitude to my publisher, PHI Learning Private Limited, for putting their trust in me and for improving the presentation of this book.

Individual social responsibility

There is no doubt that we must excel in our chosen profession. But our responsibility does not end there. Indeed, we have a greater responsibility of making the world a better place to live in—to address the challenges the world faces, to analyze, to find solutions, to share, to network, and to make a difference. You may have wondered about the diagram on the cover page; it is a plan for a city without traffic lights. There are four articles at the end of this book. You will perhaps find them interesting to read. In particular, think about Samay Daan. You are welcome to get in touch with me (agrawal.prem@gmail.com). Let us make a difference together. It is our Individual Social Responsibility.

P. K. AGRAWAL

Personnel Administration

Infotypes

1.1 INFOTYPE CONCEPTS

Functional Consultant	User	Business Process Owner	Senior Management	My Rating	Understanding Level
A	A	A	A		

SAP Personnel Administration is concerned with the life cycle activities of a company's personnel, usually employees. When a person joins a company he is created as an employee in the SAP system.

SAP lets you keep a surprisingly large amount of information about your employees. This information is organized in logically related sets called infotypes. The screenshot on the next page shows the organizational assignment (infotype 0001) of an employee. In this book, major HR and payroll infotypes are discussed. But before that let us discuss some concepts, which are common to all infotypes.

Personnel number

In SAP, each employee is uniquely identified by his eight-digit personnel number. Thus, even if two employees have identical names, you would be able to distinguish them from one another by their personnel numbers. This number can be system generated, or externally assigned. SAP does not support alphanumeric employee identification. It is also possible to generate personnel numbers in different ranges for different units of an organization.

Validity period

Consider infotype 0001, which contains the employee's organizational assignment. What happens if a person is transferred? You can modify this information in the system. But,

3

Change Organizational Assignment

| 📄 📄 👤 | Org Structure |

Pers.No.	121715		Name	Agrawal Prem
Pers.area	PNCV Pune CVBU			
EE subgrp	E4 DM		WS rule	WSRPG	G SHIFT
Start	01.01.2005	to	31.12.9999	Chng 07.07.2006 QHRPKA000137

Enterprise structure

CoCode	0100	Tata Motors Limited		
Pers.area	PNCV	Pune CVBU	Subarea	CV9Z	TTL
Cost Ctr			Bus. Area	

Personnel structure

| EE group | 1 | Permanent | Payr.area | P1 | Pune CVBU MR |
| EE subgroup | E4 | DM | Contract | | 📄 |

Organizational plan

Percentage	100.00	
Position	99999999	Integration: default po...
Job key	00000000	
Org. Unit	00000000	

Administrator

Group	PNCV
PersAdmin	
Time	
PayrAdmin	

then how do you know where he earlier was. SAP recognizes that employee's information may change over a period, and that you may want to know what it was in the past. Therefore, it lets you assign a validity period to each infotype record. You can even create infotype records for the future. Thus, if you decide that an employee is going to be promoted, and that the promotion will be effective from the next month, you can enter this information in the system. It does not interfere with the current information, or current processes.

Subtype

Some infotypes may have subtypes. For example, there may be different types of addresses. These may be stored as subtypes. SAP has defined which infotypes can have subtypes.

Time constraint

Since SAP lets you create data with validity period, sometimes you may have data conflicts. For example, can you be present and absent at the same time? To control such inconsistencies in data, SAP has a concept of time constraint. Time constraint is an important concept, which ensures that the data makes sense.

TC	Time constraint description	Explanation	Example
1	Record must have no gaps, no overlappings	One and only one record on any day.	0001
2	Record may include gaps, no overlappings	Not more than one record on any day. There may be no records on some days.	0041
3	Record may include gaps, can exist more than once	There may be 0, 1, or more records on any day.	0022
A	Infotype exists just once from Jan. 1, 1800 to Dec. 12, 9999	You can have only one record per employee. History is not maintained. Validity period is always from Jan. 1, 1800 to Dec. 12, 9999.	0003
B	Infotype exists for maximum of once from Jan. 1, 1800 to Dec. 12, 9999	You can have only one record per employee. History is not maintained. Validity period can be anything.	0031
T	Time constraint is based on subtype or subtype table	Each subtype of infotype can have different time constraints.	0006
Z	Time constraint for time management infotypes → T554Y	For some time management infotypes, the record is for a time period (which may be part of a day), and its consistency is checked not only with other records of that infotype, but also with records of other infotypes.	2001

Time constraint applies to the primary key of a table. If an infotype has a subtype, it applies to each subtype. Further, if a subtype has multiple objects it applies to each object. In infotype 0021, child is a subtype. You can have multiple children on the same day. Therefore, should time constraint be 3? No, because each child has an object id, which is part of the primary key. Therefore, time constraint is 2, but still multiple children can exist on the same day.

Action

If SAP stores information about an employee in so many infotypes, what do you do when an employee joins? The answer is obvious; enter the data in so many screens. You would appreciate a user's plight when he has to enter an employee's information in dozens of screens when an employee is hired. What if he forgets some? Running an action, using transaction PA40 partly alleviates this problem. An action presents the user a set of infotypes in predetermined sequence. This sequence is set for you at the time of customizing. Apart from presenting a set of infotypes, an action also usually creates a record in infotype 0000, which serves as a snapshot of important events in an employee's career. What actions your company will have are determined at the time of customizing, and generally include hiring, resignation, superannuation, transfer, etc.

Fast entry

Although many users are uncomfortable with the idea of having to enter the data in multiple screens (as against a single screen which some of them had in their legacy systems), they gradually come to accept it, as it is the amount of data entry that matters, and the multiplicity of screens is a minor inconvenience. However, when it comes to bulk data entry, the effort becomes too much and affects employee's productivity. SAP has provided a solution to this in the form of transaction PA70 (Fast entry). This facility, although available for only a few infotypes, is very useful.

BDC

No book on SAP can be complete without mentioning BDCs. SAP realized quite early that IT professionals are bound to seek short cuts to tedious data entry, and update the data directly in the database tables. If that happened, all the integration that SAP promised would be lost. It has found a way to prevent that. If some smart IT person updated the database tables directly, that data is not seen in SAP. However, SAP has also provided a means to address this need. Your programmers (called ABAPper in SAP parlance as they use ABAP language to write their programs) can write a program for you, which takes an excel or text file and uploads its contents in SAP using the same screens that you use in manual data entry. In this process all the checks are performed, and the accuracy of your data, by itself as well as in relation to other data, is ensured. This is just a faster way of doing the data entry. The only downside is that if you ran it in automatic mode, which everyone does, you miss out on the messages, which could highlight a potential problem. You must ensure that the BDCs created by your ABAPpers create an error file of rejected records and a log file of messages and the users look at these files whenever they run a BDC.

1.2 INFOTYPE PROCESSES

Functional Consultant	User	Business Process Owner	Senior Management	My Rating	Understanding Level
A	A	A	A		

When you use transaction PA30, and enter personnel number, infotype, and subtype if applicable, you could create, modify or delete an infotype record.

Create

If you create a new infotype record, the system gives you a blank screen to fill. You enter the start date, the end date (31.12.9999, if you don't know how long the data will remain valid), and the rest of the information.

When this data changes after sometime, you create a second record, specifying again the start date, the end date and the rest of the information. However, these two records will have overlapping period, and will not be permitted, if time constraint of the infotype is 1 or 2.

In these cases, you need to change the end date of the first record to one day before the start date of the second record. SAP does this automatically for you. Also, if you are creating a record, which overlaps with multiple existing records, SAP splits or deletes them as appropriate.

Change

If you change data in an infotype and save, the old data will be overwritten. It is not possible to know what the information was before the change was made.

If you change the start date or end date of an infotype having time constraint 1 or 2, other records will be changed, or deleted, as appropriate.

Display

Using this method, an infotype record can be displayed for viewing. If you want only to display an infotype record, you can also use transaction PA20.

Copy

If one wishes to enter data afresh, one creates a record, but if the data change is not much, it saves effort to copy and modify. Normally, create gives a blank screen, but in some cases, create also works as copy, e.g. for infotype 0002.

If object id is enabled for an infotype subtype combination, copy works very differently from create. During copy, the record is created for the same object id, whereas during create, a new object id is assigned. Thus, if you have one child and want to create record for the second child, you need to create a record, but if you want to create second record for the first child, you need to copy.

Delimit

Normally creating a new record delimits the previous one. However, when a record is to be delimited without creating another, then this method is to be used. Infotypes having time constraint 1 can be delimited only after an employee's employment status becomes withdrawn. Even then certain infotypes, e.g. 0000, 0001, 0002 cannot be delimited and must remain valid till 31.12.9999.

Delete

An employee's infotype record can be deleted. The system behaviour depends on time constraint. If the time constraint is 1, the first record cannot be deleted, and if any other record is deleted, the previous record's to-date is extended to cover the period of deleted record as well. For infotypes having time constraint 2 or 3, a record can be deleted without causing any side effect.

Overview

Overview shows all records of an infotype. One can specify the date range for which one wishes to see the records. It is also possible to select the record from the overview mode and move to maintain/display mode.

Lock/unlock

SAP permits a two-step data entry process in which one person enters the data and another approves it. Technically, the first person creates a locked record which the second person unlocks with or without modification. The locked record is not used for any purpose, and remains dormant waiting to be unlocked. When you create a new record, it could be delimiting the previous record. In case you create a locked record, this does not happen, but when you unlock it, the same action takes place.

There are two ways of creating a locked record. The user authorization could be set in such a way that when the user creates a record, it is always created locked. Alternatively, the user could create a record and lock it before saving.

Planning data

SAP keeps only part of the information in personnel administration. Some parts of employee's information is kept in personnel planning. From transaction PA20/PA30, you can display some of this information.

Delete personnel number

There may be occasions when you want to delete a personnel number. If you haven't used a personnel number further, e.g. in payroll, you can delete it by navigating from the menu in PA30.

Change entry/leaving date

In the unlikely event of a need to change entry or leaving date, you can use this menu item in transaction PA30. SAP permits this change provided it does not affect data consistency. For example, you can't change entry date of an employee if he has a payroll run prior to entry date.

Exploring SAP

Using SAP effectively requires exploring. There are so many screens and so many fields and icons on each screen that no one can hope to explain everything to you. On top of that, your screen may change, or you may get a new window, depending on the data you enter, or the icon you click. Your best guide is your experience, a spirit of exploration, on-line help, and this book.

1.3 MORE FEATURES OF INFOTYPE

Functional Consultant	User	Business Process Owner	Senior Management	My Rating	Understanding Level
A	A	A	A		

History

Whereas SAP maintains history for all infotypes, it does not maintain the history of corrections. If an infotype is corrected (changed), the new data overwrites the old data, and the old data is lost. If one is keen on maintaining the history of corrections, it can be done by switching on the log.

Reason for change

When creating, or changing an infotype, one can specify the reasons for change. During customizing, reasons for change for each infotype are created as per your needs.

Date of last change

For any infotype record, you can see the date of last change. This field is system maintained, and comes handy when one has to investigate suspect data changes.

User who changed object

For any infotype record, you can see the user who made the last change. This field is system maintained, and comes handy when one has to investigate suspect data changes.

Historical record flag

If you mark a record historical, it is permanently stored on the database and is available for reporting. However, it cannot be changed.

Storing additional information with an infotype

For many infotypes SAP allows entry of free text associated with a record (Edit ➤ Maintain Text). This text is stored elsewhere and not in the infotype. However, a flag is kept in the infotype, so that the system knows when it needs to fetch that data.

Cost assignment

In many infotypes you can create a cost assignment and charge the cost to another cost object, e.g. cost center, project, or order.

Retro accounting

If you were to change salary of an employee from a past date (for which he has already been paid), his payroll needs to run again so as to pay him the differential. Therefore, whenever an employee's master data changes, SAP determines whether his payroll or time management needs to run from a retro date. If the answer to this question is yes, this information is updated in infotype 0003.

1.4   INFOTYPE PROPERTIES

Functional Consultant	User	Business Process Owner	Senior Management	My Rating	Understanding Level
A	A	A	C		

Infotypes have several properties. Important properties are discussed here. In chapter 41, infotype properties are discussed in detail.

Time constraint

Time constraint, which is one of the properties of infotype, has already been discussed.

Subtypes

Some infotypes have subtypes. For these infotypes, SAP usually provides predefined subtypes. In addition, you can define your own subtypes. For some infotypes, subtypes are mandatory.

Additional text

You can permit, or prohibit additional text at infotype level.

Default period

Initial screen of PA30 requires you to specify the period when you create, change, or display infotype data. You can specify default values, which can vary from infotype to infotype, so that the user needs to put in less data entry effort.

Sort sequence

When there are multiple records in an infotype, they are presented in a certain sort sequence. You can assign different sort sequences to different infotypes.

Retro accounting trigger

You can specify the infotypes which trigger retro accounting of payroll and time management. You can even specify that retro accounting should take place only when certain fields of an infotype change.

Entry of past data

You can specify the infotypes in which entry of past data is allowed.

Multiple views of an infotype

SAP permits multiple views of an infotype. For example, infotype 2002 comes in five variants; Attendances, Cost Assignment (Attendances), Activity Allocation (Attendances), External Services (Attendances), and Order Confs. (Att).

Infotypes permitted for a country

In personnel administration, there are too many infotypes. You can define which infotypes (and if required subtypes) are permitted for a country.

Dynamic actions

Depending on predefined conditions, an infotype can call another infotype, set default values, send a mail, etc. These are configured as dynamic actions.

1.5 INFOTYPE SCREENS

Functional Consultant	User	Business Process Owner	Senior Management	My Rating	Understanding Level
A	A	A	C		

Infotype header

In every infotype screen, there is a header which contains information that does not necessarily come from that infotype. For example, in most infotypes, the header would show employee name, which comes from infotype 0002. Also, when you are viewing employee data for a past period, should the header information be for that past period, or should it be for the current period? SAP lets you decide what information is to be shown in the header, and whether it should be for the current period, or for the period of the infotype. The header information can vary from infotype to infotype.

Infotype screen

SAP usually has a large number of fields in each infotype. You may not need all of them. Therefore, during configuration, your consultant decides which fields should be shown on the screen, whether they are mandatory, optional, etc.

A user needs to check that unwanted fields are not shown on the screen, and that the field properties are right. If you don't like what you see, speak to your consultant. Also note that SAP provides the flexibility of having multiple screens for the same infotype. However, whether this feature is used or not, depends on how critical is your need, a management policy.

1.6   INFOTYPES CHECKS, DEFAULT VALUES AND ENHANCEMENTS

Functional Consultant	User	Business Process Owner	Senior Management	My Rating	Understanding Level
A	A	A	C		

Infotype checks

Function exit EXIT_SAPFP50M_002 in enhancement PBAS0001 (transaction SMOD) allows you to carry out your own additional check after making entries on the single screen and validating the fields.

Infotype default values

Function exit EXIT_SAPFP50M_001 in enhancement PBAS0001 (transaction SMOD) allows you to add your own default values on the single screen when creating or copying infotypes.

Infotype enhancements

You can enhance an infotype in Personnel Administration and Recruitment to add additional fields using transaction PM01. These fields are then available in the standard single screen as well as the standard list screen of the infotype.

1.7   INFOTYPES COVERED IN THIS BOOK

Functional Consultant	User	Business Process Owner	Senior Management	My Rating	Understanding Level
A	A	A	C		

Infotype	Infotype text	Area	Chapter
0000	Actions	HR	3.2
0302	Additional Actions	HR	3.3
0001	Organizational Assignment	HR	4.1
0002	Personal Data	HR	5.1
3	Payroll Status	HR	6.1
	Challenge	HR	7.1
	Addresses	HR	8.1
	ned Working Time	HR	9.1
	act Elements	HR	10.1

(Contd.)

Infotype	Infotype text	Country	Other modules/reason	
0019	Monitoring of Tasks	HR	11.1	
0021	Family Member/Dependents	HR	12.1	
0022	Education	HR	13.1	
0023	Other/Previous Employers	HR	14.1	
0024	Skills	HR	15.1	
0028	Internal Medical Service	HR	16.1	
0030	Powers of Attorney	HR	17.1	
0032	Internal Data	HR	18.1	
0034	Corporate Functions	HR	19.1	
0035	Company Instructions	HR	20.1	
0037	Insurance	HR	21.1	
0040	Objects on Loan	HR	22.1	
0041	Date Specifications	HR	23.1	
0054	Works Councils	HR	24.1	
0102	Disciplinary Action & Grievances	HR	25.1	
0105	Communication	HR	26.1	
0139	EE's Applicant No.	HR	27.1	
0553	Calculation of Service	HR	28.15	
0552	Time Specification/Employ. Period	HR	28.16	
0008	Basic Pay	Payroll	30.1	
0009	Bank Details	Payroll	31.1	
0011	External Bank Transfers	Payroll	32.1	
0014	Recurring Payments/Deductions	Payroll	33.1	
0015	Additional Payments	Payroll	34.1	
0027	Cost Distribution	Payroll	35.1	
0045	Loans	Payroll	36.1	
0078	Loan Payments	Payroll	36.2	
0057	Membership Fees	Payroll	37.1	
0128	Notifications	Payroll	38.1	
0267	Additional Off-Cycle Payments	Payroll	39.1	
0655	ESS Settings Remuneration Statement	Payroll	40.1	
0130	Test Procedures	HR	49.7	
0031	Reference Personnel Numbers	HR	51.13	
0121	Ref PerNo Priority	HR	51.14	

1.8   INFOTYPES NOT COVERED IN THIS BOOK

Functional Consultant	User	Business Process Owner	Senior Management	My Rating	Understanding Level
C	X	X	X		

There are over 600 infotypes in personnel administration. It is neither possible nor necessary to cover all of them in this book. This chapter explains which infotypes are not covered in this book and why.

Infotype	Infotype text	Country	Other modules/reason
0005	Leave Entitlement		Obsolete
0010	Capital Formation	01	
0012	Fiscal Data D	01	
0013	Social Insurance D	01	
0017	Travel Privileges		Travel Management
0020	DEUEV	01	
0025	Appraisals		Appraisals
0026	Company Insurance	01	
0029	Workers' Compensation	01	
0033	Statistics	01	
0036	Social Insurance CH	02	
0038	Fiscal Data CH	02	
0039	Add. Org. Assignment CH	02	
0042	Fiscal Data A	03	
0043	Family Allowance A	03	
0044	Social Insurance A	03	
0046	Company Pension Fund CH	02	
0048	Residence Status	02	
0049	Red. Hrs/Bad Weather	01	
0050	Time Recording Info		Time Management
0051	ASB/SPI Data	01	
0052	Wage Maintenance	01, 08	
0053	Company Pension	01	
55	Previous Employer A	03	
	Sickness Certificates A	03	
	Commuter Rate A	03	
	ial Insurance NL	05	

(Contd.)

Infotype	Infotype text	Country	Other modules/reason
0060	Fiscal Data NL	05	
0061	Social Insurance S	04	
0062	Fiscal Data S	04	
0063	Social Ins. Funds NL	05	
0064	Social Insurance F	06	
0065	Tax Data GB	08	
0066	Garnishment/Cession CA	07	
0067	Garnishment: Claim CA	07	
0068	Garnishment: Compensation CA	07	
0069	National Ins. GB	08	
0070	Court Orders GB	08	
0071	Pension Funds GB	08	
0072	Fiscal Data DK	09	
0073	Private Pension DK	09	
0074	Leave Processing DK	09	
0075	ATP Pension DK	09	
0076	Workers' Comp. NA	07, 10	
0077	Additional Personal Data	10	
0079	SI Additional Ins. D	01	
0080	Maternity Protection/Parental Leave		Time Management
0081	Military Service		Time Management
0082	Additional Abs. Data		Time Management
0083	Leave Entitlement Compensation		Obsolete
0084	SSP Control GB	08	
0085	SSP1(L) Form Data GB	08	
0086	SSP/SMP Exclusions GB	08	
0087	WFTC/DPTC GB	08	
0088	SMP/SAP/SPP GB	08	
0090	Additional Income E	04	
0092	Seniority E	04	
0093	Previous Employers D	01	
0094	Residence Status	Many	
0098	Profit Sharing F	06	
0100	Social Insurance B	12	
0101	Fiscal Data B	12	
0103	Bond Purchases	07, 10	
0104	Bond Denominations	07, 10	

(C

Infotype	Infotype text	Country	Other modules/reason
0106	Family/Related Person	10	
0107	Working Time B	12	
0108	Personal Data B	12	
0109	Contract Elements B	12	
0110	Pensions NL	05	
0111	Garnishment/Cession D	01	
0112	Garnishment Claim D	01	
0113	Garnish. Interest D	01	
0114	Garnishment Amount D	01	
0115	Garnishment Wages D	01	
0116	Garn. Transfer D	01	
0117	Garn. Compensation D	01	
0118	Child Allowance	01	
0119	Definition of child allow. (pre 1996)	01	
0120	Company pension fund transaction CH	02, 40	
0122	CA Bonus	01	
0123	Germany only	01	
0124	Disruptive Factor D	01	
0125	Garnishment B	12	
0126	Supplem. Pension D	01	
0127	Commuter Traffic NL	05	
0131	Garnishment/Cession	03	
0132	Garnishment Claim A	03	
0133	Garn. Interest A	03	
0134	Garnishment Amount A	03	
0135	Spec. Garn. Cond. A	03	
0136	Garn. Transfer A	03	
0137	Garn. Compensation A	03	
0138	Family/Rel. Person B	12	
0140	SI Basic Data JP	22	
0141	SI Premium Data JP	22	
0142	Residence Tax JP	22	
0143	Life Ins. Ded. JP	22	
	Property Accum. Sav. JP	22	
	Personnel Tax Status JP	22	
	E.A. Data JP	22	
	Appraisals JP	22	

(Contd.)

Infotype	Infotype text	Country	Other modules/reason
0148	Family JP	22	
0149	Taxes SA	16	
0150	Social Insurance SA	16	
0151	External Insurance SA	16	
0154	Social Security data (IT)	15	
0155	Additional administrative data (IT)	15	
0156	Tax Deductions (IT)	15	
0157	User Administration Data (IT)	15	
0158	Amounts paid by Third Parties (IT)	15	
0159	Seniority (IT)	15	
0160	Family allowance (IT)	15	
0161	IRS Limits USA	10	
0162	Ins. Y.E.T.A. Data JP	22	
0165	Deduction Limits	10	
0167	Health Plans		Benefits
0168	Insurance Plans		Benefits
0169	Savings Plans		Benefits
0170	Flexible Spending Accounts		Benefits
0171	General Benefits Information		Benefits
0172	Flexible Spending Account Claims		Benefits
0173	Tax card information (Norway)	20	
0177	Registration of Country of Birth NL	05	
0179	Tax SG	25	
0181	Additional Funds SG	25	
0182	Alternatative Names Asia	Many	
0183	Awards	Many	
0184	Resume Texts	25	
0185	Personal IDs	Many	
0186	CPF	25	
0187	Family Add. (TH)	26	
0188	Tax Australia	13	
0189	Construction Pay: Funds Procedure	01	
0190	Construction Pay: Previous ER	01	
0191	Construction Pay: Expenses	01	
0192	Construction Pay: Assignment	01	
0194	Garnishment Document	10	
0195	Garnishment Order	10	

(Contd.)

Infotype	Infotype text	Country	Other modules/reason
0196	Employees Provident Fund	14	
0197	Employees' Social Security	14	
0198	Schedular Deduction Tax	14	
0199	Addl. tax deduction	14	
0200	Garnishments DK	09	
0201	Basic Pension Payments CPS	01	
0202	Entitlements CPS	01	
0203	Pension/Valuation Status BAV	01	
0204	DA/DS Statistics DK	09	
0205	Tax Card Information Finland	44	
0206	Social Insurance Information Finland	44	
0207	Residence Tax Area	10	
0208	Work Tax Area	10	
0209	Unemployment State	10	
0210	Withholding Info W4/W5 US	10	
0211	COBRA-Qualified Beneficiary		Benefits
0212	COBRA Health Plans		Benefits
0213	Additional family info	14	
0214	Loan Supplement, Denmark	09	
0215	CP: Transaction Data	01	
0216	Garnish. Adjustment	10	
0217	Employment contract: addit. data	06	
0218	Membership to insurance	06	
0219	External Organizations		Benefits
0220	Superannuation Aust.	13	
0221	Payroll Results Adjustment	07, 10	
0222	Company Cars GB	08	
0224	Canadian Taxation	07	
0225	Company Car Unavail. GB	08	
0227	TFN Australia	13	
0228	Garnishments Finland	44	
0229	Value Types BAV	01	
0230	Supplement to P0008 PSG	01	
0231	Supplement to P0001 PSG	01	
0232	Child Allowance D	01	
0233	'Bilan social' (Social survey)	06	
0234	Add. Withh. Info. US	10	

(Contd.)

Infotype	Infotype text	Country	Other modules/reason
0235	Other Taxes US	10	
0236	Credit Plans		Benefits
0237	Supplement to P0052 PSG	01	
0241	Tax Data Indonesia	34	
0242	Jamsostek Insurance Indonesia	34	
0261	Loading Leave Aust.	13	
0262	Retroactive accounting	Many	
0263	Salary conversion	01	
0264	Family NL	05	
0265	Special Regulations	01	
0266	Supplement to P0027 PSG	01	
0268	Company Loans JP	22	
0269	Not used at present	10	
0270	COBRA Payments		Benefits
0271	Statistics, Public Sector Germany	01	
0272	Garnishment (F)	06	
0273	Taxes—SE	23	
0275	Garnishments—SE	23	
0277	Exceptions—SE	23	
0278	Basic Data Pension Fund	02, 05	
0279	Individual Values Pension Fund	02, 05	
0280	GB View for Contractual Elements	08	
0281	GB View for Beneficial Loans	08	
0283	Archived Objects		PA Archiving
0288	Family CH	02	
0303	Premium Reduction NL	05	
0304	Additional Basic Pay Information	01	
0305	Previous Employers (IT)	15	
0306	Family add.	15	
0309	IRD Nbr New Zealand	43	
0310	Superannuation NZ	43	
0311	Leave Balance Adj	43	
0312	Leave History Adj	43	
0313	Tax New Zealand	43	
0315	Time Sheet Defaults		Time Management
0317	Spec. Provisions NL	05	
0318	Family view Indonesia	34	

(Contd.)

Infotype	Infotype text	Country	Other modules/reason
0319	Private Insurances Indonesia	34	
0320	Official Housing	01	
0321	Employee Accommodations	01	
0322	Pension Payments	01	
0323	Entitlement Group Type CPS	01	
0326	Imputation of Pension	01	
0329	Sideline Job	01	
0330	Payment in Kind	01	
0331	Tax PT	19	
0332	Social Security PT	19	
0333	Disability PT	19	
0334	Suppl. it0016 (PT)	19	
0335	Suppl. it0021 (PT)	19	
0336	Suppl. it0002 (PT)	19	
0337	Prof.Classificat. PT	19	
0338	Absence payment clearing PT	19	
0341	DEUEV Start	01	
0342	Personal Data HK	27	
0343	Contract Elements HK	27	
0344	Additional Family HK	27	
0345	General Tax HK	27	
0346	Contribution Plan HK	27	
0347	Entitlement Plan HK	27	
0348	Appraisal & Bonus HK	27	
0349	Cont/Ent Eligibility HK	27	
0351	Country Information	27, 42	
0352	Additional Family Information (TW)	42	
0353	Income Tax (TW)	42	
0354	Labor Insurance (TW)	42	
0355	National Health Insurance (TW)	42	
0356	Empl. Stab. Fund (TW)	42	
0357	Saving Plan (TW)	42	
0358	EE Welfare Fund (TW)	42	
0359	Tax Data Ireland	11	
0360	PRSI Ireland	11	
0361	Pensions Ireland	11	
0362	Membership view Indonesia	34	

(Contd.)

Infotype	Infotype text	Country	Other modules/reason
0363	Previous Employment Period	01	
0364	Tax TH	26	
0365	Social Security TH	26	
0366	Provident Fund TH	26	
0367	SI Notification Supplements A	03	
0368	No longer used	01	
0369	Social Security Data	32	
0370	INFONAVIT Loan	32	
0371	Retenciones en otros empleos	32	
0372	Integrated daily wage	32	
0373	Loan Repayment JP	22	
0374	General Eligibility	14	
0375	HCE Information		Benefits
0376	Benefits Medical Information		Benefits
0377	Miscellaneous Plans		Benefits
0378	Adjustment Reasons		Benefits
0379	Stock Purchase Plans		Benefits
0380	Compensation Adjustment		Compensation Management
0381	Compensation Eligibility		Compensation Management
0382	Award		Compensation Management
0383	Compensation Component		Compensation Management
0384	Compensation Package		Compensation Management
0386	Health Insurance Ireland	11	
0387	Starters Details Ireland	11	
0388	Union due Ded. JP	22	
0389	Impuesto a las Ganancias AR	29	
0390	Impto.Ganancias: Deducciones AR	29	
0391	Impto.Ganancias: Otro empleador AR	29	
0392	Seguridad Social AR	29	
0393	Datos familia: Ayuda escolar AR	29	
0394	Datos familia: información adic. AR	29	
0395	External Org. Assignment		Compensation Management

(Contd.)

Infotype	Infotype text	Country	Other modules/reason
0396	Expatriation		Compensation Management
0397	Dependents BR	37	
0398	Contractual Elements BR	37	
0399	Income Tax	17	
0400	Social Insurance	17	
0401	Prestaciones/Antigüedad	17	
0402	Payroll Results		Payroll
0403	Payroll Results 2		Payroll
0404	Military Service (TW)	42	
0405	Absence Event	01	
0406	Pension Information	01	
0407	Absences (Additional information)	15	
0408	CBS NL	05	
0409	Execution of Employee Insurances	05	
0410	Transport coupon BR	37	
0411	Taxation Philippines	48	
0412	Reserved PL	25	
0415	Export Status		Interface Toolbox
0416	Time Quota Compensation		Time Management
0419	Additional tax statement info (NO)	20	
0421	Special remunerations (IT)	15	
0422	Social Security Philippines	48	
0423	HDMF Philippines	48	
0424	Work Stopped (F)	06	
0425	IJSS Summary (F)	06	
0426	Orden jurídica México	32	
0427	Deudas por órden jurídica México	32	
0428	Additional data on beneficiary	32	
0429	Position in PS	06	
0430	Fam. Allowance for Processing	06	
0431	View Basic Pay	06	
0432	View: Type of Employment	06	
0433	GB View for Bank Details	08	
0434	GB view for External Transfers	08	
0435	ITF ADP 309 Free Format	06	
0436	ITF ADP 409 Free Format	06	

(Contd.)

Infotype	Infotype text	Country	Other modules/reason
0437	Multiple employment BR	37	
0438	Annual Tax additions—SE	23	
0439	Data transfer information		Time Data Transfer to BW
0440	Receipts HK	27	
0442	Company Car	Many	
0446	Payroll US Fed Taxes	10	
0447	Payroll US Fed Taxes MTD	10	
0448	Payroll US Fed Taxes QTD	10	
0449	Payroll US Fed Taxes YTD	10	
0450	Payroll US State Taxes	10	
0451	Payroll US State Taxes MTD	10	
0452	Payroll US State Taxes QTD	10	
0453	Payroll US State Taxes YTD	10	
0454	Payroll US Local Taxes	10	
0455	Payroll US Local Taxes MTD	10	
0456	Payroll US Local Taxes QTD	10	
0457	Payroll US Local Taxes YTD	10	
0458	Monthly Cumulations	10	
0459	Quarterly Cumulations	10	
0460	Annual Cumulations	10	
0461	Tax Assignment CA	07	
0462	Provincial Tax CA	07	
0463	Federal Tax CA	07	
0464	Additional Tax Data CA	07	
0465	Documents	37	
0467	Add'l SI Notif.Data f.Comp.Agts A	03	
0468	Travel Profile (not specified)		Travel Management
0469	Travel Profile (not specified)		Travel Management
0470	Travel Profile		Travel Management
0471	Flight Preference		Travel Management
0472	Hotel Preference		Travel Management
0473	Rental Car Preference		Travel Management
0474	Train Preference		Travel Management
0475	Customer Program		Travel Management
0476	Garnishments: Order		Garnishments
0477	Garnishments: Debt		Garnishments
0478	Garnishments: Adjustment		Garnishments

(Contd.)

Infotype	Infotype text	Country	Other modules/reason
0480	Enhancement: Contracts Processing	04	
0482	Addit. data family/related person	17	
0483	CAAF data clearing (IT)	15	
0484	Taxation (Enhancement)	03	
0485	Stage	06	
0486	Military Service (PS-SG)	25	
0487	Security/Medical Clearance	25	
0488	Leave Scheme	25	
0489	Voluntary Service/ECA	25	
0490	Staff Suggestion	25	
0491	Payroll Outsourcing		Payroll Outsourcing
0493	Education (PS-SG)	25	
0494	Staff Suggestion Scheme—Evaluator	25	
0495	Retirement Benefits/Death Gratuity	25	
0496	Payroll US Benefits data	10	
0497	Payroll US Benefits data MTD	10	
0498	Payroll US Benefits data QTD	10	
0499	Payroll US Benefits data YTD	10	
0500	Statistical Data	10	
0501	Other Social Insurance Data	10	
0502	Letter of appointment	25	
0503	Pensioner Definition	12	
0504	Pension Advantage	12	
0505	Holiday certificate (B)	12	
0506	Tip Indicators	10	
0507	Superannuation	13	
0508	Prior Service	13	
0509	Activity with Higher Rate of Pay	Many	
0510	Tax-Sheltered Pension (US)		Benefits
0511	Cost-of-living allowance/amount	02	
0512	Reserved HR	01	
0521	Semiretirement D	01	
0525	Child Care	05	
0526	Work & Remuneration Confirmation A	03	
0527	Payment Upon Leaving A	03	
0528	Additional family information (CN)	28	
0529	Additional Personal Data for (CN)	28	

(Contd.)

Infotype	Infotype text	Country	Other modules/reason
0530	Public Housing Fund (CN)	28	
0531	Income Tax (CN)	28	
0532	Social Insurance (CN)	28	
0533	Personal File Management (CN)	28	
0534	Party Information (CN)	28	
0535	Project & Achievement (CN)	28	
0536	Administration Information (CN)	28	
0537	Going Abroad Information (CN)	28	
0538	Separation payment	41	
0539	Personal Data	41	
0540	Family/Related Person	41	
0541	Personnel tax status	41	
0542	Year End Adjustment Data	41	
0543	Social insurance	41	
0544	Social insurance premium	41	
0545	Disciplinary measure	41	
0546	Termination Data	25	
0547	BIK(TAX) Infotype for Malaysia	14	
0548	Supplementary pension funds (IT)	15	
0551	Termination of Contract: Gen. Data	29	
0554	Hourly Rate per Assignment	07, 10	
0555	Military service	41	
0556	Tax Treaty	10	
0557	Additional personal data	41	
0559	Commuting allowance Info JP	22	
0560	Overseas pay JP	22	
0561	Tax Data	32	
0565	Retirement Plan Valuation Results		Benefits
0566	US Pension Plan QDRO Information	10	
0567	Data Container	13	
0568	Anniversary Date History	13	
0569	Additional Pension Payments	12	
0570	Offshore Tax GB	08	
0571	Offshore Social Security GB	08	
0572	Absence Scheme Override	08, 11	
0573	Absence Infotype for Australia PS	13	
0574	Contract Elements Austria PS	03	

(Contd.)

Infotype	Infotype text	Country	Other modules/reason
0576	Seniority for Promotion	06	
0578	PBS Accumulator Correction	09	
0579	External Wage Components		Interface to Payroll
0580	Previous Employment Tax Details	40	
0581	Housing (HRA/CLA/COA)	40	
0582	Exemptions	40	
0583	Car & Conveyance	40	
0584	Income from Other Sources	40	
0585	Section 80 Deductions	40	
0586	Section 80 C Deductions	40	
0587	Provident Fund Contribution	40	
0588	Other Statutory Deductions	40	
0589	Individual Reimbursements	40	
0590	Long term reimbursements	40	
0591	Nominations	40	
0592	Public Sector—Foreign Service	01	
0593	Rehabilitants	01	
0595	Family-Related Bonuses	01	
0596	PhilHealth Philippines	48	
0597	Part Time Work During Parental Leave	01	
0598	Dismissal Protection	37	
0601	Absence History	06	
0602	Retirement Plan Cumulations		Benefits
0611	Garnishments: Management Data		Garnishments
0612	Garnishments: Interest		Garnishments
0613	Absence Donation/Withdraw (US)	10	
0614	HESA Master Data	08	
0615	HE Contract Data	08	
0616	HESA Submitted Data	08	
0617	Clinical Details	08	
0618	Academic Qualification	08	
0619	Equity and Diversity	13	
0622	Contract Elements (Public Sector BE)	12	
0623	Career History (Public Sector BE)	12	
0624	HE Professional Qualifications	08	
0626	Payment Summary	13	
0628	PAISY: USA 21 (Spec. Date Function)	99	

(Contd.)

Infotype	Infotype text	Country	Other modules/reason
0629	PAISY: P5 (Payroll Acct Carried)	99	
0630	PAISY: Other Information	99	
0631	PAISY: USA 15 (Garnishment)	99	
0632	Semiretirement A	03	
0634	Other/Previous Employers	48	
0645	Termination of contract: General data	17	
0646	FVP	05	
0647	GBA	05	
0648	Bar Point Information	08	
0649	Social Insurance (Public Sector BE)	12	
0650	BA Statements	01	
0651	SI Carrier Certificates	01	
0652	Certificates of Training	01	
0653	Certificates to Local Authorities	01	
0656	Nature of Actions	10	
0659	Personnel master record for INAIL management	15	
0661	Termination	37	
0662	Semiretirement A—Notif. Supplmnts	03	
0665	External Pension Rights	05	
0666	Planning of Pers. Costs		Management of Global Employees
0671	COBRA Flexible Spending Accounts		Benefits
0672	FMLA Event		FMLA
0694	Previous Employment Details	34	
0696	Absence Pools	10	
0697	Drug Screening	10	
0698	Loan master to supplement for KR	41	
0699	Pension Provision Act	01	
0701	End Point Australia	13	
0702	Documents		Management of Global Employees
0703	Documents on Dependants		Management of Global Employees
0704	Information on Dependants		Management of Global Employees
0705	Information on Checklists		Management of Global Employees

(Contd.)

Infotype	Infotype text	Country	Other modules/reason
0706	Compensation Package Offer		Management of Global Employees
0707	Activation Information		Management of Global Employees
0708	Details on Global Commuting		Management of Global Employees
0709	Person ID		External person IDs
0710	Details on Global Assignment		Management of Global Employees
0711	Employer number	05	
0712	Main Personnel Assignment		Concurrent Employment
0713	Termination	Many	
0715	Status of Global Assignment		Management of Global Employees
0717	Benefit point account	41	
0718	Benefit request	41	
0722	Payroll for Global Employees		Management of Global Employees
0723	Payroll for GE: Retro. Accounting		Management of Global Employees
0724	Funding Status		Management of Global Employees
0725	Taxes SA	16	
0734	View for IT Basic Pay—Brasil	37	
0735	Dimona Declarations B	12	
0736	Alimony Brasil	37	
0737	Alimony Debt Brasil	37	
0738	Alimony Adjustment Brasil	37	
0739	Stock Option (Singapore)	25	
0741	Additional Information (Singapore)	25	
0742	HDB Concession	25	
0743	Discipline	25	
0744	Blacklist	25	
0745	HDB Messages in Public Sector	01	
0746	De Only	01	
0747	DE Only	01	
0748	Command and Delegation		Structures Workbench
0751	Company Pension Plan AT	03	

(Contd.)

Infotype	Infotype text	Country	Other modules/reason
0752	Declaration of Land/Houses/Property	25	
0753	Declaration of Shares	25	
0754	Declaration of Interest in Business	25	
0755	Declaration of Non-Indebtedness	25	
0757	Tax Credit GB	08	
0758	Compensation Program		Compensation Management
0759	Compensation Process		Compensation Management
0760	Compensation Eligibility Override		Compensation Management
0761	LTI Granting		Long-term Incentive Plans
0762	LTI Exercising		Long-term Incentive Plans
0763	LTI Participant Data		Long-term Incentive Plans
0764	Perm. Invalidity Ben. Act Netherlands	05	
0768	Message Data FDI	04	
0783	ADT		HR Funds and Position Management
0793	Payment Made in Error GB	08	
0808	Salary Notification	05	
0812	Medical Expense for DME	41	
0815	Multiple Check in One Cycle		Payroll
0817	Income Tax Withholding Variation—AU	13	
0848	Bursary Payments SA	16	
0854	Savings Schemes	05	
0858	Donation Expense	41	
0900	Sales Data		Logistics
0901	Purchasing Data		Logistics
2001	Absences		Time Management
2002	Attendances		Time Management
2003	Substitutions		Time Management
2004	Availability		Time Management
2005	Overtime		Time Management
2006	Absence Quotas		Time Management
2007	Attendance Quotas		Time Management

(Contd.)

Infotype	Infotype text	Country	Other modules/reason
2010	Employee Remuneration Info		Time Management
2011	Time Events		Time Management
2012	Time Transfer Specifications		Time Management
2013	Quota Corrections		Time Management
2050	Annual Calendar		Time Management
2051	Monthly Calendar		Time Management
2052	Weekly Entry w/Activity Allocation		Time Management
2500	Personal Work Schedule Times		Time Management
2501	Employee Time and Labor Data		Time Management
2502	Quota Statuses		Time Management

Common Infotype Structure

2.1 OVERVIEW

Functional Consultant	User	Business Process Owner	Senior Management	My Rating	Understanding Level
A	A	A	C		

SAP stores employee data in logical groups called infotypes. Understanding infotypes, what data they hold and how the data is used, is critical for understanding personnel administration, payroll and time management.

Infotypes are given a four-digit number. They are stored in tables PAnnnn, where nnnn is infotype number. Thus, infotype 0008 is stored in table PA0008. Infotypes for applicants are stored in PB series tables.

The structure of any infotype table consists of client and three includes.

Client	When you log on to SAP, you log on to a specific client. The data you create there is available only in that client. Clients partition an SAP server into multiple logical servers. Most data in SAP tables is client dependent, although, there are some tables, which are client independent. However, all infotype tables are client dependent. Therefore, do not expect employee data to be the same across clients. Programs, however, are client independent.
Key for HR Master Data	This include contains fields, which uniquely identify an employee record (primary key). It includes personnel number and validity period.

(Contd.)

HR Master Record: Control Field	This include contains fields of general information, e.g. name of person who changed the object and the date of last change.
HR Master Record: Infotype nnnn	This last include contains the fields pertaining to the infotype.

2.2   KEY FOR HR MASTER DATA

Functional Consultant	User	Business Process Owner	Senior Management	My Rating	Understanding Level
A	A	A	C		

This include contains fields which form the primary key of the table.

Personnel number

Each employee in SAP is given a unique eight-digit number. This number can be system generated, or externally assigned. SAP does not support alphanumeric employee identification. The existence of an employee is checked in infotype 0003. For this reason, in all infotypes the check table for personnel number is PA0003.

Subtype

Some infotypes may have subtypes. For example, there may be different types of addresses. These may be stored as subtypes. For those infotypes where subtypes are permitted, one can define them in customizing. For some infotypes, subtypes are obligatory, for others they are not. These characteristics are defined in view V_T582A.

For most infotypes, the subtypes are defined in view V_T591A. Where time constraints are at subtype level, time constraints are also defined in view V_T591A.

For infotypes 0011, 0014, 0015, 0215, 0267, 0390 and 2010 the subtype is a wage type. For these infotypes, the subtypes are checked against view V_T512Z, in which you specify which wage types are permitted for which infotypes. For these infotypes, time constraints are at wage type level, and these are defined in view V_T591B.

Object identification

Infotype 0021 has a subtype child. However, one would not like to mix information of different children of a person. At the same time one would not like to create artificial subtypes like child1, child2, etc. This problem is solved by identifying each child with object identification. This concept is used wherever required, e.g. loans (infotype 0045), etc.

When you create a child's record in infotype 0021, SAP automatically assigns it an object id (because object id is enabled for this subtype in view V_T591A). When you create another record, it gives you the next object id. In case you want to create another record for an existing child, instead of create, you should copy. In that case, the object ids of both the records are the same, meaning that they are for the same person.

Lock indicator for HR master data record

SAP permits a two-step data entry process, in which one person enters the data, and another approves it. Technically, the first person creates a locked record, which the second person unlocks with or without modification. The locked record is not used for any purpose, and remains dormant waiting to be unlocked. When you create a new record, it could be delimiting the previous record. In case you create a locked record, this does not happen, but when you unlock it, the same action takes place.

There are two ways of creating a locked record. The user authorization could be set in such a way that when the user creates a record, it is always created locked. Alternatively, the user could create a record, and lock it before saving.

Start date and end date

The data in all infotypes is for an employee number and for a validity period. It is, therefore, possible to store employee data with history. When you create an infotype record, you know the start date. But you may not know the date till when the data will remain valid. So, the convention is to put 31.12.9999, meaning infinity. When the data changes, a new record is created from the date of change. The system automatically changes the end date of the previous record to one day prior to the start date of the new record. In SAP parlance, this is called delimiting the old record. This ensures that on any given date, only one record is valid, and there is no ambiguity about what is the correct information.

Of course, there are infotypes where more than one record can exist simultaneously, and would make sense. An employee can have two emergency addresses at the same time. For which infotypes simultaneous records are allowed, and for which they are not, depends on an infotype property called time constraint.

Number of infotype record with same key

The sequential number is used to differentiate between records that have the same key and the time constraint is 3 (any number of records at a certain point in time). Unlike the personnel object identification, this number is assigned automatically.

2.3 HR MASTER RECORD: CONTROL FIELD

Functional Consultant	User	Business Process Owner	Senior Management	My Rating	Understanding Level
A	A	A	C		

Date of last change

This field is system maintained, and comes handy when one has to investigate suspect data changes.

Name of person who changed object

This field is system maintained, and comes handy when one has to investigate suspect data changes.

Historical record flag

If you mark a record historical, it is permanently stored on the database and is available for reporting. However, it cannot be changed.

Text exists for infotype

For many infotypes SAP allows entry of free text associated with a record (Edit ➢ Maintain Text). This text is stored elsewhere and not in the infotype. However, a flag is kept in the infotype, so that the system knows when it needs to fetch that data.

Reference fields exist (primary/secondary costs)

If you create a cost assignment, this field is flagged.

Confirmation fields exist

If the infotype record is linked to confirmations, this field is flagged.

Infotype screen control

When you create an infotype, you specify not just the infotype, but also the screen control. That information is stored here. When the infotype record is retrieved for display or change, this screen control is used to decide the screen.

Reason for changing master data

When creating or changing an infotype one can specify the reasons for change, choosing from the list maintained in configuration. You define the reasons for change in view V_T530E.

Grouping value for personnel assignments

This field contains the grouping value based on which the system decides which personnel assignments of a concurrently employed person must be processed together.

2.4 NUMBER RANGE INTERVALS FOR PERSONNEL NUMBERS

Functional Consultant	User	Business Process Owner	Senior Management	My Rating	Understanding Level
A	A	A	X		

2.4.1 Purpose

When you hire an employee, you have to assign him a personnel number. If you do not want to assign personnel number to all employees in a running serial, you can create multiple intervals of personnel numbers and decide which ones are system generated and which are externally assigned. The next step is to decide which employee gets personnel number from which interval. That is determined by the feature NUMKR.

2.4.2 IMG Node

Transaction PA04—Personnel Administration Number Ranges

2.4.3 Screen

No	From number	To number	Current number	Ext
01	00600000	99999999	600000	☐
02	00100000	00299999		☑
03	00300000	00399999		☑
04	00400000	00499999		☑
05	00500000	00599999		☑

2.5 NUMBER RANGE INTERVAL DETERMINATION

Functional Consultant	User	Business Process Owner	Senior Management	My Rating	Understanding Level
A	A	C	X		

2.5.1 Purpose

When you hire an employee, you have to assign him a personnel number. If you do not want to assign personnel number to all employees in a running serial, you can create multiple intervals of personnel numbers. Then you decide which set of employees are going to be given personnel numbers from which range. In this feature you build a decision tree to determine the personnel number interval.

2.5.2 IMG Node

PE03 ➤ NUMKR

2.5.3 Screen

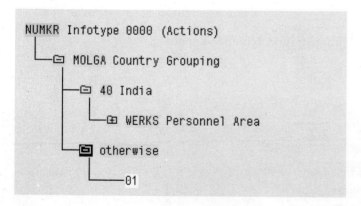

2.5.4 Fields for Decision-making

Company Code
Personnel Area
Employee Group
Employee Subgroup
Country Grouping

2.5.5 Return Value

Number range interval for personnel numbers

2.6 PERSONNEL NUMBER CHECK

Functional Consultant	User	Business Process Owner	Senior Management	My Rating	Understanding Level
A	X	X	X		

2.6.1 Purpose

In SAP, you may want each of your employees to book production against his personnel number. The personnel number he enters should be checked against personnel administration to ensure that invalid personnel numbers are not entered. But, what would you do, if you have not implemented personnel administration? Through this setting, you can switch off the check. When you are implementing personnel administration, you would probably want to switch it on. By default this check is turned on.

2.6.2 IMG Node

SM30 ≻ V_T77S0SC (PERNR + EXCHK)

2.6.3 Screen

System Switch (from Table T77S0)			
Group	Sem. abbr.	Value abbr.	Description
PERNR	EXCHK	X	Validation of personnel number from other appln

2.7 SUBTYPES

Functional Consultant	User	Business Process Owner	Senior Management	My Rating	Understanding Level
A	X	X	X		

2.7.1 Purpose

Many infotypes have subtypes. You can configure subtypes as per your requirements. For most infotypes, the subtypes are stored in view V_T591A, and you can configure the required subtypes. For an infotype, in the subtype field you can see the list of subtypes. If this list is not available, or not appropriate, you can implement BAdI HR_F4_GET_SUBTYPE.

2.7.2 IMG Node

SM30 ➤ V_T591A

2.7.3 Screen

Subty...	Name	Time constraint	ObjIDallw
1	Spouse	2	☐
11	Father	2	☐
12	Mother	2	☐
2	Child	2	☑

Subtype characteristics for Family Member/Dependents

2.7.4 Primary Key

Infotype + Subtype

2.7.5 Important Fields

Infotype

The infotype whose subtypes you are creating.

Subtype

The subtypes you want.

Time constraint

This field is shown only if time constraints are to be defined at subtype level (time constraint T in view V_T582A).

1	Record must have no gaps, no overlappings
2	Record may include gaps, no overlappings
3	Record may include gaps, can exist more than once
Z	Time constraint for time management infotypes → T554Y

Time constraint applies to the primary key of a table. If an infotype has a subtype, it applies to each subtype. Further, if a subtype has multiple objects, it applies to each object. In infotype 0021, child is a subtype. You can have multiple children on the same day. Therefore, should time constraint be 3? No, because each child has an object id, which is part of primary key. Therefore, time constraint is 2, and still multiple children can exist on the same day.

Object identification permitted for subtype

Object id allows you to differentiate between different objects within a subtype. If you keep information about employee's children in infotype 0021, in a specific subtype, how do you distinguish the data of child A from the data of child B? This can be done by using object id. Here you specify the subtypes, for which object id is allowed. This is needed, because if you allowed it for mother, one can create multiple mothers, which is not correct. This field is shown only for those infotypes for which object is allowed in view T777D.

2.8 REASON FOR CHANGE

Functional Consultant	User	Business Process Owner	Senior Management	My Rating	Understanding Level
A	X	X	X		

2.8.1 Purpose

In this view you maintain reason for change for all infotypes.

2.8.2 IMG Node

SM30 ➤ V_T530E

2.8.3 Screen

	Infotype	Infotype text	Reason	Reason text
	0001	Organizational Assignment	01	Change in department
	0001	Organizational Assignment	02	Qualification
	0008	Basic Pay	00	No Reason
	0008	Basic Pay	01	Pay scale increase
	0008	Basic Pay	02	Change in grouping

2.8.4 Primary Key

Infotype + Reason for Changing Master Data

2.9 PERSONNEL NUMBER HELP

Functional Consultant	User	Business Process Owner	Senior Management	My Rating	Understanding Level
B	X	X	X		

2.9.1 How to Find a Personnel Number

There are many occasions, when you need to find a personnel number. SAP provides you multiple ways of finding it. If you click the 🖱 icon in the personnel number field, you see the following screen.

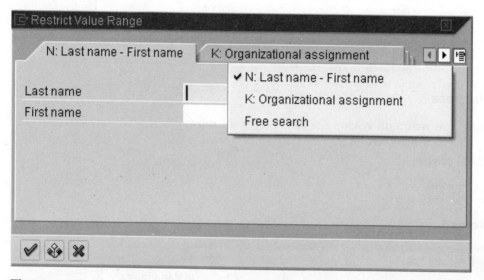

There are three tabs on this screen. Using the first tab, you can get list of personnel numbers by specifying last name, or first name, or both. Using the second tab, you can get list of personnel numbers by specifying an employee's personnel area, personnel subarea, cost center, etc. The last tab gives you maximum flexibility. Here you can search for personnel number based on information in any infotype. It gives you an ad hoc query. You can also specify the last name in the personnel number field and press Enter, e.g.

2.9.2 Personnel Number Help Tabs

SAP lets you decide which tabs you want for personnel number help and in what order. You define these in feature NSHLP using transaction code PE03. Unfortunately, this feature works only for Netherlands.

2.9.3   Hiding Free Search in Personnel Number Help

In the personnel number help, you can either show 'Free search', or hide it. If you enter 'X' in value abbreviation in the screen below, free search tab is not displayed.

System Switch (from Table T77S0)			
Group	Sem. abbr.	Value abbr.	Description
SEARK	NOAHQ		Hide Free Search for People/Applicants

2.9.4   Adding Your Own Search Help

You have seen only two search helps for personnel number

- ➢ N: Last name–First name
- ➢ K: Organizational assignment

These are from 27 search helps for personnel number that SAP provides. However, if you want to add still more search helps for personnel number, you can do that through IMG node Personnel Management ➢ Personnel Administration ➢ Basic Settings ➢ Maintain search helps.

Actions

3.1 OVERVIEW

Functional Consultant	User	Business Process Owner	Senior Management	My Rating	Understanding Level
A	A	A	A		

3.1.1 Action

Infotype 0000

During a person's employment in an organization, a number of events take place, e.g. hiring, promotion, change of address, etc. All this data is stored with history, resulting in too much data for an employee.

A manager would be interested in looking only at the important career events of an employee, e.g. hiring, promotion, salary change, disciplinary action, etc., and not at the unimportant events, e.g. change of address. This requirement is met by maintaining important events in infotype 0000.

Employment status, special payment status and customer-specific status

Infotype 0000 contains employment status, special payment status and customer-specific status. Employment status is a very important field and determines whether a person's payroll is run or not. It can only be changed through an action (transaction PA40).

On any day, there can be only one record in infotype 0000, which means that there can be only one employment status, special payment status and customer-specific status for an employee on any given date.

Infotype 0302

If multiple actions are run on the same day, one record is stored in infotype 0000, and remaining records are stored in infotype 0302. Since infotype 0302 does not store employment and other statuses; in the case of multiple actions, the one changing the statuses is stored in infotype 0000, while others are stored in infotype 0302.

Actions overwritten

If multiple actions change the status on the same day, the earlier action is overwritten.

Configuring actions

Although actions are normally recorded in infotypes 0000 and 0302, but this is configurable. Each organization identifies the actions it would like to record. Infotype 0000 is usually maintained by running actions, using transaction PA40, which presents a series of infotypes relevant for that action. Only action-reason in infotype 0000 can be changed using transaction PA30.

Reference personnel number

If a reference personnel number is entered while carrying out an action, a record in infotype 0031 is created, and appropriate infotypes are copied.

Personnel file

All actions, whether stored in infotype 0000 or in infotype 0302, can be seen in the personnel file (transaction PA10) of an employee.

Data maintained exclusively through actions

Personnel area, employee group and employee subgroup (which are fields of infotype 0001) can be changed only through actions and not through transaction PA30.

3.1.2 Infogroup

When an event, e.g. hiring, takes place, usually several infotypes need to be created/ updated. Such set of infotypes can be defined as infogroups. Infogroups can be associated with actions.

When a personnel action is run, the system runs the associated infogroup, and presents its constituent infotypes to the user.

Infogroups can be defined flexibly, and can vary depending on the employee for whom the action is run, as well as depending on the logged on user.

3.1.3 Others

Multiple personnel numbers

An employee may have multiple personnel numbers if he has multiple contracts with the company at the same time.

Data transfer from recruitment

Data can be transferred from recruitment during hiring action.

Integration with organizational management

The screen you get when running transaction PA40 is affected by integration with organizational management (OM). If integration with OM is on (value of PLOGI + ORGA is X in view V_T77S0), the position field is shown when running the action; otherwise it is not shown.

Creation of records in infotype 0000 only through actions

Unlike other infotypes, which can be created through transaction PA30, records in infotype 0000 can be created only through transaction PA40.

Multiple infotypes in a single screen

When you run an action, you are presented multiple infotypes one by one. It is always desirable from a user's perspective if the fields belonging to different infotypes can be presented in a single screen. SAP lets you design such a screen using transaction OG42. In this transaction, you can create screens only for those actions, which have been maintained in V_588B_M for menu '02'. Screens so designed can be run using transaction PA42 (fast entry for actions). You can use BAdI HR_FAST_ACTION_CHECK to set default values and checks for transaction PA42.

Action menu

When you run transaction PA40, or PA42, you see a set of actions you can perform. This is configurable, and can change depending on user.

3.2 ACTIONS (INFOTYPE 0000)

Functional Consultant	User	Business Process Owner	Senior Management	My Rating	Understanding Level
A	A	A	A		

3.2.1 Screen

Pers.No.	121715				

Name	Agrawal Prem

EE group	1 Permanent	Pers.area	PNCV Pune CVBU

EE subgroup	E4 DM

Start	01.01.2005	to	31.12.9999	Chng	07.07.2006 QHRPKA000137

Personnel action

Action Type	Z1 Hiring	🗎
Reason for Action		Other reason

Status

Customer-specific		🗎
Employment	3 Active	🗎
Special payment	1 Standard wage type	🗎

Organizational assignment

Position	99999999	Integration: default posi
Personnel area	PNCV	Pune CVBU
Employee group	1	Permanent
Employee subgroup	E4	DM

Additional actions

Start Date	Act.	Action type	ActR	Reason for acti
01.01.2005	Z1	Hiring		Other reason

3.2.2 Purpose

This infotype stores important career history events of an employee, e.g. hiring, promotion, salary change, disciplinary action, etc. If there are multiple actions on the same day, one of them is stored here, remaining are stored in infotype 0302. The important difference between these two infotypes is that infotype 0000 stores information about the employment and other statuses, whereas infotype 0302 does not have any status information. This is done to ensure that on any given day, an employee has a unique status. His employment status, for example, cannot be both 'Active' and 'Withdrawn' on the same day. If multiple actions change the status on the same day, the earlier action is overwritten.

3.2.3 Subtypes

No subtypes

3.2.4 Time Constraint

1 (Record must have no gaps, no overlappings). Infotype 0000 cannot be delimited even after the employee leaves (employment status, 'withdrawn'). End-date of the last record must be 31.12.9999.

3.2.5 Important Fields

Action type

The types of actions you propose to have in your organization, e.g. hiring, promotion, resignation, etc., are defined as action type. When you run an action using transaction PA40, you make a choice from this list.

Reason for action

The action reason defines the circumstances which have initiated a personnel action. You may or may not specify a reason for action. This list is defined while customizing your system.

Customer-specific status

You can define and use the customer-specific status as required. It is a property of action which is defined for each action during configuration. When the action is run, the employee is automatically assigned that status, and it cannot be changed.

Employment status

Employment status of an employee on a given day is very important information defining the relationship between the employee and the company. List of employment status is pre-defined by SAP, and should not be changed. Employment status is a property of action, which is defined for each action during configuration. When the action is run, the employee is automatically assigned that status, and it cannot be changed. The most important use of employment status is in payroll.

Status	Description	Explanation
0	Withdrawn	These employees have left the company forever and no relationship with the company exists. Payroll is not run for withdrawn employees. After an employee's employment status becomes withdrawn, infotypes with time constraint 1 can be delimited. Infotypes 0000, 0001 and 0002 are exceptions to this rule, and they must remain valid till 31.12.9999.
1	Inactive	These employees are not working for the company currently, but they are employed with the company, e.g. employees on study leave.
2	Retiree	These employees have left the company, but their relationship with the company continues in some form, e.g. for payment of pension.
3	Active	These employees are currently working for the company.

Special payment status

The special payment indicator is only relevant for Austria and Spain. It is a property of action, which is defined for each action during configuration. When the action is run, the employee is automatically assigned that status, and it cannot be changed.

3.2.6   Menu and Menu Bar

⊕ Execute info group   When you are executing an action, associated infogroup is run. The infogroup consists of several infotypes, which are presented to you in predefined sequence. You enter data in these infotypes and save. If for some reasons, your action gets interrupted, you can execute infogroup. The system then presents the remaining infotypes to you.

✎ Change info group   When you click this icon, the system will show the following screen, where you can change the infogroup definition for the current action.

	Inf...	S..	Su...	Name	Ope...	Text	No.
	0001			Organizational Assignment	COP	Copy	1
	0007			Planned Working Time	COP	Copy	1
	0008			Basic Pay	COP	Copy	1
	0041			Date Specifications	COP	Copy	1

Change Info Group

3.2.7 Reports

S_PH9_46000223–EEs Entered and Left

Entries and leavings

Personnel No.	First name	Last name	Entry	Leaving date	Org. Unit	Name of org...
00121715	Prem	Agrawal	01.01.2005	31.12.9999	00000000	

S_AHR_61016369–Employee List

Employee List

Pers.no.	PersIDNo.	Name	Father ...	Job title	Entry Date	Leaving
00114891	14891	Dekhane Yeshwant		DEPUTY MANAGER	01.04.1973	
00116051	16051	Hariharan Puthanpura		SENIOR OFFICER	26.04.1974	
00116667	16667	Morgaonkar Hemant		MANAGER	05.01.1975	
00119123	19123	Dharane Kashinath		SUPERVISOR	10.09.1976	

S_AHR_61016360–HR Master Data Sheet

You can use this report to print employee data as per your requirement. You need to define a form for this purpose.

S_AHR_61016362–Flexible Employee Data

In this report, you can select the fields of employee data you want. Alternatively, you may use ad hoc query.

Flexible Employee Data

Personne...	First Name	Last Name	Date of Birth	Cost Center	Employee ...	E...
00121715	Prem	Agrawal	08.12.1951		Permanent	DM

3.2.8 Deleting an Action

You may delete actions. If you delete an action, which had resulted in separation of the employee, the system proposes to extend the infotypes, which were delimited when the action was carried out.

3.3 ADDITIONAL ACTIONS (INFOTYPE 0302)

Functional Consultant	User	Business Process Owner	Senior Management	My Rating	Understanding Level
A	A	A	A		

3.3.1 Purpose

This infotype works in tandem with infotype 0000, and stores actions, which are not stored in infotype 0000. The users do not determine what entries go into this infotype. In this infotype, the records are not for a period but for a single day, i.e. from-date and to-date are same. Meaning of all fields in this infotype is same as that of infotype 0000, and no separate configuration is required for this infotype.

3.3.2 Subtypes

No subtypes

3.3.3 Time Constraint

3 (Record may include gaps, can exist more than once)

3.4 ADDITIONAL ACTIONS ACTIVATION

Functional Consultant	User	Business Process Owner	Senior Management	My Rating	Understanding Level
A	X	X	X		

3.4.1 Purpose and Overview

SAP lets you decide whether you want to use 'Additional Actions' or not. If you want to use 'Additional Actions', the system switch ADMIN+EVSUP in view T77S0 must be set to 1.

Group	Sem.abbr.	Value abbr	Description
ADMIN	EVSUP		Additional actions

If that is not the case, you need to activate this switch first. This is done by executing the IMG node Personnel Management ➤ Personnel Administration ➤ Customizing Procedures ➤ Actions ➤ Set Up Personnel Actions ➤ Activation 'Additional Actions'. When you execute this node (or SA38 ➤ RPUEVSUP), you get the following screen:

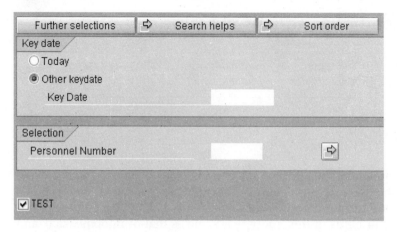

You can use this program to
> Activate 'Additional Actions' switch in view T77S0 (set ADMIN+EVSUP to 1).
> Set the indicator 'Update infotype 0302 when executing an action' for all personnel action types in view T529A. The system then logs all personnel action types that are executed for an employee and their related reasons in infotype 0302.
> Create infotype 0302 records for the specified period based on records in infotype 0000.

3.5 ACTION TYPE

Functional Consultant	User	Business Process Owner	Senior Management	My Rating	Understanding Level
A	X	X	X		

3.5.1 Purpose

This view contains master list of actions, and their properties. It determines, for example, what will be the employment status of an employee, after the action is run. It also determines which infotypes will be presented to the user and whether personnel area, position, employee group and employee subgroup are changed through actions only.

3.5.2 IMG Node

SM30 ➤ T529A

3.5.3 Screen

Actio...	Name of action type	F..	Cus...	Emp...	Spe...	Check	P	P..	E..	E..	IG	D...	U...	U...	C...
Z1	Hiring	1		3	1		✔	✔	✔	✔	Z1		✔	✔	☐
Z2	Confirmation	0					☐	✔	✔	☐	Z2		✔	✔	☐
Z3	Absorption	0					✔	✔	✔	✔	Z3		✔	✔	☐
Z4	Organization reassignm...	0		3	1		✔	✔	☐	✔	Z4		✔	✔	☐
Z5	Promotion	0					✔	✔	☐	✔	Z5		☐	✔	☐

3.5.4 Primary Key

Action type

3.5.5 Important Fields

Action type

Define the master list of actions you need in your organization here.

Function character for action

1	Initial hiring
7	Initial hiring and transfer of data from recruitment
8	Activation of pers. assignment for global employees (host)
9	Activation of pers. assignment for global employees (home)
0	Other actions

If you want to transfer applicant data from recruitment, you specify 7. When you run the action, the system asks you to enter applicant number, based on which it copies applicant data for the employee being hired.

Status (customer-specific, employment, special payment)

Each action (infotype 0000 record) has three status values, which are automatically determined based on the settings here. If a status, say employment status, is blank here, the value will be copied from the previous record to the new record.

Check feature

Here you can assign a feature which ensures logical sequence of actions, e.g. retirement cannot be before hiring.

Position, PA, EG, ESG

When you run an action, PA, EG, ESG fields are shown. These checkboxes determine which of these are allowed for input. Position field appears on this screen only if OM to PA integration (PLOGI+ORGA in view T77S0) is on.

Infogroup

The infogroup specified here is run when the action is run. Infogroups contain sequence of infotypes.

Date control

Blank	Specified date is the start date for new records.	Used for actions where the new status is applicable for the date of action also.
1	Specified date is the end date for old records.	Used for actions where the new status is not applicable for the date of action, e.g. employee leaving the organization.

Update infotype 0000

Usually you want to record an action in infotype 0000. If you don't want to record an action in infotype 0000, remove tick from the checkbox. If an action changes any of the status fields, this must be ticked.

Update infotype 0302

Infotype 0302 is used when more than one action is run on the same day. Usually you would tick it along with the previous checkbox. This field is shown only if 'Activate Additional Actions' is run.

Country reassignment

See field help for special properties of actions, which involve change in employee's country.

3.6 ACTION TYPE PRIORITY

Functional Consultant	User	Business Process Owner	Senior Management	My Rating	Understanding Level
A	X	X	X		

3.6.1 Purpose

If on a given day there are more than one actions, but no one changing status, you can decide which action will be stored in infotype 0000. This is done by assigning priority to actions where all status fields are blank and 'Update infotype 0000' is active.

3.6.2 IMG Node

SM30 ➤ V_529A_B

3.6.3 Screen

Act.	Name of action type	Priority
Z2	Confirmation	
Z3	Absorption	

3.6.4 Primary Key

Action type

3.7 ACTION REASONS

Functional Consultant	User	Business Process Owner	Senior Management	My Rating	Understanding Level
A	X	X	X		

3.7.1 Purpose

This view contains master list of reasons for each action type.

3.7.2 IMG Node

SM30 ➤ V_T530

3.7.3 Screen

Action	Name of action type	Act.reason	Name of reason for action
01			
01		01	Creation of new workplaces
01		02	Substitution of workplaces
01		03	Re-entry temporary suspension
01		04	Department reorganisation

3.7.4 Primary Key

Action type + Action reason

3.8 CUSTOMER-SPECIFIC STATUS, EMPLOYMENT STATUS, SPECIAL PAYMENT STATUS

Functional Consultant	User	Business Process Owner	Senior Management	My Rating	Understanding Level
A	X	X	X		

3.8.1 Purpose

You can define and use the customer-specific status as required. You should not change employment status, as its values are used in SAP programs.

3.8.2 IMG Node

SM30 ➤ V_T529U (Status number 1, 2, 3)

3.8.3 Customer-specific Status

Status values: Customer status	
Status	Name

3.8.4 Employment Status

Status values: Employment	
Status	Name
0	Withdrawn
1	Inactive
2	Retiree
3	Active

3.8.5 Special Payment Status

Status values: Special payment	
Status	Name
0	No special payment
1	Standard wage type
2	Special wage type

3.8.6 Primary Key

Language Key + Status number + Status indicator for actions

3.9 INFOGROUP

Functional Consultant	*User*	*Business Process Owner*	*Senior Management*	*My Rating*	*Understanding Level*
A	X	X	X		

3.9.1 Purpose and Overview

When an infogroup is run, a set of infotypes is presented in a predefined sequence. These are customized as per requirement here. Along with infotype you can also specify the screens which will be shown, subtypes if any, and whether the infotype will be copied, or blank.

The sequence of infotypes can be varied depending on the logged on user. It can also be varied depending on the employees for whom the action is being run.

While running an action, you can modify the infogroup for that particular action (see 'Change infogroup' in chapter 3.2.6).

3.9.2 IMG Node

SM30 ➤ V_T588D

3.9.3 Screen

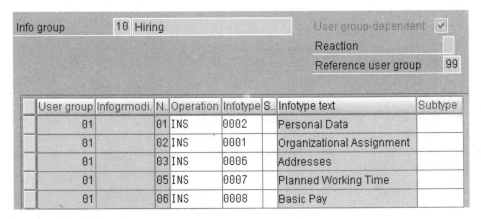

3.9.4 Primary Key

Infogroup + User group + Infogroup modifier + Sequence number

3.9.5   Important Fields

Infogroup

Infogroups are assigned to actions. When an action runs, it calls its associated infogroup. Master list of infogroups is maintained in view T588C (menu type G).

User group-dependent, reaction, reference user group

These fields are shown here from view T588C. For details, see chapter 3.12.

User group

The sequence of infotypes can be varied depending on the logged on user. User group comes from login (System ➤ User profile ➤ Own data ➤ Parameters ➤ UGR). If the infogroup is not defined for that user, reference user from view V_T588C is taken.

Infogroup modifier

The sequence of infotypes can also be varied depending on the employees for whom the action is being run. Infogroup modifier for an employee is determined by using feature IGMOD.

Sequence number

Here you specify the sequence in which infotypes are presented.

Operation

You could give the user a blank infotype record, or a copy of his last infotype, which he could modify. This is controlled through operation. You may see field help for options and exact use.

Infotype

Here you specify the infotype which is presented.

Screen control

You need this field only if you have planned to use multiple screens for an infotype. Through this field you can determine which of the multiple screens you planned to use, will be presented in this infogroup. For more details on screen control, you may see chapter 43, Infotype Screens.

Subtype

If the infotype has subtypes, you specify which subtype is to be presented.

3.10 EMPLOYEE-DEPENDENT INFOGROUP DEFINITION

Functional Consultant	User	Business Process Owner	Senior Management	My Rating	Understanding Level
A	X	X	X		

3.10.1 Purpose and Overview

Feature IGMOD provides the flexibility to run different sequence of infotypes for different group of employees based on company code, personnel area, personnel subarea, employee group, employee subgroup, infogroup, etc. This modifier is one of the key parameters which determines infogroup definition (V_T588D).

3.10.2 IMG Node

PE03 ≻ IGMOD

3.10.3 Screen

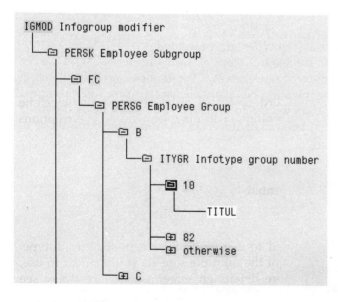

3.10.4 Fields for Decision-making

Company Code
Personnel Area
Employee Group
Employee Subgroup
Infotype Group Number
Action Type
Reason for Action

3.10.5   Return Value

Infogroup modifier

3.11   USER GROUP

Functional Consultant	User	Business Process Owner	Senior Management	My Rating	Understanding Level
A	B	C	X		

3.11.1   What Is a User Group?

SAP can behave differently based on logged on user. It is a little hard to visualize, but grant that sometimes it may be useful. Perhaps one group of users hires temporary employees, while another group of users hires permanent employees, and the hiring action needs to differ. If you have such a scenario, you can divide your users in user groups.

3.11.2   How Is User Group Determined?

When a user logs into a SAP client, he can click System ➢ User Profile ➢ Own Data. In the parameter tab user can set a number of parameters. One of them is UGR, which is user group. Depending on how the organization has planned user groups, he is assigned a user group, which is entered here. This could be done either by the user, or by the Basis team while creating user. When system behaviour depends on user group, the value is picked up from here.

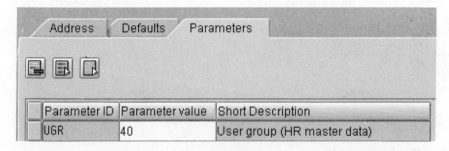

3.11.3   How Is User Group Used?

You can use user group to determine
➢ Action menu
➢ Fast action menu
➢ Infotype menu
➢ Infogroup definition

3.11.4 What Happens If there Is No User Group?

If system behaviour depends on user group, a user can face problem if he did not maintain user group. SAP solves this problem by using a reference user group, which is picked up if user group is not found. However, if you don't want to use reference user group, the system can be customized to give error, or allow use of reference user group with warning.

3.11.5 What Happens If there Is No Configuration for an User Group?

If you have specified a user group, but the system does not find configuration corresponding to that user group, the system uses the concept of reference user group as described above.

3.11.6 How to Use the Concept of User Groups?

Don't use the concept of user groups, unless you can divide your users in user groups clearly from a business perspective. If you use this concept, clearly specify the guidelines of determining user group for a user, and how their needs differ, which need to be configured in the system.

3.12 USER GROUP DEPENDENCY OF INFOGROUP

Functional Consultant	User	Business Process Owner	Senior Management	My Rating	Understanding Level
B	X	X	X		

3.12.1 Purpose and Overview

Infogroups are a sequence of infotypes. SAP lets you define your infogroups in such a way that this sequence can differ based on the logged on user. However, if you create a large number of user groups, you have to copy this configuration for each user group. To reduce this effort, SAP lets you define, a reference user group. Instead of defining the infogroup for each user group, you can define them for a few, where they differ. For other user groups, you may just specify the reference user group.

You might wonder why you would create more user groups, if you define infogroups only for a few. Assume that there is one infogroup, which has five variants. To cater to this need, you create five user groups. But all other infogroups have only one variant. If you do not have this facility, you would have to define all infogroups five times, even though they do not depend on user groups. This increases both effort and probability of error at the time of initial configuration as well as during subsequent maintenance.

3.12.2 IMG Node

SM30 ➤ VV_T588C_G_AL0

3.12.3 Screen

Menu ty.   G

	Menu	Text	User-dep.	Reaction	Ref.
	10	Hiring	✔		99
	20	Termination	✔	E	26
	25	Auto Terminations	✔	E	99
	32	Long Term Absence	✔		01

3.12.4 Primary Key

Menu Type + Menu

3.12.5 Important Fields

Menu type

View T588C is used for five different purposes. For infogroups, the menu type is G.

Menu

For menu type G, menu field contains infogroups.

User group dependent

Details of infogroup are maintained in view V_T588D. If your infogroup does not depend on user group, you should leave this checkbox blank and define an infogroup for only one user group. Otherwise, you should tick this checkbox and maintain infogroup for each user group, or reference user group.

Reaction

If you have not maintained the parameter UGR in the user defaults, the system can give an error (E), use reference user group (blank) or use it with a warning (W).

Reference user group

The infogroup definition in view V_T588D can depend on user group. If there are several user groups, maintenance of these views could become very complex. Also, if the UGR parameter is not set in user profile, the system does not know what menu to show him. This view provides the flexibility to pick up a reference user group, if parameter UGR is not set, or if there is no infogroup definition for the user's user group in view V_T588D.

3.13 USER GROUP DEPENDENCY OF PERSONNEL ACTION MENU

Functional Consultant	User	Business Process Owner	Senior Management	My Rating	Understanding Level
B	X	X	X		

3.13.1 Purpose

When you run transaction code PA40, or PA42, you see a set of actions out of which you can perform any action. This set depends on user group and is defined in view V_T588B. If your action sets are fewer than the number of user groups, you can reduce your maintenance effort by specifying a reference user group in this view.

3.13.2 IMG Node

SM30 ≻ VV_T588C_M_AL0

3.13.3 Screen

3.13.4 Primary Key

Menu Type + Menu

3.13.5 Important Fields

Menu type

View T588C is used for five different purposes. For actions, the menu type is M.

Menu

For menu type M, menu 01 is for actions, and is used in transaction code PA40. Menu 02 is for fast actions, and is used in transaction code PA42. Other menus in this view are for other modules.

User group dependent

Details of menus are maintained in view V_T588B. If your menus do not depend on user group, you should leave this checkbox blank and define the menu for only one user group. Otherwise, you should tick this checkbox and maintain menus for each user group, or reference user group.

Reaction

If you have not maintained the parameter UGR in the user defaults, the system can give an error (E), use reference user group (blank) or use it with a warning (W).

Reference user group

View V_T588B provides the flexibility to show different sequence of actions depending on the logged on user. If there are many user groups, maintenance of these views could become very complex. This view provides the flexibility to pick up a reference user group, thereby making that maintenance simpler.

3.14   ACTION SEQUENCE IN MENU

Functional Consultant	User	Business Process Owner	Senior Management	My Rating	Understanding Level
A	X	X	X		

3.14.1   Purpose

When you run transaction PA40, you get a menu. What you see there is defined here.

3.14.2   IMG Node

SM30 ➢ V_588B_M

3.14.3   Screen

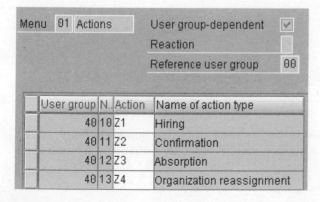

3.14.4 Primary Key

Menu type + Infotype menu + User group + Sequence number

3.14.5 Important Fields

Menu type

Menu type (M), is not displayed on the screen.

Menu

Here you can define menu for action (01), and menu for fast action (02).

User group

The sequence of actions in menu can be varied depending on the user group of the logged on user. User group comes from login (System ➢ User Profile ➢ Own data ➢ Parameters ➢ Parameter ID = UGR). If the user group is not defined for that user, reference user from view T588C is taken.

Sequence Number

Here you specify the sequence in which actions are presented in menu.

Personnel/applicant action type

The personnel action type which is run if you select this item from the menu.

Organizational
Assignment

4.1 ORGANIZATIONAL ASSIGNMENT (INFOTYPE 0001)

Functional Consultant	User	Business Process Owner	Senior Management	My Rating	Understanding Level
A	A	A	A		

4.1.1 Screen

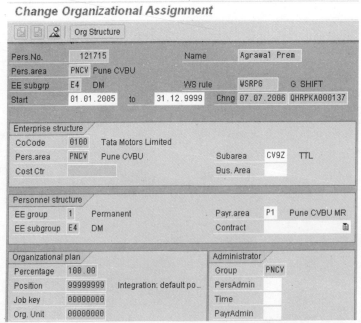

Change Organizational Assignment

4.1.2 Purpose and Overview

Infotype 0001 is a crucial infotype in SAP HR. It stores the employee's relationship with the organization. This relationship is in terms of his place in the organization (position), his physical location (enterprise structure), and the groups of employees (personnel structure) to which he belongs.

In SAP HR, there are features and personnel calculation rules, where it is possible to build customer specific logic. Many fields of infotype 0001 can be used in features and PCRs, allowing building of customer logic without programming. However, if the logic was to depend on the attribute of an employee, say personnel area, every time you add a new value of the attribute, say a new personnel area, you must review all features and PCRs to determine how they should work for the new value. It would be ideal to maintain a table of fields that are hard-coded in features and PCRs to avoid having to look at all features and PCRs, every time a new value is added in configuration of these fields.

Infotype 0001 also depends on whether you have implemented the organizational management module (OM) or not, and whether integration between OM and PA is active. If OM to PA integration is active, PA, EG, ESG, and position can be changed only through an action (transaction PA40).

Enterprise and personnel structure

SAP realized that the rules in an organization might not be uniform for all employees. It caters to this requirement by giving you flexibility in two ways. Your rules may differ based on an employee's physical location. They may also differ based on category to which an employee belongs.

A company's physical locations are divided in personnel areas, which are further subdivided in personnel subareas. Each employee is assigned to a personnel subarea. Many rules, particularly rules in time management area, can depend on the PA and PSA, and thereby can be different for different employees.

Rules may also be different, for example, for executives and for workmen. SAP provides two attributes, employee group and employee subgroup, which can be assigned to employees, and based on which different rules can be applied to different employees. Unlike PA+PSA, employee group and employee subgroup are independent attributes of an employee.

In SAP, you define rules for each PSA as well as for each combination of EG and ESG. Since both the number of PSAs as well as number of combinations of EG and ESG can be fairly large, this may become a Herculean task. Moreover, whenever a PSA, EG or ESG is added, the rules have to be defined for it. This difficulty is overcome by defining groupings of PSAs and groupings of EG+ESG. For each purpose, say appraisal, you can group the PSAs, and you can also group the EG+ESG combination. In this way, the flexibility is also retained and configuration of rules is also manageable.

4.1.3 Subtypes

No subtypes

4.1.4 Time Constraint

1 (Record must have no gaps, no overlappings). Infotype 0001 cannot be delimited even after the employee leaves (employment status, 'withdrawn'). End-date of the last record must be 31.12.9999.

4.1.5 Important Fields

Personnel area

An employee's personnel area identifies his physical/geographical location. Personnel area can be changed only through an action, which means that changes in PA are recorded in infotype 0000. It is an important attribute of an employee, and is used for the following purposes:

➤ SAP can be configured to apply different logic to different employees based on the personnel area to which they belong, particularly in the area of time management.
➤ In SAP HR, you can use Features to build customer-specific logic. Personnel area is one of the important employee characteristics, which is used in features.
➤ Usually both PA and PSA are available for decision making in features. However, PSA is not available in feature NUMKR. Therefore, employees in different PAs can be given personnel number from different personnel number intervals. PSA cannot be used for determining personnel number interval.
➤ In SAP payroll and time management, there are PCRs in which you can query employee characteristics, and perform different operations, based on the result. PA is frequently used in them.
➤ Personnel area is an important manpower reporting parameter, although it is debatable whether it should be so.
➤ The authorization of users can be limited to specified personnel areas. Note that PSA cannot be used for authorization check.
➤ Personnel area determines an employee's company code.

Personnel subarea

On the basis of physical location, a company is divided in personnel areas, which are further divided in personnel subareas. On any given day, an employee belongs to one of the personnel subareas. PSA is an important employee attribute, which is used for the following purpose:

➤ SAP provides the flexibility to build different rules for employees in different locations based on PSAs. Since PSAs could be many, these are grouped for the purpose of defining rules. For each purpose, there is a different grouping.
➤ Like personnel area, personnel subarea is often used for customizing SAP to meet customer requirements using features and PCRs.

> Personnel subarea is an important manpower reporting parameter, although it is debatable whether it should be so.
> Note that authorization cannot be granted on the basis of PSAs.

Company code

Company code of an employee in master data

Each personnel area is assigned a company code. Thus, based on an employee's personnel area, his company code is determined. It is not really necessary to store an employee's company code in infotype 0001, but it is done. Whenever an action is run assigning a personnel area to an employee, his company code is determined based on personnel area to company code linkage configured in T500P and stored in infotype 0001.

Company code of an employee in payroll run

When the payroll runs, the company code is picked by function WPBP, and stored in table WPBP. When posting takes place, the company code is picked up from table WPBP. In case an employee is partly in one company code and partly in another, the expense booking takes place in respective company codes, whereas employee payment takes place from the last company code. The system, therefore, passes a cross-company-code reconciliation entry.

Transfer of an employee across company codes

If an employee is transferred across company codes with retro effect and if employee payments are done by creating him as vendor or customer, then the system recovers from the employee in his old company code, and makes payment in new company code. If appropriate entries are not passed, the employee may get overpayment from the new company code, while debit entry would remain in the old company code.

Uses of an employee's company code

Features	Company code is a decision field in many features. It can be used to generate default values for data entry, for example, an employee's payroll area.
Reporting	Company code is a selection criterion for reporting.
Authorization	Authorization in financial accounting area can be granted based on company code.
Country	Company code determines the default country for an employee's personal data, address data, and bank data.
Currency	Company code determines the default value for the currency of employee's basic pay.
Language	Company code determines the language for text output, for example, employee remuneration information.

Business area

Whether or not you assign business area to your employees depends on how your FI module is designed. If you view your FI information business area wise, you would assign business area to an employee. This information is used to put business area in employee-related FI postings.

Business area is determined from an employee's cost center. Cost center to business area link is in table CSKS of the CO module.

If you want to maintain your financial documents business area wise, you need to decide how you are going to assign business area to postings for customers and vendors.

Cost center

Here you assign a cost center to an employee. This is called master cost center of the employee. All expenses related to an employee, e.g. his salary, are charged to this cost center, unless a more specific assignment exists.

SAP permits costs to be assigned not only to cost centers, but to any cost object, e.g. a project, a sales order, etc. These are discussed separately.

If integration with OM is on (SM30 ≻ T77S0, PLOGI+ORGA=X), the system determines it from position, otherwise it can be entered.

The cost center configuration needs to be done in table CSKS in the CO module.

An employee has a personnel area, which belongs to a company code. Company code in turn belongs to a controlling area. The employee also has a cost center, which belongs to a controlling area. If the two do not match, the system gives error.

Legal person

In this field you define the legal person for an employee. This functionality is used only in some countries. The value in this field is determined automatically by the system from view V_001P_ALL and cannot be overwritten.

Employee group and employee subgroup

SAP allows you to categorize your employees into various categories. It provides two independent attributes called employee group and employee subgroup. You can use them to categorize your employees in different categories, e.g. permanent/temporary, or executive/officer/workman, etc.

Employee subgroup is a misnomer, because they are not parts of employee groups. They are employee groups based on a second set of characteristics.

SAP provides the flexibility to build different rules for different categories of employees based on EG and ESG. Since combinations of EG and ESG could be many, they are grouped for the purpose of defining rules.

These groupings are called employee subgroup groupings. For each purpose, there is a different employee subgroup grouping. The system can process an employee differently based on his ESG for PCR. It can pay him differently based on his ESG for CAP, etc.

Employee group and employee subgroup can be changed only through an action.

Payroll area

In a large company, payroll for all employees may not be run together. SAP, therefore, lets you divide your employees into different payroll areas. A payroll area is a group of employees whose payroll is processed together, i.e. for the same period, on the same day, and by the same payroll administrator.

SAP also lets you define the payroll periods as you wish. Thus, you could have a monthly payroll, or a weekly one. Further, your months could be calendar months, or they could be from 16th to 15th of every month. You, therefore, define the pattern followed by your payroll periods, and generate the payroll periods.

Payroll area cannot be changed in the middle of the payroll period. This is not a handicap because if an employee is in one company code for part of the month, and in another company code for the rest of the month, the financial bookings take place correctly, no matter from which payroll area his payroll is run. Payroll area only determines when his payroll is run and who runs it.

Feature ABKRS can be used to default payroll area.

When you copy a record, feature DFINF determines whether the payroll area is copied from the previous record, or it gets a fresh default value as is the case when you create a new record.

Each payroll area has a payroll control record which should be created for one period prior to go live date. Payroll control record controls running of payroll for a payroll area.

Contract

Here you can specify an employee's work contract. If a person has multiple contracts with the company at the same time, he has to be given multiple personnel numbers.

Position

If you have implemented organizational management, you create positions there; otherwise you can maintain them in table T528B using transaction S_AHR_61011490. In infotype 0001, you link the position to a person. You can specify a default position number in view T77S0 (PLOGI+PRELI).

If OM is active, position can be changed only through an action (transaction PA40). Also, an employee's cost center is determined from position. If organizational management is not active, you can enter the position and cost center for an employee in infotype 0001.

You can assign one or more positions to a person, partly or fully, in OM. If OM to PA integration is on, table T528B is automatically filled when you create position in OM.

Job key

If OM to PA integration is active, the job is determined from position. Otherwise, you can assign it to a person from the master list of jobs, which you maintain in view V_T513S.

Organizational unit

If OM to PA integration is active, the lowest level organizational unit to which an employee belongs is determined from position. Otherwise, you can assign it to a person from the master list of organizational units, which you maintain in view V_T527X.

Organizational key

In SAP, you can restrict authorization of a user to specified personnel areas, employee groups and employee subgroups. However, if your company wants to restrict authorization based on other fields of infotype 0001, you can use organizational key. This topic is discussed in more detail later.

Percentage

This field shows the percentage of position occupied. This field is maintained for each position a person occupies.

Administrator group

An employee can be assigned an administrator group, from which his personnel, payroll and time administrators are picked. A value in this field can be defaulted from the feature administrator group (PINCH).

The value in the parameter ID 'SGR' of logged on user (System ➤ User Profile ➤ Own Data ➤ Parameters) is used as the default value.

Personnel administrator

The personnel administrator is the employee's administrator for HR master data. It can be used for authorization checks.

Time administrator

The time administrator is the employee's administrator for time management. It can be used for authorization checks.

Payroll administrator

The payroll administrator is the employee's administrator for payroll. It can be used for authorization checks.

Supervisor

This is a free field. For USA and Canada, it is used to store the personnel number of the supervisor.

4.1.6   Menu and Menu Bar

Org Structure   You can click this icon to see where the employee is placed in the organization structure.

4.1.7   Reports

S_L9C_94000095—Headcount Changes

This report can be used to get list of employees for a given period for selected action types. Thus you can get list of hired employees, list of promoted employees, etc.

Headcount changes

Personnel ...	First name	Last name	Entry	Act.	Name of ac...	From	Org. Unit
00122276	Deepak	Bhalerao	10.11.1978	Z8	Resignation	07.12.2005	10001318

S_AHR_61016373—Headcount Development

This report gives employee headcount. You can get the count at PA, PSA, EG, ESG level.

Headcount development

Headcount for all plants

EEGrp	12.2005
	0
1	199
2	1
3	60
4	61
*	321

4.2 PERSONNEL AREA

Functional Consultant	User	Business Process Owner	Senior Management	My Rating	Understanding Level
A	A	A	A		

4.2.1 Purpose and Overview

This view contains master list of personnel areas. An employee's personnel area identifies his physical/geographical location. It can be changed only through an action, which means that changes in PA are recorded in infotype 0000. It is an important attribute of an employee, and is used for the following purposes:

➤ SAP can be configured to apply different logic to different employees based on the personnel area to which they belong, particularly in the area of time management.

➤ In SAP HR, you can use Features to build customer-specific logic. Personnel area is one of the important employee characteristics, which is used in features.

➤ Usually both PA and PSA are available for decision making in features. However, PSA is not available in feature NUMKR. Therefore, employees in different PAs can be given personnel number from different personnel number intervals. PSA cannot be used for determining personnel number interval.

➤ In SAP payroll and time management, there are PCRs in which you can query employee characteristics, and perform different operations, based on the result. PA is frequently used in them.

➤ Personnel area is an important manpower reporting parameter, although it is debatable whether it should be so.

➤ The authorization of users can be limited to specified personnel areas. Note that PSA cannot be used for authorization check.

➤ Personnel area determines an employee's company code.

4.2.2 IMG Node

SM30 ➢ T500P

4.2.3 Screen

Personnel area	Personnel Area Text	
AR01	Oficina central Argentina	
AR02	Plantas Zona Norte Argentina	
AR03	Plantas Zona Sur Argentina	
AT01	Personnel Area AT01	
AU01	Personnel Area AU01	Personnel Area AU01-Australia
AU02	Personnel Area Au02	Personnel Area Au02-Australia

4.2.4 Primary Key

Personnel Area

4.2.5 Important Fields

Personnel area text

Here you specify the code and name of the personnel area.

Address

Here you maintain address of a personnel area. You need to configure master lists required for addresses. For details see chapter 8.

4.3 PERSONNEL AREA TO COMPANY CODE ASSIGNMENT

Functional Consultant	User	Business Process Owner	Senior Management	My Rating	Understanding Level
A	A	A	A		

4.3.1 Purpose and Overview

This view of personnel area table, T500P, stores the linkage between personnel area and company code. Once you have assigned a company code to a personnel area, and posted payroll results, you should never change personnel area to company code linkage. If you do, you would face problem in the case of retro payroll run. If you have such a need, create new personnel area, link it to the new company code, and transfer all employees to the new personnel area. This is needed because there is no date validity in the personnel area table.

4.3.2 IMG Node

SM30 ➤ V_T500P

4.3.3 Screen

Pers.area	Personnel Area Text	Company Code	Company Name	Ctry Grpg
AT01	Personnel Area AT01	AT01	Country Template AT	03
AU01	Personnel Area AU01	AU01	Country Template AU	13
AU02	Personnel Area Au02	AU01	Country Template AU	13
BE01	Personnel area BE01	BE01	Country Template BE	12

4.3.4 Primary Key

Personnel Area

4.3.5 Important Fields

Company code

In SAP, company code is determined from personnel area. Employees are paid by their respective company codes.

Country grouping

Company code determines the default country for an employee's personal data, address data, and bank data.

4.4 PERSONNEL SUBAREA

Functional Consultant	User	Business Process Owner	Senior Management	My Rating	Understanding Level
A	A	A	A		

4.4.1 Purpose

On the basis of physical location, a company is divided in personnel areas, which are further divided in personnel subareas. On any given day, an employee belongs to one of the personnel subareas. This view contains the master list of PSAs and their names.

4.4.2 IMG Node

SM30 ➢ V_T001P

4.4.3 Screen

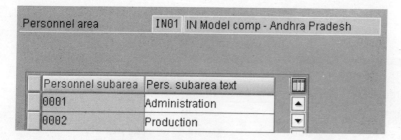

4.4.4 Primary Key

Personnel Area + Personnel Subarea

4.5 PERSONNEL SUBAREA GROUPINGS

Functional Consultant	User	Business Process Owner	Senior Management	My Rating	Understanding Level
A	C	C	X		

4.5.1 Purpose

On the basis of physical location, a company is divided in personnel areas, which are further divided in personnel subareas. On any given day, an employee belongs to one of the personnel subareas. This view contains the list of PSAs.

SAP provides the flexibility to build different rules for employees in different locations based on PSAs. Since PSAs could be many, they are grouped for the purpose of defining rules. For each purpose, there is a different grouping. This view contains all the groupings for the PSAs.

These groupings should be defined based on the needs of the user systems. While implementing personnel administration, you may keep one default value for each grouping. When other systems, e.g. time management, or appraisal get implemented, the groupings can be changed based on their requirements.

Table T001P does not have a validity period. Once you define PSA grouping for a PSA, and it gets used in time management/appraisal, etc., you should never change them. For example, you have one holiday calendar for all PSAs, and you are in production environment for several years. Then you decide that some of your PSAs will have a different holiday calendar. If you change PSA to holiday calendar assignment, you have a problem with retro. You will have to create the holiday calendar from the day you went live, generate work schedules, make all the adjustments you did in those work schedules (e.g. change in off days). Alternatively, you create a new PSA, assign it the new holiday calendar, and shift all employees to the new PSAs. You also have to enforce the discipline, or write a user exit, not to use the old PSA from the date it is made invalid.

Some countries also have country specific PSA groupings, e.g. those in table T7IN0P for India.

4.5.2 IMG Node

SM30 ➤ V_001P_ALL

4.5.3 Screen

PA	PA text	PSu...	PS text	Pr...	P...	A...	L...	T...	W...	H...	A...	TR...	A...	S...	PS	P...	L...	S...
IN01	IN Model ...	0001	Admin		1	40	40	40	40	IN	40	01	40		01	01		
IN01	IN Model ...	0002	Produ...		1	40	40	40	40	IN	40	01	40		03	01		
IN02	IN Model ...	0001	Admin		1	40	40	40	40	IN	40	01	40		01	01		
IN03	IN Model ...	0001	Admin		1	40	40	40	40	IN	40	01	40		01	01		

4.5.4 Primary Key

Personnel Area + Personnel Subarea

4.5.5 Important Fields

Personnel area, personnel subarea

Personnel area and personnel subarea for which the groupings are being defined.

PSA grouping for leave types

This grouping is now obsolete.

Pay scale area

This is used to default pay scale area in infotype 0008. However, feature TARIF takes precedence over it.

Pay scale type

This is used to default pay scale type in infotype 0008. However, feature TARIF takes precedence over it.

PSA grouping for absence and attendance types

Different types of leaves in a company are defined as absence types. Similarly, attendance types include training, business tour, etc. The properties of absence and attendance types are defined in view T554S based on this grouping. For example, you could specify that minimum duration of privilege leave is 3 days. SAP lets you configure different properties for different PSAs. For example, in one state the minimum duration may be 3 days, but in another state it may be 4 days. You could create 2 groups of PSAs, one for the first state and another for the second state, and configure these rules in SAP.

PSA grouping for substitution/availability types

The properties of substitution types (T556) and availability types (T557) can be different based on this grouping.

PSA grouping for attendance and absence counting

Rules for attendance/absence counting and leave deduction (T554X) depend on this grouping. This is an obsolete grouping. It was used when leave entitlement was kept in infotype 0005. Table T554X is also obsolete now.

Legal person

If you maintain legal person here, it defaults in infotype 0001.

PSA grouping for time recording

This grouping is a key field in most tables related to time types, important among them being T555A Time Types, T555E Time Evaluation Messages, T555J Transfer to Time Types, T555K Transfer to Time Wage Types and T555L Transfer to Absence Quotas.

PSA grouping for time quota types

This grouping is a key field in most tables related to time quotas, important among them being T556A Absence Quota Types, T555L Transfer to Absence Quotas, T556C Counting Rule for Attendances and Absences, T556P Attendance Quotas, T556R Rules for Deduction Sequence for Absence Quotas, T556U Attendance/Absence Quota Compensation Types and T556W Wage Type Assignment for Att./Absence Quota Compensations.

PSA grouping for premiums

You can define different premiums for different groups of employees based on this grouping, which is a key field in table T510P (Premium Table).

PSA grouping for primary wage type and wage maintenance

This grouping is used to allow/restrict a wage type to certain PSAs. The values must be from 0 to 9 only. It is used in view V_511_B (Define Wage Type Permissibility for each PS and ESG).

Statistics modifier

This field has country-specific use.

PSA grouping for appraisals

This grouping is a key field in tables related to appraisals; T513G Appraisal Groups, T513H Appraisal Criteria, T510B Appraisal Constants and T513PAPD PA-PD: Assign Appraisal Models to EE (sub)area/(sub)group.

Public holiday calendar

Here the public holiday calendar is defined for each PSA.

PSA grouping for work schedules

This grouping is a key field in tables T508A Work Schedule Rules and T508Z Assignment of PS Grouping for Work Schedules to Daily WS. Through the latter table, it is a key for T550A Daily Work Schedule, T550P Break Schedules, T551A Period Work Schedules, T551C Period Work Schedule Valuation, T552V Dynamic Daily Work Schedule Assignment, and T552W Dynamic Daily WS Assignment: Planned/Actual Overlap.

4.6 EMPLOYEE GROUP

Functional Consultant	User	Business Process Owner	Senior Management	My Rating	Understanding Level
A	A	A	A		

4.6.1 Purpose and Overview

Employee groups let you categorize your employees for identification and reporting. Employee groups can be used in features and PCRs.

In features you can generate data entry default values, e.g. payroll accounting area. In PCRs, you can apply different rules to different employee groups. User authorization can be restricted based on employee groups.

You should use employee group to capture an important characteristic of employee, e.g. permanent, temporary, etc. Since rules can be based on employee group, the employee attribute it represents should be chosen very carefully.

4.6.2 IMG Node

SM30 ➤ T501

4.6.3 Screen

Employee group	Name of Employee Grp
1	Permanent
2	Probationer
3	Temporary
4	Trainee

4.6.4 Primary Key

Employee Group

4.7 EMPLOYEE SUBGROUP

Functional Consultant	User	Business Process Owner	Senior Management	My Rating	Understanding Level
A	A	A	A		

4.7.1 Purpose and Overview

Employee subgroups let you categorize your employees for identification and reporting. Employee subgroups can be used in features and PCRs.

In features you can generate data entry default values, e.g. payroll accounting area. In PCRs, you can apply different rules to different employee subgroups. User authorization can be restricted based on employee subgroups.

Employee subgroup is an independent categorization of employees, and is not a further classification under employee group.

Use this field to capture an important characteristic of employee, e.g. grade, etc. Since rules can be based on employee subgroup, the employee attribute it represents should be chosen very carefully.

It is often useful to use a good naming convention. For example, your employee grades may be classified in executive, officer, supervisors and operatives. If you followed a naming convention, which helps you identify the group of grades from the first character, it could help you while defining authorizations by specifying, for example, E* rather than list each individual grade in that category.

4.7.2 IMG Node

SM30 ➤ T503K

4.7.3 Screen

Employee subgroup	Name of EE Subgroup
B1	Hourly worker
B2	Monthly worker
B3	Hrly salaried empl.
B4	Mthly salaried empl.
B5	Partner

4.7.4 Primary Key

Employee Subgroup

4.8 EMPLOYEE GROUP/SUBGROUP TO COUNTRY ASSIGNMENT

Functional Consultant	User	Business Process Owner	Senior Management	My Rating	Understanding Level
A	X	X	X		

4.8.1 Purpose

This view contains the list of valid EG, ESG combinations. You define employee groups and employee subgroups independently. But in your organization, certain combinations may not be valid. For example, you may not have Temporary Executives, while you may have Temporary Workmen. For each combination of employee group and employee subgroup, you tick the field 'Allowed' for each country in which it is valid. Certain combinations may not be valid in any country.

4.8.2 IMG Node

SM30 ➤ V_T503Z

4.8.3 Screen

EE group	1	Permanent
EE subgroup	1A	1A

	C..	Name of HR country grpg	Allowed
	01	Germany	☐
	02	Switzerland	☐
	03	Austria	☐
	04	Spain	☐
	05	Netherlands	☐

4.8.4 Primary Key

EG + ESG + Country Grouping

4.9 EMPLOYEE SUBGROUP GROUPINGS

Functional Consultant	User	Business Process Owner	Senior Management	My Rating	Understanding Level
A	C	C	X		

4.9.1 Purpose

Various SAP functionalities can be configured to work differently for different categories of employees. The employees can be categorized based on EG ESG combination. There is a category (grouping) for each purpose. This view defines the linkage between EG ESG combination and these groupings. The ESG groupings need to be defined carefully, and the linkage built.

4.9.2 IMG Node

SM30 ➤ V_503_ALL

4.9.3 Screen

E.	EE Gp Na...	ESgrp	EE ...	A...	E...	Tr...	E...	C...	E...	Pr...	A...	T...	WS...	Parti...
1	Permanent	1A	1A	1	2	2		3	A	1	1	1	2	☐
1	Permanent	1B	1B	1	2	2		3	3	1	1	1	2	☐
1	Permanent	2A	2A	1	2	2		3	3	1	1	1	2	☐
1	Permanent	2B	2B	1	2	2		3	3	1	1	1	2	☐

4.9.4 Primary Key

EG + ESG

4.9.5 Important Fields

ESG grouping for personnel calculation rule

Personnel calculation rules (PCRs) are used in payroll and time management. Using these rules you can apply different logic to different employees based on ESG for PCR. In this field you may assign the ESG for PCR to each combination of EG and ESG. Master list of ESG for PCR is predefined by SAP. The meanings of these groupings are fixed and must not be changed. ESG for PCR for salaried employees is 3.

ESG grouping for primary wage types

This grouping is used to allow/restrict a wage type to certain employee groups and subgroups. The values must be from 0 to 9 only. It is used in view V_511_B (Define Wage Type Permissibility for each PS and ESG).

Employee category

This data element is no longer used. It is now possible to define country-dependent work contracts in view T542A.

ESG grouping for collective agreement provision

In SAP, you define different components of an employee's salary under different wage types. Since some payments can be based on employee attributes, e.g. grade, SAP allows a wage type to be indirectly valuated based on five employee characteristics. ESG for CAP (ESG grouping for collective agreement provision) is one of them; others are pay scale type, pay scale area, pay scale group and pay scale level, which are defined in infotype 0008 at employee level.

ESG grouping for work schedules

You need to determine which work schedules are permissible for which employee groups and subgroups using the employee subgroup grouping for work schedules. This grouping is a key field in view T508A, Work Schedule Rules.

Activity status

Activity status is the status of an account in relation to the activities carried out by the account holder.

Employment status

This field is for Belgium.

Training status

This may be a country-specific field.

ESG grouping for time quota types

This grouping is a key field in most tables related to time quotas, important among them being T556A Absence Quota Types, T555L Transfer to Absence Quotas, T556C Counting Rule for Attendances and Absences, T556P Attendance Quotas, T556R Rules for Deduction Sequence for Absence Quotas, T556U Attendance/Absence Quota Compensation Types and T556W Wage Type Assignment for Att./Absence Quota Compensations.

ESG grouping for appraisal

One can set up appraisal criteria depending on employee subgroup using the employee subgroup grouping for appraisal. This grouping is a key field in tables related to appraisals; T513G Appraisal Groups, T513H Appraisal Criteria and T513PAPD PA-PD: Assign Appraisal Models to EE (sub)area/(sub)group.

Participation in incentive wages

Very often, incentive wages are restricted to certain groups of employees. Here, for every EG ESG combination, you can define whether incentive wages are permitted or not. This indicator can be queried in payroll by the operation OUTWP with feature INWID. In this way, you can check in payroll whether an employee participates in incentive wages (see PCR XW3). Incentive wage averages formed with function AVERA are only available for employee subgroups that participate in incentive wages.

4.10 EMPLOYEE SUBGROUP GROUPING FOR WORK SCHEDULES

Functional Consultant	User	Business Process Owner	Senior Management	My Rating	Understanding Level
A	X	X	X		

4.10.1 Purpose

This view contains master list of employee subgroup grouping for work schedules. It is assigned to an EG ESG combination in view V_T503_ALL. Thus for an employee, whose EG and ESG values are determined from infotype 0001, ESG for work schedules is determined from view V_T503_ALL. Although this table is not a check table for table T503, do not use any value in table T503, unless it is specified in this table.

For an employee, this grouping is used to access table T508A, Work Schedule Rules. If a work schedule rule is applicable to an ESG for work schedules, it must be defined in table T508A and work schedules generated, which are stored in table T552A. Through the above linkage, you find the work schedules of an employee.

4.10.2 IMG Node

SM30 ➢ V_T508T

4.10.3 Screen

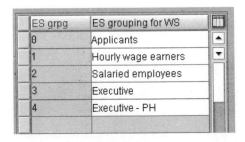

4.10.4 Primary Key

Language Key + Employee Subgroup Grouping for Work Schedules

4.11 PAYROLL AREA

Functional Consultant	User	Business Process Owner	Senior Management	My Rating	Understanding Level
A	A	A	A		

4.11.1 Purpose

This view contains the master list of payroll areas. In a large company, payroll for all employees may not be run together. SAP, therefore, lets you divide your employees into different payroll areas.

A payroll area is a group of employees whose payroll is processed together, i.e. for the same period, on the same day, and by the same payroll administrator. Configuration of payroll area is done by your payroll consultant. He chooses the appropriate period parameter and date modifier for each payroll area.

4.11.2 IMG Node

SM30 ➤ V_T549A

4.11.3 Screen

Payroll area	Payroll area text	Period parameters	Name	Run payroll	Date modifier
01	Monthly	01	Monthly	✔	
02	Semi-monthly	02	Semi-monthly	✔	
03	Weekly	03	Weekly	✔	
04	Bi-weekly	04	Bi-Weekly	✔	

4.11.4 Primary Key

Payroll Area

4.11.5 Important Fields

Payroll area and text

Here you define the master list of payroll areas.

Period parameters and name

Period parameters are used to create different payroll periods for the same time unit. For example, while two payroll areas may run monthly payroll, in one case the period may be the calendar month, while in another it may be from 21st of a month till 20th of the next month.

Run payroll

If you remove this tick, you cannot run payroll for this payroll area.

Date modifier

There are a number of dates specified for a payroll area. However, they are not defined at payroll area level, but at period parameter + date modifier level (T549S). This combination is then assigned to a payroll area (T549A), thereby associating these dates to a payroll area.

4.12 DEFAULT PAYROLL AREA

Functional Consultant	User	Business Process Owner	Senior Management	My Rating	Understanding Level
A	X	X	X		

4.12.1 Purpose

This feature is used to default payroll area in infotype 0001.

4.12.2 IMG Node

PE03 ≻ ABKRS

4.12.3 Screen

```
ABKRS Default value for payroll area
    └─⊟ TCLAS Transaction class for data storage
        ├─⊟ B Applicant data
        │     └─99
        └─⊟ otherwise
              └─⊞ MOLGA Country Grouping
```

4.12.4 Fields for Decision-making

Company Code
Personnel Area
Personnel Subarea
Employee Group
Employee Subgroup
Country Grouping
Transaction Class for Data Storage

4.12.5 Return Value

Payroll area

4.13 WORK CONTRACT

Functional Consultant	User	Business Process Owner	Senior Management	My Rating	Understanding Level
A	X	X	X		

4.13.1 Purpose

The work contract is used in statistical reporting. It enables you to group employees together in survey groups. In this view you maintain the master list for each country.

4.13.2 IMG Node

SM30 ➤ V_T542A

4.13.3 Screen

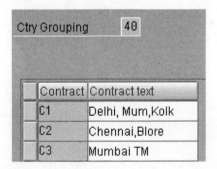

4.13.4 Primary Key

Country Grouping + Work Contract

4.14 ORGANIZATIONAL KEY

Functional Consultant	User	Business Process Owner	Senior Management	My Rating	Understanding Level
A	C	C	X		

4.14.1 Overview

In SAP, you can restrict authorization of a user to specified personnel area, employee group and employee subgroup. However, if your company wants to restrict authorization based on other fields of infotype 0001, you can use organizational key.

You can control authorization at employee level. To do so, you can divide your employees in groups, give each group an organizational key, and give authorization to users for one or more organizational keys. In these cases, you maintain the organizational key at employee level in infotype 0001.

However, in most cases, you would not like to control authorization at employee level. Instead, you would like it to depend on other employee parameters, e.g. PSA, cost center, etc. SAP lets you define the logic for creating groups of employees. This is done in feature VDSK1. This feature returns a variable key. Each variable key is a group of employees, to whom same authorization control would apply.

For each group of employee, you can define the following:

➢ Is the organizational key optional or required?
➢ Does the system propose a default value? If yes, under which creation rule this logic is specified?
➢ Can the user enter the value, or overwrite the default value proposed.
➢ Does the system ensure that the organizational key is from a predefined list, so as to prevent entry of unwanted values? This is particularly important if you do not plan to have any user with global authorization, as no user is then able to deal with the data of employees who have a wrong organizational key.

If you want the system to propose default values, you define the logic in creation rules. If you want the system to validate the organizational keys, you need to maintain the master list of organizational keys.

4.14.2 Employee Grouping for Authorization Control

SAP lets you define the logic for creating groups of employees for authorization check. This is done in feature VDSK1 using transaction PE03. This feature returns a variable key. Each variable key is a group of employees, to whom the same authorization control applies.

```
VDSK1 VDSK1  Organizational key
    |
    └─☐ MOLGA Country Grouping
           |
           └─☐ otherwise
                   |
                   └────01
```

4.14.3 Organizational Key Rules

Organizational key rules are maintained in view T527.

Variable key	Default/validation	Creation rule
01	5	01
19	5	19

Variable key

Variable key represents a group of employees. For each employee, feature VDSK1 returns the variable key, which is matched with this field.

Default/validation

You select from the following predefined values:

Code	Description	Optional	Default	User entry	Validation
1	Optional entry without validation	Y		Y	
2	Optional entry with validation	Y		Y	Y
3	Required entry with validation			Y	Y
4	Default that cannot be overwritten without validation		Y	N	
5	Default that can be overwritten without validation		Y	Y	
6	Default that can be overwritten with validation		Y	Y	Y
7	Default that cannot be overwritten with validation		Y	N	Y

Here you define whether the system proposes an organizational key by default. If yes, you need to have a creation rule. You define creation rule in view T527A, and assign it to the variable key in the 'Creation rule' column of this view.

You also define whether the system validates the organizational key entered. If yes, the organizational key must be maintained in view T527O.

Creation rule

In this field a creation rule is assigned to the group of employees identified by variable key returned by feature VDSK1. The creation rule is specified in view T527A.

4.14.4 Organizational Key Creation Rules

View T527A contains the creation rules, which define how to create organizational key from various fields of infotype 0001.

Creation rule	Serial no.	Field Name	Length	Offset
01	01	P0001-WERKS	04	
01	02	P0001-KOSTL	10	
19	01	P0001-BTRTL	04	
19	02	P0001-KOSTL	10	

Creation rule

Here you specify the creation rule which is being defined.

Serial number

The sequence in which the fields are combined to form the organizational key.

Field name

Field from which the data is picked up. Fields of only infotype 0001 are available. Available fields include hidden fields, e.g. employee name. You can also specify a constant value.

Length and offset

Only specified length of the field is picked up after leaving the specified offset. If you want to take substring of a field, the naming convention for that field must be meticulously followed. If you do not make an entry in the fields length and offset, the system automatically proposes the length of the field that is defined in the ABAP/4 Dictionary and the offset is 0.

4.14.5 Organizational Key Master

View T527O contains the master list of organizational keys with short and long text. It is used for validation of organizational keys entered in infotype 0001, where such a validation is specified in view T527. Field 'Hierarchy' is not used in the SAP standard system and always has value 1.

Hierarchy	Org.key	Short text	Name
1	002	SACHZ	SACHBEAR. ZEIT
1	007	SACHZ	SACHBEAR. PERS
1	01	SACHZ	SACHBEAR. ABR
1	010100001	KST 00001	BU 01 WK 01 KST ***00001
1	010100110	KST 00110	BU 01 WK 01 KST ***00110
1	CA01	H.O.-Mktg.	Marketing - Head Office Toronto
1	CA02	H.O.-Fin	Finance - Head Office Toronto

4.15 ADMINISTRATORS

Functional Consultant	User	Business Process Owner	Senior Management	My Rating	Understanding Level
A	X	X	X		

4.15.1 Overview

In infotype 0001, you can assign a personnel administrator, a time administrator and a payroll administrator to each employee. You can design authorization checks so that an employee's data is accessed only by his administrators. For each employee, an administrator group is determined by using feature PINCH. All administrators in that administrator group are available for selection in personnel administrator, time administrator and payroll administrator fields in infotype 0001.

4.15.2 Administrator Group

Feature PINCH helps you to determine the administrator group for an employee, based on the fields of infotype 0001. If you specify **** instead of a specific administrator group, the personnel area of the employee is returned as the administrator group.

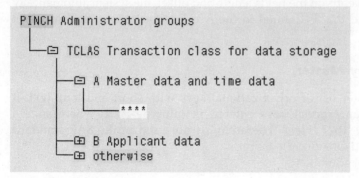

4.15.3 Administrators

View T526 contains the master list of administrators.

Group	Administrator	Administrator name	Title	Telephone no.	SAP name
APPL	AJ	Anjali Joshi	Ms		ANJALI
APPL	DR	Deepika Rao	Ms		DEEPIKA
APPL	EB	Edrina Boyle	Ms		EDRINA

Administrator group

An administrator group combines all administrators who are responsible for one organizational area in personnel administration or recruitment. The administrator group is determined by feature PINCH. Alternatively, the value in the parameter ID 'SGR' of your user master record is used as the default value. This value is populated in infotype 0001.

Administrator

This field contains a three-character administrator code, which can be assigned in personnel administrator, time administrator and payroll administrator fields of infotype 0001. Administrator fields in infotype 0001 can be used for authorization checks.

Administrator name, title, telephone number

These fields contain the name, form of address and telephone number of the administrator.

SAP name

The system can be configured to send internal mail to administrators. These mails go to the inbox of the user's SAP business workplace. The user id of the administrator is taken from this field.

4.16 POSITIONS

Functional Consultant	User	Business Process Owner	Senior Management	My Rating	Understanding Level
B	X	X	X		

4.16.1 Purpose and Overview

Usually you would implement OM along with personnel administration. However, if you decide to implement personnel administration without OM, you can still maintain positions.

You can use transaction code S_AHR_61011490 to maintain positions in personnel administration. If you are using OM and integration of OM and PA is on, you maintain positions in OM, and SAP automatically creates entries in table T528B.

4.16.2 IMG Node

SM30 ≻ V_528B_C

Transaction S_AHR_61011490—Change view "Positions: Organizational Assignment"

4.16.3 Screen

O..	Position	Position Text	Valid From	End Date	O..	Job	Job title	WM	WM	Gen.	HL
A	50007378	ABC WORK CENT..	21.08.2006	31.12.9999	P						
O	99999999		01.01.1800	31.12.9999							
S	00003007	GENERAL MANAG..	13.09.2006	31.12.9999	P						
S	20000026	Managing Director..	29.07.2005	31.12.9999	P						

4.16.4 Primary Key

Object Type + Position + End Date

4.16.5 Important Fields

Object type

Object type for position is S.

Position and position text

These fields contain position number and its description.

Valid from and end date

Here you specify the validity period of the position record.

Maintenance of table entry in OM

Positions, which have been maintained in OM, cannot be changed manually.

Job and job title

Here you maintain the job, which is performed by the position.

Work methods

You can define up to two work methods for a position.

Gender key

If you want the position to be occupied by only males, or only females, you can specify that here.

Hard labor

Here you can specify whether the position involves heavy labor on night shifts. If this is the case, it also specifies whether an employee earns additional leave or a special retirement pension.

4.17 POSITION-BASED PAYMENTS

Functional Consultant	User	Business Process Owner	Senior Management	My Rating	Understanding Level
B	X	X	X		

4.17.1 Purpose and Overview

SAP lets you pay your employees based on the positions they occupy. If you want to use this functionality, you specify the wage types and their amounts for a position. The wage types can also be indirectly valuated. Indirect valuation requires pay scale type, area, group, level and ESG for CAP. You, therefore, need to specify these for the position. Position-based payments can be maintained by users using transaction S_AHR_61011401.

4.17.2 IMG Node

SM30 ➤ V_T528C_B

4.17.3 Screen

Object type	S
Position	00003007

	No	Wage type	Long text	Valid From	End Date	Amount	Currency

4.17.4 Primary Key

Object Type + Position + End Date + Sequence Number

4.17.5 Important Fields

Object type

Object type for position is S.

Position

Here you enter the position number for which you are specifying payment.

Sequence number

Since the position-based payments may have multiple wage types, you put them in multiple lines and give a sequence number to each line.

Wage type and text

Wage type for making payment. Some wage types may be indirectly valuated.

Valid from and end date

Here you specify the validity period of the record, as the payments for a position may change over a period of time. While making payment for a day, only records which are valid on that day are considered.

Amount and currency

If the wage type is directly valuated, you enter the amount. If it is indirectly valuated, leave it blank.

4.18 INDIRECT VALUATION OF POSITION-BASED PAYMENTS

Functional Consultant	User	Business Process Owner	Senior Management	My Rating	Understanding Level
B	X	X	X		

4.18.1 Purpose and Overview

SAP lets you pay your employees based on the positions they occupy. If you want to use this functionality, you specify the wage types and their amounts for a position. The wage types can also be indirectly valuated. Indirect valuation requires pay scale type, area, group, level and ESG for CAP. You, therefore, need to specify these for the position. Position-based payments can be maintained by users using transaction S_AHR_61011401.

4.18.2 IMG Node

SM30 ➤ V_528B_D

4.18.3 Screen

O.	Position	Po...	Valid From	End Date	C...	Ty.	PS type	Ar.	PS area	Grpg	P...	Lv	O.
S	20000026	Man...	29.07.2005	31.12.9999									P
S	20000030	GE...	01.01.2001	29.02.2004									P
S	20000032	MC...	01.01.2001	15.07.2004									P
S	20000033	MC...	01.01.2001	08.06.2005									P

4.18.4 Primary Key

Object Type + Position + End Date

4.18.5 Important Fields

Object type

Object type for position is S.

Position and position text

Here you enter the position number for which you are specifying pay scale type, area, group, level and ESG for CAP.

Valid from and end date

Here you specify the validity period of the record, as the pay scale type, area, group, level and ESG for CAP for a position may change over a period of time.

Country grouping

Pay scale is defined for a country grouping. After you specify the country grouping, choose the pay scale.

Pay scale type, area, group, level and ESG for CAP

Indirect valuation of wage types is defined based on these parameters. The values specified here are used for indirect valuation of wage types for the position.

OM

If you maintain positions in OM and OM to PA integration is on, entries are automatically created in this table and this field is marked P. You can delete or change those positions only in OM. However, even for these positions, you can maintain parameters for indirect valuation.

4.19 JOBS

Functional Consultant	User	Business Process Owner	Senior Management	My Rating	Understanding Level
B	X	X	X		

4.19.1 Purpose and Overview

Usually you would implement OM along with personnel administration. However, if you decide to implement personnel administration without OM, you can still maintain jobs. You can use transaction code S_AHR_61011475 to maintain jobs in personnel administration. If you are using OM and integration of OM and PA is on, you maintain jobs in OM, and SAP automatically creates entries in table T513.

4.19.2 IMG Node

SM30 ➤ T513, V_T513S

Transaction S_AHR_61011475—Change view "Job Title"

4.19.3 Screen T513

Job key	Job title	Start Date	End Date	OM
00000001	Accountant	01.01.1900	31.12.9999	
00000002	Bank employee	01.01.1900	31.12.9999	
00000003	Administrator	01.01.1900	31.12.9999	
00000004	Bank clerk	01.01.1900	31.12.9999	

4.19.4 Screen V_T513S

Job key	Job title	Start Date	End Date	OM
00000001	Accountant	01.01.1900	31.12.9999	
00000002	Bank employee	01.01.1900	31.12.9999	
00000003	Administrator	01.01.1900	31.12.9999	
00000004	Bank clerk	01.01.1900	31.12.9999	

4.19.5 Primary Key

Job + End Date

4.19.6 Important Fields

Job and title

These fields contain the job key and its description.

Start date and end date

Here you specify the validity period of the job record.

OM

Jobs, which have been maintained in OM, can be changed only in OM.

4.20 ORGANIZATIONAL UNITS

Functional Consultant	User	Business Process Owner	Senior Management	My Rating	Understanding Level
B	X	X	X		

4.20.1 Purpose

Usually you would implement OM along with personnel administration. However, if you decide to implement personnel administration without OM, you can still maintain organizational units. You can use transaction code S_AHR_61011474 to maintain organizational units in personnel administration. If you are using OM and integration of OM and PA is on, you maintain organizational units in OM, and SAP automatically creates entries in table T527X.

4.20.2 IMG Node

SM30 ➤ V_T527X

Transaction S_AHR_61011474—Change view "Organizational Units"

4.20.3 Screen

Organizational unit	Organizational Unit Text	Start Date	End Date	OM
00000001	Temp Truck-I Div Pool	01.01.1900	31.12.9999	
00000002	Planning department	01.01.1900	31.12.9999	
00000003	Printshop	01.01.1900	31.12.9999	
00000004	Data processing	01.01.1900	31.12.9999	
00000005	Production	01.01.1900	31.12.9999	

4.20.4 Primary Key

Language Key + Organizational Unit + End Date

4.20.5 Important Fields

Organizational unit and text

These fields contain an organizational unit's id and its description.

Start date and end date

Here you specify the validity period of the organizational unit's record.

OM

Organizational units, which have been maintained in OM, cannot be changed manually.

4.21 OM–PA INTEGRATION

Functional Consultant	User	Business Process Owner	Senior Management	My Rating	Understanding Level
A	C	X	X		

4.21.1 Overview

There are two places, where SAP keeps data about a person's relationship in the organization: organizational management and personnel administration. Ideally, it should store it in only one place. But what would SAP do if an organization were implementing only one of the two sub modules? Therefore, SAP has decided to store it in two places. But, to overcome the problem created by storing the data in two places, SAP has provided some facilities. If integration between OM and PA is on and you create the data in one, it is automatically duplicated in the other.

SAP also permits you to maintain partial integration between OM and PA. Through feature PLOGI, you can specify which group of employees participate in integration, and which do not.

If you are using OM and want to implement PA, you can run reports RHINTE10 or RHINTE30 to create the data in PA.

If you are using PA and want to implement OM, you can run report RHINTE00 to create the data in OM.

You can check consistency between OM and PA using RHINTECHECK and create missing objects on both sides by using RHINTE20 and RHINTE20_ALT.

4.21.2 IMG Node

SM30 ➤ V_T77S0

4.21.3 Screen

Group	Sem.abbr.	Value abbr	Description
PLOGI	ORGA	X	Integration Switch: Organizational Assignment
PLOGI	PDCON		HR: Context Authorization Check in PD
PLOGI	PLOGI	01	Integration Plan Version / Active Plan Version
PLOGI	PRELI	99999999	Integration: default position
PLOGI	PRELU		Integration: PA update online or batch
PLOGI	QUALI	1 A032 Q	Integration switch for qualifications
PLOGI	SPLIT		Integration: New IT 0001 record at name change
PLOGI	TEXTC		Integration: transfer short text of job
PLOGI	TEXTD		Integration: Selection Date for OM Texts (IT0001)
PLOGI	TEXTO		Integration: transfer short text of org.unit
PLOGI	TEXTS		Integration: transfer short text of position
PLOGI	TIME		Integration switch: Training and Event Mgmt/ Time

4.21.4 Integration Parameters

Group	Sem. abbr.	Description	Explanation
PLOGI	ORGA	Integration Switch: Organizational Assignment	This is the main integration switch between OM and PA. If integration between OM and PA is on and you create the data in one, it is duplicated automatically in the other.
PLOGI	PLOGI	Integration Plan Version/Active Plan Version	Since you can have multiple plan versions in OM, you need to specify integration plan version here, if integration is on.
PLOGI	PRELI	Integration: default position	This position is used for those employees, for whom OM to PA integration is not active.
PLOGI	PRELU	Integration: PA update online or batch	You can decide whether changes made in OM are updated in PA immediately or not. If they are to be updated in batch, use RHINTE30.
PLOGI	SPLIT	Integration: New infotype 1 record at name change	Sometimes you could change description of jobs, positions or organizational units, without changing the objects themselves. Till some date, there is old description, after which there is new description. If you wish that the description were correctly shown in PA, before and after the date of change,

(Contd.)

Group	Sem. abbr.	Description	Explanation
			then the PA record needs to be split, otherwise it shows new description for the entire period. This choice is controlled by this integration switch. If this switch is set ('X'), and you change the description of jobs, positions or organizational units, new infotype 0001 records for the personnel numbers concerned are created on the date of change.
PLOGI	TEXTC	Integration: transfer short text of job	In OM, objects have a short text, and a long text. If this switch is blank, long text of the job is shown. If it is 'X', short text is shown.
PLOGI	TEXTD	Integration: Selection Date for OM Texts (IT0001)	If you do not create split when the OM text changes (PLOGI + SPLIT), whether the OM text should be shown for the latest period or earliest period is controlled by this.
PLOGI	TEXTO	Integration: transfer short text of org.unit	If this switch is blank, long text of the organizational unit is shown. If it is 'X', short text is shown.
PLOGI	TEXTS	Integration: transfer short text of position	If this switch is blank, long text of the position is shown. If it is 'X', short text is shown.

4.22 PARTIAL OM–PA INTEGRATION

Functional Consultant	User	Business Process Owner	Senior Management	My Rating	Understanding Level
A	B	B	X		

4.22.1 Purpose

Sometimes organizations do not wish to maintain organization structure for all their employees. SAP permits you to maintain partial integration between OM and PA. Through feature PLOGI, you can specify which groups of employees participate in integration, and which groups of employees do not.

4.22.2 IMG Node

PE03 ≻ PLOGI

4.22.3 Screen

```
PLOGI Control: Integration of personnel planning and master data

  └─⊟ PERSG Employee Group

       ├─⊟ 1 Permanent

       │      └───X

       └─⊞ 2 Probationer
```

4.22.4 Fields for Decision-making

Transaction Class for Data Storage
Country Grouping
Company Code
Personnel Area
Personnel Subarea
Employee Group
Employee Subgroup

4.22.5 Return Value

X	Integration on
Blank	Integration off

Personal Data

5.1 PERSONAL DATA (INFOTYPE 0002)

Functional Consultant	User	Business Process Owner	Senior Management	My Rating	Understanding Level
A	A	A	A		

5.1.1 Screen

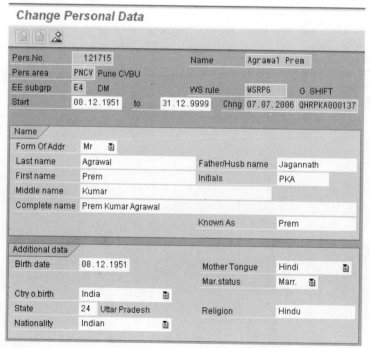

Change Personal Data

Pers.No.	121715
Pers.area	PNCV Pune CVBU
EE subgrp	E4 DM
Start	08.12.1951 to 31.12.9999

Name: Agrawal Prem
WS rule: WSRPG G SHIFT
Chng 07.07.2006 QHRPKA000137

Name

Form Of Addr	Mr		
Last name	Agrawal	Father/Husb name	Jagannath
First name	Prem	Initials	PKA
Middle name	Kumar		
Complete name	Prem Kumar Agrawal		
		Known As	Prem

Additional data

Birth date	08.12.1951	Mother Tongue	Hindi
		Mar.status	Marr.
Ctry o.birth	India		
State	24 Uttar Pradesh	Religion	Hindu
Nationality	Indian		

5.1.2 Purpose and Overview

This infotype stores personal information of an employee. It has time constraint 1, which means that an infotype data record must exist in the system at all times. The validity start for the first record of the infotype 0002 is determined from the employee's date of birth, and not from the date of his joining the organization, as is the case for most other infotypes.

The number of children entered in infotype 0002 can differ from the number of children stored in infotype 0021, Family/Related Person. In some countries, number of children field triggers a dynamic action for taking in the details of the children in infotype 0021.

The employee's name is also stored in infotype 0001, when data is entered in infotype 0002.

5.1.3 Subtypes

No subtypes

5.1.4 Time Constraint

1 (Record must have no gaps, no overlappings). Infotype 0002 cannot be delimited even after the employee leaves (employment status, 'withdrawn'). End-date of the last record must remain 31.12.9999.

5.1.5 Important Fields

Form of address

Gender is determined from the form of address and stored in the gender field, which is not displayed normally.

Name format

This field is used to permit name formatting depending on the group to which the employee belongs, e.g. north Indian names vs. south Indian names. For more details on name formatting, see chapter 5.4.

Name affixes

SAP provides a number of fields for storing name prefixes, suffixes and affixes. Which of these are seen on the screen depends on customizing of the screen.

Birth date

The employee's date of birth determines the start date of the first record of infotype 0002.

Number of children

The number of children entered here is not validated against the number of children stored in infotype 0021. In some countries, this field triggers a dynamic action for taking in the details of the children in infotype 0021.

Religion

If the holiday calendar contains religious holidays, the employee gets them on the basis of the religion assigned to him here.

5.1.6 Reports

S_PH9_46000221–Birthday List

You can use this report to get a list of employees whose birthday falls in the specified period.

Birthday list

Personnel No.	Last name	First name	Day	Month
00121715	Agrawal	Prem	08	12

S_AHR_61016374–Nationalities

This report gives a summary of nationality of employees with gender break-up.

Nationalities   1

Key date 03.12.2006

Nationality	- Male -		- Female -		= Total =	
	Number	%	Number	%	Number	%
IN Indian	322	100.0			322	100.0
***	322	100.0			322	100.0
Non-EU members	322	100.0			322	100.0

S_PH9_46000218–Statistics: Gender Sorted by Age

This report gives agewise, genderwise count of employees.

Age/gender

Age	Gender	Σ Number	Σ Share in %
20		14	2.0
	Male	33	4.8
21		33	4.8
	Male	44	6.4

5.2 NAME AFFIXES

Functional Consultant	User	Business Process Owner	Senior Management	My Rating	Understanding Level
A	X	X	X		

5.2.1 Purpose

This view contains the master list of name affixes.

5.2.2 IMG Node

SM30 ➤ V_T535N

5.2.3 Screen

AT	Name affix	Output text
S	B.A.	B.A.
S	B.SC.	B.Sc.
S	CPA	CPA
S	D.D.	D.D.

5.2.4 Primary Key

Type of name affix + Name affix

5.2.5 Important Fields

Type of name affix

You can store following types of name affixes in this view.

S	Titles which come after the name (suffix)
T	Titles which come before the name (prefix)
V	Name prefixes
Z	Name affixes

Name affix

This field contains the code of name affix.

Output text

This field contains the text which is affixed in the name.

5.3 FORM OF ADDRESS

Functional Consultant	User	Business Process Owner	Senior Management	My Rating	Understanding Level
A	X	X	X		

5.3.1 Purpose

This view contains master list of forms of address.

5.3.2 IMG Node

SM30 ➤ T522G

5.3.3 Screen

FOA key	Title	Long text	Gender
1	Mr	Mr	1
2	Mrs	Mrs	2
3	Ms	Ms	2
4	Dr	Doctor	1
5	DrMs	Doctor Ms	2

5.3.4 Primary Key

Form-of-Address Key

5.3.5 Important Fields

Form-of-address key

This field contains the code for form-of-address key.

Title

This field contains the short text for Form-of-Address.

Long text

This field contains the long text for Form-of-Address.

Gender

Gender is determined from the form-of-address, and stored in infotype 0002. The values are:

Blank	Unknown
1	Male
2	Female

5.4 NAME FORMATTING

Functional Consultant	User	Business Process Owner	Senior Management	My Rating	Understanding Level
A	B	B	B		

5.4.1 Requirement

In all manpower related reports/letters/communications, employee name is an important information. The employees need to be addressed differently depending on the context. Sometimes you would congratulate them, sometimes warn. Sometimes you would address them in a personal tone, sometimes you would be formal.

People are also sensitive to how their name is written, and may mind if not addressed properly. Different communities in the world follow different practices in naming people.

SAP has met this requirement by providing a number of name component fields, and customer defined rules to combine these components in different sequences to give desired names. To take full advantage of SAP's power and to delight your employees, you need to understand the data model for name format.

5.4.2 Data Model for Name Format

Types of use

The name you print depends on the type of use. The table below lists some of the possible uses. Type of use is a characteristic of a program. This link is maintained in view T522F.

Code	Uses of names
01	Reports
02	Payslip
03	Cheque
04	Formal letter
05	Informal (personal) letter
06	E-mail
08	Rewards
09	Disciplinary action

Styles of names

Names come in various styles. North Indian names are different from south Indian names. This is an employee characteristic and is specified in the name format field of infotype 0002.

01	North India	First, middle, last
02	North India	First, last
03	North India	First, middle
11	Maharashtra/ Gujarat	First, father/husband, last
21	Andhra	Surname, first, caste
22	Andhra	Surname, first
41	Tamil Nadu	Village, father/husband, own, caste
42	Tamil Nadu	Father/husband, first, caste
43	Tamil Nadu	Village, father/husband, own
44	Tamil Nadu	Father/husband, own
51	Kerala	Family, father, first, last
52	Kerala	Family, father, first
53	Kerala	Family, first, last
54	Kerala	Father, first, last
55	Kerala	First, father/husband, last

Name assembly logic

Depending on the types of use and styles of names, specify what name components are assembled and in which sequence. The logic can also differ for employee name and family member name. It can vary for different countries. This is specified in view V_T522N.

Name components

Name components used in name assembly logic come from infotype 0002 or infotype 0021. You need to have a clear guideline on which field is used for what purpose.

Field name	SAP description	Your use
VORNA	First name	
MIDNM	Middle Name	
NACHN	Last Name	
ANRED	Form-of-Address	
NAME2	Name at Birth	
INITS	Initials	
CNAME	Full Name	
RUFNM	Known As	

5.4.3 How a Program Prints a Name

When a program runs, it determines what type of name it has to print. This information is picked up from view T522F, which specifies what type of name has to be printed in that program.

For each employee, the program gets the name format from infotype 0002, which specifies what is the style of that particular employee's name.

Then the program fetches the name assembly logic from view V_T522N for that name-type and name-style.

It then fetches the name components required from infotype 0002, and assembles it as per logic fetched earlier. This is the name printed by the program.

If the name to be printed is of employee's family member, infotype 0021 is referred everywhere instead of infotype 0002.

5.4.4 Keeping Name Formatting Simple

While SAP provides a lot of flexibility in assembling names, in real life the combinations may become too many and difficult to maintain. Here is a simple solution you may like to use. SAP has the following seven fields for name:

➤ Last Name
➤ First Name
➤ Name at Birth
➤ Second Name
➤ Full Name
➤ Known As
➤ Middle Name

Define a maximum of seven types of names, you wish to use in your organization.

Type of name	Use	SAP field
First name	Informal address	First name
Last name	Formal address	Last name
Full name	Cheque	Full name
Name followed by initials	Reports	
Initials followed by name	Identity card, payslip	
Name for bank	Bank	
Passport/official documents	Nominations	

You may customize this matrix as per your needs. Rename data elements where required, so that there is no confusion later. Ask each employee to give all the names. Update all the names of an employee in SAP. In each program, use the appropriate name.

5.5 PROGRAM TO NAME TYPE LINK

Functional Consultant	User	Business Process Owner	Senior Management	My Rating	Understanding Level
A	X	X	X		

5.5.1 Purpose

You can assign different types of use of names to different programs. Thus, one program may be a letter, which addresses the employee using his first name, whereas another program may be a report, where the name is the last name followed by the first name.

5.5.2 IMG Node

SM30 ➤ T522F

5.5.3 Screen

Program	For...
RPC190E0	02
RPCALCJ0	02
RPCEDTJ0	02
RPCKOCN0	04
RPCKVCN0	04
RPCLGA00	06

5.5.4 Primary Key

ABAP program name

5.5.5 Important Fields

ABAP program name

This field contains the program name for which the name format is specified.

Format for HR name editing

This field contains the 'type of use' of the program. View V_T522N contains the rule for assembling the name from its components for each 'type of use'.

5.6 HR NAME FORMAT

Functional Consultant	User	Business Process Owner	Senior Management	My Rating	Understanding Level
A	X	X	X		

5.6.1 Purpose

This view contains rules to assemble names from its components.

5.6.2 IMG Node

SM30 ➤ V_T522N

5.6.3 Screen

HR Name Format

Format	Prefix	Nam...	Serial...	Field name	Con...	Alt.pr...
0	0002	0	1	NACHN		
0	0002	0	2	VORNA	99	
1	0002	0	1	TITEL		
1	0002	0	2	VORNA		
1	0002	0	3	NAMZU		
1	0002	0	4	VORSW		
1	0002	0	5	NACHN		

5.6.4 Primary Key

Country Grouping + Format for HR name editing + Prefix for field names (origin) + Name Format of Employee + Sequence Number

5.6.5 Important Fields

Format for HR name editing

This field contains the 'Types of use' your organization wants to have. Examples of 'Types of use' are given in the table on the next page.

Code	Uses of names
01	Reports
02	Payslip
03	Cheque
04	Formal letter
05	Informal (personal) letter
06	E-mail
08	Rewards
09	Disciplinary action

Depending on the program, which needs to assemble a name, this field is determined from view T522F, and used for accessing this view.

Prefix for field names (origin)

This field specifies the infotype from which the fields are to be read. For employees the data is read from infotype 0002, whereas for family members it is read from infotype 0021. Within a program, there may be employee names, as well as the names of family members, and the formatting requirement for the two may be different; hence, this field is part of primary key.

Name format of employee

This field contains the style of name. Style of name is an employee characteristic and is specified in the name format field of infotype 0002. The name assembly logic has to be defined for each style (called name format by SAP). The name format of the employee in infotype 0002 is matched with this field. If no name format is specified for the employee, name format 00 is taken.

Sequence number

Here you specify the sequence in which the name fields are taken.

Field name

Sequence number and field name combination decide how the name is assembled from its constituents. You may also specify a literal in this field. If you want the name to appear as Ayer, Ravi you would put a comma in sequence number 2.

Conversion for field editing

These rules are applied to prevent silly looking name assembly. In the above example, if the first name is not present, you would want to suppress the comma.

Alternative prefix for field names

If you enter an infotype here, this supercedes the infotype given in 'Prefix for field names (origin)'. This field is used only for Japan.

5.7 MARITAL STATUS

Functional Consultant	User	Business Process Owner	Senior Management	My Rating	Understanding Level
A	X	X	X		

5.7.1 Purpose

In this view you define the master list of marital status, which you assign to an employee in infotype 0002.

5.7.2 IMG Node

SM30 ➤ V_T502T

5.7.3 Screen

Mar.stat.	Marital status
0	Single
1	Marr.
2	Wid.
3	Div.

5.7.4 Primary Key

Language Key + Marital Status Key

5.7.5 Important Fields

Marital status key and marital status description

Here you maintain the marital status keys and their corresponding descriptions.

5.7.6 Longer Description of Marital Status

View V_T502T can hold only six-character description of marital status. If you want to keep a longer description, you can do so in view V_T7BRE1.

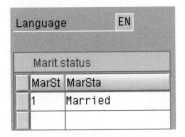

5.8 RELIGIOUS DENOMINATIONS

Functional Consultant	User	Business Process Owner	Senior Management	My Rating	Understanding Level
A	X	X	X		

5.8.1 Purpose

In this view you define the master list of religions with four character abbreviation and text, which you assign to an employee in infotype 0002.

5.8.2 IMG Node

SM30 ➤ V_T516T

5.8.3 Screen

Key	Abbr.	Denomination text
00	- -	No church tax liability
01	EV	Evangelical
02	RC	Roman Catholic
03	RF	Reformed (Evangelical)

5.8.4 Primary Key

Language Key + Religious Denomination Key

5.9 CONSISTENCY OF FORM-OF-ADDRESS AND GENDER

Functional Consultant	User	Business Process Owner	Senior Management	My Rating	Understanding Level
A	X	X	X		

5.9.1 Purpose

Infotype 0002 contains two fields, form-of-address and gender. Gender is also derived indirectly from the form-of-address. You can use this feature to give a warning, or error, if the two are contradictory.

5.9.2 IMG Node

PE03 ➤ 27GMS

5.9.3 Screen

```
27GMS HR-HK: Set message type for inconsistency of Address and Gender
   └─🗀 MOLGA Country Grouping
       └─🗀 27 Hong Kong
           └─🗀 BUKRS Company Code
               ├─🗀 HK01 Country Template HK
               │   └─W
               └─🗀 otherwise
                   └─W
```

5.9.4 Fields for Decision-making

Company Code
Country Grouping

5.9.5 Return Value

Warning message (W), or Error message (E).

Payroll Status

6.1 PAYROLL STATUS (INFOTYPE 0003)

Functional Consultant	User	Business Process Owner	Senior Management	My Rating	Understanding Level
A	A	A	A		

6.1.1 Screen

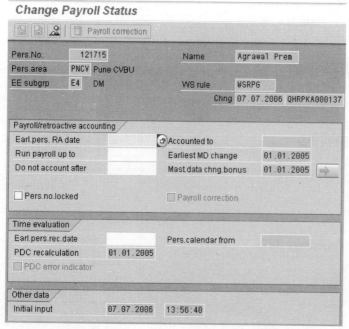

6.1.2 Purpose and Overview

Infotype 0003 contains control data for an employee's payroll and time accounting. The system automatically creates this infotype when an employee is hired. Whenever an infotype is updated, which requires that the employee's payroll, or time evaluation is to be run for a past period (see chapter 41, infotype properties), the system automatically updates this infotype.

You can prevent retro accounting before a given date at employee level for payroll and time management. You can temporarily stop the payroll of an employee by updating lock indicator.

This infotype controls whether an employee's payroll is run or not. There is no history maintained for this infotype. There is only one record, which has the current status. Table PA0003 is the check table for all other infotypes.

When you maintain this infotype through transaction PA30, certain fields cannot be edited as shown in the screen shot. In exceptional circumstances, if you wish to edit these fields you may use transaction PU03. However, you must do so only if you fully understand the implication of the changes you propose to make.

6.1.3 Subtypes

No subtypes

6.1.4 Time Constraint

A (Infotype exists just once from Jan. 1, 1800 to Dec. 12, 9999)

6.1.5 Important Fields

Earliest personal retro accounting date

The retroactive accounting limit defines the date in the payroll past up to which master and time data changes are allowed as well as the date up to which the system carries out retroactive accounting.

Earliest personal retroactive accounting date can be used to prevent retro accounting before a given date at employee level. It is one of the following three dates which determine the retroactive accounting limit.

➤ The earliest period for which retroactive accounting can be run (specified in the payroll control record).
➤ The earliest personal retroactive accounting date for a particular employee specified in infotype 0003.
➤ The employee's hiring date.

The system determines the latest date as the retroactive accounting limit. You can't run payroll for the employee before this date. But this is not the date from which the payroll is run. Normally, it is run from the 'earliest master data change date' in infotype 0003. However, if you run forced retro and specify an earlier date, it runs from that date.

Run payroll up to

Normally, payroll is not run for withdrawn, inactive or retiree employees. If you wish to override this default, and run payroll even for these employees, you can specify here the date till when the payroll will run. This date must be in a period in which the employee is not active, because for active employees the payroll runs anyway.

Do not account after

Normally, payroll is not run for withdrawn, inactive or retiree employees. However, for an employee, if master data is changed for a period when he was active, his payroll needs to be run. In that case payroll is run up to the current month because payment to employee can happen only in the current month.

If you do not want to run payroll for a withdrawn employee, without your explicit authorization, even though there is change in master data during active period, you can do so by specifying a date here. This forcibly stops the payroll. This date must be in an inactive period. This field is not to be used for stopping payroll of an active employee.

Accounted to

This field is system maintained and contains the date up to which payroll has been run for an employee. You cannot have gaps in payroll run. You also cannot run payroll for a person for a period twice, except in retroactive mode.

You can run payroll for a person for a period up to 99 times before exiting payroll. This is counted as only one payroll run, because each subsequent payroll run overwrites the previous payroll run.

Earliest MD change

When you change employee data that triggers retro accounting in payroll, the system stores the earliest date from which the master data change is valid. Note that all master data changes do not trigger retro accounting in payroll. This date is used for running his payroll from a retro period if necessary. This date can be a future date after the last payroll run.

When the payroll runs for an employee, this date is blanked out. Since, the payroll does not run for locked employees, this date is not blanked out for locked employees.

Master data change—bonus

This field, like the 'earliest master data change' field, is set when master data is changed. It is deleted by bonus payments in the payroll program.

Personnel number locked

If you flag the personnel number locked indicator, the employee is excluded from payroll, i.e. the employee's personnel number is then not selected for processing. However, when the lock is removed, the payroll is run for all the periods for which it had not run. Hence, it should be used only where temporary locking is to be achieved, and not when the intention is not to pay the employee. If the intention is not to pay the employee, infotype 0008 should be updated appropriately.

You cannot lock a personnel number if payroll for the current period has already been run for him. However, you may delete the payroll result and then lock him. You must do so before exiting payroll.

Payroll correction

The system automatically activates the payroll correction indicator, if a personnel number was rejected in the payroll run or if changes were made to payroll-relevant data in the correction phase of payroll. At the same time, the system writes this personnel number into the payroll correction run search help (matchcode W). This search help is installed as a search help for personnel numbers in personnel administration.

By calling up the search help, you can select personnel numbers that have previously been rejected by the payroll program and run the payroll again. The payroll correction indicator is removed from infotype 0003 for all personnel numbers that are accepted in the new payroll run.

Earliest personal recalculation date for time evaluation

If you don't want to run time evaluation for an employee before a certain date, you can maintain it here.

Personal calendar from

This field specifies the date as of which the employee's personal calendar must be generated.

PDC recalculation

This field specifies the date from which the next time evaluation run would start. When time evaluation is complete, the date is set to the first day for which time evaluation has not been run. This field is system maintained and is updated whenever any data comes in the system, which requires time evaluation to start from an earlier date.

PDC error indicator

The system automatically updates this field if a personnel number is rejected in time evaluation.

Initial input date and time

These fields show the date and time when the record was created.

6.1.6 Menu and Menu Bar

Delete correction run, set correction run

Through these actions, you can remove payroll correction tick, or mark it.

Payroll area list

Through this menu item you can access the payroll control record.

Valid From	End Date	PArea	PP	PayY	Valid From	End Date	Control record status
01.01.2005	31.12.9999	P1	5	2006	01.08.2006	31.08.2006	Payroll correction

Challenge

7.1 CHALLENGE (INFOTYPE 0004)

Functional Consultant	User	Business Process Owner	Senior Management	My Rating	Understanding Level
B	B	B	B		

7.1.1 Screen

Create Challenge

Pers.No.	121715		Name	Agrawal Prem
Pers.area	PNCV Pune CVBU			
EE subgrp	E4 DM		WS rule	WSRPG G SHIFT
Start	01.01.2005	to	31.12.9999	

Challenge data

Challenge group	☑	ID end date
Degree of challenge		
Credit factor		
Type of challenge		

Issuing authority

Official agency

Challenge cert.date

Reference number

Second authority

7.1.2 Purpose

This infotype stores information about the challenged employees.

7.1.3 Subtypes

No subtypes

7.1.4 Time Constraint

2 (Record may include gaps, no overlappings)

7.1.5 Important Fields

Challenge group

You can classify challenged employees in challenge groups based on degree of challenge, e.g. severely challenged employees, etc. Here you specify the challenge group to which an employee belongs.

Degree of challenge

Here you specify the exact degree of challenge of the employee.

Credit factor

If the employee is expected to get a credit because he is challenged, specify here.

Type of challenge

Challenge types are used to distinguish employees based on type of challenge, e.g. orthopedic, hearing, etc. You define a master list of types of challenge and assign it to an employee here.

ID end date

The end date of the ID is used in the directory for severely challenged persons. This field is useful only in certain countries. For more details, see field help.

Issuing authority and second authority

Enter data about challenge certificates in these fields. These fields are not validated.

7.2 CHALLENGE GROUPS

Functional Consultant	User	Business Process Owner	Senior Management	My Rating	Understanding Level
B	X	X	X		

7.2.1 Purpose

You can classify challenged employees in challenge groups based on degree of challenge, e.g. severely challenged employees, etc.

7.2.2 IMG Node

SM30 ➤ T543

7.2.3 Screen

Challenge group	01	Severely challenged

Challenge Groups

Permissible range for degree of challenge

Min.degree of challnge	50 %
Max.degree of chllnge	100 %

Permissible credit range for compulsory work centers for challenged persons

Minimum creditable	1.0
Maximum creditable	1.0

Official abbreviation of challenge group *   SB

7.2.4 Primary Key

Challenge group

7.2.5 Important Fields

Minimum and maximum degree of challenge

In infotype 0004 you enter challenge group as well as degree of challenge. The degree of challenge you enter there must lie within the minimum and maximum degree of challenge for the challenge group.

Minimum and maximum credit factor

In infotype 0004 you enter challenge group as well as credit factor. The credit factor you enter there must lie within the minimum and maximum credit factor for the challenge group.

Official abbreviation

If your country has officially defined challenge groups, and they have official abbreviations, here you can maintain the link between your challenge groups and official abbreviations.

7.3 CHALLENGE TYPES

Functional Consultant	User	Business Process Owner	Senior Management	My Rating	Understanding Level
B	X	X	X		

7.3.1 Purpose

Challenge types are used to distinguish employees based on type of challenge, e.g. orthopedic, hearing, etc. Here you define the master list of types of challenge.

7.3.2 IMG Node

SM30 ➤ V_T523T

7.3.3 Screen

Type of challenge	Challenge
01	Unlim.wrk.capability
02	Lim.work capability
03	Sitting jobs only
04	Perm. Part.Disab. MX

7.3.4 Primary Key

Type of challenge

Addresses

8.1 ADDRESSES (INFOTYPE 0006)

Functional Consultant	User	Business Process Owner	Senior Management	My Rating	Understanding Level
A	A	A	A		

8.1.1 Screen

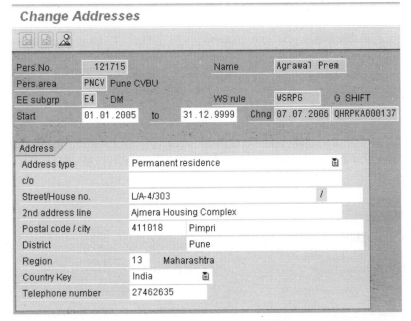

8.1.2 Purpose and Overview

This infotype is used to store employee's address information. All employees for whom you want to run payroll must have a permanent address. You can maintain different types of addresses of an employee, e.g. permanent address, present address, emergency address, etc. Different types of addresses are maintained as subtypes of infotype 0006 and stored in address type field.

Time constraints are at subtype level. Thus, you may permit multiple emergency addresses, but allow only one permanent address.

An employee's personnel area determines his company code, which in turn determines his default country. Based on the country, the system shows the appropriate screen. If the employee is living in a different country, you need the screen for that country. SAP provides feature CSSCR to define the default country for entering employees' addresses. However, if you are not getting the required screen even after this mechanism, you can click 'Foreign address' and specify the country while creating the address.

8.1.3 Subtypes

Address type

8.1.4 Time Constraint

T (Time constraint is based on subtype or subtype table)

8.2 ADDRESS TYPE

Functional Consultant	User	Business Process Owner	Senior Management	My Rating	Understanding Level
A	X	X	X		

8.2.1 Purpose

This view contains master list of address types. Address types are subtypes of infotype 0006. You can have different time constraints for different address types which you specify here.

8.2.2 IMG Node

SM30 ➤ VV_T591A_0006___AL0

8.2.3 Screen

Subtype characteristics for Addresses		
Subtype	Name	Time constraint
1	Permanent residence	1
2	Temporary residence	3
3	Present Address	2
4	Emergency address	2
5	Mailing address	2

8.2.4 Primary Key

Infotype + Subtype

8.3 COUNTRIES

Functional Consultant	User	Business Process Owner	Senior Management	My Rating	Understanding Level
A	X	X	X		

8.3.1 Purpose

Here you specify country level parameters.

8.3.2 IMG Node

SM30 ➤ V_T005

8.3.3   Screen

Country	IN

General data

Altern.country key	664
Name	India
Long name	
Nationality	Indian
Nationality (Long)	
Vehicle country key	IND
Index-based curr.	

Language Key	EN English
Hard currency	

Properties

EU Country	☐	ISO code	IN
Trde stat.short name	INDIEN	ISO code 3 char	IND
Procedure	TAXIN	Intrastat code	
Capital Goods Ind.	☐		

Address format

Address Layout Key	010	Print Country Name	☑
Standard name format			

Date format

- ⦿ DD.MM.YYYY
- ◯ MM/DD/YYYY
- ◯ MM-DD-YYYY
- ◯ YYYY.MM.DD
- ◯ YYYY/MM/DD
- ◯ YYYY-MM-DD

Decimal format

- ◯ 1.234.567,89
- ⦿ 1,234,567.89
- ◯ 1 234 567,89

8.3.4   Primary Key

Country Key

8.3.5   Important Fields

Address layout key

This key determines the way address is formatted from its component fields. There are country-specific routines to do that. For more details, see field help.

Print country name

The address format of post from many European countries does not usually use the country name in the last line of the address. This checkbox gives you a choice of printing country names even for those countries. For more details, see field help.

Standard name format

This standard natural person name format is used in Business Address Services (for example, in user addresses) and in the SAP business partner. Note that this name format is not used for employees. Name format of employees is discussed in chapter 5.4.

Date format

Different countries have different conventions in which they write date. Here you specify your choice.

Decimal format

Different countries have different conventions in which they write numbers with decimal values. Here you specify your choice.

8.4 COUNTRY FIELD CHECKS

Functional Consultant	User	Business Process Owner	Senior Management	My Rating	Understanding Level
A	X	X	X		

8.4.1 Purpose and Overview

When you enter data in SAP, the data is checked for correctness. There are certain data items for which different countries follow different conventions. For example, in India postal code is always a 6-digit number, while in the USA postal code has a variable length, can be alphanumeric, and can be up to 10 characters long. These rules are defined in this view. Normally these checks are correctly pre-built by SAP for each country, but you can change them if you want to.

8.4.2 IMG Node

SM30 ➤ V_005_B

8.4.3   Screen

| Country Key | IN | India |

Key for the bank directory

| Bank Key | 4 | Assign externally |

Formal checks

	Length	Checking rule	
Postal code length	6	4	Length to be kept to exactly, numerical, with
Bank account number			
Bank number length	15	5	Maximum value length
Post bank acct no.			
Tax Number 1			
Tax Number 2			
VAT registration no.			
Bank Key	11	1	Maximum value length, without gaps

Further checks

- ☐ Bank data
- ☐ Other data
- ☐ Postal code req. entry
- ☐ P.O.box code req. entry
- ☐ City file active
- ☐ Street postcode

8.4.4   Primary Key

Country Key

8.5   REGIONS/STATES

Functional Consultant	User	Business Process Owner	Senior Management	My Rating	Understanding Level
A	X	X	X		

8.5.1   Purpose

Here you maintain master list of states/regions in each country.

8.5.2   IMG Node

SM30 ➤ V_T005S

8.5.3   Screen

Country	Region	Description
AR	00	Capital Federal
AR	01	Buenos Aires
AR	02	Catamarca
AR	03	Córdoba

8.5.4   Primary Key

Country Key + Region (State, Province, County)

8.6   COUNTIES

Functional Consultant	User	Business Process Owner	Senior Management	My Rating	Understanding Level
A	X	X	X		

8.6.1   Purpose

Here you maintain master list of counties within a region of a country.

8.6.2   IMG Node

SM30 ➢ V_T005E

8.6.3   Screen

Country	Region	Description	County cde	Description
HK	KLN	Kowloon	TSW	Tsuen Wan
HK	KLN	Kowloon	WTS	Wong Tai Sin
HK	KLN	Kowloon	YMT	Yau Ma Mei
HK	NT	New Territories	FL	Fanling
HK	NT	New Territories	MOS	Ma On Shan
HK	NT	New Territories	SHA	Shatin

8.6.4   Primary Key

Country Key + Region (State, Province, County) + County Code

8.7 SCREENS FOR FOREIGN ADDRESSES

Functional Consultant	User	Business Process Owner	Senior Management	My Rating	Understanding Level
B	X	X	X		

8.7.1 Purpose

If an employee works in one country and lives in another, you can get an appropriate screen to maintain his address.

8.7.2 IMG Node

PE03 ≻ CSSCR

8.7.3 Screen

```
CSSCR Assignment between screen type and country for foreign addresses

    └─ 🗀 LAND1 Country Key

        ├─ 🗀 AT

        │      └───03

        ├─ 🗀 BE

        │      └───12
        │
```

8.7.4 Fields for Decision-making

Country Key

8.7.5 Return Value

Screen type

Planned Working Time

9.1 PLANNED WORKING TIME (INFOTYPE 0007)

Functional Consultant	User	Business Process Owner	Senior Management	My Rating	Understanding Level
A	A	A	A		

9.1.1 Screen

Change Planned Working Time

Work schedule

Pers.No.	121715		Name	Agrawal Prem	
Pers.area	PNCV Pune CVBU				
EE subgrp	E4 DM		WS rule	WSRPG	G SHIFT
Start	15.08.2006	To 31.12.9999	Chg.	31.10.2006	QHRPKA000137

Work schedule rule

Work schedule rule	WSRPG	G SHIFT
Time Mgmt status	0 - No time evaluation	

☑ Part-time employee

Working time

Employment percent	100.00	☐ Dyn. daily work schedule		
Daily working hours	8.00	Min.	Max.	
Weekly working hours	48.00	Min.	Max.	
Monthly working hrs	208.00	Min.	Max.	
Annual working hours	2496.00	Min.	Max.	
Weekly workdays	6.00			

9.1.2 Purpose and Overview

Infotype 0007 stores information relating to an employee's planned working time and time management status.

The employee is assigned to a work schedule rule, which is a condensed specification of planned working time. The relationship between a work schedule rule and the planned working time is configured in time management.

Time management status determines whether an employee is expected to record attendance, or whether he is assumed to be working as per his work schedule, and is expected to merely record his absences, or whether he is not evaluated for time management at all.

Before the time evaluation program can be run for a particular employee, you must specify the time management status in infotype 0007. Otherwise, the system cannot account the employee's time data with the time evaluation program.

Configuration for this infotype is done in time management and is out of scope of this book.

9.1.3 Subtypes

No subtypes

9.1.4 Time Constraint

1 (Record must have no gaps, no overlappings)

9.1.5 Important Fields

Work schedule rule

Work schedule rule and related configuration determines when the employee is supposed to work. This includes shift timings, break timings, grace periods, weekly offs, holidays, etc.

Time management status

Time management status determines whether the employee's time data is evaluated by time evaluation or not.

Part-time employee

You select this option if you want to reduce the planned working time of an existing full-time work schedule rule to the percentage specified in the employment percent field. You also select this option if you have created a special work schedule rule for part-time employees.

Employment percent

If you select part-time employee, enter employment percentage here. This is used to determine working hours per day, week, month and year. You may need to adjust the capacity utilization level in infotype 0008.

If you enter employment percentage without ticking part-time employee, system automatically ticks it, opens all relevant fields, and ticks dynamic daily work schedule by default.

Daily/weekly/monthly/annual working hours

Out of these four fields, only one is open for entry, others are automatically calculated. Employment percent is also automatically calculated. Which field is open for input is decided by configuration.

Weekly workdays

This field is calculated automatically based on the work schedule rule. Changing this does not change weekly/monthly/annual working hours. When you create an infotype 0007 record, the default value of weekly workdays field comes from work schedule rule.

Dynamic daily work schedule (for part-time workers)

This option is available when you select the part-time employee option and press Enter. If you choose this option, the system reduces the planned working time determined by the work schedule rule to the percentage you enter in the employment percent field. While calculating an employee's new working time, the system uses the specifications from the daily work schedule for the work schedule rule. The system takes the start of work time from the daily work schedule as its starting point and taking into account the break schedule, adds the new number of planned hours. The end of work time from the daily work schedule is then brought forward in accordance with the percentage you specify.

Minimum and maximum fields (for part-time workers)

These are specified at day, week, month and year level for part-time workers. These fields are optional. They can be queried in time evaluation but have no influence on an employee's daily work schedule. To enter values in these fields, you must select the dynamic daily work schedule option.

9.1.6 Reports and Other Features

PT_DSH20–Daily work schedule

If you want to see the details of a daily work schedule, you can see it by running transaction PT_DSH20. The user sees all the details of a daily work schedule which has been configured by the consultant.

Work schedule

When you click 🖩 Work schedule in any infotype, SAP shows you the work schedule for a month. For each day, it shows the daily work schedule, the daily work schedule variant, and the day type. It also shows the holiday class, if it is not blank.

PT63–Personal work schedule

Personal work schedule shows the daily work schedule, daily work schedule variant, day type, holiday class, period work schedule, holiday calendar and a number of time infotypes.

PT_UTPR00–Revaluate daily work schedule

Daily work schedule has an embedded break schedule. Paid breaks in the break schedule are included in planned working hours. If you change a break schedule such that hours of paid breaks are changed, then you need to update this field appropriately. This is done by executing transaction PT_UTPR00.

PT_UWSH00–Revaluate planned working time

Infotype 0007 contains information about daily/weekly/monthly/annual working hours of an employee. These are based on his work schedule rule. If the definition of work schedule rule changes, infotype 0007 should be appropriately updated. Transaction PT_UWSH00 is used to do that. In the rare event of this happening, your consultant will ask you to run this transaction.

PT_BPC00–Generate personal calendar

You can use this transaction to generate personal calendar. However, it is better to set 'Admissibility indicator PC' field in view T582Z to 1. In that case the personal calendar is automatically maintained, and there is no need to use this transaction.

PT_CLSTPC–Display personal calendar

You can see one-year calendar at a glance—showing absences, holidays, etc. from cluster PC.

PT_REOPC–Personal calendar reorganization

You can use this report to rectify inconsistencies in personal calendar, if any, from cluster PC.

Contract Elements

10.1 CONTRACT ELEMENTS (INFOTYPE 0016)

Functional Consultant	User	Business Process Owner	Senior Management	My Rating	Understanding Level
B	B	B	B		

10.1.1 Screen

Pers.No.	121715		Name	Agrawal Prem	
Pers.area	PNCV	Pune CVBU			
EE subgrp	E4	DM	WS rule	WSRPG	G SHIFT
Start	01.01.2005	to	31.12.9999		

Contractual regulations

Contract type	Temporary	Valid to	
☐ Sideline job			
☐ Competition clause			

Payment period from beginning of illness

Continued pay	
Sick pay supplement	

Periods

Probationary period
Notice period for ER
Notice period for EE
Work Permit

Entry

Initial entry date
Entry into group
Corporation

10.1.2 Purpose and Overview

You can use infotype 0016 to maintain employee's contractual relations with the company. Note that the work contract defined for an employee in infotype 0001 is independent of this.

When you create an infotype 0016 record, the contract type, notice period, continued pay, additional sick pay, and probationary period can be populated by default using feature CONTR.

When an applicant from recruitment module is hired in personnel administration, the relevant data is transferred; this infotype is one of them.

10.1.3 Subtypes

No subtypes

10.1.4 Time Constraint

1 (Record must have no gaps, no overlappings)

10.1.5 Important Fields

Contract type

In your company, you may have different types of contract for employees. Here you specify the contract type applicable to the employee.

Valid to

Here you can specify the end date of the employee's contract. This field appears on the screen only if the contract is of fixed-term type.

Sideline job

If the work contract contains permission to practice sideline jobs, you tick this checkbox.

Competition clause

This checkbox indicates whether the employee is bound by a non-competition clause, which restricts the employees from taking up a job with the company's competitors after termination of employment.

Continued pay: number and unit

The continued pay period is used for certain absences in infotype 2001.

Sick pay supplement: number and unit

The sick pay supplement period defines the period in which the employer pays the employee a sick pay supplement. The sick pay supplement period starts at the beginning of the employee's illness. The employer does not pay a sick pay supplement during the period of continued pay.

Probationary period: number and unit

Here you can specify a probationary period for the employee.

Notice period for employer

If the employer needs to give a notice to the employee, before terminating his contract, that period is specified here.

Notice period for employee

If the employee needs to give a notice to the employer, before resigning his job, that period is specified here.

Work permit

Here you can maintain the date on which the employee's work permit expires.

Initial entry date

There are occasions when an employee is with the company for several non-continuous periods. While determining his joining date, normally his last employment is considered. However, you may want to consider the date when he first joined the company as his joining date. In SAP, date of joining is determined by function module HR_ENTRY_DATE. If you want to consider the first date of joining as the joining date of an employee, you can maintain that date here, and maintain feature ENTRY appropriately.

Entry into group

There are occasions when an employee's joining date is not the date of joining the company, but that of joining the group of companies. In SAP, date of joining is determined by function module HR_ENTRY_DATE. If you want to consider the date of joining the group as the joining date of an employee, you can maintain the date of joining the group in this field, and maintain feature ENTRY appropriately.

Corporation

If an employee came from a subsidiary or a sister company, you may give him a particular contract. You may maintain the name of that company in this field.

10.2   CONTRACT TYPES

Functional Consultant	User	Business Process Owner	Senior Management	My Rating	Understanding Level
B	X	X	X		

10.2.1   Purpose

In your company, you may have different types of contracts for employees. You maintain the master list here. If you tick the field 'Fixed-term contract', you can specify contract end date in infotype 0016.

10.2.2   IMG Node

SM30 ➤ V_T547V

10.2.3   Screen

Contract type	Text - contract type	Fixed-term contract
01	Permanent	☐
02	Probationary	☐
03	Temporary	☐
04	Contract	☐
10	Trainee	☐

10.2.4   Primary Key

Contract type

10.3 PERIODS OF NOTICE

Functional Consultant	User	Business Process Owner	Senior Management	My Rating	Understanding Level
B	X	X	X		

10.3.1 Purpose

Here you maintain master list of notice periods. In infotype 0016, this list is available for selection in notice period for employee, as well as notice period for employer.

10.3.2 IMG Node

SM30 ➤ V_T547T

10.3.3 Screen

Period of notice	Description
01	Daily
02	Every 2 weeks
03	2 weeks/weekend
04	Monthly/weekend
05	6 weeks/quarter

10.3.4 Primary Key

Language Key + Period of notice

10.4 CORPORATIONS

Functional Consultant	User	Business Process Owner	Senior Management	My Rating	Understanding Level
B	X	X	X		

10.4.1 Purpose

Here you maintain a list of corporations, from which you can select, when you maintain infotype 0016 for an employee. You can maintain corporation field in infotype 0016 provided you have an understanding with that corporation and the contract has some link to the employee's relationship with that corporation.

10.4.2 IMG Node

SM30 ➤ T545T

10.4.3 Screen

	Corporation key	Corporation	Corporation name
	01	WINTERSH	WINTERSHALL AG
	02	K+S	KALI + SALZ AG
	03	ICI	ICI GMBH
	04	BURDA	BURDA GMBH
	05	G+H	GRUENZWEIG & HART...
	06	SAP	SAP GMBH

10.4.4 Primary Key

Corporation key

10.5 DEFAULT VALUES FOR CONTRACT ELEMENTS

Functional Consultant	User	Business Process Owner	Senior Management	My Rating	Understanding Level
B	X	X	X		

10.5.1 Purpose

This feature can be used to obtain default values in infotype 0016 for contract type, notice period, continued pay, additional sick pay, and probationary period.

10.5.2 IMG Node

PE03 ≻ CONTR

10.5.3 Screen

```
CONTR Default values for contract elements
    └─▣ TCLAS Transaction class for data storage
         └─▣ A Master data and time data
              └─▣ MOLGA Country Grouping
                   └─▣ 01 Germany
                        └─▣ PERSG Employee Group
                             └─▣ 1 Permanent
                                  └─▣ PERSK Employee Subgroup
                                       └─▣ DU
                                            └──42/010-1/013-6/012-13-13-01-01
                                  └─▣ otherwise
```

10.5.4 Fields for Decision-making

Company Code
Personnel Area
Personnel Subarea
Employee Group
Employee Subgroup
Country Grouping
Transaction Class for Data Storage

10.5.5 Return Value

Contract type, notice period, continued pay, additional sick pay, and probationary period.

Monitoring of Tasks

11.1 MONITORING OF TASKS (INFOTYPE 0019)

Functional Consultant	User	Business Process Owner	Senior Management	My Rating	Understanding Level
A	A	A	A		

11.1.1 Screen

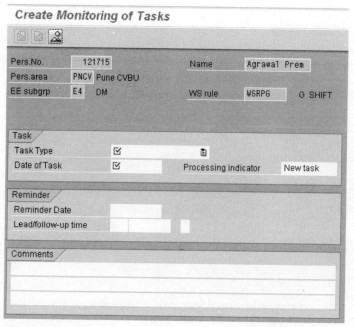

11.1.2   Purpose and Overview

Purpose

This infotype is used for tracking the status of the tasks you are required to perform and for generating reminders.

Types of tasks

You can define different types of tasks, which you want to track. Depending on the properties of a task type, you may be restricted from creating a task on a public holiday, or from creating it in the past period.

Date of task

Infotype 0019 records do not have a validity period. They have a 'date of task'. You do not find from date/to date on the screen. However, the system populates both these dates and they are the same as the 'date of task'.

Status of task

As the status of the task changes you can update the record, marking it as new task, task in process, task completed, etc., thus keeping track, whether the action is completed or not.

Reminder date

For a task, you can set the reminder date. Depending on the configuration of a task type, the system can determine the default reminder date based on the task date, which may be in the past or future. The default reminder date can be changed. Depending on the configuration of a task type, you can also be prevented from creating a task, whose reminder is in the past period.

Control of quota deduction using tasks

You can use tasks to prevent deduction from absence quota. For example, you can specify that privilege leave can be taken only after probation is completed and resignation is not submitted. Thus, you can specify the task type before which quota deduction is not permitted and also the task type after which quota deduction is not permitted.

Difference between infotype 0041 and 0019

The key difference between infotype 0041 and 0019 is that while infotype 0041 can be read during payroll processing, infotype 0019 cannot be. Also, in infotype 0041 the focus is on events, while in infotype 0019 the focus is on tasks.

11.1.3   Subtypes

Task types

11.1.4 Time Constraint

2 (Record may include gaps, no overlappings)

11.1.5 Important Fields

Task type

You can create different types of task. The types of task you are allowed to create are configured during implementation of SAP as per the requirement. Depending on the type of task you want to perform, the system may create default reminder date, and validate task date and reminder date.

Date of task

The date on which the task is to be performed.

Processing indicator

This indicator identifies the completion status of the task, viz. new task, task in process, and task completed. Processing indicator may be used in creating reminder lists; it does not make sense to create reminder for completed tasks.

Reminder date

Here you can specify the date on which you want to be reminded. The system suggests a default date depending on the task type. For certain task types, reminders in past may be prohibited.

Lead/follow-up time

Very often reminder date is in relation to the task date; you may want to be reminded of a task three days before the task date. Instead of computing the reminder date, you can specify it in the same form. You specify the number, the time unit, and whether you want to be reminded before, or after. Depending on these, the system determines the reminder date. If you leave the last field (lead/lag indicator) blank, the system takes the default value, which you have specified for the type of task. If you specify both the reminder date as well as the lead/follow-up time, the reminder date is ignored.

Comments

All infotypes have the facility to maintain text with an infotype record. Comments are not stored in infotype tables, but elsewhere. In infotype 0019, you can enter the comment on the screen. It is stored in the same way. Comments are not available for reporting.

11.1.6   Reports

S_PH0_48000450—Date Monitoring

You can generate this report based on task dates, task types, reminder dates, task status, etc. you can also restrict the employees in various ways.

Task Monitoring

Task	Reminder	Pl	Processi...	TT	Task Type	Personne...	First name	Last name
01.10.2003	01.09.2003		New task	01	Expiry of probation	00212801	Prashant	Pare
	01.09.2003		New task	01	Expiry of probation	00212802	Pavan	Pachauri
	01.09.2003		New task	01	Expiry of probation	00212803	Yekambara	Allanki
	01.08.2003		New task	01	Expiry of probation	00212804	Bhagwan	Bhosale
03.10.2003	03.04.2003		New task	01	Expiry of probation	00322992	Siva Kumar	Ramagiri

11.2 TASK TYPES

Functional Consultant	User	Business Process Owner	Senior Management	My Rating	Understanding Level
A	X	X	X		

11.2.1 Purpose and Overview

You can create various types of tasks in infotype 0019. The properties of these tasks are defined here. You can specify whether tasks of a type can be created on a public holiday, or in the past period. You can propose a default reminder date in infotype 0019 which depends on the task type. It can be before or after the task date. You can also specify, how much before or after the task date, the reminder date should be. You can specify whether tasks of a type can have reminders in the past period or not. In time management, there are absence quotas. These quotas have deduction intervals in view V_T559D. These intervals can be linked to certain task types.

11.2.2 IMG Node

Personnel Management ➤ Personnel Administration ➤ Evaluation Basis ➤ Monitoring of tasks ➤ Determine Task Type (view V_T531).

11.2.3 Screen

```
Task Type            01  Expiry of probation


 Deadline Types
 Lead/follow-up time      6  Months      Date < today's date
 Operator                              Remind.< day's date
 ☐ Check public holiday calendar
```

11.2.4 Primary Key

Task Type

11.2.5 Important Fields

Task type and text

You can create different types of task in infotype 0019. The types of task and their property are defined here.

Lead/follow-up time and unit

This determines the default interval between the task date and reminder date.

Operator for task types

This operator decides whether the time in the earlier field is a lead time, or follow-up time.

Blank	Standard: Lead time
–	Lead time: The reminder will take place before date/deadline
+	Follow-up time: The reminder takes place after the deadline

Reaction indicator if date precedes today's date

Some tasks make no sense, if you were to enter a past date. You cannot enter a task saying a meeting is to take place yesterday. Through this indicator you can control such behaviour.

Blank	Allowed
E	Error
W	Warning

Reaction indicator if reminder date precedes day's date

This field is similar to the one above. But, instead of checking task date, this field is used to check reminder date.

Check public holiday calendar

If you tick this field, and if the task falls on a public holiday, then the date is changed to the next working day.

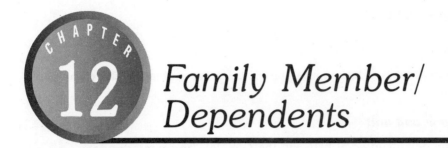

Family Member/ Dependents

12.1 FAMILY MEMBER/DEPENDENTS (INFOTYPE 0021)

Functional Consultant	User	Business Process Owner	Senior Management	My Rating	Understanding Level
A	A	A	A		

12.1.1 Screen for Child

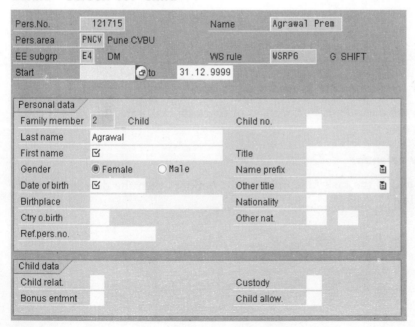

12.1.2 Screen for Other Family Member/Dependent

Create Family Member/Dependents

Pers.No.	121715			Name	Agrawal Prem
Pers.area	PNCV Pune CVBU				
EE subgrp	E4 DM			WS rule	WSRPG G SHIFT
Start	☑	to	31.12.9999		

Family Member/Dependents

Family member	Spouse		📄	Number
Last name	Agrawal	Birth name		
First name	☑	Initials		
Gender	⦿ Female ○ Male			
Date of birth	☑			
Birthplace				
Nationality	📄			

12.1.3 Purpose

Infotype 0021 stores data of an employee's family members as well as for other related persons.

12.1.4 Subtypes

Family members (mandatory)

12.1.5 Time Constraint

T (Time constraint is based on subtype or subtype table)
Father (TC 1), Mother (TC 1), Spouse (TC 2), Child (TC 2), Brother (TC 2), Sister (TC 2). Time constraint applies to the primary key of a table. If an infotype has a subtype, it applies to each subtype. Further, if a subtype can have multiple objects the time constraint applies to each object. In infotype 0021, child is a subtype. You can have multiple children on the same day. Therefore, should time constraint be 3? No, because each child has an object id, which is part of primary key. Therefore, time constraint is 2, and still multiple children can exist on the same day.

12.1.6 Important Fields

Most fields of this infotype are similar to infotype 0002 and require no further explanation. Some fields are explained here which may be used in some countries.

Reference personnel number of family member

This field is not used in the SAP standard system. If this family member of employee is also employed with the company, you can use this field to keep his personnel number.

Child relationship

You can have different types of child relationships, e.g. biological child, stepchild, foster child, etc. You can select the appropriate relationship here. The master list of child relationship is defined in view V_T577 (Family characteristic 1).

Bonus/extra pay entitlement

If you pay your employees child bonus, you can specify it here. You may have different types of child bonuses, e.g. normal child bonus, challenged child bonus, etc. You can maintain the master list in view V_T577 (Family characteristic 2).

Custody/address

Here you can specify whether the child lives with the employee, or with employee's spouse, etc. You can maintain the master list in view V_T577 (Family characteristic 3).

Child allowance

If you pay your employees child allowance, you can specify it here. You may have different types of child allowances. You can maintain the master list in view V_T577 (Family characteristic 4).

12.1.7 Name Formatting

Note that the name formatting discussion in infotype 0002, applies to infotype 0021 as well.

12.1.8 Reports

S_PH9_46000222—Family Members

You can use this report to generate a list of family members. If you want, you can restrict it to specified type of family members, e.g. child.

Family members

Personnel n...	Name of empl...	Entry	Family r...	First ...	Last na...	Date of Birth
00121715	Agrawal Prem	01.01.2005	Spouse	Urmila	Agrawal	17.07.1953

12.2 FAMILY MEMBERS

Functional Consultant	User	Business Process Owner	Senior Management	My Rating	Understanding Level
A	X	X	X		

12.2.1 Purpose

When you create a record in infotype 0021, you do so for a family member/dependent. Whereas you cannot allow more than one father or mother, you would allow multiple children. Further, you must know which record is for which child. These characteristics are specified here.

12.2.2 IMG Node

SM30 ➢ VV_T591A_0021___AL0

12.2.3 Screen

	Subtype	Name	Time constraint	ObjIDallw
	1	Spouse	2	☐
	11	Father	2	☐
	12	Mother	2	☐
	2	Child	2	☑

Subtype characteristics for Family Member/Dependents

12.2.4 Primary Key

Infotype + Subtype

12.2.5 Important Fields

Subtype

For infotype 0021, subtypes are relations.

Time constraint

Time constraint applies to the primary key of a table. If an infotype has a subtype, it applies to each subtype. Further, if a subtype can have multiple objects the time constraint applies to each object. In infotype 0021, child is a subtype. You can have multiple children on the same day. Therefore, should time constraint be 3? No, because each child has an object id, which is part of primary key. Therefore, time constraint is 2, and still multiple children can exist on the same day.

Object identification permitted for subtype

If you keep information about employee's children in infotype 0021, in a specific subtype, how would you distinguish the data of child A from the data of child B? This can be done by using object id.

If, for an infotype-subtype, object id is enabled, copy works very differently from create. During copy, the record is created for the same object id, whereas during create, a new object id is assigned. Thus, if you have one child and want to create record for the second child, you create a record, but if you want to create second record for the first child, you copy.

12.2.6   Naming Convention

You may like to adopt the following naming convention:

Code	Description
F	Father
M	Mother
B	Brother
C	Sister
S	Son
D	Daughter
H	Husband
W	Wife

Further relations can be built by combining these, e.g. Father's brother's son (FBS). Stepmother would be Father's wife (FW). If you also need relationships, which cannot be defined using this naming convention, you may define them additionally.

12.3   FAMILY CHARACTERISTICS

Functional Consultant	User	Business Process Owner	Senior Management	My Rating	Understanding Level
A	X	X	X		

12.3.1   Purpose

There are several fields in infotype 0021, where you can keep details of employees' family. You can maintain their master lists in this view.

12.3.2   IMG Node

SM30 ➤ V_T577

12.3.3 Screen

	Character.	Proficien.	Description	Internal key
	1	01	Legitimate	
	1	02	Stepchild	
	1	03	Foster child	
	1	04	Sibling	
	2	00	Unauthorized	0
	2	01	Up to 16 years old	2

12.3.4 Primary Key

Country Grouping + Family characteristic + Specification for family characteristic

12.3.5 Important Fields

Characteristic

In this view you can maintain master lists for various family characteristics. For each family characteristic, you have a one-digit code in this field. For example, the following values are configured for Germany.

---

1 Relationship to child
2 Reason for entitlement to child element of family-related, cost-of-living and social bonuses
3 Child care
4 Reason for entitlement to increase in children's allowance (special bonus)
6 Authorized to receive child allowance
7 Reason for entitlement to child allowance and entitlement clearing amount according to Public Sector Pensions Act
8 Employer competition for element of family-related, cost-of-living and social bonuses

---

Proficiency and description

Here you define the master list for each family characteristic. You specify a two-digit code and a description.

Internal key

For each proficiency of a characteristic, you can specify an internal key. Each key has a specific meaning. In many cases they are used in payroll.

12.4 DEFAULT VALUES IN FAMILY MEMBERS

Functional Consultant	User	Business Process Owner	Senior Management	My Rating	Understanding Level
A	X	X	X		

12.4.1 Purpose

This feature allows you to determine whether or not default values are proposed for last name, name prefix, name at birth, etc. in infotype 0021.

12.4.2 IMG Node

PE03 ≻ NLNAM

12.4.3 Screen

```
NLNAM Determine Method for Default Values in Infotype 0021

    └──⊟ BUKRS Company Code

        └──⊟ NL01 Country Template NL

            └──11

    └──⊟ otherwise

        └──00
```

12.4.4 Fields for Decision-making

Company Code
Personnel Area
Personnel Subarea
Employee Group
Employee Subgroup
Infotype
Subtype
Number of the Following Screen

12.4.5 Return Value

The return value indicates the fields for which default values are proposed and from where these default values are picked up. You may see feature documentation for details.

Education

13.1 EDUCATION (INFOTYPE 0022)

Functional Consultant	User	Business Process Owner	Senior Management	My Rating	Understanding Level
A	A	A	A		

13.1.1 Screen

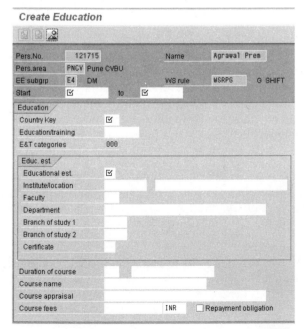

Create Education

Pers.No.	121715		Name	Agrawal Prem	
Pers.area	PNCV	Pune CVBU			
EE subgrp	E4	DM	WS rule	WSRPG	G SHIFT
Start	☑	to ☑			

Education
- Country Key ☑
- Education/training
- E&T categories 000

Educ. est.
- Educational est. ☑
- Institute/location
- Faculty
- Department
- Branch of study 1
- Branch of study 2
- Certificate

- Duration of course
- Course name
- Course appraisal
- Course fees _____ INR ☐ Repayment obligation

13.1.2 Purpose

This infotype displays information relating to education of an employee.

13.1.3 Subtypes

Educational establishments

13.1.4 Time Constraint

3 (Record may include gaps, can exist more than once)

13.1.5 Important Fields

Start and end dates

These fields do not indicate when the education started and ended. What these indicate is the period of validity of education. Usually the validity starts when the result is declared and has no end date, in which case as per convention the end date is 31.12.9999. In case the certificate has a defined validity, the end date is the end of the validity period.

Country key

Here you specify the country where the education took place.

Education/training and E&T categories

You can use these two fields to classify the education of the employee. You may use them for the levels of education if you like (since there is no attribute of certificate from which you can derive the level of education).

Educational establishment

Educational establishment is a provider of education, e.g. a university. It grants certificates, has branches of study, and has schools/institutes under it. Once you specify the educational establishment, certificates, branches of study, and schools/institutes are shown only for that educational establishment. Educational establishment is the subtype of infotype 0022.

Institute

Here you specify the institute where the person has studied. You choose from a master list, which is defined for each educational establishment.

Location

If you are not using the institute field, you can use this field to enter the institute's name and its location. This field is not validated.

Faculty and department

Usually an educational establishment has multiple faculties, or departments. You can specify that here. Note that the master list of faculty codes is a common one, and not educational establishment wise. This may present some difficulty in case faculty names of different educational establishments are similar, but not identical. If you don't have a close enough faculty name, you may enter a descriptive text in department field.

Branch of study 1 and 2

Here you can maintain the employee's branches of study. Branches of study are defined for each educational establishment. Note that you can keep information on what a person has studied in faculty and branch of study. SAP does not provide more layers for keeping this information.

Certificate

Upon successful completion of education, a person is usually given a certificate. For each educational establishment, the certificates awarded by it are defined. You choose from that master list.

Duration of course and time unit

Here you specify how long the person took to complete the course.

Course name

You can enter the course name here.

Course appraisal

You can enter the course appraisal in free text.

Course fees and currency

Here you can enter the amount and currency of course fees.

Repayment obligation

If the employee is expected to repay the course fee, you tick this checkbox.

Final mark

Table PA0022 contains a four-character final mark field, which may be present on some screens, where you can keep the marks obtained by the person. Since it is a character field, you can store a percentage, a CGPA, or a class. But different types of marks will get mixed up and it will not be possible to use them for ranking, summarization, etc.

13.1.6 Reports

S_PH9_46000224—Education and Training

You can use this transaction code to generate a report containing education of your employees. You can do so for specified certificates, branches of study, etc.

Education and training

Personnel ...	First ...	Last ...	Education ...	Certificat...	Educ./...	Department	Institute/I...	Cost...
00100001	Arvind	Bapat	Premium ...	Full Time	BCom	Commerce	Pune Univ	

13.2 EDUCATION/TRAINING

Functional Consultant	User	Business Process Owner	Senior Management	My Rating	Understanding Level
A	X	X	X		

13.2.1 Purpose

You can use education/training and E&T categories to classify the education of your employees. You may use them for the levels of education if you like (since there is no attribute of certificate from which you can derive the level of education). Education/ training is specified for an employee's education in infotype 0022. E&T categories are derived from education/training.

13.2.2 IMG Node

SM30 ➤ T518A

13.2.3 Screen

E & T	Educ./train. text
00120001	BE
00120002	BTech
00120003	BSc Engg
00150004	AMIE
00220004	BA

13.2.4 Primary Key

Education/training

13.3 EDUCATION/TRAINING CATEGORIES

Functional Consultant	User	Business Process Owner	Senior Management	My Rating	Understanding Level
A	X	X	X		

13.3.1 Purpose

You can use education/training and E&T categories to classify the education of your employees. You may use them for the levels of education if you like (since there is no attribute of certificate from which you can derive the level of education). Education/training is specified for an employee's education in infotype 0022. E&T categories are derived from education/training. In this view you maintain master list of E&T categories.

13.3.2 IMG Node

SM30 ➤ T518D

13.3.3 Screen

E&T categories	E&T category text
001	Engineering Graduate
002	Other Graduate
003	Engineering Post Graduate
004	Other Post Graduate

13.3.4 Primary Key

Education/training categories

13.4 EDUCATION/TRAINING LINKAGE TO CATEGORIES

Functional Consultant	User	Business Process Owner	Senior Management	My Rating	Understanding Level
A	X	X	X		

13.4.1 Purpose

You can use education/training and E&T categories to classify the education of your employees. You may use them for the levels of education if you like (since there is no attribute of certificate from which you can derive the level of education). Education/

training is specified for an employee's education in infotype 0022. E&T categories are derived from education/training. In this view you maintain the link between education/ training and E&T categories.

13.4.2 IMG Node

SM30 ➤ V_T518E

13.4.3 Screen

E & T	Educ./train. text	E&T categories	E&T category text
00120001	BE	001	Engineering Graduate
00120002	BTech	001	Engineering Graduate
00120003	BSc Engg	001	Engineering Graduate
00150004	AMIE	001	Engineering Graduate
00220004	BA	002	Other Graduate
00220005	BCom	002	Other Graduate

13.4.4 Primary Key

Education/training categories + Education/training

E&T category should have been an attribute of education/training. Alternatively, E&T category should have been stored in infotype 0022. It is recommended that only one E&T category be maintained for each education/training.

13.5 EDUCATIONAL ESTABLISHMENT

Functional Consultant	User	Business Process Owner	Senior Management	My Rating	Understanding Level
A	X	X	X		

13.5.1 Purpose and Overview

This view contains the master list of educational establishments which are subtypes of infotype 0022. An educational establishment has branches of study (T517Z). It also awards certificates (T517A). It has institutes/schools (T5J65). It is, therefore, like universities or school boards. You should create each body, which has authority to grant education/ training certificate as an educational establishment. The data element 'Course' is no longer used.

13.5.2 IMG Node

SM30 ➤ V_T517T

13.5.3 Screen

	Educ. est.	Educ. est. text	Course
	01	Other Colleges/Unive	✔
	02	State Board	✔
	03	CBSE	✔
	04	Reg/National Engg C	✔

13.5.4 Primary Key

Language Key + Educational establishment

13.6 INSTITUTES/SCHOOLS

Functional Consultant	User	Business Process Owner	Senior Management	My Rating	Understanding Level
A	X	X	X		

13.6.1 Purpose

This view contains the master list of institutes/schools. You can classify institutes/schools into different types.

13.6.2 IMG Node

SM30 ➤ V_T5J65

13.6.3 Screen

Educational est.   14   Premium Mgmt Inst

	Ins./Sc. code	T	Ins./school type	Institute/location	Institute/school (Katakana)
	1	1	National	FMS, Delhi	
	2	1	National	ICAI	
	3	1	National	IIFT, Delhi	
	4	1	National	IMI Delhi	

13.6.4 Primary Key

Educational establishment + Institute/school code

13.6.5 Important Fields

Educational establishment and description

An educational establishment can have multiple institutes/schools attached to it. Here you specify the educational establishment whose institutes/schools you are defining.

Institute/school code

Here you specify the code of the institute/school.

Type of institute/school and description

You can use this field to categorize the institutes/schools.

Institute/location of training

Here you specify the name and location of the institute.

Institute/school (Katakana)

13.7 INSTITUTE/SCHOOL TYPE

Functional Consultant	User	Business Process Owner	Senior Management	My Rating	Understanding Level
A	X	X	X		

13.7.1 Purpose

You can create master list of institute/school types here if you want to classify institutes/schools.

13.7.2 IMG Node

SM30 ➤ V_T5J66

13.7.3 Screen

T	Ins./school type
1	National
2	Regional
3	State
4	International
5	Others

13.7.4 Primary Key

Type of institute/school

13.8   FACULTY

Functional Consultant	User	Business Process Owner	Senior Management	My Rating	Understanding Level
A	X	X	X		

13.8.1 Purpose

This view contains master list of faculties.

13.8.2 IMG Node

SM30 ➤ V_T5J68

13.8.3 Screen

Faculty code	Faculty
1	Entry With Highest
2	Entry Level
3	highest
4	Others

13.8.4 Primary Key

Faculty code

13.9 BRANCH OF STUDY

Functional Consultant	User	Business Process Owner	Senior Management	My Rating	Understanding Level
A	X	X	X		

13.9.1 Purpose

This view contains master list of branches of study.

13.9.2 IMG Node

SM30 ➤ T517Y

13.9.3 Screen

Branch of study	Branch of study text
00010	Classical languages/Hindi
00011	Modern languages
00012	Math/natural sciences
00013	Liberal/Commercial/Fine arts
01000	Science

13.9.4 Primary Key

Branch of study

13.10 BRANCHES OF STUDY IN AN EDUCATIONAL ESTABLISHMENT

Functional Consultant	User	Business Process Owner	Senior Management	My Rating	Understanding Level
A	X	X	X		

13.10.1 Purpose

This view contains branches of study in each educational establishment.

13.10.2 IMG Node

SM30 ➤ V_T517Z

13.10.3   Screen

Educ. est.	Educ. est. text	Branch of study	Branch of study text
01	Other Colleges/Unive	00010	Classical languages/Hindi
01	Other Colleges/Unive	00011	Modern languages
01	Other Colleges/Unive	00012	Math/natural sciences
01	Other Colleges/Unive	00013	Liberal/Commercial/Fine arts
01	Other Colleges/Unive	01000	Science
01	Other Colleges/Unive	01010	Physics

13.10.4   Primary Key

Educational establishment + Branch of study

13.11   CERTIFICATES

Functional Consultant	User	Business Process Owner	Senior Management	My Rating	Understanding Level
A	X	X	X		

13.11.1   Purpose

This view contains master list of certificates.

13.11.2   IMG Node

SM30 ➤ V_T519T

13.11.3   Screen

Certificate	Certificate text
Z1	Full Time
Z2	Part Time
Z3	Correspondence/External
Z4	Non Formal

13.11.4   Primary Key

Language Key + Certificate

13.12 CERTIFICATES GIVEN BY AN EDUCATIONAL ESTABLISHMENT

Functional Consultant	User	Business Process Owner	Senior Management	My Rating	Understanding Level
A	X	X	X		

13.12.1 Purpose

This view contains master list of certificates given by an educational establishment.

13.12.2 IMG Node

SM30 ➢ V_T517A

13.12.3 Screen

Educ. est.	Educ. est. text	Certific.	Certificate text
01	Other Colleges/Unive	Z1	Full Time
01	Other Colleges/Unive	Z2	Part Time
01	Other Colleges/Unive	Z3	Correspondence/External
01	Other Colleges/Unive	Z4	Non Formal
02	State Board	Z1	Full Time
02	State Board	Z2	Part Time

13.12.4 Primary Key

Educational establishment + Certificate

Other/Previous Employers

14.1 OTHER/PREVIOUS EMPLOYERS (INFOTYPE 0023)

Functional Consultant	User	Business Process Owner	Senior Management	My Rating	Understanding Level
B	B	B	B		

14.1.1 Screen

Create Other/Previous Employers

Pers.No.	121715	Name	Agrawal Prem
Pers.area	PNCV Pune CVBU		
EE subgrp	E4 DM	WS rule	WSRPG G SHIFT
Start	☑	to ☑	

Other/previous employers

Employer	☑
City	
Country Key	☑ ▤
Industry	▤
Job	▤
Work contract	▤

14.1.2 Purpose

One can store information about where an employee worked before starting work with your company in infotype 0023. You can store information about all the employers of an employee by creating multiple data records in this infotype, each with its respective validity period.

14.1.3 Subtypes

No subtypes

14.1.4 Time Constraint

3 (Record may include gaps, can exist more than once)

14.1.5 Important Fields

Employer

Here you specify the name of the previous employer of your employee.

City

Here you specify the city where the employee worked when he was with the above employer.

Country key

Here you specify the country in which the employee worked when he was with the above employer.

Industry

Here you specify the industry in which the employee was working earlier. Identification of industry gives you the perspective of employee's work environment.

Job

One of the most important things you want to know about an employee's previous employment is the nature of work or job he did. You choose from the master list created for this purpose.

Work contract

Master list of work contracts should be defined after careful consideration. You choose the one which best explains the employee's work contract with his previous employer.

14.2 INDUSTRY SECTORS

Functional Consultant	User	Business Process Owner	Senior Management	My Rating	Understanding Level
B	X	X	X		

14.2.1 Purpose

Industry in which an employee has worked gives you the broad perspective of employee's work environment. You define the master list here as per your requirements. You can make finer division of industries, which are similar to your industry, while a coarser division can be done for dissimilar industries. For example, a media company would want to distinguish between print media and television media, while for a steel company this distinction is not important.

14.2.2 IMG Node

SM30 ➢ V_T016

14.2.3 Screen

Indus.	Description
0001	Advertising / Market
0002	Automobile / Vehicle
0003	Financial Services
0004	Construction

14.2.4 Primary Key

Industry key

14.3 JOBS WITH PREVIOUS EMPLOYERS

Functional Consultant	User	Business Process Owner	Senior Management	My Rating	Understanding Level
B	X	X	X		

14.3.1 Purpose

One of the most important things you want to know about an employee's previous employment is the kind of work or job he did. You need to pay some attention to create this master list. Many of the jobs you define here may be similar to your own jobs, so that people can readily relate to them. Jobs, which are common to your industry sector, or other industry sectors, need to be included as well.

14.3.2 IMG Node

SM30 ➢ V_T513C

14.3.3 Screen

Job	Text
00000001	Sales & Marketing
00000002	After SS / Dealer Mgt
00000003	Spare Parts
00000004	Design
00000005	Manuf/Prodn/Operations

14.3.4 Primary Key

Job at former employer(s)

14.4   WORK CONTRACTS WITH PREVIOUS EMPLOYERS

Functional Consultant	User	Business Process Owner	Senior Management	My Rating	Understanding Level
B	X	X	X		

14.4.1   Purpose

The work contracts defined by you depends largely on the kind of industry you are in and information which is important for you. For example, you may want to distinguish among permanent employment, fixed-time contracts of different durations, temporary employment, etc. Or, you may want to capture the employee's salary in one of the various buckets you define. Which information is most useful to you will determine this master list.

14.4.2   IMG Node

SM30 ➤ T542C

14.4.3   Screen

Work Contract - Other.	
C...	Text
01	< 8 K
02	8 K to 10 K
03	11 K to 15 K
04	16 K to 20 K

14.4.4   Primary Key

Work Contract—Other Employers

Skills

15.1 SKILLS (INFOTYPE 0024)

Functional Consultant	User	Business Process Owner	Senior Management	My Rating	Understanding Level
A	A	A	A		

15.1.1 Screen

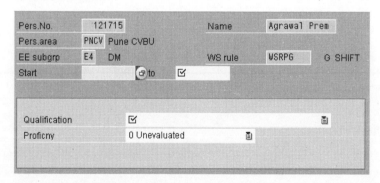

15.1.2 Purpose

This is one of the most important infotypes for personnel development. Here, you store the skills of your employees. You can use them to

- ➢ Create development plan for the employee
- ➢ Compare the competencies of a person and his current position
- ➢ Find the best candidates if you are trying to fill a position
- ➢ Career planning
- ➢ Succession planning

15.1.3 Subtypes

No subtypes

15.1.4 Time Constraint

3 (Record may include gaps, can exist more than once)

15.1.5 Important Fields

Qualification

This field contains the skills/competencies of the employee.

Proficiency

This field contains the proficiency level of the skill/competency.

15.2 QUALIFICATIONS/SKILLS/COMPETENCIES

Functional Consultant	User	Business Process Owner	Senior Management	My Rating	Understanding Level
A	A	A	A		

15.2.1 Purpose

This view contains the master list of competencies. A position has requirements, which are a set of competencies. A person has skills, which are also a set of competencies. The competencies thus provide the common ground for determining the match between a position and a person. They are also used to determine which training programmes can fill the gap between what is required and what is available.

15.2.2 IMG Node

SM30 ➤ T574A

15.2.3 Screen

Qualification	Qualification text
00000001	English language skills
00000002	French language skills
00000003	Spanish language skills
00000004	Computer sciences degree (university)
00000005	Computer sciences degree (tech.college)
00000006	Mathematics degree (university)

15.2.4   Primary Key

Qualification key

15.3   SKILLS/COMPETENCIES WHEN INTEGRATION WITH PD IS ON

Functional Consultant	User	Business Process Owner	Senior Management	My Rating	Understanding Level
A	A	A	A		

15.3.1   Screen

15.3.2   Purpose

Employee competencies are one of the most important areas for HR, and SAP has rich functionality in this area. However, this functionality is a part of Personnel Development (PD) and not a part of Personnel Administration (PA).

If you have implemented PD, you can access as well as create data in PD from infotype 0024 of PA. For this you need to turn the integration on. To get a clearer understanding, it would be better if you understand how SAP stores data for the PD module.

15.3.3   Data Model of Personnel Planning

Data model

This data model applies to Organizational Management, Personnel Development and Training. The data is stored in Objects (HRP1000), Relationships (HRP1001), and other related infotypes (HRP1nnn series).

Objects

SAP has created a variety of objects, e.g. organizational unit, position, job, qualification, applicant, business event, etc. The master list of object types is in table T778O. When an object of a particular type, e.g. an organizational unit, is created, the data is stored in table HRP1000.

Relationships

The objects are linked to each other through relationships. Master list of relationships is maintained in table T778V. When two objects are related to each other through a relation, this data is stored in table HRP1001. The permitted relationships between two object types are maintained in table T777E.

Infotypes

Depending on the object type, there may be a need to store additional data. This data is stored in infotypes. The master list of infotypes is in table T778T. Which infotype is allowed for which object type, is kept in table T777I.

Competencies infotype

With this background, let us understand infotype 0024, which shows us the data about a person's skills, his potential, likes and dislikes, etc.

15.3.4 Overview of Skills/Competencies when Integration with PD is On

When integration with PD is on, infotype 0024 shows the following tab pages on the screen. These are described below.

> Qualifications
>
> Potentials
>
> Preferences
>
> Dislikes
>
> Appraisals where appraisee
>
> Appraisals where appraiser
>
> Individual development
>
> ✔ Development plan history

Qualifications

This tab page shows the skills, or competencies of a person. Competencies are the common scales on which a job's requirements are compared with a person's abilities. In the relationships table, they are stored as relation A032 between the object Person (P) and the object Qualification (Q). When you open infotype 0024 for a person, the data is fetched from that table and shown. If you create or delete data here, the change takes place in table HRP1001.

Potentials

This tab page shows the areas where the employee is identified to have a potential. This data is stored in table HRP1001 as relationship A038 between object of type P and any type of related object. In table T777E, SAP has defined that a person can have potential for a job, a position, a qualification, a task or a work center. Hence, if you try to specify a potential for the employee, the system asks you what the potential is for, and after you have specified the category, you answer the next question, e.g. which specific position or job.

Preferences

Like potential, you can record an employee's preferences. The relationship created is A042.

Dislikes

Dislikes are stored under relationship A043.

Appraisals where appraisee

Unlike other tabs, you do not create or delete appraisals in this infotype. You can see which persons have created which appraisals for you. These persons are identified from the same relationship table HRP1001, through a two-step operation. First the appraisals received by the employee are identified (A046). Then the persons who created those appraisals (B045) are identified. These are then shown on this tab page.

Appraisals where appraiser

Items displayed on this tab page also follow a two-step process like the previous tab page. Here you find the appraisals using relation A045, and then find the persons using relation B046.

Individual development

Individual developments are stored in table HRP1001 as A049. A person is developed by an appraisal model, a business event type, a job, a location, an organizational unit, a position, or a work center. If some of these are not applicable in your company, you can change it in table T777E.

Development plan history

This tab page is like the earlier tab page, but contains historical data.

15.3.5 Menu and Menu Bar

| 品 Career planning | You can do career planning for a person from infotype 0024. The system shows positions, which are a good match for this person. If you save it, the information is saved in the relationships table, HRP1001.

▎▎ Current position You can also compare the qualifications of a person with requirements of his current position, and create the necessary development plan.

15.3.6 Integration

Integration switch

To set the switch on, first specify the plan version in PLOGI + PLOGI in view T77S0. Then use the IMG node: Personnel Management ➤ Personnel Development ➤ Integration ➤ Set Up Integration with Personnel Admin. and Recruitment. This shows the following two entries.

Group	Sem. abbr.	Value abbr.	Description
PLOGI	APPRA	0	Integration switch for appraisal
PLOGI	QUALI	0 A032 Q	Integration switch for qualifications

Integration of appraisal

The PLOGI + APPRA entry determines the integration between Personnel Administration infotype 0025 (Appraisals) and Personnel Development. It should be set to 1 to activate integration.

Integration of qualification

The PLOGI + QUALI entry determines the integration between Personnel Administration infotype 0024 (Skills) and Personnel Development. It should be set to '1 A032 Q' to activate integration.

Moving qualification data from PA to PD

If you were moving from un-integrated to integrated scenario, you would like to move qualification data from PA to PD. SAP provides a transaction OOQI for this purpose. For more details, you may see the documentation of transaction OOQI.

Moving appraisal data from PA to PD

Similarly, appraisal data can be moved from infotype 0025 to PD using transaction OOAI.

Internal Medical Service

16.1 INTERNAL MEDICAL SERVICE (INFOTYPE 0028)

Functional Consultant	User	Business Process Owner	Senior Management	My Rating	Understanding Level
B	B	B	B		

16.1.1 Screen

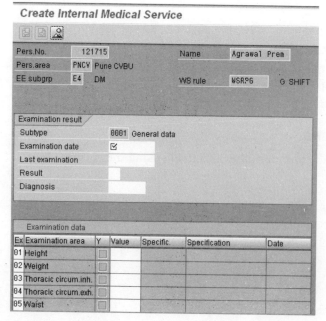

16.1.2   Purpose and Overview

Medical examination data

One can store data pertaining to employees' medical examination in infotype 0028, e.g. height, weight, blood group, etc.

Examination date

The data stored in this infotype is the result of a medical examination, and hence is for an examination date, and not for an interval.

Examination type

The medical examination is carried out under various examination types. You can create the examination types required by you in view V_T591A.

Examination area

For each examination type, you define the examination areas.

Examination result

For each examination area, you can define whether the examination result is a yes/no answer, a numeric value, or choice from a list.

Overall result

Apart from detailed results of a medical examination, you can also have an overall result, which you can configure in V_T578Y. Unfortunately, you cannot define the overall result at the level of examination type.

Diagnosis

You can also enter diagnosis. But, in the absence of a master list, the length of this field (8 characters) is inadequate.

16.1.3   Subtypes

Examination types (mandatory)

16.1.4   Time Constraint

T (Time constraint is based on subtype or subtype table)

Depending on the type of medical examination, the time constraint is either 2 or 3.

16.1.5 Important Fields

Examination type (subtype)

A person can have various types of medical examinations. Depending on the type of medical examination, the examination areas vary.

STyp	Name
0001	General data
0002	Habits
0003	Dermatological exam
0004	Reproductive organs and urinalysis

Examination date

Here you specify the date on which the examination took place.

Last examination

Here you specify the last date when health examination of the same type was held.

Result

Apart from detailed results of a medical examination, you can also have an overall result, which you can configure in V_T578Y. Unfortunately, you cannot define the overall result at the level of examination type.

Diagnosis

You can enter the diagnosis here. But, in the absence of a master list, the length of this field (8 characters) is inadequate.

Examination area

For each type of medical examination, the examination areas are defined in view V_T578Z. This list is shown in the lower part of the screen, and the results of examination are recorded against them. Under each type of medical examination, up to 30 examination areas can be defined.

Yes/no, value, specification

Depending on the type of a medical examination, its result can be expressed in different ways.

Yes/no	For some medical examinations, the answer is either yes or no, e.g. a hole in the heart. You would enter that result in the yes/no field in infotype 0028.
Value	For other medical examinations, the result is a number, e.g. height of a person. You would enter that result in the value field in infotype 0028.
Specification	For some other medical examinations, the value could be a choice from a list, e.g. for blood group. In these cases, the result is entered in the specification field in infotype 0028. The list is maintained in view V_T578X. SAP lets you specify, whether values outside the list are permitted or not, during configuration.

In order to ensure that you do not enter junk data, SAP lets you decide the type of result expected for each examination area. Others are disabled during configuration. However, if you think that for some examination area, the result can be put in more than one field, SAP lets you enable multiple fields also. It is for you to decide the format of the result.

Examination date

For certain examination areas, you may be allowed to enter examination date. This is needed where the examination is carried out over several days, or a specific examination is carried out on a different date. Depending on whether you want to allow this or not, you would do the configuration in view V_T578Z, which would enable/disable this field.

16.2 EXAMINATION TYPE

Functional Consultant	User	Business Process Owner	Senior Management	My Rating	Understanding Level
B	X	X	X		

16.2.1 Purpose

This view contains subtypes of infotype 0028, internal medical service.

16.2.2 IMG Node

SM30 ➤ VV_T591A_0028___AL0

16.2.3 Screen

	Subtype	Name	Time constraint
	0001	General data	2
	0002	Habits	2
	0003	Dermatological exam	2
	0004	Reproductive organs and urinalysis	2
	0005	Endocrinological exam	2

Subtype characteristics for Internal Medical Service

16.2.4 Primary Key

Infotype + Subtype

16.3 EXAMINATION AREA

Functional Consultant	User	Business Process Owner	Senior Management	My Rating	Understanding Level
B	X	X	X		

16.3.1 Purpose

Each type of medical examination can have several examination areas. The master list of these examination areas, for each type of medical examination, is defined in this view.

16.3.2 IMG Node

SM30 ➤ V_T578Z

16.3.3 Screen

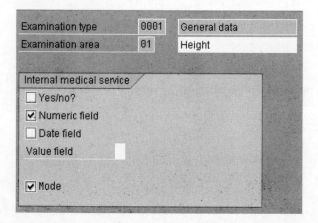

16.3.4 Primary Key

Subtype + Examination area

16.3.5 Important Fields

Examination type, examination area

Each medical examination type can have several examination areas. For each examination area, the properties are set here.

Yes/no?

If you tick this field, the yes/no field in infotype 0028 is in the input mode. Otherwise, it is disabled.

Numeric field

If you tick this field, the value field in infotype 0028 is in the input mode. Otherwise, it is disabled.

Date field

If you tick this field, the date field in infotype 0028 is in the input mode. Otherwise, it is disabled.

Value field

Here you determine whether the specification field in infotype 0028 is disallowed (Blank), allowed without restriction (X), or allowed but checked against view V_T578X (T). If it is disallowed, the field will be disabled. In the other two cases, the list of values is shown from view V_T578X. If the field is validated, you must choose a value from this list. If it is not validated, you can enter a value, which is not in the list.

Mode

If you tick this field, the examination area is stored irrespective of whether an entry is made. If not ticked, the examination area is stored only if an entry is made.

16.4   EXAMINATION AREA: PERMISSIBLE VALUES

Functional Consultant	User	Business Process Owner	Senior Management	My Rating	Understanding Level
B	X	X	X		

16.4.1   Purpose

For those medical examinations, where the results are from a fixed list, the list is maintained in this view.

16.4.2   IMG Node

SM30 ➤ V_T578X

16.4.3   Screen

Examination type	0001	General data
Examination area	08	Blood group

	Proficiency	Description
	A+	A RH Positive
	A -	A RH Negative
	AB+	AB RH Positive
	AB -	AB RH Negetive
	B+	B RH Positive
	B -	B RH Negetive
	0+	O RH Positive
	0 -	O RH Negetive

16.4.4   Primary Key

Subtype (Examination type) + Examination area + Proficiency

16.5   EXAMINATION RESULTS

Functional Consultant	User	Business Process Owner	Senior Management	My Rating	Understanding Level
B	X	X	X		

16.5.1 Purpose

Apart from detailed results of a medical examination, you can also have an overall result, which you can configure here. Unfortunately, you cannot define the overall result at the level of examination type.

16.5.2 IMG Node

SM30 ➤ V_T578Y

16.5.3 Screen

	Result	Examination result
	01	Fit for work
	02	Unable to work
	03	Deceased
	04	Convalescent
	05	Without after-effect

16.5.4 Primary Key

Language Key + Result

CHAPTER 17

Powers of Attorney

17.1 POWERS OF ATTORNEY (INFOTYPE 0030)

Functional Consultant	User	Business Process Owner	Senior Management	My Rating	Understanding Level
B	B	B	B		

17.1.1 Screen

Pers.No.	121715		Name	Agrawal Prem	
Pers.area	PNCV	Pune CVBU			
EE subgrp	E4	DM	WS rule	WSRPG	G SHIFT
Start	☑	to	☑		

Power of attorney

Power of attorney	☑
Organizational unit	

Comments

17.1.2 Purpose

You can use this infotype to specify the powers of attorney given to the employees and the organizational unit for which these powers are given.

17.1.3 Subtypes

Power of attorney type

17.1.4 Time Constraint

3 (Record may include gaps, can exist more than once)

17.1.5 Important Fields

Power of attorney

In this field you specify what power of attorney is given to the employee.

Organizational unit

Here you specify the organizational unit for which this power is given.

Comments

All infotypes have the facility to maintain text with an infotype record. Comments are not stored in infotype tables, but elsewhere. In infotype 0030, you can enter the comment on the screen. It is stored in the same way. Comments are not available for reporting.

17.1.6 Reports

S_PH9_46000225—Powers of Attorney

You can use this report to view the list of powers of attorney given to your employees. You can generate this list for specified power of attorney type.

Powers of attorney

Personnel ...	Last n...	First ...	Power of attorney	Po...	Org. Unit	Name of org...
00121715	Agrawal	Prem	General commer...	02	00000000	

17.2 POWER OF ATTORNEY TYPE

Functional Consultant	User	Business Process Owner	Senior Management	My Rating	Understanding Level
B	X	X	X		

17.2.1 Purpose

In your company, you may have different types of power of attorney. You maintain the master list here.

17.2.2 IMG Node

SM30 ➤ VV_T591A_0030___AL0

17.2.3 Screen

	Subtype characteristics for Powers of Attorney	
	Subtype	**Name**
	01	Limited commercial powers of attorney
	02	General commercial power of attorney
	03	P.of attorney for banking transactions

17.2.4 Primary Key

Infotype + Subtype

Internal Data

18.1 INTERNAL DATA (INFOTYPE 0032)

Functional Consultant	User	Business Process Owner	Senior Management	My Rating	Understanding Level
B	B	B	B		

18.1.1 Screen

Pers.No.	121715		Name	Agrawal Prem		
Pers.area	PNCV Pune CVBU					
EE subgrp	E4 DM		WS rule	WSRP6	G SHIFT	
Start	01.01.2005	to	31.12.9999			

Employee identification

Prev. personnel no.

Company ID

Company car

Car regulation

Car Value   INR

License plate number

Asset Number

Work center

Building number

Room number

In-House Tel.Number   /

18.1.2   Purpose

In this infotype, you can maintain an employee's legacy personnel number, his identity card number, his car details and his work location.

18.1.3   Subtypes

No subtypes

18.1.4   Time Constraint

2 (Record may include gaps, no overlappings)

18.1.5   Important Fields

Previous personnel number

In this field you can maintain an employee's legacy personnel number. Unlike SAP's personnel number, which is a numeric field, this is a character field.

Company ID

Here you can maintain the employee's ID card number. Note that if you are using time recording system, you usually maintain the employee's ID card number in infotype 0050.

Car regulation

For certain countries, you can use this field to compute imputed income for tax purposes.

Car value and currency

Here you maintain the list price of the company car for calculating the imputed income.

License plate number

Here you maintain the license plate number of the company car given to the employee, or his personal car. You can get a report of the license plate numbers of the employees using SAP standard report S_PH9_46000220—Vehicle Search List.

Asset number

If the employee's company car has an asset number, you can maintain it here. The asset number you enter here can be checked against the asset database if you so desire. The decision to check the asset database can depend on employee characteristics and is specified in feature ANLAC. If checking against the asset table ANLA is activated, this field should contain company code (4 digits) + main asset number (12 digits) + asset subnumber (4 digits).

Building number, room number, in-house telephone numbers

Here you can specify the work location and telephone numbers of an employee. Based on this field, you can generate a telephone directory using SAP standard report S_AHR_61016354—Telephone Directory.

18.1.6 Menu and Menu Bar

Communication By clicking this icon, you can see the details of infotype 0105 of the employee.

18.1.7 Reports

S_PH9_46000220—Vehicle Search List

You can use this report to view the list of vehicles of your employees. You can also specify the license plate number and find the person to whom the vehicle belongs.

Vehicle search list

Personnel No.	First ...	Last na...	Licens...	Tel.	BirNo	Room	Payr...	CoCd	Cost ctr
00121715	Prem	Agrawal					P1	0100	

S_AHR_61016354—Telephone Directory

You can use this report to view the list of telephone numbers of your employees. You can generate this report with address. You can also generate it in telephone directory format.

Telephone Directory

Name	Tel01	Tel02
Saraf Papia	2218	

18.2 CAR RULE FOR TAX

Functional Consultant	User	Business Process Owner	Senior Management	My Rating	Understanding Level
B	X	X	X		

18.2.1 Purpose

In this view you maintain different car rules applicable in your country. This list is used in infotype 0032.

18.2.2 IMG Node

SM30 ➢ V_T544A

18.2.3 Screen

Car	Car rule (text)
	Imputed income not calculated
1	Imputed income taxed individually
2	Imputed income taxed partly on a lump sum basis
3	Partial lump sum control for imputed income (ER)

18.2.4 Primary Key

Country Grouping + Car rule

18.3 ASSET NUMBER CHECK AGAINST ASSET MASTER

Functional Consultant	User	Business Process Owner	Senior Management	My Rating	Understanding Level
B	X	X	X		

Refer to chapter 22.3.

Corporate Functions

19.1 CORPORATE FUNCTIONS (INFOTYPE 0034)

Functional Consultant	User	Business Process Owner	Senior Management	My Rating	Understanding Level
B	B	B	B		

19.1.1 Screen

Pers.No.	121715		Name	Agrawal Prem

Pers.area PNCV Pune CVBU

EE subgrp E4 DM   WS rule WSRPG   G SHIFT

Start ☑   to ☑

Corporate function

Corporate Function ☑

Acquired on ☑

19.1.2 Purpose and Overview

If your company has a list of corporate functions, you can assign them to employees in this infotype. You can also maintain its start date and store remarks/comments.

19.1.3 Subtypes

Corporate function

19.1.4 Time Constraint

T (Time constraint is based on subtype or subtype table)

19.2 CORPORATE FUNCTION

Functional Consultant	User	Business Process Owner	Senior Management	My Rating	Understanding Level
B	X	X	X		

19.2.1 Purpose

Here you maintain the master list of corporate functions of your company. These are subtypes of infotype 0034.

19.2.2 IMG Node

SM30 ➤ VV_T591A_0034___AL0

19.2.3 Screen

Subtype	Name	Time constraint
SAT	Satisfactory	2
SUP	Superior	2
USAT	Unsatisfactory	2

19.2.4 Primary Key

Infotype + Subtype

Company Instructions

20.1 COMPANY INSTRUCTIONS (INFOTYPE 0035)

Functional Consultant	User	Business Process Owner	Senior Management	My Rating	Understanding Level
B	B	B	B		

20.1.1 Screen

Create Company Instructions

Pers.No.	121715	Name	Agrawal Prem
Pers.area	PNCV Pune CVBU		
EE subgrp	E4 DM	WS rule	WSRPG G SHIFT
Start	☑	to ☑ '	

Instructions

Instruction type	☑
Received on	☑

Comments

20.1.2 Purpose

If you want to keep a record of instructions given to employees, you can use this infotype. The instruction is a free text. Its only attributes are instruction type and the date of instruction.

20.1.3 Subtypes

Instruction types

20.1.4 Time Constraint

T (Time constraint is based on subtype or subtype table)

20.1.5 Important Fields

Instruction type

Instruction type specifies what type of instruction is given. Instruction types are subtypes of infotype 0035.

Instruction date

Here you specify the date on which the instruction is given.

Instruction (comments)

This is free text. It is stored separately. In the infotype, only the 'Text Exists for Infotype' field is flagged.

20.2 INSTRUCTION TYPES

Functional Consultant	User	Business Process Owner	Senior Management	My Rating	Understanding Level
B	X	X	X		

20.2.1 Purpose

Here you maintain the master list of types of company instruction. These are subtypes of infotype 0035.

20.2.2 IMG Node

SM30 ➢ VV_T591A_0035___AL0

20.2.3 Screen

	Subtype characteristics for Company Instructions	
Subtype	Name	Time constraint
01	Accident prevention	3
02	Other instructions	2

20.2.4 Primary Key

Infotype + Subtype

Insurance

21.1 INSURANCE (INFOTYPE 0037)

Functional Consultant	User	Business Process Owner	Senior Management	My Rating	Understanding Level
B	B	B	B		

21.1.1 Screen

Pers.No.	121715		Name	Agrawal Prem
Pers.area	PNCV Pune CVBU			
EE subgrp	E4 DM		WS rule	WSRPG G SHIFT
Start	☑	to	31.12.9999	

Insurance data

Insurance type	☑
Insurance company	☑
Insurance number	☑
Insurance tariff	
Currency	INR
Insurance total	☑ INR
1st different total	INR
2nd different total	INR
Premium base	INR
Insurance premium	☑ INR
Fully vested on	

21.1.2 Purpose and Overview

In this infotype you can maintain data of insurance taken by your employees. This infotype is for customer-specific functionality. It is not used in standard SAP reports. Note that there are several country-specific infotypes for insurance data.

21.1.3 Subtypes

Insurance types

21.1.4 Time Constraint

3 (Record may include gaps, can exist more than once)

21.1.5 Important Fields

Insurance type

There may be different types of insurance. You choose the one which the employee has taken.

Insurance company

There may be different insurance companies providing insurance to your employees. You choose the insurance company from which the employee has taken insurance.

Insurance number

The insurance companies assign an insurance number to each insurance policy. You enter that here.

Insurance tariff

If the insurance company has different pricing policies (tariffs), here you store the tariff under which the insurance was given to the employee.

Currency

Here you specify the currency, which is applicable to all amount fields on the screen.

Insurance total, 1st different total, 2nd different total

In these fields you maintain the amount insured.

Premium base

Here you store the basis amount for calculation of insurance premium.

Insurance premium

The premium payable by the employee for insurance is entered in this field.

Fully vested on

This field is for Germany only.

21.2 INSURANCE TYPES

Functional Consultant	User	Business Process Owner	Senior Management	My Rating	Understanding Level
B	X	X	X		

21.2.1 Purpose

Here you maintain the master list of insurance types in your company. These are subtypes of infotype 0037.

21.2.2 IMG Node

SM30 ➢ VV_T591A_0037___AL0

21.2.3 Screen

Subtype characteristics for Insurance	
Subtype	Name
0001	Company insurance
0002	Group accident insurance
0003	Life insurance
0005	Supplementary insurance
0010	Not liable
0011	Risk

21.2.4 Primary Key

Infotype + Subtype

21.3 INSURANCE COMPANIES

Functional Consultant	User	Business Process Owner	Senior Management	My Rating	Understanding Level
B	X	X	X		

21.3.1 Purpose

In this view you maintain the master list of insurance companies for use in infotype 0037.

21.3.2 IMG Node

SM30 ➤ V_T564T

21.3.3 Screen

	IC	Insurance company	Ins.comp.
	01	Gerling Ins., 6 Frankfurt	GERLIN
	02	Allianz Ins., 1 Berlin	ALLIAN
	03	Company pension fund...	
	04	Bochum Association	
	05	Duisburg Association	
	06	Company pension fund...	
	07	DB support fund	
	08	Essen Association	
	09	Bavarian Ins. Chamber	BAYERN
	10	Winterthur AG, Winterth...	WINTER

21.3.4 Primary Key

Language Key + Insurance companies

Objects on Loan

22.1 OBJECTS ON LOAN (INFOTYPE 0040)

Functional Consultant	User	Business Process Owner	Senior Management	My Rating	Understanding Level
B	B	B	B		

22.1.1 Screen

Create Objects on Loan

Pers.No.	121715	Name	Agrawal Prem
Pers.area	PNCV Pune CVBU		
EE subgrp	E4 DM	WS rule	WSRPG G SHIFT
Start	☑	to ☑	

Objects on Loan

Object on loan	☑
Number/unit	
Loan object no.	

Comments

Line 1
Line 2
Line 3

22.1.2 Purpose and Overview

In this infotype, you can record which company assets an active employee has received on loan. On the start-date of the infotype record, the employee must be active, i.e. his employment status must be 3. Object on loan field identifies the type of object.

You can decide whether the objects on loan are to be validated against the assets in SAP. You can decide whether you want to validate all types of object, or only some. You can also decide to validate only for employees in certain company codes, personnel areas, etc.

It is also possible to keep the information on which asset is given to which employee in the asset master itself. To do so, use transaction code AS02, and go to 'Time-dependent' tab. At the bottom, you can specify the personnel number. If the asset changes hands, you can add an interval, and specify the new personnel number. Just as in HR, a new record delimits the old record. Thus, you have a choice of either using infotype 0040 or this method.

22.1.3 Subtypes

Types of object on loan

22.1.4 Time Constraint

3 (Record may include gaps, can exist more than once)

22.1.5 Important Fields

Object on loan

The type of object an employee has taken on loan. The master list is defined in view V_T591A.

Number/unit

Number of objects with unit (restricted to pieces).

Loan object number

This field contains a 20-character loan object number. If the employee and object type combination qualify for validation of asset against asset master as defined in feature ANLAC, then the validation is done as follows. First four characters are checked against the company code; characters 5 to 16 are checked against the main asset number, and characters 17 to 20 are checked against the asset subnumber.

Comments

All infotypes have the facility to maintain text with an infotype record. Comments are not stored in infotype tables, but elsewhere. In infotype 0040, you can enter the comment on the screen. It is stored in the same way. Comments are not available for reporting.

22.1.6   Assets with an Employee in Asset Master

It is also possible to keep the information on which asset is given to which employee in the asset master itself. To do so use transaction code AS02, and go to 'Time-dependent' tab. At the bottom, you can specify the personnel number. If the asset changes hands, you can add an interval, and specify the new personnel number. Just as in HR, a new record delimits the old record. Thus, you have a choice of either using infotype 0040, or this method.

| Asset | 32000001105 | 0 |
| Class | 32 | |

| General | Time-dependent | Allocation |

Cost center	☑
Resp. cost center	
Activity type	
Int. order	
Maintenance order	
Location	
Room	
License plate number	
Personnel number	141146

22.2 TYPES OF OBJECTS ON LOAN

Functional Consultant	User	Business Process Owner	Senior Management	My Rating	Understanding Level
B	X	X	X		

22.2.1 Purpose

Here you maintain the master list of types of objects on loan in your company. These are subtypes of infotype 0040.

22.2.2 IMG Node

SM30 ➤ VV_T591A_0040___AL0

22.2.3 Screen

Subtype	Name
01	Laptop
02	Personal computer
03	Inkjet printer
04	Laser printer
05	Calculator

Subtype characteristics for Objects on Loan

22.2.4 Primary Key

Infotype + Subtype

22.3 ASSET NUMBER CHECK AGAINST ASSET MASTER

Functional Consultant	User	Business Process Owner	Senior Management	My Rating	Understanding Level
B	X	X	X		

22.3.1 Purpose

This feature determines whether or not the system checks the asset number field in infotype 0032 (Internal Control) and loan object number in infotype 0040 (Objects on Loan) against assets table ANLA.

22.3.2 IMG Node

PE03 ≻ ANLAC

22.3.3 Screen

```
ANLAC Check number of object on loan and asset number
   └────N
```

22.3.4 Fields for Decision-making

Company Code
Personnel Area
Personnel Subarea
Infotype
Subtype
Country Grouping

22.3.5 Return Value

Y	Asset is checked against asset table ANLA
Any other	Asset is not checked against asset table ANLA

Date Specifications

23.1 DATE SPECIFICATIONS (INFOTYPE 0041)

Functional Consultant	User	Business Process Owner	Senior Management	My Rating	Understanding Level
A	A	A	A		

23.1.1 Screen

Create Date Specifications

Pers.No.	121715		Name	Agrawal Prem
Pers.area	PNCV Pune CVBU			
EE subgrp	E4 DM		WS rule	WSRPG G SHIFT
Start	01.01.2005	to	31.12.9999	

Date Specifications

Date type	Date	Date type	Date

23.1.2   Purpose and Overview

Storing and querying important dates

This infotype stores dates which are important for the company and which cannot be derived from the organizational assignment history. These dates can be queried in payroll and time management schemas, and logic can be built on their basis.

Date indicator

Some date types may have a date indicator attached to it, which gives it a specific meaning, and is used in programs. The meaning of the date indicators should not be changed. Also, once the date indicators are assigned to date types and data created in infotype 0041, if the linkage is changed, then the data in infotype 0041 has to be revamped.

Difference between infotype 0041 and 0019

An important difference between infotype 0041 and 0019 is that the dates of infotype 0019 cannot be queried in payroll and time management schemas, whereas those of infotype 0041 can be. On the other hand, tracking of task completion and reminders are not available in infotype 0041.

Time constraint of infotype 0041

You can store up to 12 date types for an employee on a given date in this infotype. If you need to maintain more than 12 date types, you can store them in different records by changing time constraint of this infotype to 3.

Keeping track of the use of date types

You should maintain a user-guideline for this infotype. This document should have three columns; date type, meaning and use (in programs, PCRs and manual processes).

23.1.3   Subtypes

No subtypes

23.1.4   Time Constraint

2 (Record may include gaps, no overlappings)

23.1.5   Important Fields

Date type and date

You define the date types you propose to use in view V_T548Y. You can specify the date types applicable to an employee and the corresponding date in infotype 0041. You can maintain up to 12 date types for an employee.

23.2 DATE TYPES

Functional Consultant	User	Business Process Owner	Senior Management	My Rating	Understanding Level
A	X	X	X		

23.2.1 Purpose

Here you maintain master list of date types.

23.2.2 IMG Node

SM30 ≻ V_T548Y

23.2.3 Screen

Date type	Date type	Date indicator
01	Techn. date of entry	01
02	Techical entry SPF	
03	Pension fund entry	
04	Start interim bonus	02
05	strt cst-of-liv.adj.	03

23.2.4 Primary Key

Date type

23.2.5 Important Fields

Date type and description

Here you specify the type of dates, which can be stored in infotype 0041.

Date indicator

Some date types may have a date indicator attached to it, which gives it a specific meaning, and is used in programs. The meaning of the date indicators should not be changed. Also, once the date indicators are assigned to date types and data created in infotype 0041, if the linkage is changed, then the data in infotype 0041 has to be revamped.

23.3 DEFAULT VALUE FOR DATE SPECIFICATIONS

Functional Consultant	User	Business Process Owner	Senior Management	My Rating	Understanding Level
A	X	X	X		

23.3.1 Purpose

In this feature you can make multiple entries for date types (T548Y). When you create infotype 0041 record, the dates are shown in that sequence.

23.3.2 IMG Node

PE03 ➢ DATAR

23.3.3 Screen

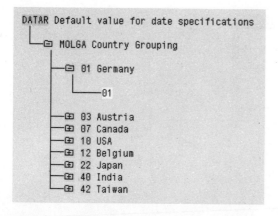

23.3.4 Fields for Decision-making

Company Code
Personnel Area
Employee Group
Employee Subgroup
Country Grouping

23.3.5 Return Value

Table of date types

23.3.6 Remarks

Maximum of 10 dates are defaulted at the time of entering data. In case you want to create more than 10 entries, click create again and select Return table ➢ Add rows. The dates are shown in the order in which you put in this feature. They don't get sorted.

Works Councils

24.1 WORKS COUNCILS (INFOTYPE 0054)

Functional Consultant	User	Business Process Owner	Senior Management	My Rating	Understanding Level
B	B	B	B		

24.1.1 Screen

Pers.No.	121715		Name	Agrawal Prem	
Pers.area	PNCV Pune CVBU				
EE subgrp	E4 DM		WS rule	WSRPG	G SHIFT
Start	01.01.2005	to	31.12.9999		

Works Councils

1st Personnel Number

2nd Personnel Number

3rd Personnel Number

24.1.2 Purpose and Overview

Infotype 0054 contains three comparable personnel numbers, which are called up when running the payroll for a semi-autonomous works council. Because this employee loses his night work and overtime bonuses due to his duties as a works council representative, he should receive compensation. The system calculates this compensation by using the bonuses received by the comparable personnel numbers specified.

24.1.3 Subtypes

No subtypes

24.1.4 Time Constraint

2 (Record may include gaps, no overlappings)

25 Disciplinary Action and Grievances

25.1 DISCIPLINARY ACTION AND GRIEVANCES (INFOTYPE 0102)

Functional Consultant	User	Business Process Owner	Senior Management	My Rating	Understanding Level
B	B	B	B		

25.1.1 Screen

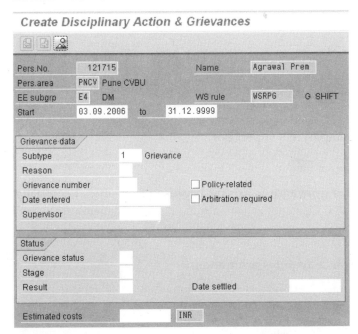

Create Disciplinary Action & Grievances

Pers.No.	121715	Name	Agrawal Prem
Pers.area	PNCV Pune CVBU		
EE subgrp	E4 DM	WS rule	WSRPG G SHIFT
Start	03.09.2006 to 31.12.9999		

Grievance data

Subtype   1   Grievance
Reason
Grievance number   ☐ Policy-related
Date entered   ☐ Arbitration required
Supervisor

Status

Grievance status
Stage
Result   Date settled

Estimated costs   INR

25.1.2 Purpose and Overview

This infotype stores disciplinary action and grievances of employees. Each record in this table is a separate entity, and is not related to any other.

25.1.3 Subtypes

Subtype

25.1.4 Time Constraint

3 (Record may include gaps, can exist more than once)

25.1.5 Important Fields

Subtype

You can use infotype 0102 for several purposes, e.g. grievance, discipline, or harassment. These are created as subtypes of infotype 0102. This category is recorded here.

Reason

This field contains a specific type of grievance, discipline, or harassment. You decide the types of grievance, discipline, and harassment your company requires and define in V_T505O. Here, you choose from that master list.

Grievance number

Here you can assign a three-digit number to identify specific grievance.

Date entered

Here you enter the date on which the employee filed the grievance.

Supervisor

Here you enter the name of the employee's supervisor.

Policy-related

Here you can specify whether this grievance is arising because of an official company policy.

Arbitration required

Here you can specify if the grievance requires arbitration.

Grievance status

In this field, you store the status of the grievance, e.g. investigation not yet started, investigation in progress, investigation completed, etc. The whole cycle of investigation may restart, if the stage changes.

Stage

You may have escalation procedures built into your handling of grievances, disciplinary actions, etc. If an employee's grievance is rejected by local management, he may have the option to go to corporate management. Failing there, he may go to a court of law. Similarly, in the case of disciplinary actions, the case may be escalated, either by the employee, or by the management.

Result

Here you indicate what finally happened. In the case of disciplinary actions, the employee may be exonerated, warned, or dismissed. In the case of grievances, the grievance may be dismissed, or redressed.

Date settled

This date indicates when the grievance, or disciplinary action, was finally closed.

Estimated costs

If you enter this data, it can be summarized for management information.

25.2 DISCIPLINARY ACTION/GRIEVANCE TYPE

Functional Consultant	User	Business Process Owner	Senior Management	My Rating	Understanding Level
B	X	X	X		

25.2.1 Purpose

In this view you define the broad categories, under which you want to maintain grievances, disciplinary actions, etc. These are subtypes of infotype 0102.

25.2.2 IMG Node

SM30 ➢ VV_T591A_0102___AL0

25.2.3 Screen

Subtype characteristics for Disciplinary Action _Grievances		
Subtype	Name	ObjIDallw
1	Grievance	☐
2	Discipline	☐
3	Harassment	☐

25.2.4 Primary Key

Infotype + Subtype

25.2.5 Important Fields

Subtype and subtype name

For infotype 0102, you define grievance, discipline, harassment, etc. as subtypes.

Object identification permitted for subtype

An employee can have multiple grievances. Each grievance is identified by an object type, which distinguishes that grievance from other grievances.

25.3 GRIEVANCE REASONS

Functional Consultant	User	Business Process Owner	Senior Management	My Rating	Understanding Level
B	X	X	X		

25.3.1 Purpose

This view contains the master list of grievance/disciplinary action. When a record in infotype 0102 is created the reason is specified.

25.3.2 IMG Node

SM30 ➤ V_T505O

25.3.3 Screen

Grievance Reasons Overview		
Art	Begründung	Description
1	01	With supervisor
1	02	With co-worker
2	01	Abatement or Attempt
2	02	Habitual abs fr work
3	01	Sexual
3	02	Mental
3	03	Physical

25.3.4 Primary Key

Subtype + Grievance reason

25.3.5 Important Fields

Subtype

This field contains the broad category, e.g. grievance, disciplinary action, harassment, etc.

Grievance reason code and description

This field contains the specific type of grievance, disciplinary action or harassment. When a record in infotype 0102 is created the reason is specified.

25.4 GRIEVANCE LEVELS

Functional Consultant	User	Business Process Owner	Senior Management	My Rating	Understanding Level
B	X	X	X		

25.4.1 Purpose and Overview

A grievance, or disciplinary action, has three attributes; stage, status and result. This view contains possible values for each of these. It is important to understand the difference between stage, status and result.

Stage	A disciplinary action or grievance may go through multiple stages, or levels of escalation, e.g. supervisor, management, court of law.
Status	Within each stage, a grievance, or disciplinary action would have a status, e.g. 'proceedings not started', 'proceedings in progress', and 'proceedings completed'.
Result	Within each stage, there may be a result, e.g. 'employee exonerated', 'caution letter issued', 'employee suspended', and 'employee dismissed'.

25.4.2   IMG Node

SM30 ➢ V_T505K

25.4.3   Screen

Art	Grievance level	Description
A	01	Case was dismissed
A	02	Case is still open
A	03	Case was resolved
R	01	Exonerated
R	42	Dismissal
S	01	Supervisor
S	02	Review board

Disciplinary Levels

25.4.4   Primary Key

Grievance Level Type + Grievance Level

25.4.5   Important Fields

Grievance level type

This field identifies, whether the master list in the next field is for stage (S), status (A), or result (R).

Grievance level and description

This contains the permitted values of stage, status and result which can be assigned in infotype 0102.

Communication

26.1 COMMUNICATION (INFOTYPE 0105)

Functional Consultant	User	Business Process Owner	Senior Management	My Rating	Understanding Level
A	A	A	A		

26.1.1 Screen

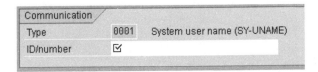

26.1.2 Purpose and Overview

In this infotype, you can maintain details of various methods of communication with the employee, e.g. office phone, residence phone, mobile, office e-mail, personal e-mail, SAP user id, etc. Subtype 0001 has special significance. It links the user code to personnel number. If you need to determine personnel number from user code, e.g. in employee self-service, or user code from personnel number, as in SAP-office, SAP business workflow, this linkage is used.

26.1.3 Subtypes

Communication type

26.1.4 Time Constraint

T (Time constraint is based on subtype or subtype table)

26.1.5 Important Fields

Communication type

Here you specify the type of communication, selecting from a predefined list.

ID/number

Here you specify the phone number, e-mail id, etc. In the case of subtype 0011 (Credit card numbers), first two characters identify the credit card company, e.g. AX (American Express), DI (Diners Club), EC (Euro Card), TP (Lufthansa AirPlus), VI (Visa).

26.2 COMMUNICATION TYPE

Functional Consultant	User	Business Process Owner	Senior Management	My Rating	Understanding Level
A	X	X	X		

26.2.1 Purpose

A company needs various methods through which it can communicate with its employees. Communication types are subtypes of infotype 0105. Communication type 0001 has a special significance. It links the user code to personnel number. If you need to determine personnel number from user code as in employee self-service, or user code from personnel number, as in SAP-office, SAP business workflow, this linkage is used.

26.2.2 IMG Node

SM30 ➢ VV_T591A_0105___AL0

26.2.3 Screen

Subtype characteristics for Communication		
Subtype	Name	Time constraint
0001	System user name (SY-UNAME)	2
0002	SAP2	2
0003	Netpass	2
0004	Direct Line	2
0005	Fax	2
0006	Voice mail	2

26.2.4 Primary Key

Infotype + Subtype

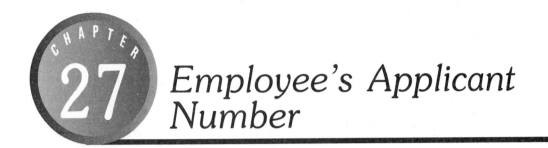

Employee's Applicant Number

27.1 EMPLOYEE'S APPLICANT NUMBER (INFOTYPE 0139)

Functional Consultant	User	Business Process Owner	Senior Management	My Rating	Understanding Level
A	A	A	A		

27.1.1 Screen

Pers.No.	121715		Name	Agrawal Prem
Pers.area	PNCV Pune CVBU			
EE subgrp	E4 DM		WS rule	WSRPG G SHIFT

Applicant master data interface

Applicant number

27.1.2 Purpose

This infotype is the link between the personnel administration and recruitment modules of SAP. When a person is hired using an action which transfers his data from applicant database to employee database, this infotype is created automatically.

27.1.3 Subtypes

No subtype

27.1.4 Time Constraint

B (IT exists for maximum of once from Jan. 1, 1800 to Dec. 12, 9999)

27.1.5 Important Fields

Applicant number

In this field the system maintains the employee's applicant number when his data is copied from applicant database to employee database. You can also maintain this field manually.

27.2 RECRUITMENT TO PA INTEGRATION

Functional Consultant	User	Business Process Owner	Senior Management	My Rating	Understanding Level
A	A	A	A		

27.2.1 Purpose

This feature determines whether recruitment data can be transferred to PA or not.

27.2.2 IMG Node

PE03 ≻ PAPLI

27.2.3 Screen

```
PAPLI Integration of Personnel Administration and Recruitment
   └───.*
```

27.2.4 Fields for Decision-making

None

27.2.5 Return Value

1st Character

*	Integration activated—Both applications in the same system
D	Integration activated—The applications are in different systems but can be accessed by RFC
N	Integration deactivated—The applications are in different systems and cannot be accessed by RFC.

2nd to 33rd characters: Target system.

28 Calculation of Employment Period

28.1 OVERVIEW

Functional Consultant	User	Business Process Owner	Senior Management	My Rating	Understanding Level
B	B	B	B		

28.1.1 Overview of Employment Period Calculation

Business scenarios

While computing employment period, you may have to consider several scenarios, e.g.

➢ The employee was hired, separated, and rehired.
➢ The employee was on unpaid leave for some period, which is not to be counted in the employment period.
➢ The employee was on study leave, and he gets only 50% credit for that period.
➢ The employee joined from another group company, and his service period in that company also needs to be considered.
➢ The employee had a break in service, and period prior to that needs to be ignored.

SAP provides you the flexibility to consider all these, and more, scenarios while calculating employment period. The concepts described below are the major building blocks of this calculation. Each of these is detailed further in this chapter, where you will find more features. Some of the features are deliberately not included in this overview, so that you understand major concepts easily.

Selection rule

For computing employment period, the first step is to select the periods. Information about all the business scenarios described above is stored in SAP in some infotype. If some information is not stored in any infotype, you can use infotype 0552 to store that information. In selection rules, you specify how to extract this information.

Selection class

The periods selected by selection rules are classified in selection classes. All periods, which are to be evaluated in the same way, are assigned the same selection class. When you assign a selection class to a valuation model, you can assign weightings. Thus, you can give partial credit to an employee, e.g. for study leave, or you may give more credit than the actual period, e.g. for hazardous work.

Gaps in periods

What happens if there are gaps in selected periods, e.g. an employee who was hired, separated, and rehired? Nothing! The gaps are not counted in employment period.

Overlapping of periods

Since there may be several selection rules, it is possible that you may get overlapping periods. For example, an employee's active period and unpaid leave period may overlap. If the overlapping periods are in the same selection class, only one is taken. Which period is taken and which is left is unimportant, because they are evaluated in the same way. But when periods across selection classes overlap, you need to decide what to do. SAP provides two alternatives.

> Eliminate the overlapping period of the selection class, which has lower priority. For this purpose, selection classes are assigned priority.
> Keep the overlapping periods and multiply their weightings. If you have a selection class, which is never to be considered in employment period, no matter what else happened during those periods, just give it a zero weighting.

Interruption

Sometimes there are clauses that the employment must be uninterrupted. A company's policy may be that if an employee left the company, and joined again, the company will consider both the periods for determining the length of service, provided he did not work with a competitor in the interim. If he did, his earlier service will not be considered. Similarly, an act of indiscipline leading to suspension may result in break in service. SAP lets you classify a selection class as interruption relevant. It also lets you specify a value, which if crossed will reset the employment period to zero.

Limits on calculated employment period

SAP lets you define a maximum value, and a threshold value (below which the period is ignored). This can be done at two levels.

> When periods are selected by selection rule, you can apply a maximum value, and a threshold value.
> You can also apply a maximum value, and a threshold value, when periods selected by selection rules are grouped at selection class level.

Note that both maximum value as well as threshold value can only reduce the employment period.

Rounding

You can assign a rounding rule to a calculation process, or process step.

Employment period calculation for various purposes

You may want to compute employment period for various purposes, which have different rules for employment period calculation. For example, you may want to compute employment period for

➢ Confirming a probationer employee
➢ Giving long service award

SAP lets you define various calculation processes, which can be called from different applications (by calling function module HR_SEN_CALCULATE_COMPLETE). Alternatively, you can create multiple records of infotype 0553 for an employee, one for each calculation process.

28.1.2 Reports

S_PH9_46000216—Service Anniversaries

This report gives service anniversaries of your employees. Note that this report takes into account the settings for entry date and employment period calculation.

Service Anniversaries

Personnel No.	Last name	First name	Entry	Year
00205184	Chandwani	Rohit	07.07.2002	03
00502027	Champavat	B	04.08.1986	17
00502746	Joshi	V	01.02.1995	09
00504019	Saraswat	Amit	01.07.1995	10
00504151	Jain	Vikram	01.07.2000	04

S_PH9_46000217—Statistics: Gender Sorted by Seniority

This is a summary report giving years of service wise number of employees. It also gives gender wise break up. Note that this report also takes into account the settings for entry date and employment period calculation.

Seniority/gender			
yea...	Gend...	ΣNumb...	Σ Share in %
04	Male	1	20.0
🔲 04	▪	1 ▪	**20.0**
06	Male	1	20.0
🔲 06	▪	1 ▪	**20.0**
11	Male	2	40.0
🔲 11	▪	2 ▪	**40.0**
20	Male	1	20.0
🔲 20	▪	1 ▪	**20.0**
🔲	▪ ▪	5 ▪ ▪	**100.0**

PSEN_IMG_XX_CUST—Settings for Employment Period Calculation

This utility shows the settings for employment period calculation in a structured way. You can view it for a valuation model, or entire calculation process.

Settings for Valuation Model

Emp. per. evaluation	Name
▽ 🗀 Select valuation model	
▽ 🗀 Valuation model 1SVY	Seniority
▽ 🗀 Selection class ACTI	Active periods (with tech. start date)
📄 Weight factor: 1.000	
▽ 🗀 Assigned selection rules	
🗀 Selection rule DT01	Tech. start date (01) up to 1st action
🗀 Selection rule ST23	Employment status: active
▽ 🗀 Selection class ST21	Employment status: suspended
📄 Weight factor: 0.000	
▽ 🗀 Assigned selection rules	
🗀 Selection rule ST21	Employment status: suspended
▽ 🗀 Selection class ST22	Employment status: retiree
📄 Weight factor: 0.000	
▽ 🗀 Assigned selection rules	
🗀 Selection rule ST22	Employment status: retiree

Settings for Calculation Process

Emp. per. evaluation	Name
▽ ☐ Select calc. processes	
▽ ☐ Calc. process 1SVY	Seniority
📄 Conversion rule 0100	Years, months, days: Variant A
▽ ☐ Valuation model 1SVY	Seniority
▽ ☐ Selection class ACTI	Active periods (with tech. start date)
📄 Weight factor: 1.000	
▽ 📁 Assigned selection rules	
☐ Selection rule DT01	Tech. start date (01) up to 1st action
☐ Selection rule ST23	Employment status: active
▷ ☐ Selection class ST21	Employment status: suspended
▷ ☐ Selection class ST22	Employment status: retiree
📄 Rounding rule 1YM1	Round up (decimal) days >0

S_PH9_46000454—Test Utility for Employment Period Calculation

Since calculation of employment period is complex, SAP has provided a test utility. It shows all the intermediate steps of calculation, so that you can clearly understand how the employment period was calculated.

Reporting
▽ ☐ Calculation Process 1SVY Seniority
Personnel Number 00121715 Agrawal Prem
Selection date 24.09.2006
Conversion rule 0100 Years, months, days: Variant A
Result : 1.00 Years 9.00 Months 0.00 Days
▽ ☐ Process step
Calculate employment period to
Valuation model 1SVY Seniority
▷ ☐ Import infotypes (005)
▷ ☐ Processing of periods overridden by duration (010)
▷ ☐ Processing according to selection rule (020)
▷ ☐ Distribute periods among simultaneous personnel assignments (028)
▷ ☐ Priority rules for selection classes (030)
▷ ☐ Check interruption periods (040)
▷ ☐ Threshold and max. value for selection class (050)
▷ ☐ Determine remaining periods (060)
▷ ☐ Assign weighting factor (070)
▷ ☐ Determine partial periods (080)
▷ ☐ Sum of simultaneous part periods (085)
▷ ☐ Maximum weighting factor (087)
▷ ☐ Weight durations (100)
▷ ☐ Table of imputed times
Rounding rule 1YM1 Round up (decimal) days >0
Result of calculation

You may note that the calculation takes place in the following hierarchy.

Calculation process
    Process steps
        Valuation model
            Selection classes
                Selection rules

28.2 SELECTION RULE

Functional Consultant	User	Business Process Owner	Senior Management	My Rating	Understanding Level
B	C	X	X		

28.2.1 Purpose and Overview

The selection rule identifies the employee data which is selected for the employment period calculation. All four types of selection rules are discussed in this chapter. Regardless of the category of selection rule, you can specify a minimum and a maximum threshold. You can also specify if the first day, or the last day, is to be moved, to the beginning or end of calendar month for example. Selection rules can return a period, a weighted period, or a date based duration. Selection rules are maintained in view V_T525A_A.

28.2.2 Period Selection based on Start Date and End Date

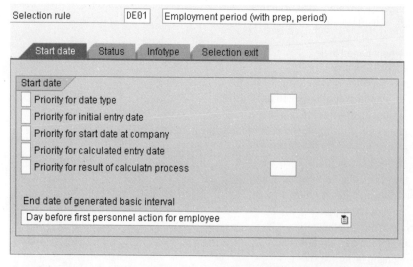

A selection rule may select a period by determining the start date and the end date according to the specification in the 'Start date' tab. These selection rules are used mostly for periods for which there is no data about the employee in the system, e.g. working for a group company.

Start date

The start date can be determined

> From a date type in the Date Specifications infotype (0041)
> From an initial entry date in the Contract Elements infotype (0016)
> From the Entry into group date in the Contract Elements infotype (0016)
> Using the function module HR_ENTRY_DATE
> From the result of a calculation process in the Employment Period infotype (0553)

Each of these methods is assigned a priority (priority 1 is the highest). The assigned priorities specify the sequence in which the system searches for the dates. The search ends when the first date is found. If no priority is assigned to a field, the system does not evaluate the accompanying infotype when the start date is determined.

Function module HR_ENTRY_DATE along with feature ENTRY offers a lot of flexibility in determining the start date of a period. Read the documentation of these objects to determine their suitability to your needs. You can use BAdI HRPAD00_ENTRY_LEAVE to calculate an employee's entry and/or leaving date according to your requirements. Note the information in SAP Note 621634. In the standard system, this is done using the HR_ENTRY_DATE and HR_LEAVING_DATE function modules.

End date

Most often, the employee is created in the system through a joining personnel action. Periods prior to that date are selected through selection rules of this type, and the end date for such periods is one day before the first personnel action of the employee. Other options are 'End of reporting period' and 'Day before start of evaluation period'. However, if the start date is after the generated end date, it is ignored.

28.2.3 Period Selection based on Status

Selection rule	DE01	Employment period (with prep, period)

Start date	Status	Infotype	Selection exit

Status	
Status	
Status indicator	

Status

You can select periods based on the employee's status in infotype 0000.

Status indicator

Here you can specify the value of the status field. For example, to determine active period of an employee, you would specify Employment in the status field, and Active in the status indicator field.

28.2.4 Period Selection based on Infotype

Selection rule	DE01	Employment period (with prep, period)

Start date	Status	Infotype	Selection exit

Infotype

- ○ Infotype existence
  - Infotype   ☐
  - Subtype   ☐

- ◉ Infotype content
  - Selection condition   GAB1   Absences not contributing to service

Infotype existence

You can select periods based on infotypes. If you specify infotype and subtype in infotype existence, infotype records matching the specification are selected and their validity period is taken for employment period calculation. You can restrict the infotypes which can be entered in this field in view V_T525Z.

Infotype	Infotype text	Permissib
0000	Actions	☑
0001	Organizational Assignment	☑
0007	Planned Working Time	☑
0008	Basic Pay	☑
0016	Contract Elements	☑
0022	Education	☑
0023	Other/Previous Employers	☑
0041	Date Specifications	☑
0081	Military Service	☑
0145	Personnel Tax Status JP	☑
0294	Work book RU	☑
0429	Position in PS	☑
0495	Retirement Benefits/Death Gratuity	☑
0552	Time Specification/Employ. Period	☑
0623	Career History (Public Sector BE)	☑
2001	Absences	☑
2006	Absence Quotas	☑

Infotype content

If you want to select periods from infotype data based on more complex conditions, you can specify a selection condition in infotype content. Selection conditions are defined in view cluster VC_T525I_A.

Selection Condition

Selection condition	GAB1	Absences not contributing to service
Infotype	2001	Absences
Subtype		

Selection condition: Definition

Seq	Field	Short text	Relational	Value in IT field	Field length	Logical link
1	AWART	Attendance or Absence Type	EQ Equal ▤	0700	4	▤
			▤			▤

Selection conditions can only use infotypes specified in view V_T525Z.

28.2.5   Period Selection based on Selection Exit

Selection rule   DE01   Employment period (with prep, period)

| Start date | Status | Infotype | Selection exit |

Selection exit

Selection exit

Selection exit

Selection value

This option provides maximum flexibility. You can write your own logic for period selection in a selection exit and specify the selection exit here. You can also enter a value in selection value, which is passed to the selection exit. Selection exits are defined in view T525V.

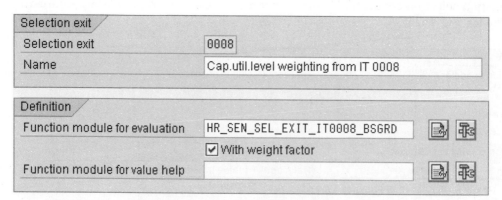

You specify the function module which determines the employment period in the field 'Function module for evaluation'. The function module can take a selection value, which is specified in the selection rule. Permissible selection values are determined by the function module which is specified in the field 'Function module for value help'. In infotype 0552, you can specify a multiplier, or weight factor, to be associated with a period. If you want the selection exit to return weighted period, you tick the field 'With weight factor'.

28.2.6 Minimum and Maximum Threshold

Minimum and maximum threshold

○ None
◉ Threshold value
  ☐ Only complete calendar units
  ☐ Round off under threshold value
  Years [ ]   Months [ ]   Days [ ]
○ Maximum amount
  ☑ Round off above maximum amount
  Years [0]   Months [0]   Days [0]

None

If you select this radio button, you cannot specify threshold value or maximum amount.

Threshold value

You can specify threshold value in years, months and days. If the period is smaller than the threshold value, it is not passed to the valuation model. If you tick 'Round off under threshold value', the period is rounded off to the threshold value. If you tick 'Only complete calendar units', you can only specify years and months, the days field is disabled. Also, 'Round off under threshold value' is disabled.

Maximum amount

You can specify maximum amount in years, months and days. If the period is larger than the maximum amount, maximum amount is passed to valuation model instead of the actual period. The field 'Round off above maximum amount' is always ticked and disabled.

28.2.7 Moving Start and End Date

```
Move start and end date
☑ Move start date to first day
    ◉ of the current month
    ○ of the following month
        ☐ With exception of first day of calendar unit
    ○ of the current year
    ○ of the following year
        ☐ With exception of first day of calendar unit
☑ Move end date to last day
    ◉ of the current month
    ○ of the previous month
        ☐ With exception of last day of calendar unit
    ○ of the current year
    ○ of the previous year
        ☐ With exception of last day of calendar unit
```

Sometimes companies want to move the first day of a period to coincide with the beginning of a calendar month or year. Similarly, they may want to move the last day of a period to coincide with the end of a calendar month or year. You can define that here for all periods selected by a selection rule.

28.3 SELECTION CLASS

Functional Consultant	User	Business Process Owner	Senior Management	My Rating	Understanding Level
B	X	X	X		

28.3.1 Selection Class

A selection class may have many selection rules. All periods selected through different selection rules in a selection class are processed in the same manner. You define selection classes in view T525N of view cluster V_T525N.

	Selection class	Name		With weight factor	Special class
	ACTI	Active periods (with tech. start dates)		☐	📋
					📋

With weight factor is an attribute that a selection class inherits from the selection rules assigned to it. Selection rules with weight factor and without weight factor cannot be assigned to the same selection class. If a selection class contains selection rules with a weighting factor, no generated periods can overlap when the selection classes are evaluated in the valuation model. If you specify a special class for a selection class, it is evaluated in the valuation model.

28.3.2 Selection Rules in a Selection Class

You assign selection rules to selection classes in view V_T525M_A of view cluster V_T525N. A selection rule can be assigned to multiple selection classes.

Selection class	ACTI	

Assignment of Selection Rules		
Selection rule	Name	Wi
DE01	Employment period (with prep, period)	☐

28.3.3 Indicator for Selection Class

Indicators for selection classes are defined in view T525NI of view cluster VC_T525NI. They are used in Pension Administration.

	Indicator	Name
	D4	Increased Release Par. 14 Sec. 4
	D9	F91 Neutral.Release.n90, Verdict 2005/05
	DA	Fictitious Compl. Imputation Quota Arrgt

Selection classes are assigned to the Indicator for selection classes in view V_T525NJ of view cluster VC_T525NI.

Indicator for Selection Class		D4
Increased Release Par. 14 Sec. 4		
Assigned Selection Class		
Selection class	Name	

28.3.4 Legal Regulations

Legal regulations are defined in view T525OL. When selection classes are assigned to valuation models in view V_T525O_B, legal regulation can be specified.

Legal Regulations	Description
DEVA10	P.10 BeamtVG (Germany only!)
DEVA10A	P.10 i.V.m. P.12b BeamtVG (Germany only!)
DEVA10C	P.10 Satz 1 Nr. 2 BeamtVG (Germany only!)
DEVA10D	P.10 Satz 1 Nr. 1 BeamtVG (Germany only!)
DEVA11	P.11 BeamtVG (Germany only!)
DEVA11A	P.11 Nr. 1a u. Nr. 3 BeamtVG (Germany only!)
DEVA11B	P.11 i.V.m. P.12b BeamtVG (Germany only!)

28.4 VALUATION MODEL

Functional Consultant	User	Business Process Owner	Senior Management	My Rating	Understanding Level
B	X	X	X		

28.4.1 Purpose and Overview

For each selection class you can specify a weighting factor. This weighting factor is different from the weight factor, which is already applied when the period is selected using selection rule. Selection rule weight factor is applicable only when infotype 0552 is used in selection.

Interruption periods are more critical than gaps. During a gap, the employment period does not increase; it remains constant. But a large enough interruption makes it zero. Although the weighting factor in a valuation model is defined at selection class level, you can also specify a maximum weighting factor for a day at valuation model level.

28.4.2   Valuation Model

Valuation models are defined in view V_T525L of view cluster VC_T525L.

Valuation model	
Valuation model	1SVY
Name	Seniority

Maximum weighting of a day	
⦿ None	
○ Counter	1.000
Denominator	1.000
Quotient	1.000

Interruption period	
Years	
Months	
Days	

Maximum weighting of a day

Here you can specify maximum weighting for valuation model which applies to all periods, regardless of the selection class through which they come.

Interruption period

Here you can specify the interruption period in years, months and days. When the continuous interruption from interruption relevant selection classes reaches this value, the employment period is reset to zero.

28.4.3 Assignment of Selection Classes to Valuation Model

Valuation model		
Valuation model	1SVY	Seniority
Selection class	ACTI	Active periods (with tech. start dates)

Weighting factor

☐ With weight factor

Numerator	1.000
Denominator	1.000

Quotient	1.000

Upper and lower limit for selection class

○ None

◉ Threshold value

     ☐ With consideration of weighting factor

     Years [ ]   Months [ ]   Days [ ]

○ Maximum amount

     ☐ With consideration of weighting factor

     Years [0]   Months [0]   Days [0]

Other settings

☐ Interruption-relevant

Priority [ ]

Selection classes are assigned to valuation classes in view V_T525O_A of view cluster V_T525L_A. They have following properties.

Weighting factor

You can specify weighting factor for the selection class in the valuation model.

None

If you select this radio button, you cannot specify threshold value or maximum amount.

Threshold value

You can specify threshold value in years, months and days. If the period is smaller than the threshold value, it is not passed to the valuation model. If you tick 'With consideration of weighting factor', threshold is checked after multiplying the weighting factor; otherwise, threshold is checked before multiplying the weighting factor.

Maximum amount

You can specify maximum amount in years, months and days. If the period is larger than the maximum amount, maximum amount is passed to valuation model instead of the actual period. If you tick 'With consideration of weighting factor', maximum amount is checked after multiplying the weighting factor; otherwise, maximum amount is checked before multiplying the weighting factor.

Interruption relevant

If you specify a selection class as interruption relevant, then the periods during that selection class is considered an interruption, and the employment period does not build up during those periods. Moreover, you can specify an interruption period at valuation model level. When the continuous interruption reaches this value, the employment period is reset to zero.

Priority

When the periods from different selection classes overlap, you need to decide which selection class gets priority (because they may be evaluated differently). Periods with lower priority selection class are ignored. Selection classes without priority (priority 0) are not compared, and are transferred for evaluation irrespective of the other priorities.

Note that SAP does not eliminate overlapping periods. If there are overlapping periods with priority 0, they would come in. Also, a period with priority 0 can co-exist with an overlapping period with different priority. What SAP would do is multiply all the weightings.

You need to carefully design the weightings and priorities. You use priority if you want to exclude overlapping periods of lower priority. But, if you want certain periods never to be counted, you assign it zero weighting and blank priority.

28.4.4 Valuation Model for Add-On HR-VADM

SAP has refined valuation model for Pension Administration. It is defined in view cluster VC_T525L.

```
Dialog Structure
 ▽  🗁 Valuation model for employee data
   ▽  🗀 Assignment of selection classes to valuation model
       🗀 Period-dependent characteristics of an assignment
```

The valuation model view V_T525L remains the same. Assignment of selection classes to valuation model view V_T525O_B is slightly different from the classical view V_T525O_A. View V_T525OT for period dependent characteristics of selection classes to valuation model assignment has been added.

28.5 CALCULATION PROCESS

Functional Consultant	User	Business Process Owner	Senior Management	My Rating	Understanding Level
B	X	X	X		

28.5.1 Calculation Process

Service period calculation is controlled by a calculation process defined in view V_T525P. There are two ways of doing service period calculation.

Call function module	You may call function module HR_SEN_CALCULATE_COMPLETE in a program. You pass calculation process as a mandatory parameter to this function module.
Specify in infotype 0553	For an employee, you may specify different types of service periods in infotype 0553. For each record of infotype 0553, you specify calculation process as its subtype.

Thus, no service period calculation can take place without a calculation process. A calculation process may have process steps. These are controlled by the function module for calculation process.

A calculation process has a valuation model and a rounding rule. If a calculation process has steps, it is possible to associate different valuation models and rounding rules to different process steps of the same calculation process. It is also possible to have different valuation models and rounding rules for different group of employees.

SAP provides standard calculation processes, but you can create your own process definition without changing the name of the calculation process. SAP calls calculation processes in standard SAP programs. Therefore, it is necessary that the name of the calculation process remains the same, but the customer is able to create his own definition for it.

Calculation Process		
Calculation Process	1SVY	Start Time Exit
Name	Seniority	> 01.01.1800 31.12.9999

Control calculation of employment period	
Conversion rule	Years, months, days: Variant A
Function module for calculation process	
☑ Authorization check	

Employment Period Calculation infotype
☐ Individual override for valuation model
☐ Save result as

Calculation process and name

Here you enter the calculation process you are defining.

Start time, exit

Here you specify the validity period of calculation process definition, as calculation process definition can change with time.

Conversion rule

Here you specify the conversion rule for the calculation process. For more details of conversion rule, see chapter 28.6.

Function module for calculation process

If a calculation process consists of multiple process steps, this function module controls those steps. It is also required if the result of the calculation process is saved in infotype 0553.

Authorization check

Calculation of employment period requires reading of several infotypes. If you want the system to check that the user has read authorization on these infotypes, you tick this checkbox.

Individual override for valuation model

Each calculation process, or process step, has a valuation model. However, SAP gives you the flexibility of overriding these valuation models for specific employees by specifying alternate valuation model in infotype 0553. If you want your users to have this flexibility, you tick this checkbox.

Save result as

Here you specify whether users can save the result in infotype 0553; and if yes whether it is saved as duration or a key date.

28.5.2 Override Attributes for Calculation Process

SAP provides standard calculation processes, which are defined in V_T525P. You can maintain your own calculation processes there in customer name space. However, if you want to use SAP defined calculation processes (same name), but want to change its definition, you can define that in view V_T525Q. If a calculation process is found here, it is taken from here, otherwise from V_T525P. The screens of V_T525Q and V_T525P are identical.

28.5.3 Process Step

In view V_T525R you specify process steps, if any, for a calculation process. Note that the logic and sequence for executing the steps is defined in the function module associated with the calculation process.

	Calculation Process	Name	Process step	Name

28.5.4 Assignment of Valuation Model to Process Step

In view V_T525S you define the valuation model and rounding rule for each calculation process. If a calculation process consists of multiple steps, you can define the valuation model and rounding rule at process step level. If you want the valuation model and rounding rule to be different for different groups of employees, you can group your employees using feature SENOR, and define different valuation models and rounding rules based on the return value of the feature. You should only use a rounding rule if the calculation process is evaluated in years–months–days with the conversion rule. Otherwise, the rounding rule generates unwanted results.

	Calcu...	Process step	Feature return	Start Date	End Date	Valuation ...	Rounding rule
	1SVY			01.01.1800	31.12.9999	1SVY	1YM1
	SENI			01.01.1800	31.12.9999	SENI	0YM0

28.5.5 Employee Grouping for Valuation Model Determination

You define the valuation model and rounding rule for each calculation process. If a calculation process consists of multiple steps, you can define the valuation model and rounding rule at process step level. If you want the valuation model and rounding rule to be different for different groups of employees, you can group your employees using feature SENOR, and define different valuation models and rounding rules based on the return value of the feature.

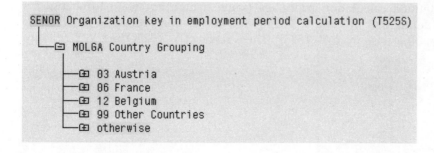

```
SENOR Organization key in employment period calculation (T525S)
  └─⊟ MOLGA Country Grouping
        ├─⊞ 03 Austria
        ├─⊞ 06 France
        ├─⊞ 12 Belgium
        ├─⊞ 99 Other Countries
        └─⊞ otherwise
```

28.6 CONVERSION RULE

Functional Consultant	User	Business Process Owner	Senior Management	My Rating	Understanding Level
B	X	X	X		

28.6.1 Conversion Rule

A calculation process has a conversion rule which specifies how the durations are computed, how they are weighted, how they are cumulated, etc. With known duration, you need start date to know end date, or end date to know start date. These tasks require exact logic, which is defined in the function modules specified in a conversion rule. Conversion rules are defined in view T525U

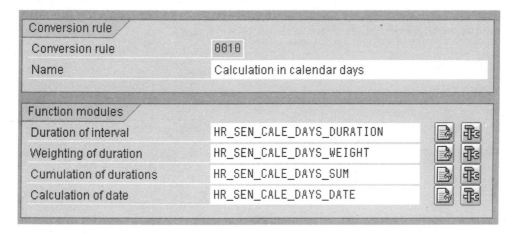

28.6.2 Conversion Rule for Infotype 0552

In infotype 0552, SAP calculates the duration from a given validity period. For calculating duration, you can use a conversion rule. In feature CRULE, you can define a conversion rule based on the time specification type of infotype 0552.

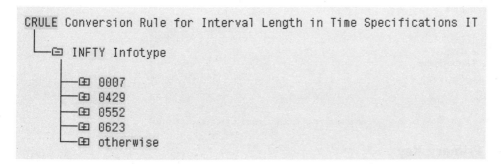

28.7 ROUNDING RULE

Functional Consultant	User	Business Process Owner	Senior Management	My Rating	Understanding Level
B	X	X	X		

28.7.1 Purpose and Overview

Here you define whether rounding is not to take place, or whether you want to always cut off rather than round, or if you want to round up what value you want to round up to. This is defined for part of a day, days, and months.

The rounding rule converts 30 days to one month and 12 months to one year. Only use a rounding rule if the calculation process is evaluated in years, months, and days using the conversion rule. Otherwise, the rounding rule may generate unwanted results. Rounding rules are attached to calculation processes and process steps.

28.7.2 IMG Node

SM30 ➤ V_T525E

28.7.3 Screen

28.7.4 Primary Key

Rounding rule for time intervals

28.8   CALCULATION OF SERVICE (INFOTYPE 0553)

Functional Consultant	User	Business Process Owner	Senior Management	My Rating	Understanding Level
B	B	C	X		

28.8.1   Screen

```
Pers.No.        121715              Name        Agrawal Prem
Pers.area    PNCV  Pune CVBU
EE subgrp    E4   DM                WS rule     WSRPG        G SHIFT
Start        01.01.2005  To    31.12.9999


Calculation Process          XGDZ   Pensionable employment periods


┌ Different valuation model ─────────────────────────────────────
│ Diff. valuation model │Valuation model│ Valuation model │ Valuation model │
│                       │               │                 │                 │
│                       │               │                 │                 │
│                       │               │                 │                 │
│ ◄ ►                                                                        │
└────────────────────────────────────────────────────────────────

┌ Result ────────────────────────────────────────────────────────

        [▦]    Run calculation        [⋯]      Simulation
```

28.8.2   Purpose and Overview

You can use infotype 0553 to assign a different valuation model and to save the result. Both these features are controlled by the configuration of calculation process. If neither is allowed, you cannot create an infotype 0553 record. If both are allowed, you see the above screen. If only one is allowed, you see only the relevant part of the screen.

You can run calculation and save the result only if a function module is associated with the calculation process. If you save the result in infotype 0553, it can be used for other functions and processes in SAP.

28.8.3 Subtypes

Calculation process (T525P)

28.8.4 Time Constraint

2 (Record may include gaps, no overlappings)

28.9 TIME SPECIFICATIONS FOR EMPLOYMENT PERIOD (INFOTYPE 0552)

Functional Consultant	User	Business Process Owner	Senior Management	My Rating	Understanding Level
B	B	C	X		

28.9.1 Screen

The screen you get for infotype 0552 depends on the subtype you select. The screen below is for a subtype where you specify weighting in numerator and denominator. If your subtype is of 'percentage rate' type, you specify weighting directly, instead of numerator and denominator.

Pers.No.	121715		Name	Agrawal Prem	
Pers.area	PNCV	Pune CVBU			
EE subgrp	E4	DM	WS rule	WSRPG	G SHIFT
Start	☑	To ☑			

Time specifications/employment period

Time spec.	0110	Part-time employment, Public Sector
Weighting	100.000 / 100.000	100.00 %
☐ Do not evaluate		

Duration of validity period

Years	0
Months	0
Days	0

Comments

If your subtype specification requires imputed period entry, you get additional fields as shown below.

Normally the duration is determined from the validity period of infotype 0552 record, and displayed on the screen. However, SAP lets you override this period, and enter your own period. This is defined at the level of time specification type. If you are permitted to override the period, you see the fields where you can enter the imputable period.

Duration of validity period		Imputable period	
Years	0	Years	
Months	0	Months	
Days	0	Days	

28.9.2 Purpose and Overview

When you calculate employment period, you pick up data from various infotypes. However, you may want to consider some aspects of a person's employment, e.g. employment in public sector, which is not in any infotype. SAP provides infotype 0552 for capturing such data.

Unlike periods coming from other infotypes, which can be given a weighting only at selection class level, periods coming from infotype 0552 can have their own weightings, which may be assigned either as percentage, or by specifying a numerator and a denominator.

Alternatively (but not in addition), you can specify the period that should be considered for employment calculation directly in imputable period fields. Instead of specifying a period, you can also specify a key date and imputable period. The system then gives date-based duration.

Thus you receive either a period, or a weighted period, or a date-based duration. You can also specify that this record should not be considered in calculation of employment period by ticking the 'Do not evaluate' checkbox.

28.9.3 Subtypes

Time specification type (T525T)

28.9.4 Time Constraint

2 (Record may include gaps, no overlappings)

28.9.5 Important Fields

Time specification type

You may store different types of time specification in infotype 0552; e.g. employment in public sector, employment in sister company, etc.

Duration of imputation in years, months and days

You can override the validity period by entering an imputable duration in years, months, and days. This is only possible if it is permitted for the selected time specification type. The permissibility is defined in Customizing.

If you have entered an imputable duration in at least one of the three fields, it is taken into account instead of the duration of the validity period when the time specifications are evaluated in the employment period calculation.

For example, an employee studied in the period from January 01, 1995 to December 31, 1998. Four years are displayed in the Duration of validity period group. However, of these 4 years, only 3 years and 6 months should be imputed to the employment period. Enter 3 years and 6 months in the Imputable period group.

Imputation factor: numerator and denominator

Here you can define imputation factor in numerator denominator form.

Renewal number of a time entry sequence

If there are two consecutive records of infotype 0552, they may be treated as two separate records, or as a single record. If the value in this field is the same in both records, they are treated as a single period (the second record being an extension or renewal of the first). The weighting in the two records may be different. If the value in this field is different in the two records, they are treated as two different records.

Approval date of time specification type

Time data that requires approval (employment period), such as parental leave is approved by the approval date. If an employment period requiring approval such as parental leave is approved by entering the approval date, this can be taken into account for the employment period. This field is displayed if the time specification type requires approval.

Occasion for time specification type

The evaluation of the employment period can be dependent on the occasion (reason) when calculating the length of service. For example, in Germany, employees can be part-time employees because of parental leave.

Do not evaluate

If this checkbox is ticked, the infotype record is not taken into account in the calculation of the employment period.

28.10 TIME SPECIFICATION TYPES

Functional Consultant	User	Business Process Owner	Senior Management	My Rating	Understanding Level
B	X	X	X		

28.10.1 Purpose

You may store different types of time specification in infotype 0552; e.g. employment in public sector, employment in sister company, etc. Master list of time specification types is defined here.

28.10.2 IMG Node

SM30 ➤ T525T

28.10.3 Screen

Ti...	Time spec. type	Period/key ...	Addition
0100	Employment in Public Sector	Period	No additional speci...
0110	Part-time employment, Public Sector	Period	Factor with counter...
0200	Employment in private enterprise	Period	Duration in years, m...
0300	Parental leave before entry		Duration in years, months, and days
0400	Employment period bonus		Percentage Rate
DE01	Employment period (with prep. period)		Factor with counters and denominators
			No additional specifications
DE02	Parental leave	Period	No additional speci...

Time Specification Type for Employment Period Calculation

28.10.4 Primary Key

Time specification type for employment period calculation

28.10.5 Important Fields

Time specification type and description

You may store different types of time specification in infotype 0552; e.g. employment in public sector, employment in sister company, etc. Time specification type is the subtype of infotype 0552.

Period/key date

This determines whether data in infotype 0552 is for a period, or for a key date.

Addition

This field determines the screen you get for infotype 0552.

Duration in years, months, and days	Time period is not computed from start date and end date. It is directly specified in years, months and days.
Percentage rate	Time period is computed from start date and end date. Weighting is specified as %.
Factors with counters and denominators	Time period is computed from start date and end date. Weighting is specified as numerator divided by denominator.
No additional specifications	Time period is computed from start date and end date. No weighting can be specified.

You can only select a weighting with a percentage rate or with a factor with numerator and denominator for period. Always choose duration in years, months, and days for the key date.

28.11 APPROVAL OF TIME SPECIFICATION TYPES

Functional Consultant	User	Business Process Owner	Senior Management	My Rating	Understanding Level
B	X	X	X		

28.11.1 Purpose

Here you define whether the time specification type requires approval. This configuration is required for Add-On HR-VADM.

28.11.2 IMG Node

SM34 ➤ VC_T525T (view V_T525TD)

28.11.3 Screen

Time spec.	0100 Employment in Public Sector

Define Additional Properties of Time Data Type

Start Date	End Date	Approval Condition	R	Part-Time Condition for Renewal
01.01.2000	31.12.9999	Not Subject to Approval ▤	☑	No Renewal ▤

28.11.4 Primary Key

Time specification type for employment period calculation + End Date

28.11.5 Important Fields

Time specification type and description

You may store different types of time specification in infotype 0552; e.g. employment in public sector, employment in sister company, etc. Time specification type is the subtype of infotype 0552.

Start and end date

The properties of time specification type can change with time.

Approval condition

If you specify that a time specification type requires approval, the approval date field is displayed in infotype 0552. Only if the approval date is entered, infotype 0552 record is considered for service period calculation. If a time specification type does not require approval, the approval date field is not displayed in infotype 0552.

Blank	No Approval
Y	Subject to Approval
P	Part-Time Work Subject to Approval

Required entry approval date

You tick this checkbox, if the time specification type requires approval. If you tick this checkbox; the field for approval must be filled in infotype 0552.

Part-time condition for renewal

You choose from the following options.

Blank	No Renewal
N	No Additional Condition
P	Same Part-Time Percentage
Q	Different Part-Time Percentage

28.12 OCCASIONS FOR TIME SPECIFICATION TYPE

Functional Consultant	User	Business Process Owner	Senior Management	My Rating	Understanding Level
B	X	X	X		

28.12.1 Occasion for Time Specification Type

In infotype 0552, along with time specification type, you can specify an occasion or reason for time specification type. The occasion can be used to specify time types closer. Thereby it is possible, for instance to differentiate with a part-time employment after the reason for the reduction of the working hours (e.g., education vacation). The occasion can also be taken into consideration in the assessment of business hours. Master list of occasion for time specification type is defined in view T525TR. You can also specify whether an occasion for time specification type is a parental leave.

Cause	Name	Parental Leave
		☐
		☐
		☐

28.12.2 Consideration of the Occasion for Time Specification Type

In view V_T7DEPBS25TR, you can define more properties of the occasion for time specification type. These properties are useful only for certain countries.

Cause	Bezeichnung	Neutral Quotierung	Neutral Abschlag 84	Neutral Abschlag 80
01	Social Upliftment	☐	📋	📋

28.12.3 Occasion to Time Specification Type Assignment

In view T525TRP a time specification type can be associated with one or more reasons/causes/occasions. After you specify the time specification type, you may select from one of the permitted causes defined here.

Time spec. type	Text	Start Date	End Date	Cause	Name

29 Wage Type

29.1 WAGE TYPE OVERVIEW

Functional Consultant	User	Business Process Owner	Senior Management	My Rating	Understanding Level
A	A	A	A		

29.1.1 Wage Type

Wage type is the instrument of payments and deductions in SAP payroll. Wage types have multiple properties, e.g.

- ➢ Payment to/deduction from employees
- ➢ Financial posting
- ➢ Taxability

These can be varied independently, giving enormous power in the hands of consultants to meet client requirement. In addition, you may note the following.

- ➢ You may specify the value of a wage type directly at the employee level, or let the system determine it from employee attributes.
- ➢ Wage types are printed on payslips.
- ➢ Some wage types are meant for intermediate calculations.

Wage types are always created by copying an appropriate model wage type, which creates entries in several tables. Choosing an appropriate model wage type helps assign suitable properties to a wage type. The system maintains a record of the model wage type from which a wage type was copied in view V_T52DZ.

29.1.2 Wage Type Properties

There are many properties associated with wage types. The value of a wage type can be restricted within a minimum and maximum range. A wage type has number, amount and rate fields. For a wage type, you can specify the fields in which a user can enter data. There are many other properties of wage types, which are beyond the scope of this book.

29.1.3 Wage Type Permissibilities

You can specify

➤ Wage types which are permitted in an infotype and the time constraint for these wage types in that infotype.
➤ Wage types which are permitted for different employees based on employee subgroup grouping and personnel subarea grouping.
➤ Wage types which can or cannot be entered in the payroll past.

29.1.4 Wage Type Entry in Master Data

Regular employee payment wage types are entered in infotype 0008 (maximum 40 on a given date). Payment and deduction wage types are also entered in infotypes 0014, 0015, 0057, 0267, etc.

For infotypes 0011, 0014, 0015, 0215, 0267, 0390 and 2010, the subtype is a wage type. For these infotypes, the subtypes are checked against view V_T512Z, in which you specify the wage types permitted in an infotype. For these infotypes, time constraints are at wage type level, and these are defined in view V_T591B.

29.1.5 Wage Type Valuation

The amount of a wage type can be directly entered, or it may be indirectly valuated. In indirect valuation, the value of a wage type depends on pay scale type, pay scale area, pay scale group, pay scale level, and ESG for CAP. The first four are specified for an employee in infotype 0008, whereas the last is determined from employee group and employee subgroup, which are specified in infotype 0001. The combination of these five factors is called allowance grouping.

SAP provides many methods of indirect valuation. You may specify a fixed amount at allowance grouping level, or you may determine value of a wage type from the values of other wage types.

Indirect valuation is period dependent. The parameters of calculation can change with time. They can be changed even with retroactive effect. Indirect valuation takes place both during payroll, as well as during display of master data. If the amount is indirectly valuated, whether the amount so valuated can be overwritten or not can be specified.

29.1.6 Wage Types Generated in Payroll and Time Management

Usually wage types come from master data. But certain wage types also get generated during time evaluation and payroll processing, e.g.

➤ Time wage types
➤ Secondary wage types
➤ Wage types created through PCRs

29.1.7 Wage Types in Payroll

During payroll run, SAP reads the master data, and makes appropriate payment or deduction. SAP permits multiple rates for a wage type during a payroll period. The computation is done for each partial period. During payroll run, SAP constantly keeps working on wage types, transforming them as appropriate. It also creates certain predefined wage types, called secondary wage types. These wage types start with '/', and are also called '/' wage types.

29.1.8 Deduction Wage Types

A wage type may be defined as a deduction wage type. The value entered for such a wage type is automatically reversed when the payroll is run, although in infotypes the value is shown without reversal, and with deduction indicator.

If the value of a deduction wage type changes for past period, the difference may be carried forward, or ignored, or only the positive or negative value may be carried forward.

Sometimes an employee may not have enough salary for all the deductions. To cater to these requirements, SAP allows deduction priority to be specified for deduction wage types. You can also specify whether in the case of insufficient salary partial amount is to be deducted or not.

29.1.9 Wage Type Posting

Wage types can be posted to Accounting in SAP. During configuration it must be ensured that the principle of double entry book keeping is followed, and the net effect of posting a wage type is zero. However, one of the postings may be direct, whereas the second posting may be indirect, through another wage type. There may be wage types, which are not posted.

A wage type posts to a symbolic account, which can translate to different general ledger accounts, based on employee groupings. A wage type can also post to sub ledger accounts.

29.1.10 Wage Types and Retroactive Accounting

The value of a wage type in master data can change with retroactive effect, and SAP would recompute the employee's payroll from that month onward. It is possible to prevent the entry of a wage type in payroll past.

In case a wage type is indirectly valuated, and the calculation procedure changes with retroactive effect, you need to perform a forced retro run of payroll for that period.

Deduction wage types have special properties pertaining to retroactive accounting.

29.2 WAGE TYPE CHARACTERISTICS

Functional Consultant	User	Business Process Owner	Senior Management	My Rating	Understanding Level
A	A	A	A		

29.2.1 Purpose

In this view you specify the basic characteristics of a wage type. Records are inserted in this table during wage type copy. Changes are done through IMG nodes. This table does not contain all wage types, e.g. loan wage types, carry forward and brought forward wage types.

29.2.2 IMG Node

SM30 ➢ V_T511

29.2.3 Screen

Wage type	M230 House Rent Allowance	Start Time Exit
		➢ 01.01.1998 31.12.9999

Amount
- ☐ Deduction WT
- Minimum amount ___ INR
- Maximum amount ___ INR
- ☑ Add to total

Input combination
- Amount +
- Number/unit -

Time leveling and time sheet
- Basic hours ___

Number/unit
- Time unit/meas. Percent
- Minimum number ___
- Maximum number ___

Indirect valuation
- Indirect eval.module INVAL
- Module variant B
- Red.method ___
- Rounding type ___
- Rounding div. ___
- ☑ Rewritable

29.2.4 Primary Key

Country Grouping + Wage type + End Date

29.2.5 Important Fields

Wage type and text

Wage type whose characteristics are being set.

Start time, exit

Here you specify the validity period of wage type characteristics. Wage type characteristics can change with time.

Deduction wage type

In the amount field of a wage type, you can enter a positive amount, or a negative amount. Normally, positive amounts are paid, while negative amounts are recovered.

However, certain wage types are normally meant for deduction, e.g. insurance premium. SAP lets you specify a wage type as a deduction wage type. If you enter a positive amount for these wage types, it gets recovered, while negative amount gets paid.

You tick this checkbox if the wage type is a deduction wage type. Deduction wage types remain unchanged in retro processing of payroll. Value changes may be recovered/paid in current month as specified in table T51P6.

Minimum and maximum amount

Through these fields you can restrict the wage type amount within a range. This is useful for control purpose.

Add to total

Infotype 0008 screen displays a total of wage type amounts. If this field is not ticked, amount of this wage type is not added to the total.

Input combination: amount and number/unit

You may want to control what data one enters for a wage type. For some wage type, you want that amount must be entered, while number and unit must not be entered. For another wage type, it is OK if one enters either the amount, or number and unit. These characteristics are controlled by these fields. These restrictions apply only during online data entry. These fields can be populated during time evaluation and payroll processing.

Basic hours

This indicator is used for time leveling. Here you specify whether the wage type is for basic hours, overtime hours, or bonus.

Time/measurement unit

In a wage type for overtime, the user may enter five days, and computation of amount may be done by the system. Each wage type has an amount field and a number field. In this case, five is entered in the number field. But what is its unit, because for some wage types the unit may be days while for some it may be hours. You can even have a wage type called petrol, where the unit may be liters, and the amount field may never be used. In this field you specify the unit associated with the number field.

Minimum and maximum number

You can use these fields to restrict the values that can be entered in number field within a range.

Indirect evaluation module and module variant

Sometimes the amount of a wage type is rule based. For example, you may pay a transport allowance of Rs. 1000 to all managers, and Rs. 500 to all workmen. SAP lets you specify that the amount of a wage type should be computed based on employee characteristics. This is called indirect valuation of a wage type. There are many methods of indirect valuation to choose from. If the wage type is indirectly valuated, you specify the module and variant here.

Reduction method

If there are employees who work lesser hours than normal, e.g. part time workers, you may want the amount derived through indirect valuation to be reduced. You can specify that here.

Rounding type and rounding divisor

Here you can specify whether the amount is to be rounded off, or rounded up, or rounded down, and to what amounts.

Rewritable

Sometimes a company wants a wage type to be indirectly valuated, but wants an option to overwrite in exceptional cases. Unless you tick this checkbox, a user cannot overwrite the amount of an indirectly valuated wage type.

29.3 WAGE TYPE TEXTS

Functional Consultant	User	Business Process Owner	Senior Management	My Rating	Understanding Level
A	B	B	C		

29.3.1 Purpose and Overview

You can change the text of a wage type in view V_T512T. Note that table T512T does not have period validity. If you change the text of a wage type, changed text shows even for earlier periods, for example in remuneration statement.

Wage type text can also be changed in view V_512W_T. If you do so, do not change the start date in this view. You would split a record in table T512W without any benefit, as both records would be identical except for validity period.

29.3.2 IMG Nodes

SM30 ➤ V_T512T
SM30 ➤ V_512W_T

29.3.3 Screen V_T512T

WT	Wage Type Long Text	Text
/001	Valuation basis 1	Val.1
/002	Valuation basis 2	Val.2
/02A	Frozen averages	FrozAvrg
/101	Total gross amount	TotGross

29.3.4 Screen V_512W_T

WT	Info	Wage Type Long Text	Text	Start Date	End Date
M230	ℹ	House Rent Allowance	HRA Alln	01.01.1998	31.12.9999
M231	ℹ	Company leased accom	CLA Alln	01.01.1998	31.12.9999
M232	ℹ	Company owned accom	CLA Alln	01.01.1998	31.12.9999
M233	ℹ	Hotel Accom	HotelAcc	01.01.1998	31.12.9999
M260	ℹ	Children Education Allow.	ChEduAll	01.01.1998	31.12.9999

29.3.5 Primary Key

Language Key + Country Grouping + Wage type

29.4 PERMISSIBILITY OF WAGE TYPES IN INFOTYPES

Functional Consultant	User	Business Process Owner	Senior Management	My Rating	Understanding Level
A	A	A	A		

29.4.1 Purpose

This view maintains the list of permitted wage types in an infotype. Unless there is an entry in this view, a wage type cannot be used in an infotype.

29.4.2 IMG Node

SM30 ➤ V_T512Z

29.4.3 Screen

Allowed wage types for Basic Pay

Wage ty...	Wage Type Long Text	Start Date	End Date
0100	Consolidated Salary	01.01.1998	31.12.9999
0110	Basic	01.01.1998	31.12.9999
0120	Basic Salary	01.01.1998	31.12.9999
0140	Stipend	01.01.1998	31.12.9999

Allowed wage types for Recurring Payments/Deductions

Wage type	Wage Type Long Text	Start Date	End Date	once	Sev.times
0440	Transport Recovery	01.01.1998	31.12.9999	○	◉
0503	House Rent Allowance Adj	01.01.1998	31.03.2005	○	◉
0563	House Rent Allowance Adj	01.01.1998	31.03.2005	○	◉
0600	LTA - Fixed	01.01.1998	31.12.9999	○	◉
0605	LTA - Fixed	01.04.2004	31.12.9999	○	◉

29.4.4 Primary Key

Country Grouping + Infotype + Wage type + End Date

29.4.5 Important Fields

Country grouping

The wage type permissibility can be dependent on country grouping. You specify the country grouping in the initial dialog box.

Infotype

This can be any infotype, which has wage types in it, e.g. 0008, 0014, 0015, 0057, 0267, etc. First you specify the infotype, and then the wage types permitted in it.

Wage type

The wage types listed here are permitted in the infotype and country grouping given in the initial dialog box.

Start date and end date

The wage type permissibility can change over a period of time.

Time constraint

If the subtype of an infotype is wage type (e.g. infotype 0014, but not infotype 0008), then you can specify time constraint for the wage type in the infotype. However, note that the validity period is only for permissibility, and not for time constraint. Actually time constraint is stored in view V_T591B, which does not have validity period.

29.5 PERMISSIBILITY OF WAGE TYPE ENTRY IN THE PAST

Functional Consultant	User	Business Process Owner	Senior Management	My Rating	Understanding Level
A	A	A	A		

29.5.1 Purpose

In view V_T582A, it is defined whether an infotype is changeable in the past. If it is not, then you cannot change it from the past date. However, if it is changeable, and its subtypes are wage types, you can prevent past entry for specified wage types through this view. This is applicable only for those infotypes whose subtype is a wage type. Thus, it does not control infotype 0008.

29.5.2 IMG Node

SM30 ➤ V_T591B

29.5.3 Screen

Wage type	Wage Type Long Text	N...
0103	Consolidated Salary Adj	☐
0113	Basic Adj	☐
0143	Stipend Adj	☐
0175	Basic ESS	☐

29.5.4 Primary Key

Infotype + Country Grouping + Wage type

29.5.5 Important Fields

Infotype and country grouping

These are specified while maintaining the view.

Wage type

Wage type for which retro permissibility is being specified.

No wage-type-dependent indicator entry in payroll past

In view V_T582A, it is defined whether an infotype is changeable in the past. If it is not, then you cannot change it from the past date. However, if it is changeable, and its subtypes are wage types, you can prevent past entry for specified wage types, by ticking this field.

29.6 PERMISSIBILITY OF WAGE TYPES FOR EMPLOYEES

Functional Consultant	User	Business Process Owner	Senior Management	My Rating	Understanding Level
A	A	A	A		

29.6.1 Purpose and Overview

SAP lets you control which wage types can be used for which employees. Each employee has an employee group and employee subgroup. For each combination of employee group and employee subgroup, you define employee subgroup grouping for primary wage type in view V_503_ALL. Similarly, each employee has a personnel subarea. For each personnel subarea, you define personnel subarea grouping for primary wage type in view V_001P_ALL.

In this view you define the employee subgroup grouping for primary wage type and the personnel subarea grouping for primary wage type for which the wage type can be used. You can also permit the use of wage type with a warning.

Do not use this functionality unless your employee subgroup grouping for primary wage type and personnel subarea grouping for primary wage type are stable.

29.6.2 IMG Node

SM30 ➤ V_511_B

29.6.3 Screen

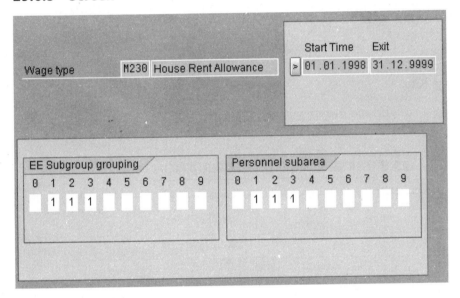

29.6.4 Primary Key

Country Grouping + Wage type + End Date

29.7 ASSIGNMENT OF WAGE TYPES TO WAGE TYPE GROUPS

Functional Consultant	User	Business Process Owner	Senior Management	My Rating	Understanding Level
B	X	X	X		

29.7.1 Purpose

In this view you assign wage types to wage type groups. Wage type groups must exist in table T52D5.

29.7.2 IMG Node

SM30 ➤ V_T52D7

29.7.3 Screen

WT group	Wage type group text	WType	Wage Type Long Text
0008	Basic pay	M211	Medical amount
0008	Basic pay	M212	Medical insurance
0008	Basic pay	M220	Conveyance Allowance
0008	Basic pay	M230	House Rent Allowance
0008	Basic pay	M231	Company leased accom
0008	Basic pay	M232	Company owned accom
0008	Basic pay	M233	Hotel Accom

29.7.4 Primary Key

Country Grouping + Wage type group + Wage type

29.8 BASE WAGE TYPE VALUATION

Functional Consultant	User	Business Process Owner	Senior Management	My Rating	Understanding Level
A	A	A	A		

29.8.1 Purpose

This view contains wage types, which are indirectly valuated from other wage types. When a wage type is deleted, it does not get deleted from here. You have to specifically delete it.

29.8.2 IMG Node

SM30 ➤ V_T539J

29.8.3 Screen

Mod.n	Valua...	Wage Type L...	N.	Start Date	End Date	Base WT	Wage Type L...	Percent
PRZNT	0150	Basic (Derived..	1	01.04.2001	31.12.9999	0110	Basic Pay	100.00
PRZNT	0150	Basic (Derived..	2	01.04.2001	31.12.9999	0180	Personal Pay	100.00
PRZNT	0200	C.D.A.	1	01.11.2005	31.12.9999	0100	Consolidated ...	10.00
PRZNT	0210	C.D.A.	1	01.04.2001	31.12.9999	0110	Basic Pay	

29.8.4 Primary Key

Indirect evaluation module + Country Grouping + Wage type + Sequence Number + End Date

29.8.5 Important Fields

Indirect evaluation module

Here you specify the indirect evaluation module, e.g. PRZNT, SUMME, etc.

Valuated wage type and text

The wage type being indirectly valuated is entered here.

Sequence number

Valuation of a wage type can depend on more than one wage type, e.g. HRA = 30% (Basic + DA). You give a sequence number to each wage type.

Start date and end date

Valuation formula of a wage type can change with time.

Base wage type and text

Here you specify the base wage type, which is used for valuating the current wage type.

Percent

The value of the base wage type is multiplied by the percentage specified here.

Basic Pay

30.1 BASIC PAY (INFOTYPE 0008)

Functional Consultant	User	Business Process Owner	Senior Management	My Rating	Understanding Level
A	A	A	A		

30.1.1 Screen

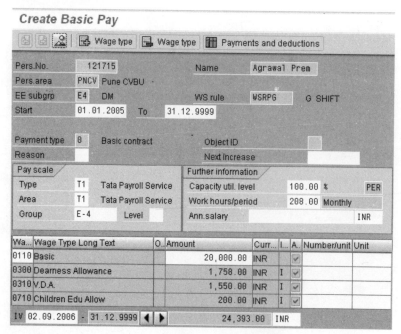

Create Basic Pay

Wa...	Wage Type Long Text	O..	Amount	Curr...	I..	A.	Number/unit	Unit
0110	Basic		20,000.00	INR		✓		
0300	Dearness Allowance		1,758.00	INR	I	✓		
0310	V.D.A.		1,550.00	INR	I	✓		
0710	Children Edu Allow		200.00	INR	I	✓		

IV 02.09.2006 - 31.12.9999 ◀ ▶   24,393.00 INR

30.1.2 Purpose and Overview

Salary of an employee

Infotype 0008 contains an employee's salary, which is paid in every payroll period. It contains all wage types, which are to be paid regularly to an employee, except reimbursements and time wage types.

Payments/deductions are specified in wage types. Wage types of infotype 0008 are paid for a payroll period. It is not necessary that the rate must be the same for the entire period. Whenever the rate changes, the payroll period is split into partial periods. The amount is computed for each partial period by multiplying the rate with the partial period factor.

Wage type

Wage types can have multiple properties. Important among them being

➢ Payment to/deduction from employees
➢ Financial posting
➢ Taxability

These can be varied independently, giving enormous power in the hands of consultants to meet client requirement. You may specify the value directly at employee level, or let the system determine the value based on pay scale type, area, group, level and ESG for CAP, which are employee attributes. Some wage types are also used for intermediate calculations.

Indirect valuation of a wage type

Depending on the properties of a wage type, you may be either required to specify the value of the wage type, or it may be indirectly valuated. Indirect valuation is based on pay scale and ESG for CAP. Pay scale has four components: pay scale type, area, group and level. These are specified for an employee in infotype 0008. ESG for CAP is determined from EG and ESG of the employee which are specified in infotype 0001.

Where a wage type is indirectly valuated, you would see an 'I' in the column 'Indicator for indirect valuation'. If the period of an infotype 0008 record is such that, an indirectly valuated wage type in it has more than one value, the value shown is determined by your configuration, and the validity period for indirect valuation is shown near the bottom of the screen.

Wage types permitted for infotype 0008

You can specify which wage types can be entered in infotype 0008, thus preventing unwanted wage types from entering in this infotype.

Deduction of salary for absences

Wage types in infotype 0008 can be factored for absences in payroll.

Salary data after employee separation

When an employee leaves a company you are not permitted to delimit infotype 0008. Basic payroll data must remain in the system. This is the only way of ensuring the accuracy of any retroactive accounting runs that need to be performed.

Change log

This infotype is so important that it is worthwhile to track all changes to the infotype by enabling log.

Distinction between infotype 0008 and other payroll infotypes

There are multiple routes through which wage types come in payroll. They come from master data entered by users in infotypes 0008, 0014, 0015, 0057, and 0267. Wage types are also generated by time evaluation from where they are taken in payroll. The purpose and use of each of these must be understood clearly so that they are properly used.

> Infotype 0008 is for regular payments.
> Infotype 0014 is for recurring payments/deductions.
> Infotype 0015 is for one time payments/deductions.
> Infotype 0057 is for deductions, which are to be paid to defined payees.
> Infotype 0267 is for off-cycle payments/deductions.
> Time wage types are generated in time management and stored in table ZL.

The main difference between infotype 0008 and other infotypes is that the wage types of infotype 0008 are for a period. Consequently, they can be factored for service period and absences. In contrast, a payment in infotype 0014, 0015 or 0267 is a lump sum payment, which is payable on a certain day, and therefore gets paid during a payroll period. It is not for a payroll period, and hence cannot be factored for service period and absences.

Pay scale reclassification

Pay scale reclassification allows you to update the information on the pay scale group and pay scale level in infotype 0008. The data is updated automatically when a situation meriting a reclassification arises for a specific employee. You can specify various reclassification criteria, in addition to the date of the next increase.

You can do pay scale reclassification according to master data using transaction RPITUM00. If you want to do pay scale reclassification according to time worked, you can use transaction RPITIG00. You can also use reports RPLTRF00, RPLTRF10, and RPSTRF00.

Pay scale reclassification is not covered in this book, as it is part of compensation management.

Standard pay increase

For indirectly valuated wage types, pay scale based amounts are specified in view V_T510. If these amounts change, you can make the change in that view. However, SAP also provides a program, RPU51000 (transaction PC00_M99_U510). This program takes company decision as input, determines what new values in the view should be, and updates the same.

If your company's pay increase is not only for indirectly valuated wage type, but includes directly valuated wage types as well, you can run program RPITRF00 (transaction PC00_M99_ITRF) to effect 'Enhanced standard pay increase'. In these cases, you have to maintain tables T510D and T510E, where you specify details of increase.

Standard Pay Increase is not covered in this book, as it is part of compensation management.

30.1.3 Subtypes

Payment type (subtype field of infotype 0008)

30.1.4 Time Constraint

T (Time constraint is based on subtype or subtype table)
For subtype 0 (Basic Contract): 1 (Record must have no gaps, no overlappings)

30.1.5 Important Fields

Payment type

This field contains the subtype of infotype 0008. Usually, you would use subtype 0 (Basic contract). Master list of subtypes is maintained in view V_T591A.

Object ID

This field is generally not used.

Reason

Here you maintain reason for changing infotype 0008. Master list of reasons for change are maintained in view V_T530E.

Next increase

SAP provides for pay scale reclassification based on customizing settings. However, if you want to override that criteria, and specify the date on which pay scale reclassification should take place for an employee, you can specify that here. Once pay scale reclassification takes place, this field is blanked out.

Pay scale type, area, group, level

Pay scale determines the value of a wage type for an employee, where the wage type is indirectly valuated. For indirect valuation, apart from pay scale, you also need ESG for CAP, which is determined from V_503_ALL based on EG and ESG of the employee specified in infotype 0001.

The pay scale also determines the wage type model, which specifies what wage types are going to default in infotype 0008.

Pay scale type and area can be defaulted based on PA PSA combination if defined in view V_001P_ALL (see chapter 4.5). However, feature TARIF takes precedence over this.

When you copy a record, feature DFINF determines whether the pay scale type and area is copied from the previous record, or it gets a fresh default value which happens when you create a new record.

If you want to use pay grade instead of pay scale, choose 'Edit ➤ Change remuneration type'.

Capacity utilization level

Here you specify what percentage of standard working time an employee works. This field gets a default value from employment percentage in infotype 0007.

When you copy a record, feature DFINF determines whether the capacity utilization level is copied from the previous record, or it gets a fresh default value which happens when you create a new record.

Work hours/period

This field contains the number of hours an employee works in one payroll period. It gets default value from the number of hours entered in infotype 0007.

When you copy a record, feature DFINF determines whether the work hours/period is copied from the previous record, or it gets a fresh default value which happens when you create a new record.

Annual salary and currency

In the USA, Canada, and Australia, this value is computed. For other countries, it can be input.

Wage type, amount, currency, number and unit

Wage types are used mainly for payments and deductions, but can also be used for other purposes, e.g. perquisites, intermediate values, etc. A wage type can have an amount with currency or number with unit. In infotype 0008, a person can have up to 40 wage types on any given day. For indirectly valuated wage types the amount field may be blank, in which case the value is determined by the system. Or, the amount may have a value indicating that the value has been overwritten. If a wage type is indirectly valuated, and its value cannot be overwritten, the amount field is not in input mode.

Wage type long text

In this field wage type description is displayed.

Operation indicator for wage types

For payment wage types this field is blank, for deduction wage types it is 'A'. However, wage types can have negative values, whereby a payment wage type can be deducted, and deduction wage type can be paid. This indicator is defined at wage type level, but is also stored in infotype 0008.

Indirect valuation indicator

Some wage types are configured for indirect valuation. SAP also lets you specify whether you want the flexibility of overwriting it. If a wage type is indirectly valuated, and its value is not overwritten, this field shows 'I'. If the value is overwritten, 'I' disappears. If overwritten value is deleted, 'I' reappears.

Add to total amount

This is a wage type property, which is picked from view V_T511. The value of wage types, for which this field is ticked, is totalled and shown at the bottom of the screen.

Start and end of validity period for indirect valuation

An infotype 0008 record is created only if the content of infotype 0008 changes. Suppose, for an employee there is an infotype 0008 record which is valid from 01.01.2005 to 31.12.2005. This contains an infotype which is indirectly valuated and its value changes on 01.07.2005. SAP shows only one record, which is valid for the entire year. However, it faces problem in doing indirect valuation. SAP gives you two options. You may specify that indirect valuation should be on the start date of the infotype record. Alternatively, you may specify that the valuation should be on a date as near the current date as possible. You make this choice in view T77S0 (PCOMP + BPIVT).

Total of all wage type amounts

This field shows total of all wage types, for which 'Add to total amount' field is ticked. This is only a screen field, and is not stored.

30.1.6 Caution, Tips, Workaround

One should not use 'No factoring' for infotype 0008 wage types in payroll. Because, in the case of two partial periods, the amount will become double.

In case the amount is not to be reduced, one should link it to service period. This would ensure correct payment. However, in the joining and separation months, the amount would be proportionate to the service period.

Payments/deductions in other infotypes are not for a period. They are paid/recovered in full whenever incurred. This distinction should guide what goes into infotype 0008 and what in infotype 0014.

There may be situations, e.g. study leave, when the employee is not to be paid. In such situations, one should not lock the employee; because when the employee is unlocked, his payroll will run even for those periods during which he was locked. His employment status should be made inactive, so that factoring becomes zero.

Factoring will also become zero when an employee separates, hence there is no change required in infotype 0008.

30.1.7 Menu and Menu Bar

| 📥 Wage type | | 📤 Wage type | Using these icons, you can add or delete a wage type.

🎛 Payments and deductions If you click this icon, you can see a summarized view of infotypes 0008, 0014 and 0015.

30.1.8 Reports

S_AHR_61016356—Time Spent in Each Pay Scale Area/Type/Group/Level

You can use this report to see how much time an employee has spent in different pay scales.

Time spent in pay scale group/level

Pers.No.	ID nu...	Name	Ar.	Ty.	PS group	PS level	since	Years	Months
00100001	100001	Bapat Arvind	T1	T1	1B		01.07.2006	00	05

S_AHR_61016357—Defaults for Pay Scale Reclassification

This report displays the next standard pay scale reclassification for individual employees. You can use this report to determine whether you have forgotten to reclassify an employee or to determine when and who is due for a reclassification.

S_AHR_61016376—Salary According to Seniority

This report calculates the employees' average annual salary according to cost centers or organizational units and employee seniority.

```
Salary Information

Cost center   0100 0001422242

Seniority       Number of employees  Average salary

02                    1              INR    187,596.00

Total salary                         INR    187,596.00
Average salary per employee          INR    187,596.00
Employee(s)                                      1
```

S_AHR_61016378—Assignment to Wage Level

This report gives pay scalewise, genderwise count of employees.

```
Assignment to Wage Level
───────────────────────────────── Key date 03.12.2006 ─────────────────

PS area: T1 Tata Payroll Service
PS type:    T1 Tata Payroll Service
```

Pay scale				Male		Female		All		Associated
Area	Type	Group	Level	Number	%	Number	%	Number	%	years
T1	T1	MF-OPTMP		62	19.3	0	0.0	62	19.3	1.39
T1	T1	MM1	05	15	4.7	0	0.0	15	4.7	1.65
T1	T1	MM2	05	4	1.2	0	0.0	4	1.2	1.67
T1	T1	MM3	05	2	0.6	0	0.0	2	0.6	1.67
T1	T1	MM4	05	1	0.3	0	0.0	1	0.3	1.67
T1	T1	MM5	05	1	0.3	0	0.0	1	0.3	1.67
T1	T1	MOP		123	38.2	0	0.0	123	38.2	3.67
T1	T1	RMS1		21	6.5	0	0.0	21	6.5	3.45
T1	T1	RMS2		16	5.0	0	0.0	16	5.0	2.73
T1	T1	RMS3		17	5.3	0	0.0	17	5.3	3.38
T1	T1	TR		60	18.6	0	0.0	60	18.6	1.99
T1	T1	********	**	322	100.0	0	0.0	322	100.0	2.70

30.2 PAYMENT TYPE

Functional Consultant	User	Business Process Owner	Senior Management	My Rating	Understanding Level
A	C	C	X		

30.2.1 Purpose

In infotype 0008, you can not only keep basic salary, but also comparable salary, etc. However, it is subtype 0, which is used for salary payment.

30.2.2 IMG Node

SM30 ➤ V_T591A (infotype 0008)

30.2.3 Screen

	Subtype	Name	Time constraint
	0	Basic contract	1
	1	Increase basic contract	2
	2	Comparable domestic pay	2
	3	Refund of costs in foreign currency	2
	4	Local weighting allowance	3
	BR01	Increase Basic Contract - Brasil	3
	ERA	Germany Only	2
	FS	Secondary assignment	2
	HG		2
	HG54		2

Subtype characteristics for Basic Pay

30.2.4 Primary Key

Infotype + Subtype

30.3 PAY SCALE TYPE

Functional Consultant	User	Business Process Owner	Senior Management	My Rating	Understanding Level
A	C	C	X		

30.3.1 Purpose

This view contains the master list of pay scale types. It is assigned to an employee in infotype 0008 and used for indirect valuation of wage types and for determination of wage type model. Pay scale type should be used to distinguish between pay scales at the highest levels. For example, if your implementation is for a group of companies, and their pay scales are very different, then you could distinguish between them by pay scale type.

30.3.2 IMG Node

SM30 ≻ V_T510A

30.3.3 Screen

P.scale type	Pay scale type text
01	Fin Ad Department
02	Developers
03	Production

30.3.4 Primary Key

Country Grouping + Pay scale type

30.4 PAY SCALE AREA

Functional Consultant	User	Business Process Owner	Senior Management	My Rating	Understanding Level
A	C	C	X		

30.4.1 Purpose

This view contains the master list of pay scale areas. It is assigned to an employee in infotype 0008 and used for indirect valuation of wage types and for determination of wage type model. If your employees are geographically scattered and your pay scales depend on geographic locations, pay scale areas can be based on geography. If there are different business units, or divisions, and your pay scales depend on them, then pay scale areas can also be based on the same.

30.4.2 IMG Node

SM30 ➤ V_T510G

30.4.3 Screen

Pay Scale Area	Pay scale area text
01	Bangalore
02	Rest of India
C1	Delhi, Mumbai, Kolka
C2	Chennai, Bangalore

30.4.4 Primary Key

Country Grouping + Pay Scale Area

30.5 DEFAULT PAY SCALE TYPE AND AREA

Functional Consultant	User	Business Process Owner	Senior Management	My Rating	Understanding Level
A	B	B	X		

30.5.1 Purpose

Feature TARIF is used to default pay scale type and pay scale area in infotype 0008. This has precedence over the default pay scale type and pay scale area specified in V_001P_ALL.

30.5.2 IMG Node

PE03 ≻ TARIF

30.5.3 Screen

```
TARIF Default pay scale type and area in basic pay
 └────T1/T1
```

30.5.4 Fields for Decision-making

Company Code
Personnel Area
Personnel Subarea
Employee Group
Employee Subgroup
Country Grouping

30.5.5 Return Value

Pay scale type and area

30.6 PAY SCALE GROUPS AND LEVELS

Functional Consultant	User	Business Process Owner	Senior Management	My Rating	Understanding Level
A	A	A	A		

30.6.1 Purpose

If your wage type has a fixed value for a group of employees, you specify that here. Employee groups are formed by a combination of pay scale type, area, group, level, and ESG for CAP.

Table T510 is also used to show valid values for pay scale group and level in infotype 0008. Hence an entry in this table is a must for every allowance grouping even if there is no wage type which needs indirect valuation.

Deleting a wage type does not delete it from table T510. You have to do it from this view.

30.6.2 IMG Node

SM30 ➤ V_T510, V_T510_B (Same as V_T510. Only PS group is modifiable)

30.6.3 Screen

P.scale type	T1	Tata Payroll Service
P.Scale Area	T1	Tata Payroll Service

Grpg	PS group	Lv	Wage type	Start Date	End Date	Amount	Currency
3	CVH1		0600	01.09.2003	31.12.9999	8,440.00	INR
3	CVH1		0700	01.04.2001	31.12.9999	200.00	INR
3	CVH1		0800	01.09.2003	31.12.9999	340.00	INR
3	CVH1		0900	01.09.2003	31.12.9999	675.00	INR
3	CVH1		0910	01.09.2003	31.12.9999	3,600.00	INR

30.6.4 Primary Key

Country Grouping + Pay scale type + Pay Scale Area + ES grouping for collective agreement provision + Pay Scale Group + Pay Scale Level + Wage type + End Date

30.7 SETTING THE INDIRECT VALUATION PERIOD

Functional Consultant	User	Business Process Owner	Senior Management	My Rating	Understanding Level
A	B	B	X		

30.7.1 Purpose

An infotype 0008 record is created only if the content of infotype 0008 changes. Suppose, for an employee there is an infotype 0008 record which is valid from 01.01.2005 to 31.12.2005. This contains an infotype which is indirectly valuated and its value changes on 01.07.2005. SAP shows only one record, which is valid for the entire year. However, it faces problem in doing indirect valuation. SAP gives you two options. You may specify that indirect valuation should be on the start date of the infotype record. Alternatively, you may specify that the valuation should be on a date as near the current date as possible. You make this choice in view T77S0 (PCOMP + BPIVT).

30.7.2 IMG Node

SM30 ➢ T77S0 (PCOMP + BPIVT)

30.7.3 Screen

Group	Sem.abbr.	Value abbr	Description
PCOMP	BPIVT	S	Basic Pay: Set Indirect Valuation Period

30.7.4 Important Fields

Value of semantic abbreviation

B	Start date of the infotype record.
S	As near the current date as possible (SY-DATUM). If the record is entirely in the past, the end-date of the record. If the record is entirely in the future, the start-date of the record. Otherwise, today's date.

30.8 DEFAULT WAGE TYPES FOR BASIC PAY

Functional Consultant	User	Business Process Owner	Senior Management	My Rating	Understanding Level
A	B	B	X		

30.8.1 Purpose and Overview

When you create an infotype 0008 record, you have to enter all appropriate wage types. SAP helps you by giving a set of wage types by default. However, the set of wage types may not be same for all employees. Therefore, SAP lets you define wage type models, which contain a set of wage types, in view V_T539A. It also lets you build the logic of determining wage type model for an employee in feature LGMST.

30.8.2 IMG Node

PE03 ➤ LGMST

30.8.3 Screen

```
LGMST Planned payment specification
   └─▣ MOLGA Country Grouping
       ├─▣ 01 Germany
           └─▣ PERSG Employee Group
               ├─▣ 1 Permanent
                   └─▣ PERSK Employee Subgroup
                       ├─▣ DE MS5
                           └──────20/──────1DE-
```

30.8.4 Fields for Decision-making

Company Code
Personnel Area
Personnel Subarea
Employee Group
Employee Subgroup
Transaction class for data storage
Subtype
Country Grouping

30.8.5   Return Value

The return value format is XX/YYYYYYYY, where XX is maximum number of wage types per record and YYYYYYYY is the name of the wage type model from table T539A.

30.9   WAGE TYPE MODEL FOR BASIC PAY

Functional Consultant	User	Business Process Owner	Senior Management	My Rating	Understanding Level
A	B	B	X		

30.9.1   Purpose and Overview

When you create an infotype 0008 record, you have to enter all appropriate wage types. SAP helps you by giving a set of wage types by default. However, the set of wage types may not be same for all employees. Therefore, SAP lets you define wage type models in view V_T539A, which contain a set of wage types. It also lets you build the logic of determining wage type model for an employee in feature LGMST, or in India payroll by assigning a wage type model to payroll grouping in table T7INA5. For India payroll, all wage types required for infotypes 0581 and 0583 must be present in wage type model.

30.9.2   IMG Node

SM30 ➤ V_T539A

30.9.3   Screen

Wage type model	S...	Start Date	End Date	Mode	Wage type	Wage Type Long Text
1B-4B	1	01.04.2005	31.12.9999	0	0100	Consolidated Salary
1B-4B	2	01.04.2005	31.12.9999	0	0180	Personal Pay
1B-4B	3	01.04.2005	31.12.9999	F	2010	Executive Allow
1B-4B	4	01.04.2005	31.12.9999	F	0900	Uniform Maint Allow
1B-4B	5	01.04.2005	31.12.9999	F	0500	House Rent Allow

30.9.4   Primary Key

Country Grouping + Wage type model + Sequence Number + End Date

30.9.5   Important Fields

Wage type model

For defaulting wage types in infotype 0008, wage type model for an employee is determined through feature LGMST. That is matched with this field and all wage types picked up from this view.

Sequence number

This field determines the sequence in which wage types are defaulted in infotype 0008.

Start date and end date

Here you specify the validity period of the record as the wage type model can change over a period of time.

Mode

If the mode is F, the wage type field in infotype 0008 is grayed out and you cannot change it. If it is in O mode, the wage type field in infotype 0008 can be changed.

Wage type and long text

Here you specify the wage types in the wage type model.

30.10   PAY SCALE CONVERSION FOR BASIC PAY

Functional Consultant	User	Business Process Owner	Senior Management	My Rating	Understanding Level
B	X	X	X		

30.10.1   Purpose

In infotype 0008, you show the values of wage types in monthly or hourly rates depending on whether your ESG for PCR is monthly (e.g. 2 or 3) or hourly (e.g. 1). However, if the time unit of your ESG for CAP is different, you need to convert from monthly rate to hourly rate, or vice versa. That is defined here.

30.10.2   IMG Node

SM30 ➢ T546

30.10.3 Screen

ES grouping for PCR	SGTx	Long text	ESG for CAP	Reaction
1	STD	Hourly	1	
1	STD	Hourly	2	2
1	STD	Hourly	4	
1	STD	Hourly	5	
2	PER	Periodic (wage)	0	
2	PER	Periodic (wage)	1	1
2	PER	Periodic (wage)	2	

30.10.4 Primary Key

ESG grouping for PCR + ESG grouping for CAP

30.10.5 Important Fields

ESG grouping for PCR, short text and long text

Here you specify the employee subgroup grouping for PCR.

ESG grouping for CAP

Here you specify the employee subgroup grouping for collective agreement provision.

Reaction

Here you specify the conversion rule. Possible values are:

Blank	No conversion
1	Recalculate table value on monthly basis
2	Recalculate table value on hourly basis

30.11 SIMULATION VARIANT FOR THE PAYROLL PROGRAM

Functional Consultant	User	Business Process Owner	Senior Management	My Rating	Understanding Level
B	X	X	X		

30.11.1 Purpose

When you run payroll simulation from infotype 0008, which variant is run depends on this feature.

30.11.2 IMG Node

PE03 ≻ PM004

30.11.3 Screen

```
PM004 Determining the Simulation Variant for the Payroll Program

    └──🗀 SCODE Simulation Code

         ├──🗀 GV Taxation of Pensions
         │      └──GMVS

         ├──🗇 IT Basic Pay infotype
         ├──🗇 PM HR Funds and Position Management
         └──🗇 VA Pension Administration (public sector Germany)
```

30.11.4 Fields for Decision-making

Personnel Area
Personnel Subarea
Employee Group
Employee Subgroup
Payroll Area
Simulation Code

30.11.5 Return Value

Payroll program variant.

30.12 PAY SCALES FOR ANNUAL SALARIES

Functional Consultant	User	Business Process Owner	Senior Management	My Rating	Understanding Level
C	X	X	X		

30.12.1 Purpose

In infotype 0008, there is a field where you can specify annual salary of an employee. If you have a salary range for each pay scale, which you want to check, and give warning or error, you can specify that here.

30.12.2 IMG Node

SM30 ≻ V_T510N

30.12.3 Screen

30.12.4 Primary Key

Country Grouping + Pay scale type + Pay Scale Area + ESG grouping for collective agreement provision + Pay Scale Group + Pay Scale Level + End Date

30.12.5 Important Fields

Pay scale type, area, ESG for CAP, pay scale group, level

Here you specify the allowance grouping for which annual salary limit is being defined.

Start and end date

These fields contain the validity period of annual salary.

Minimum annual salary

Here you specify the minimum annual salary for an allowance grouping.

Maximum annual salary

Here you specify the maximum annual salary for an allowance grouping.

Warning/error

If the annual salary is outside the specified limit, whether the system gives warning or error is specified here.

Maximum increase %

Here you can specify maximum % increase in annual salary. This field is for information only.

30.13 STANDARD WORKING HOURS

Functional Consultant	User	Business Process Owner	Senior Management	My Rating	Understanding Level
C	X	X	X		

30.13.1 Purpose

Here you can define number of working hours per week, and number of working days per week, for a combination of pay scale type, pay scale area and ESG for CAP.

30.13.2 IMG Node

SM30 ➤ V_T510I

30.13.3 Screen

P.scale type	Pay ...	P.Scale Area	Pay ...	ESG/CAP	Start Date	End Date	Hours	Days

30.13.4 Primary Key

Country Grouping + Pay scale type + Pay Scale Area + ESG grouping for collective agreement provision + End Date

30.13.5 Important Fields

Pay scale type, area and ESG for CAP

Here you specify the combination of pay scale type, pay scale area and ESG for CAP for which number of working hours and days per week are being defined.

Start date and end date

These fields contain the validity period for standard working hours and days.

Hours

Here you specify the standard weekly working time in hours.

Days

Here you specify the number of working days per week.

Bank Details

31.1 BANK DETAILS (INFOTYPE 0009)

Functional Consultant	User	Business Process Owner	Senior Management	My Rating	Understanding Level
A	A	A	A		

31.1.1 Screen

Create Bank Details

Pers.No.	121715	Name	Agrawal Prem	
Pers.area	PNCV Pune CVBU			
EE subgrp	E4 DM	WS rule	WSRPG	G SHIFT
Start	01.01.2005 to	31.12.9999		

Bank details

Bank Details Type	Main bank
Payee	Agrawal Prem
Postal code / city	411018 Pimpri
Bank Country	India
Bank Key	
Bank Account Number	
Payment method	U
Purpose	
Payment currency	INR

Additional fields

House bank	

31.1.2   Purpose and Overview

Infotype 0009 stores information related to the employee's method of payment, e.g. direct deposit in bank or cheque. Normally salary payments go to the main bank (subtype 0). However, you can specify that part of your salary goes to other bank (subtype 1), by specifying standard value or standard percentage. These fields are not shown on the screen for bank details type 0. Rest of the salary goes to the main bank. You can specify where your travel payments should go in subtype 2 of infotype 0009. You can also specify a main bank and an other bank for off-cycle payments.

31.1.3   Subtypes

Type of Bank Details Record.
Standard subtypes are: 0—Main bank, 1—Other bank, 2—Travel expenses, 5—Main bank details for off-cycle, 6—other bank details for off-cycle.

31.1.4   Time Constraint

T (Time constraint is based on subtype or subtype table)
For subtype 0 (Main bank): 1 (Record must have no gaps, no overlappings)

31.1.5   Important Fields

Bank details type

You can maintain various types of bank for an employee, e.g. for salary payment, travel expenses payment, etc. Normally salary payments go to the main bank (bank details type 0). However, you can specify that part of your salary goes to other bank (bank details type 1), by specifying standard value or standard percentage. These fields are not shown on the screen for bank details type 0. Rest of the salary goes to the main bank.

Payee

The system defaults the employee to be the payee. Employee's name is taken from infotype 0002. However, the payee does not have to be same as employee, and you can change it.

Postal code, city

The system defaults the information supplied in infotype 0006.

Bank country

The system defaults the information supplied in infotype 0006. This is used to validate the bank key and account numbers.

Bank key

Bank key is the combination of bank and branch. You need to define the bank keys and associated properties in table BNKA before they can be used in infotype 0009. This configuration is an FI activity, and should be completed before implementing PA.

Bank account number

Here you enter the employee's bank account number.

Payment method

You need to define the payment methods in table T042Z before they can be used in infotype 0009. This configuration is an FI activity, and should be completed before implementing PA. If this field is blank, the payment is assumed to be in cash.

Purpose

The purpose entered here is indicated on the bank transfer form.

Payment currency

Here you specify the currency of payment.

Standard value, standard percentage

If you wish to transfer a part of your salary to a bank, other than your main bank, you can specify that in bank details type 1. You can either specify a fixed amount in standard value field, or a fixed percentage in standard percentage field. You must specify a value in one and only one of these fields. If the salary to be credited is less than the amount in the standard value field, then the salary to be credited is transferred and not the amount in the standard value field.

31.2 BANK DETAILS TYPE

Functional Consultant	User	Business Process Owner	Senior Management	My Rating	Understanding Level
A	X	X	X		

31.2.1 Purpose

SAP lets you specify one or more banks where your salary is deposited. You can specify the share either in value, or percentage terms. SAP also lets you specify the bank where your travel reimbursement is deposited, if you want it to be deposited in a bank different from your main bank. Bank details types are subtypes of infotype 0009.

31.2.2 IMG Node

SM30 ➤ VV_T591A_0009___AL0

31.2.3 Screen

Subtype characteristics for Bank Details		
Subtype	Name	Time constraint
0	Main bank	1
1	Other bank	3
2	Travel expenses	2
5	Main bank details for Off-Cycle	3
6	Other bank details for Off-Cycle	3

31.2.4 Primary Key

Infotype + Subtype

31.3 DEFAULT PAYMENT METHOD

Functional Consultant	User	Business Process Owner	Senior Management	My Rating	Understanding Level
A	B	C	X		

31.3.1 Purpose and Overview

You can use this feature to default payment methods in various infotypes where it is relevant.

31.3.2 IMG Node

PE03 ≻ ZLSCH

31.3.3 Screen

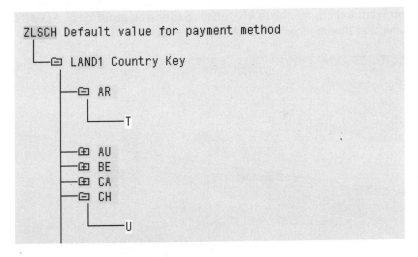

31.3.4 Fields for Decision-making

Infotype
Subtype
Country Grouping
Country Key

31.3.5 Return Value

Payment method.

31.4 INTERNATIONAL BANK ACCOUNT NUMBER

Functional Consultant	User	Business Process Owner	Senior Management	My Rating	Understanding Level
A	B	C	X		

13.4.1 Purpose and Overview

The International Bank Account Number (IBAN) is a European standard, developed by the International Organization for Standardization (ISO) and the European Committee for Banking Standards (ECBS), that identifies the bank and the account number.

Bank details are identified in various ways in different countries. With IBAN, it is possible to determine the account number, bank and country of the payee in the same way in each country, thus avoiding problems in cross-border payment transactions.

The IBAN is a combination of the country key, check digit, and country-specific account number. The IBAN can be used instead of the bank details so that an account can be uniquely identified. If you want to activate the IBAN functionality, you enter 'S' in ADMIN + IBAN in view T77S0. After that the infotype screen includes the IBAN field as shown below.

31.4.2 IMG Node

SM30 ➤ V_T77S0SC

31.4.3 Screen

Group	Sem.abbr.	Value abbr	Description
ADMIN	IBAN	S	Activate IBAN Function for HR

External Bank Transfers

32.1 EXTERNAL BANK TRANSFERS (INFOTYPE 0011)

Functional Consultant	User	Business Process Owner	Senior Management	My Rating	Understanding Level
B	B	B	B		

32.1.1 Screen

Pers.No.	121715	Name	Agrawal Prem	
Pers.area	PNCV Pune CVBU			
EE subgrp	E4 DM	WS rule	WSRPG	G SHIFT
Start	01.01.2006 to	31.12.9999		

Payment data

Wage type	☑
Amount	INR
Number/unit	
1st payment period	or 1st payment date
Interval in periods	Interval/Unit

Payee

Payee key	
Postal code / city	
Bank Country	
Bank Key	
Bank Account Number	
Payment method	Cash Payment
Purpose	Priority

32.1.2   Purpose and Overview

SAP provides the facility to pay to different payees on behalf of employees. Infotype 0011 contains how much to pay (payment data) and whom to pay it to (payee).

Payment data is specified in the same way as in infotype 0014. For payee, either you can enter a payee key, or enter the payee's name, address, bank details and payment method manually. You can also write a purpose and priority. These fields are not used by SAP.

When payroll is run, infotype 0011 is processed by function P0011, which puts the amount to be transferred in table BT. PCR X055 which is used with function P0011 looks at processing class 24 of the wage type, which specifies whether the amount is to be reduced in case the net pay of an employee is less than the amount of external bank transfer.

32.1.3   Subtypes

Wage type

32.1.4   Time Constraint

T (Time constraint is based on subtype or subtype table)

Recurring Payments/ Deductions

33.1 RECURRING PAYMENTS/DEDUCTIONS (INFOTYPE 0014)

Functional Consultant	User	Business Process Owner	Senior Management	My Rating	Understanding Level
A	A	A	A		

33.1.1 Screen

Create Recurring Payments/Deductions

Pers.No.	121715	Name	Agrawal Prem	
Pers.area	PNCV Pune CVBU			
EE subgrp	E4 DM	WS rule	WSRPG	G SHIFT
Start	☑ to	31.12.9999		

Recurring Payments/Deductions

Wage type	☑
Amount	INR Ind.val.
Number/unit	
Assignment number	
Reason for Change	

Payment dates

1st payment period	or	1st payment date
Interval in periods		Interval/Unit

33.1.2 Purpose and Overview

Recurring payment/deduction

Infotype 0014 is used for making recurring payment/deduction to employees through payroll. There are two methods of specifying the frequency of recurrence.

In the first method you specify the 1st payment period and interval in periods. Through this option, you could make payment/deduction, every payroll period, alternate payroll periods, and so on.

The second option is more flexible. In this option you specify 1st payment date and recurrence interval. Through this option you can make a payment every 21 days, for example. Depending on the 1st payment date and interval, the system determines how many entries to put in each payroll period. Thus, the recurrence frequency need not necessarily be once per payroll period.

No factoring

Note that wage types in infotype 0014 are payable/deductible on a particular date and hence are not subjected to factoring.

Payment/deduction for current, past, or future periods

You may enter payment/deduction in infotype 0014 for current, past, or future periods. You may also change/delete entries for any of these periods.

If you enter data for future periods, payment/deduction takes place in those periods. Thus, if you have such a need, you can enter the data and forget it. There is no need to keep manual record, and wait for the period to enter data.

If changes are made for past periods, the differences may be paid or recovered, but it will not be evident from infotype records. Hence, it may be better not to change or delete past data, but to make adjustment entries through infotype 0015.

Assignment number field

You can use assignment number field for reference information. However, this field is not stored in table RT, and cannot be printed in payslip. If you wish to print reference information in the payslip, you can use the number field.

Wage types permitted in infotype 0014

You can specify which wage types can be entered in infotype 0014, thus preventing unwanted wage types from entering in this infotype.

Time constraint

The time constraint can be defined at the wage type level.

Cost assignment

You can specify cost assignment of an infotype 0014 record.

33.1.3 Subtypes

Wage type

33.1.4 Time Constraint

T (Time constraint is based on subtype or subtype table)

33.1.5 Important Fields

Wage type

Here you enter the wage type for payment or deduction.

Operation indicator for wage types

If you enter a deduction wage type, an 'A' is shown before the amount field. It is determined from the wage type and stored in this infotype.

Amount and currency

Here you enter the wage type amount and the currency.

Indirect valuation

Indicator for indirect valuation 'I' is shown only if the wage type is indirectly valuated, i.e. it is a wage type for indirect valuation, and its value has not been overwritten by updating the amount field.

If the wage type is indirectly valuated, and the indirect valuation rule changes from a certain date in the past, you need to run forced retro payroll for all employees from that date. If retro is not run, the payment/recovery due to change in indirect valuation does not take place.

Number and unit

These fields are used when the stored data is not an amount, but number with unit. You must enter either the amount with currency or number with unit.

Assignment number

You can use this field for reference information. However, this does not enter RT, and cannot be printed in payslip. If you wish to print reference information, you can use number field.

Reason for change

You can maintain a master list of reasons for creating infotype 0014 records in view V_T530E and assign a reason here.

Payment dates

Recurring payments and deductions are for an interval, which is controlled by the start date and end date of the record. Within this period, there may be multiple payments. When would they occur can be defined in the following two ways.

1st payment period and interval in periods

In this method, you define in which payroll period the payment should take place first time, and at what interval, in payroll periods, it should repeat. If you want the payment every payroll period, both 1st payment period and interval in periods should be 1. If you specify the 1st payment period to be other than 1, in those periods no payment will be made each year, even though the infotype record is valid. Similarly, by specifying interval other than 1, you can skip payments.

1st payment date and interval with unit

This method gives even more flexibility in deciding the recurrence of payments. You could decide to make a payment every 11 days, starting from a certain day. In each payroll, the system determines how many payments are due. No payment is made for the period when the employee's status changes to 'Withdrawn'.

33.1.6 Menu and Menu Bar

When you click this icon, you get the following dialog box, where you can maintain cost assignment for the current record of infotype 0014. For more details, you may see chapter 45, Cost Assignment.

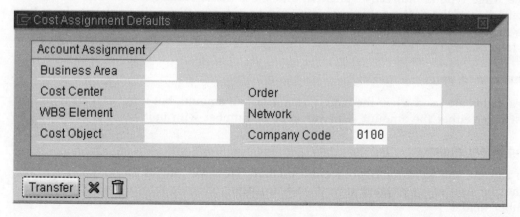

33.2 WAGE TYPE MODEL

Functional Consultant	User	Business Process Owner	Senior Management	My Rating	Understanding Level
B	C	X	X		

33.2.1 Purpose

In this step, you define the wage types that are created as default values in fast entry for infotype 0014. If you want to use this function, assign wage types to a wage type model here. You can then create all wage types assigned to this model as defaults in the fast entry with defaults screen.

33.2.2 IMG Node

SM30 ➤ V_T511M

33.2.3 Screen

Model	No	Wage type	Wage Type Long Text
M1	01	M640	Meals (lump sum EE)
M1	02	M790	Transport allow. (LS EE)
M2	01	MM00	Base overtime remun.
M2	02	MM10	Overtime 25%
M2	03	MM20	Overtime 50%
M3	01	0100	Night work performed BAT
M3	02	0110	12.24&12.31 after 12 BAT

33.2.4 Primary Key

Country Grouping + Wage Type Model + Sequence Number

Additional Payments

34.1 ADDITIONAL PAYMENTS (INFOTYPE 0015)

Functional Consultant	User	Business Process Owner	Senior Management	My Rating	Understanding Level
A	A	A	A		

34.1.1 Screen

Create Additional Payments

Pers.No.	121715	Name	Agrawal Prem
Pers.area	PNCV Pune CVBU		
EE subgrp	E4 DM	WS rule	WSRPG G SHIFT

Additional Payments

Wage type	☑
Amount	INR
Number/unit	
Date of origin	31.08.2006
Default Date	
Assignment number	
Reason for Change	

34.1.2 Purpose and Overview

One time payment/deduction

Infotype 0015 can be used for making one time payment/deduction to employees through payroll. These occur only once, unlike payments in infotype 0014, which have multiple occurrences.

Date of origin

Since these are one time payments/deductions, there is just one date for these records. You do not find from date/to date on the screen. However, the system populates both these dates same as the date of origin which is entered in the screen.

No factoring

Note that wage types in infotype 0015 are payable/deductible on a particular date and hence are not subjected to factoring.

Payment/deduction for current, past, or future periods

You may enter payment/deduction in infotype 0015 for current, past, or future periods. You may also change/delete entries for any of these periods.

If you enter data for future periods, payment/deduction take place in those periods. Thus, if you have such a need, you can enter the data and forget it. There is no need to keep manual record, and wait for the period to enter data.

If changes are made for past periods, the differences may be paid or recovered, but it will not be evident from infotype records. Hence it may be better not to change or delete past data, but to make adjustment entries in infotype 0015.

Assignment number field

You can use assignment number field for reference information. However, this field is not stored in table RT, and cannot be printed in payslip. If you wish to print reference information in the payslip, you can use the number field.

Wage types permitted in infotype 0015

You can specify which wage types can be entered in infotype 0015, thus preventing unwanted wage types from entering in this infotype.

Time constraint

The time constraint can be defined at wage type level.

Cost assignment

You can specify cost assignment of an infotype 0015 record.

34.1.3 Subtypes

Wage type

34.1.4 Time Constraint

T (Time constraint is based on subtype or subtype table)

34.1.5 Important Fields

Wage type

Here you enter the wage type for payment or deduction.

Operation indicator for wage types

If you enter a deduction wage type, an 'A' is shown before the amount field. It is determined from the wage type and stored in this infotype.

Amount and currency

Here you enter the wage type amount and the currency.

Indirect valuation

Indicator for indirect valuation 'I' is shown only if the wage type is indirectly valuated, i.e. it is a wage type for indirect valuation, and its value has not been overwritten by updating the amount field.

If the wage type is indirectly valuated, and the indirect valuation rule changes from a certain date in past, you need to run forced retro for all employees from that date. If retro is not run, the payment/recovery due to change in indirect valuation does not take place.

Number and unit

These fields are used if the data stored is not an amount, but number with unit. You must enter either the amount with currency or number with unit.

Date of origin

The date on which the payment/deduction is to be made. The system enters the last day of the current payroll period as the new value. If the employee has left the company, the date of origin is identical to the last active day of the payroll period. It can be past, present or future. But, it is better not to create, change or delete records in this infotype for past periods, even if system permits, as it is difficult to explain payroll results from what you see in the infotype.

Default date (payroll period and year)

If your payment/deduction is not for current period, you may enter the payroll period and year here. The system uses this information to determine the date of origin.

Assignment number

You can use this field for reference information. However, this does not enter RT, and cannot be printed in payslip. If you wish to print reference information, you can use number field.

Reason for change

You can maintain a master list for creating infotype 0015 records in view V_T530E, and assign the reason here.

34.1.6   Menu and Menu Bar

When you click this icon, you get the following dialog box, where you can maintain cost assignment for the current record of infotype 0015. For more details, you may see chapter 45, Cost Assignment.

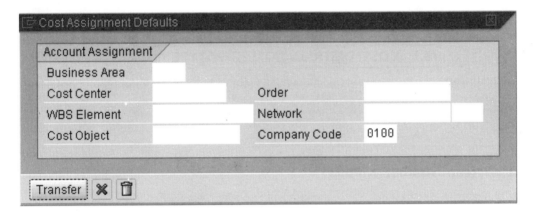

Cost Distribution

35.1 COST DISTRIBUTION (INFOTYPE 0027)

Functional Consultant	User	Business Process Owner	Senior Management	My Rating	Understanding Level
A	A	A	A		

35.1.1 Screen Number 2500

Pers.No.	121715		Name	Agrawal Prem	
Pers.area	PNCV Pune CVBU				
EE subgrp	E4 DM		WS rule	WSRPG	G SHIFT
Start	01.01.2005 To	31.12.9999			

Distrib. ☑

Master cost center

Cost distribution

CoCd	Cost ctr	Order	WBS element	Name	Pct.	Name of aux. account	BusA

35.1.2 Screen Number 2100

Pers.No.	121715		Name	Agrawal Prem	
Pers.area	PNCV Pune CVBU				
EE subgrp	E4 DM		WS rule	WSRPG	G SHIFT
Valid	01.01.2005	To	31.12.9999		

Distribution ☑

	No	CoCd	BusA	Cost Ctr		Funds Ctr		Fund		Prcnt.

35.1.3 Purpose and Overview

SAP provides rich functionality to charge costs to appropriate cost objects.

Cost assignment to master cost center

At the most gross level, the cost incurred on an employee is charged to the cost center to which an employee is assigned in infotype 0001. If an employee is in more than one cost centers during a payroll period, the salary cost is appropriately apportioned.

Cost distribution

However, if an employee works on a specific assignment, and it is desired to charge his cost to a more specific cost object, you can do so by creating an entry in infotype 0027.

SAP lets you charge the cost to a variety of cost objects, e.g. cost center, functional area, orders, or WBS elements. You also specify which costs you want to distribute, e.g. wage/ salary or trip costs. This infotype creates a WPBP split.

You can apportion a cost to multiple cost objects, specifying the percentage for each. The sum of percentages cannot exceed 100. If the sum is less than 100, the balance cost goes to the employee's master cost center.

Assignment of a specific cost

SAP also lets you charge specific expenses, e.g. one time payment in infotype 0015, to the cost object you specify.

Distribution of costs incurred on organizational objects

You can also do cost distribution of various organizational objects, e.g. positions, organizational units, etc. To do so, you specify the cost distribution of those objects. SAP finds the persons associated with those organizational objects and distributes their costs as specified. For this functionality to work, you have to activate integration between organizational management and personnel administration for cost distribution (PLOGI+COSTD = 'X' in view T77S0).

35.1.4   Subtypes

Costs to be distributed.

The costs to be distributed are predefined by SAP. If you add your own types, SAP does not know what to do with them.

35.1.5   Time Constraint

T (Time constraint is based on subtype or subtype table)

Time constraint is 2 (Record may include gaps, no overlappings) for both subtypes.

35.1.6   Important Fields

Costs to be distributed

You can use this infotype to distribute salary cost or travel cost. You specify which cost you want to distribute here.

Company code, business area, cost center

You can enter up to 25 sets.

Funds center, fund, functional area, grant

You can enter up to 12 sets.

Order number

You can enter up to 25 sets.

WBS element

You can enter up to 25 sets.

Percentage

The sum of percentages should not exceed 100, but can be less than 100. The balance cost will go to the employee's master cost center.

35.1.7 Menu and Menu Bar

⊞ If you position the cursor on any line of the distribution list, and click this icon, a line is inserted there, and that line and all lines below it is moved down.

⊟ If you position the cursor on any line of the distribution list, and click this icon, that line is deleted, and all lines below it are moved up.

Append lines After filling all lines of the distribution list, if you want to add more lines in the distribution list, you click this icon.

35.2 COSTS TO BE DISTRIBUTED

Functional Consultant	User	Business Process Owner	Senior Management	My Rating	Understanding Level
A	X	X	X		

35.2.1 Purpose

In infotype 0027, you can distribute salary cost or travel cost. These are created as subtypes of infotype 0027.

35.2.2 IMG Node

SM30 ➤ V_T591A (infotype 0027)

35.2.3 Screen

Subtype	Name	Time constraint
01	Wage/salary	2
02	Trip costs	2

Subtype characteristics for Cost Distribution

35.2.4 Primary Key

Infotype + Subtype

Loans

36.1 LOANS (INFOTYPE 0045)

Functional Consultant	User	Business Process Owner	Senior Management	My Rating	Understanding Level
A	A	A	A		

36.1.1 Purpose and Overview

Loans

This infotype is used for recording loans given to an employee. You can have several types of loans. An employee can be given different types of loan. They can also be given same type of loan multiple times, which are given different sequence numbers.

Loan categories

The loans in SAP come under one of the following categories which determine their repayment behaviour:

➤ Annuity loan (fixed periodic repayment. The interest is recovered first, balance goes towards principal repayment)
➤ Installment loan (fixed principal repayment + variable interest)
➤ Recurring advance (no repayment, no interest)

Eligibility for loan

When a loan is created, the system checks whether the employee is eligible to get this loan. There are several checks you can build in the system. These are described in chapter 36.10, 'Loan Approval'. Apart from the eligibility to get a loan, the system also checks the amount you are eligible for. These are also described in chapter 36.10.

Loan condition

Loans are given under a 'Loan condition', which specifies the important properties of the loan. These include interest rate, interest calculation method, and whether and how the imputed income is to be computed. It also defines the interest and principal repayment cycles.

Principal and interest recovery

Based on the properties of the loan, the system recovers installment and interest during payroll run. It also computes imputed income.

Date of principal and interest recovery

Since payroll is run for a period, you need to decide the date on which the payment of loan, or recovery of installment, has happened. SAP lets you decide whether it is first day of the payroll period, last day, middle of the period, or payment date. This impacts interest computation.

Simulation of principal and interest recovery

You can use 🎲 icon, for an existing loan, to see the full details of payments and repayments of the loan, considering entries in infotype 0078. Usually, for the past period, you see actual data, and for the future the proposed data.

You can also use 🎲 icon, for a proposed loan. This serves as a simulation tool. You can vary the parameters, e.g. payment amount and date, installment, etc. and see how the payments and repayments will take place, what will be the balance during each period, when the loan will end, etc.

If you want, you can change the layout, and save it as a variant. The variant name must start with a '/'. In future, you can specify the variant while seeing the repayment plan.

36.1.2   Subtypes

Loan type

36.1.3   Time Constraint

2 (Record may include gaps, no overlappings)

It may be thought that there cannot be more than one loan on any given day. Actually, that is not the case. The time constraint includes the sequence number of the loan.

36.1.4 Basic Data

Loan type	0100 Building loan with payment by instalment
Sequence number	01 External reference no.

Basic data	Conditions	Payments

Approval date	01.09.2003
Loan amount granted	☑ ☑
Amount paid	0,00
Loan balance	0,00 on
End of loan	

Loan type

Your company may have different types of loans, which may be for different purposes and may charge different interest rates. SAP supports multiple loan types, and their properties are defined at the time of configuration. For every loan record in infotype 0045, loan type must be specified. Loan types are subtypes of infotype 0045. Master list of loan types and their properties are defined in view V_T591A.

Sequence number

SAP permits you to give multiple loans of the same type to an employee. For example, an employee may have two housing loans. They are distinguished by sequence number. SAP automatically generates this when you create a loan.

External reference number

SAP does not use this field. You can use it to keep useful information, e.g. loan approval number, or loan application number. This can be used for reporting purpose.

Approval date

System defaults first day of the month in which you create the loan as the approval date. You can overwrite this default value.

Loan amount granted with currency

This gives loan amount granted to an employee. The system ensures that the total payment does not exceed the loan amount granted. You can increase the loan amount granted. However, if you are decreasing the approved loan amount, the system ensures that it cannot become less than the total payment already made. If you have configured eligibility checks on loan amounts, these are observed.

Loan amount paid with currency

The system displays the total loan payment made to the employee till now in infotype 0078.

Loan balance with currency

This field shows the loan amount balance after last payroll run. The employee still owes this amount to the company.

On

This field shows the date of the loan balance.

End of loan

This field displays the last day of the payroll period in which repayment of the loan is expected to be completed. This takes into account, the current loan balance, installment, and entries in infotype 0078.

36.1.5 Conditions

Loan type	0100 Building loan with payment by instalment
Sequence number	01	External reference no.

| Basic data | Conditions | Payments |

Loan conditions ☑ 🗎 ⊞

Indiv. interest rate ___ %

Effective interest rte 0,0000 %

Repayment start 01.09.2003

Rpymnt instl. ___ ☑ 🔧🗗

🖊🔧

Loan conditions

In SAP, a loan is given under a loan condition. SAP lets you define multiple loan conditions for a loan type, and lets you select the loan condition you would like to apply when you create a record in infotype 0045. A loan condition is a set of properties, e.g. interest rate. For the same loan condition, these properties may change over a period of time. The changed properties automatically apply to the employee's loan. If you click the icon ⊞, you can see the details of loan condition for each period. For a better understanding of loan conditions, you may see chapter 36.5.

Individual interest rate

SAP not only lets you select from different loan conditions you have specified for a loan type when you create a loan record in infotype 0045 but also lets you specify an interest rate, which is applicable only to a specific loan given to a specific employee.

If you enter an interest rate here, the system uses this value (as opposed to the debit interest rate, defined in customizing for the existing loan type) to calculate interest and imputed income. If your company policy does not permit interest rate determination at individual level, you should hide this field to prevent accidental entry in it. This field can get a default value, or fixed value, or maximum value depending on the employee and configuration in chapter 36.8.

Effective interest rate

Depending on the debit interest rate, and loan condition, the system computes an effective interest rate. If you update loan conditions with retro effect, you need to open the infotype 0045 record in change mode and save, for the effective interest rate to change.

Repayment start date

Here you define the repayment start date. The system defaults it to the start date of the month. If your repayment starts later, your loan balance will become more than the loan payment on account of interest.

Repayment installment with currency

This field contains the installment paid every payroll period. Out of this, first the interest is charged, and the balance goes towards principal repayment. If the interest is more than the installment, the principal repayment is negative, and the loan balance increases.

This icon is used to calculate loan installment based on the loan period and payment made. This is particularly useful in the case of annuity loans, where the computation is complex. If there are several infotype records for one loan, this function is available only for the last infotype record.

This icon is used to do the reverse, i.e. calculate the loan period depending on loan installment and payment made. Depending on the computed period and start date, the end date is changed. If there are several infotype records for one loan, this function is available only for the last infotype record.

If you click this icon, it shows the proposed disbursement schedule.

This icon shows how much penal interest will be charged in the case of special repayment.

Exemption for interest rate advantage with currency

This field is not on screen. Where applicable, it could be used to give exemption on imputed income.

36.1.6   Guidelines on Classifying a Loan

SAP lets you give your employee different types of loan. It also lets you give your employee same type of loan multiple times. It also lets you make multiple payments for a loan. These guidelines help you decide the most appropriate category when you make a loan payment.

Selection of a loan type should be intuitive. You should not create different loan types, e.g. 1st Housing loan, 2nd Housing loan, etc. unless the loan conditions for the two are different.

For a given loan type, if you create a second loan, you will be recovering two installments, they can have different repayment periods, and there will be two separate balances.

If you want to recover a single installment, which may be increased after second payment, you should not create a second loan.

36.1.7   Employee Transferred to Another Company Code

If an employee is transferred from one company code to another within your group, he can not transfer his loan to the new company code. This is due to the fact that he would no longer make repayments to the company that awarded him the loan but to the new company.

For this reason you must delimit the infotype 0045 to the date of the change of company code. To do this, you change the end date of the infotype record so that the infotype record is only valid until the date of the change of company code. You must also close the infotype with a complete repayment.

Finally, you create a new loan for the employee from the point in time that he belongs to the new company code.

36.1.8   Employee Leaving the Company

If an employee leaves the company, you must deduct total loan from his salary by entering complete repayment in infotype 0078 on the day of separation.

36.1.9   Employee Becoming Inactive

If an employee becomes inactive, you will not be able to deduct installment from his salary. You should, therefore, make his installment zero for that period. The interest accrued during this period will increase the loan balance. When the employee becomes active again, you should reinstate the installment amount.

36.1.10   Deletion of a Loan

A loan can be deleted before payroll run. Once an employee has been paid loan, and payroll run, you cannot delete it.

36.1.11 Menu and Menu Bar

When you create a loan, or want to change a loan, you may want to know how the repayment would happen. On clicking the repayment plan icon, you can specify the parameters in the screen below, and the system will show you complete details of payment, repayment, interest, etc. for each period.

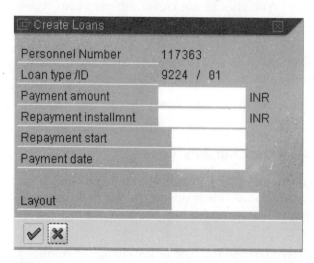

This icon shows you details of loan condition, which you have selected. You can also see it by clicking 'overview of conditions' in menu.

After you give a loan and specify repayment start date and period, the system computes the installment by clicking this icon on the conditions tab, or installment calculation menu item.

Alternatively, you may specify the installment and compute the end date by clicking this icon.

If you are using event-based loan disbursement, you can see the proposed loan disbursement schedule by clicking this icon.

In case an employee wants to foreclose the loan, he may want to know how much penal interest he has to pay (if you charge penal interest). You can click this icon to compute that.

Loan overview: If you click this menu item, you can see payments and repayments for each period for each loan of an employee.

Bank statement: If you click this menu item, the system calls transaction code PC00_M99_CLOF Account statement for company loans, which is explained in the next section.

36.1.12 Reports

PC00_M40_LON1—Loans Summary Report

You can use this program to get loan summary of your employees. This report is a list. The screenshot below shows detail of one line. This program is useful for answering employee queries. However, it does not show loan balance.

HR-IN: Loan Report
Details

Group description	Cell Content
Personnel Number	117363
Name of employee or applicant	Menon Sasidharan
Loan Type	9225
Seq No	01
Principal Latest month	1,014.10
Principal for the Period	8,088.14
Interest Latest month	70.90
Interest for the Period	591.86
Interest Subsidy Latest month	70.90
Interest Subsidy for the period	591.86
Maturity date	31.03.2010

PC00_M40_LON2—Batch Program for Penal Interest

This report is used to update infotype 0015 with the penal interest amount in the case of foreclosure of a loan.

PC00_M99_CLOF—Account Statement for Company Loans

You can use this program to create account statements for employer loans, which can be given to employees. It shows periodwise debits, credits and balances. It also shows summary at the end of each financial year.

Posting text	Period	Transaction	Status
Transfer loan balance	01.2002	139,414.62	139,414.62
Interest for curr.period	01.2002	456.41	139,871.03
Annuity	01.2002	1,424.00	138,447.03
Interest for curr.period	02.2002	453.24	138,900.27
Annuity	02.2002	1,424.00	137,476.27
Interest for curr.period	03.2002	450.06	137,926.33

You can also generate the report in debit memo–credit memo layout.

Posting text	Period	Debit memo	Credit memo
Transfer loan balance	01.2002	139,414.62	
Interest for curr.period	01.2002	456.41	
Annuity	01.2002		1,424.00
Interest for curr.period	02.2002	453.24	
Annuity	02.2002		1,424.00
Interest for curr.period	03.2002	450.06	

PC00_M99_CLOG—Overview of Company Loans

You can use this program to see overview of company loans. This program goes by evaluation period, and in the case of retro run, it shows multiple records for the same period. Finally, you don't know the current status of loan. You may see program documentation for more details. You may like program PC00_M22_CLOG Overview of Company Loans (Japan) better.

Pers.No.	Type	Ob	R	PP	PayY	01.01.1800	Payment	Repayment	31.01.2007	Crcy
110014	9370	01		5	2003	0.00	38,332.00	4,264.00	0.00	INR
110014	9370	01		6	2003	0.00	0.00	4,264.00	0.00	INR
110014	9370	01		7	2003	0.00	0.00	4,264.00	0.00	INR
110014	9370	01		8	2003	0.00	0.00	4,264.00	0.00	INR
110014	9370	01		9	2003	0.00	0.00	4,264.00	0.00	INR
110014	9370	01		10	2003	0.00	0.00	4,264.00	0.00	INR
110014	9370	01		11	2003	0.00	0.00	4,264.00	0.00	INR
110014	9370	01		12	2003	0.00	0.00	4,264.00	0.00	INR
110014	9370	01		1	2004	0.00	0.00	4,220.00	0.00	INR
* 110014	9370	01				0.00	38,332.00	38,332.00	0.00	INR
** 110014	9370					0.00	38,332.00	38,332.00	0.00	INR
*** 110014						0.00	38,332.00	38,332.00	0.00	INR

PC00_M22_CLOG—Overview of Company Loans (Japan)

You can use this program to see the overview of company loans. You may like this program better than PC00_M99_CLOG Overview of Company Loans, as it contains loan balance column.

Pers.No.	Type	ObjID	PerPa	PayY	PP	Payment	Loan repayment	Loan balance
110014	9370	01	11	2003	5	38,332.00	4,264.00	34,068.00
110014	9370	01	11	2003	6	0.00	4,264.00	29,804.00
110014	9370	01	11	2003	7	0.00	4,264.00	25,540.00
110014	9370	01	11	2003	8	0.00	4,264.00	21,276.00
110014	9370	01	11	2003	9	0.00	4,264.00	17,012.00
110014	9370	01	11	2003	10	0.00	4,264.00	12,748.00
110014	9370	01	11	2003	11	0.00	4,264.00	8,484.00
110014	9370	01	11	2003	12	0.00	4,264.00	4,220.00
110014	9370	01	11	2004	1	0.00	4,220.00	0.00

PC00_M99_CLOH—Calculate Present Value for Company Loans

Many companies offer loans to employees at a concessional rate. They may need to determine the net present value (NPV) of these loans at current interest rate to show it in their books of accounts. You can use this program to do that.

DLART	Incrse	Dep	Book value
9221	82,363.47	3,982.22	78,381.25
9223	100,230.61	4,564.19	95,666.42
9225	43,938.39	2,860.20	41,078.19
****	226,532.47	11,406.61	215,125.86

36.2 LOAN PAYMENTS (INFOTYPE 0078)

Functional Consultant	User	Business Process Owner	Senior Management	My Rating	Understanding Level
A	A	A	A		

36.2.1 Purpose and Overview

Loan payments and special repayments

When you create a loan in SAP, and specify installment, it is recovered in payroll. However, before the installment can be recovered, first the payment for loan must take place. This is recorded in infotype 0078. Apart from loan payments, which can happen through payroll, or externally; special repayments, loan fee, loan remission, etc. can also be created in infotype 0078.

Loan wage types

In payroll, entries in infotype 0078 generate loan wage types which depending on their predefined behaviour may result in

> ➢ Payment to/deduction from the employee
> ➢ Income tax change (imputed income wage type)
> ➢ Entries in the FI system

Regular installments

Infotype 0078 does not contain regular installments deducted in payroll. Hence, you cannot determine loan balance by looking at this infotype alone.

Infotype maintenance

Infotype 0078 is not maintained directly, but through infotype 0045. The payment tab, shown in infotype 0045, is actually infotype 0078.

Disbursement schedule

When you create a loan payment, the system checks whether the employee is eligible for payment, provided that a loan disbursement schedule has been defined for that loan type.

Penal interest

When an employee makes a special repayment, a penal interest may be charged as per configuration.

Processing fee

You can charge a loan processing fee through infotype 0078.

Complete repayment

If an employee wants to make complete repayment, you select this option and the system determines the amount automatically.

Changing payments/repayments already made

Payments that have already been included in the payroll run are inactive and cannot be changed, as you usually do not make changes to such payments. However, if you want to process a payment that has already been accounted, select it and choose Change. The payment is then released for processing.

Payments and deductions in an interval

Usually, the payments and deductions entered in infotype 0078 are one time. SAP has a provision to let you enter an interval. This is described in chapter 36.20.6.

36.2.2 Subtypes

Payment type

36.2.3 Time Constraint

3 (Record may include gaps, can exist more than once)

36.2.4 Payments

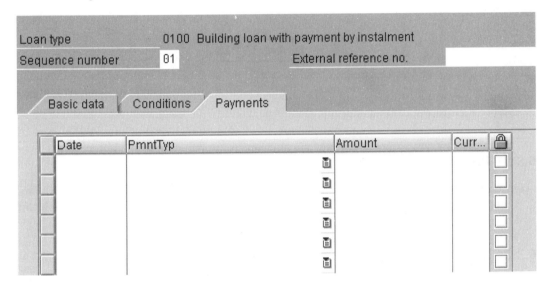

Date

This date determines when the payment or recovery through payroll takes place. You can enter a future date, if you want to pay a loan, or recover a repayment, in a future month. If data is entered for the past month, retro payroll run takes place.

Payment type

The payment type determines whether it is a payment or repayment, and whether it is through payroll or external. This list is predefined by SAP. These are subtypes of infotype 0078.

Amount and currency

This field contains the payment or repayment amounts for the payment type. The total of payment amounts which you enter here, should not exceed the amount that you have entered in the approved loan amount field on the 'Basic data' tab page. The system checks this.

Lock indicator

Unless a record is unlocked, it has no effect in the system.

36.3   LOAN TYPES

Functional Consultant	User	Business Process Owner	Senior Management	My Rating	Understanding Level
A	X	X	X		

36.3.1   Purpose

A company may give its employees multiple types of loan, e.g. housing loan, car loan, etc. These are created as loan types. If you want to permit multiple loans of a type to an employee at the same time, you tick the object id checkbox.

36.3.2   IMG Node

SM30 ➤ VV_T591A_0045___AL0

36.3.3   Screen

Subtype characteristics for Loans		
Subtype	Name	Objl...
0100	Building loan with payment by instalment	☐
0110	Car loan with payment by instalment	☐
0120	Personal loan with payment by instalment	☐
0130	Recurring advance	☐
0200	Building loan with annuity payment	☐

36.3.4   Primary Key

Infotype + Subtype

36.4 LOAN CATEGORIES

Functional Consultant	User	Business Process Owner	Senior Management	My Rating	Understanding Level
A	A	A	A		

36.4.1 Purpose

In this view, you specify whether a loan type is an annuity loan, or installment loan, or recurring advance. The repayment of loan depends on the loan category.

36.4.2 IMG Node

SM30 ➤ V_T506A

36.4.3 Screen

Loan type	Name	Loan category
0100	Building loan with payment by instalment	Instalment loan
0110	Car loan with payment by instalment	Instalment loan
0120	Personal loan with payment by instalment	Instalment loan
0130	Recurring advance	Instalment loan
0200	Building loan with annuity payment	Annuity loans
0210	Car loan with annuity payment	Annuity loans

36.4.4 Primary Key

Loan type

36.4.5 Important Fields

Loan type and name

Here you enter the loan types and their description.

Loan category

Annuity loans (EMI)	The total of repayment and interest payment remains constant for this loan type. When the loan continues to be repaid, the repayment share increases and the interest share decreases.
Installment loan	In this case, the repayment of principal remains constant. The interest is added in every period, but decreases when the loan continues to be repaid.
Recurring advance	In this case, a certain amount is paid to the employee. The recurring advance is not repaid, and no interest incurs. The employee only has to repay the amount when he leaves the company.

36.5 LOAN CONDITIONS

Functional Consultant	User	Business Process Owner	Senior Management	My Rating	Understanding Level
A	A	A	A		

36.5.1 Purpose

In this view you define the interest rate, repayment characteristics, etc. for each loan type. These attributes are clubbed together under loan condition. The loan conditions are period dependent, and their attributes can change over a period of time. Moreover, you can create multiple loan conditions for a loan type, and assign different loan conditions to different employees. This could be useful, for example, if your company charges the officers different interest rate for housing loan than the workers.

36.5.2 IMG Node

SM30 ➢ V_T506D

36.5.3 Screen

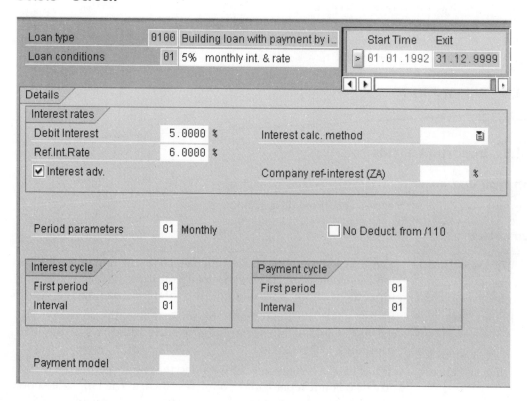

36.5.4 Primary Key

Loan type + Loan conditions + End date. Note that loan conditions are period-dependent.

36.5.5 Important Fields

Loan type

Here you enter the loan type whose loan condition is being specified.

Loan conditions

A loan type can have multiple predefined loan conditions. Different employees can be given the same loan under different conditions.

Start time and exit

If the interest rate that your company charged to the employees for a loan changes, you are not required to create a new loan condition, and assign it to all loan records from the new date. The attributes of loan conditions in SAP are period-dependent. For the same loan condition, the interest rate can differ from period to period. This validity period is specified here.

Debit interest rate

Here you enter the interest rate charged by the company. If you have a legacy system, which is computing interest, you have to test whether those values match with SAP computed interest. If there is a mismatch, and you wish to continue with old values, it may be necessary to adjust this marginally.

Interest calculation method

SAP lets you decide which of the following methods you want to use for interest computation:

```
B 30/365
7 30/360
2 act/360
3 act/365
6 act/actY
```

You can also specify the interest calculation method in feature INTLO. This helps if you have too many loan conditions, and a uniform interest calculation method. However, if the interest calculation method is entered in this field, that gets precedence.

Reference interest rate

If the law in your country requires that in the case of a concessional loan, you pay tax on imputed income, you specify the reference interest rate here. If you do not do so, the reference interest rate is taken from the REFIN constant in view V_T511K. The system calculates imputed income, for which the employee must effect statutory payments, on the basis of the difference between reference interest and debit interest.

Interest advantage

The imputed income is computed only if you tick this checkbox.

Company reference interest rate

The system calculates the employee's benefit amount, based on the difference between the reference interest and the debit interest. If there is no entry in this field, the company reference interest rate is taken from the REFIN constant in view V_T511K.

Period parameters

Period parameter determines how often the interest and principal repayment of loan would take place. It is recommended that the period parameter for loan should be same as the period parameter for the payroll area.

No deduction of interest and repayment from wage type /110

Usually, /LID (Interest Due), /LRP (Regular Repayment) and /LEP (Special Repayment Payroll) are deducted from wage type /110 (Net Payments/Deductions). You can disable that and specify the wage type from which these wage types are deducted in program PLO_NATIO.

Repayment cycles

SAP gives you flexibility in defining when the repayments should take place. In a yearly cycle, you can define the first period when the repayment should take place, and the interval at which subsequent repayments should take place. In the case of annuity loans, you specify one set of values, but in the case of installment loans you specify one set for principal repayment, and one set for interest repayment.

Payment model

This is even more flexible method of defining repayments. You define payment models in T549W, and assign it to a loan condition here.

36.6 DEFAULT INTEREST CALCULATION METHOD

Functional Consultant	User	Business Process Owner	Senior Management	My Rating	Understanding Level
A	B	B	X		

36.6.1 Purpose

Different countries have different practices on how to calculate interest. You can set that here. You can also vary them by loan type and loan condition. You can also specify interest calculation method in V_T506D. If it is specified in V_T506D, that takes precedence.

36.6.2 IMG Node

PE03 ≻ INTLO

36.6.3 Screen

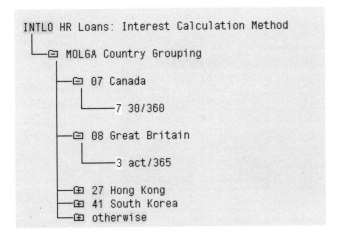

36.6.4 Fields for Decision-making

Country Grouping
Loan type
Loan conditions

36.6.5 Return Value

Interest calculation method

36.7 LOAN VALUE DATES

Functional Consultant	User	Business Process Owner	Senior Management	My Rating	Understanding Level
A	B	B	X		

36.7.1 Purpose

Loan payments and repayments through payroll must have a date on which they are paid or recovered. This date is needed for interest calculation. SAP offers you a choice of start date of the payroll period, end date, middle of the period, and payment date. These are associated to a payroll area in this view.

36.7.2 IMG Node

SM30 ➤ V_T506S

36.7.3 Screen

P..	Payroll area text	Start Date	End Date	Value date	
C0	HR-CH: Monthly	01.01.1900	31.12.9999	End of period	
C1	HR-CH: Hourly	01.01.1900	31.12.9999	End of period	
C8	HR-CH: Retirees	01.01.1900	31.12.9999	End of period	
C9	HR-CH: No payroll	01.01.1900	31.12.9999	End of period	
D1	HR-D: Indus. workers	01.01.1900	31.12.9999	End of period	
D2	HR-D: Sal. employees	01.01.1900	31.12.9999	End of period	

HR Loans: Define Value Date for Each Payroll Area

36.7.4 Primary Key

Payroll Area + End Date

36.7.5 Important Fields

Payroll area

The date for loan payments and repayments through payroll depends on payroll area.

Start and end date

The indicator for determining value date for a payroll area can change with time. These fields determine the validity period of that assignment.

Indicator for determining value date

```
Start of period
End of period
Middle of period (15th)
In accordance with payment day (T549S)
```

36.8 LOAN ALLOCATION CONTROL (INTERNATIONAL)

Functional Consultant	User	Business Process Owner	Senior Management	My Rating	Understanding Level
A	B	B	X		

36.8.1 Purpose and Overview

When you create a loan for an employee in infotype 0045, this view determines what you can, or cannot do. All controls in this view are at employee category + loan type level. The employee category in this view is different from the employee category in view V_T7INJ3.

Certain loan types may not be available to certain category of employees. Through this view, you can prevent them from getting that loan.

You can limit the maximum loan amount available to a category of employees for a loan type. Similar functionality is also available through view V_T7INJ3. You may decide which one you want to use.

You can determine the default values of loan conditions, repayment installment, and individual interest rate. These can be changed while creating a record in infotype 0045.

If you give fixed values of loan conditions, repayment installment, and individual interest rate, then they cannot be changed while creating a record in infotype 0045.

If you specify maximum value, then repayment installment and individual interest rate are accordingly restricted.

While there is no doubt that this view gives a lot of flexibility in controlling allocation of loan to employees, it can be argued that these indicators should apply to each field individually, rather than to the whole set. Also, the indicators should include a minimum value. It would also be useful, if you could specify whether the restriction is a warning, or an error.

36.8.2 IMG Node

SM30 ➤ T506C

36.8.3   Screen

Controlling Loan Allocation							
Lo...	Lo...	Loan amount	Curr...	C..	Instllment	Int. Rate	Indicators
P001	0100	30,000.00	DEM	01	500.00		Default value 📋
				.			📋
							📋

36.8.4   Primary Key

Loan grouping + Loan type

36.8.5   Important Fields

Loan grouping

You can categorize your employees for the purpose of controlling loan allocation. This logic can be built in feature ALOAN, which returns the loan grouping. Based on that loan grouping, the controlling values from this view get picked up.

Loan type

Restrictions differ depending on loan type.

Maximum loan amount and currency

Here you define the maximum loan amount an employee can get for this loan type.

Loan conditions

In this field you specify the loan condition. Depending on the employee category and loan type, this loan condition applies.

Repayment installment

Repayment installment can also depend on the employee category and loan type.

Individual interest rate

If your interest rates do not depend on employee category, leave this blank. The interest rate is picked up from loan condition. The value entered here has precedence over that.

Indicators

This indicator determines the nature of the fields: loan conditions, repayment installment, and individual interest rate.

Default value	Fields will default while creating a loan record in infotype 0045, and the user can change them.
Fixed value	Fields will default while creating a loan record in infotype 0045, and the user cannot change them.
Maximum value	Fields will default while creating a loan record in infotype 0045, and the user cannot increase them.
Non-permitted loan type	The employee cannot be given this loan.

36.9 LOAN GROUPING (INTERNATIONAL)

Functional Consultant	User	Business Process Owner	Senior Management	My Rating	Understanding Level
A	B	B	X		

36.9.1 Purpose

You can categorize your employees for the purpose of controlling loan allocation. This logic can be built in feature ALOAN, which returns the loan grouping. Based on that loan grouping, the controlling values from view T506C get picked up.

36.9.2 IMG Node

PE03 ≻ ALOAN

36.9.3 Screen

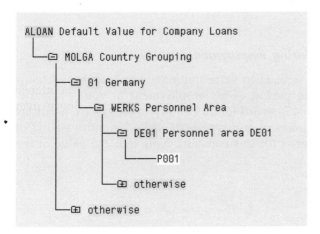

36.9.4 Fields for Decision-making

Company Code
Personnel Area
Personnel Subarea
Employee Group
Employee Subgroup
Country Grouping
User group

36.9.5 Return Value

Loan Grouping (International)

36.10 LOAN APPROVAL

Functional Consultant	User	Business Process Owner	Senior Management	My Rating	Understanding Level
A	A	A	A		

36.10.1 Overview

Companies often have a number of rules to determine the eligibility of employees for loans. Some of these rules are for specific loan types, whereas others apply to all types of loan taken together. Here the overview of controls provided by SAP is discussed. These are followed by details of specific control where appropriate.

Maximum number of loans allowed at a time

The constant LMNL1 in view V_T511K is used to store the maximum number of loans allowed at a time for an employee. When you populate the loans infotype (0045) record for an employee, the system performs a check to see that the total number of active loans at that time does not exceed the number entered for this constant. Note that the value of the constant can change over time.

Maximum number of loans allowed during employment

The constant LMNL2 in view V_T511K is used to store the maximum number of loans that an employee can avail in the entire period of his employment in your company. When you populate the loans infotype (0045) record for an employee, the system performs a check to see that the total number of loans of any type availed in the entire period of service does not exceed the number entered for this constant. Note that the value of the constant can change over time.

Maximum amount of outstanding loans at any time

The constant LMVAL in view V_T511P is used to store the maximum amount of outstanding loans of all types, for an employee at any given point of time. When you populate the loans infotype (0045) record for an employee, the system performs a check to see that the total outstanding amount does not exceed the amount entered for this constant. Note that the value of the constant can change over time.

Additional loan approval conditions for India

SAP lets you control loan allocation through view T506C. However, this view offers limited functionality. For an employee and a loan type, it gives you loan amount, loan condition, installment and interest rate. It also tells you whether they are default value, maximum value, or fixed value. But you can't specify that the loan amount is maximum value, but installment is fixed value.

SAP India has developed rich functionality for loan approval. There is no reason why you can't take advantage of it. It lets you decide whether a loan is to be granted or not, depending on the following factors:

➢ Maximum number of loans at a time
➢ Maximum number of loans till date
➢ Maximum outstanding amount
➢ Minimum service period
➢ Upper limit on age
➢ Minimum gap between current and previous loan

Restriction on loan amount

Apart from these, the loan amount can also be restricted based on

➢ The employee's salary
➢ Value of asset to be created by the loan
➢ A fixed amount

Configuration for additional loan approval functionality

Configuration	Description
V_T7INA1	You first define master list of allowance grouping.
V_T7INA3	Then you assign the combination of pay scale (type, area, group and level) and ESG for CAP to allowance grouping.
Feature 40LGR	From allowance grouping, and other employee attributes, you determine loan grouping.
V_T7INJ3	For each loan grouping, you define the loan approval rules.
Feature 40LSL	Since the loan amount can be controlled based on the employee's salary, you need to define the wage types that constitute employee's salary.

(Contd.)

Configuration	Description
BAdI HR_IN_LOANS_VALID	Since the loan amount can depend on the asset you are going to build with the loan, you need to capture the asset value in infotype 0045. But there is no field in infotype 0045 for this purpose. To capture this data you implement this BAdI.
V_T7INJ5	Based on loan grouping, you can also define a loan disbursement schedule.
V_T7INJ6	Since loan disbursement can depend on events, e.g. purchase of land, you may need to define event codes.

36.11 ALLOWANCE GROUPING

Functional Consultant	User	Business Process Owner	Senior Management	My Rating	Understanding Level
A	B	B	X		

36.11.1 Purpose

In SAP, you can define the value of an indirectly evaluated wage type for a combination of pay scale type, area, group, level and ESG for CAP. This combination is called allowance grouping. You define the master list of allowance groupings in V_T7INA1. You assign pay scale type, area, group, level and ESG for CAP to an allowance grouping in V_T7INA3.

36.11.2 IMG Node

SM30 ➤ V_T7INA1

36.11.3 Screen

36.11.4 Primary Key

Country Grouping + Pay scale grouping for allowances

36.12 ALLOWANCE GROUPING ASSIGNMENT

Functional Consultant	User	Business Process Owner	Senior Management	My Rating	Understanding Level
A	B	B	X		

36.12.1 Purpose

This view contains the assignment of allowance grouping to pay scale type, area, group, level and ESG for CAP.

36.12.2 IMG Node

SM30 ➤ V_T7INA3

36.12.3 Screen

	Associating pay parameters to pay scale grouping				
PS area	PS type	ESG/CAP	PS group	PS level	AlGrp
01	01	1	MANAGER	0	MN01
01	01	1	MANAGER	5	MN02

36.12.4 Primary Key

Country Grouping + Pay Scale Area + Pay scale type + ESG for CAP + Pay Scale Group + Pay Scale Level

36.13 LOAN GROUPING

Functional Consultant	User	Business Process Owner	Senior Management	My Rating	Understanding Level
A	B	B	X		

36.13.1 Purpose and Overview

This feature is used to define the loans groupings. These loans groupings are used as a key to maintain the views loans eligibility checks and limits (V_T7INJ3) and loans disbursement schedule (V_T7INJ5). Note that loans groupings are combination of employee grouping and loan type. Also note that the employee grouping is determined primarily from allowance grouping of infotype 0008, rather than fields of infotype 0001.

36.13.2 IMG Node

PE03 ≻ 40LGR

36.13.3 Screen

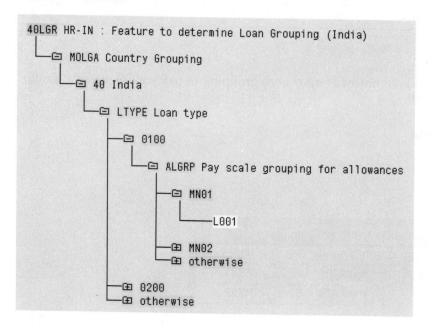

```
40LGR HR-IN : Feature to determine Loan Grouping (India)
    └─▭ MOLGA Country Grouping
        └─▭ 40 India
            └─▭ LTYPE Loan type
                ├─▭ 0100
                │   └─▭ ALGRP Pay scale grouping for allowances
                │       ├─▭ MN01
                │       │   └────L001
                │       ├─⊞ MN02
                │       └─⊞ otherwise
                ├─⊞ 0200
                └─⊞ otherwise
```

36.13.4 Fields for Decision-making

Country Grouping
Pay scale grouping for allowances
Personnel Number
Loan type

36.13.5 Return Value

Loan Grouping

36.14 LOANS ELIGIBILITY CHECKS AND LIMITS

Functional Consultant	User	Business Process Owner	Senior Management	My Rating	Understanding Level
A	B	B	X		

36.14.1 Purpose and Overview

This view is used to check an employee's eligibility to get loans. The restrictions can be varied depending on loan grouping. The loan grouping, for the purpose of this view, is determined by feature 40LGR. The grouping depends on employee category and loan type.

SAP lets you decide whether a loan is to be granted or not, depending on the following factors:

➢ Maximum number of loans at a time
➢ Maximum number of loans till date
➢ Maximum outstanding amount
➢ Minimum service period
➢ Upper limit on age
➢ Minimum gap between current and previous loan

Apart from these, the loan amount can also be restricted based on

➢ The employee's salary
➢ Value of asset to be created by loan
➢ A fixed amount

It would have been be useful, if you could specify whether the restriction is a warning, or an error.

36.14.2 IMG Node

SM30 ➢ V_T7INJ3

36.14.3 Primary Key

Loan Grouping (includes employee grouping and loan type) + End Date

36.14.4   Loan Grouping

Loan Grouping [   ]   Start Time   Exit

Loan grouping

In this view, the loan grouping includes employee grouping and loan type. It is determined by feature 40LGR. Note that if loan type is included in loan grouping, all restrictions listed here apply only to that loan type.

Start date and end date

The restrictions you apply through this view can change with time.

36.14.5   Employees' Eligibility for a Loan

Employees' eligibility for a loan	
Minimum experience	
Maximum age	

Minimum experience

Here you specify the minimum service which the employee must put in before he is eligible for a loan.

Maximum age

If your company does not give loans to employees above certain age, enter the age limit here.

36.14.6   Limit on Number of Loans Taken

Limit on number of loans taken	
Max. no. of loans at a time	
Max. no. of loans till date	

Maximum number of loans at a time

Here you specify the maximum number of loans that can be taken by an employee at a time.

Maximum number of loans till date

Here you specify the maximum number of loans that can be taken by an employee.

36.14.7 Limiting Parameters—Loan Amount Approved

Limit. parameters-loan amt. approved	
Sal. multi.factor	
Asset percentage	
Fixed amount	

The loan approval amount is the minimum of the amounts computed below. However, it is only a warning.

Salary multiplication factor

Some companies have a policy, e.g. the housing loan cannot be more than 20 times the salary. If you have such a policy, the multiplying factor can be defined here. The components of salary are defined in feature 40LSL and are taken from infotype 0008.

Asset percentage

Some companies have a policy, e.g. the housing loan cannot be more than 80% of the value of the house. If you have such a policy, you can define the asset percentage here. Since the asset value is not captured in infotype 0045, to capture the asset value, you must configure the GET_ASSET_VALUE method in the Business Add-In HR_IN_LOANS_ VALIDITY, through the IMG under Payroll India: Company Loans ➢ Master Data ➢ BAdI: Loans Eligibility.

Fixed amount

Regardless of an employee's salary-based eligibility and asset value-based eligibility, the companies often have a maximum amount that can be granted as loan. This limit is specified here.

36.14.8 Limit on Outstanding Amount

Limit on outstanding amount		
Max. outstanding amount		

Maximum outstanding amount with currency

Some companies allow another loan of the same loan type, if the outstanding balance of the previous loan is below a certain amount. That limit can be entered here. If a person is not able to get loan because of this restriction, he can prepay an amount which brings down his outstanding balance within acceptable limit, and avail the new loan.

36.14.9 Minimum Time Interval between Current and Previous Loan

Min. time interval between curr. and prev. loan	
Prev. loan reference date	📋
Min. months b/w curr. and prev loan	

If your company policy is to maintain a minimum gap between two loans of the same type, you can specify that here.

Previous loan reference date

While determining the gap with current loan, whether you want to take the end date of the previous loan, or the start date, needs to be specified here.

Minimum months between current and previous loan

If the time gap between the previous and current loan, of the same loan type, is less than the number of months in this field, the loan is not approved.

36.15 SALARY COMPONENTS FOR LOAN ELIGIBILITY

Functional Consultant	User	Business Process Owner	Senior Management	My Rating	Understanding Level
A	B	B	X		

36.15.1 Purpose

This feature is used to define the wage types, which constitute salary for the purpose of granting loan. The wage type values are taken from infotype 0008, added to compute salary, and multiplied by salary multiplying factor to determine one of the limits on loan approval amount.

36.15.2 IMG Node

PE03 ➤ 40LSL

36.15.3 Screen

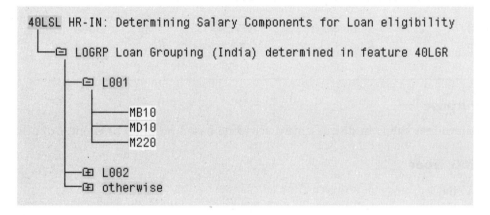

```
40LSL HR-IN: Determining Salary Components for Loan eligibility

    └─🗁 LOGRP Loan Grouping (India) determined in feature 40LGR

        ├─🗁 L001

        │       ├──────MB10
        │       ├──────MD10
        │       └──────M220

        ├─🗄 L002
        └─🗄 otherwise
```

36.15.4 Fields for Decision-making

Personnel Number
Loan Grouping (India) determined in feature 40LGR

36.15.5 Return Value

Table of wage types

36.16 BADI: LOANS ELIGIBILITY

Functional Consultant	User	Business Process Owner	Senior Management	My Rating	Understanding Level
B	X	X	X		

36.16.1 Purpose

If you wish to determine loan eligibility based on asset value, you need to use Business Add In HR_IN_LOANS_VALID to capture the asset value, as infotype 0045 does not capture asset value.

36.16.2 IMG Node

Payroll ➢ Payroll: India ➢ Company Loans ➢ Master Data ➢ BAdI: Loans Eligibility

36.17 LOANS DISBURSEMENT SCHEDULE

Functional Consultant	User	Business Process Owner	Senior Management	My Rating	Understanding Level
B	C	C	X		

36.17.1 Purpose

This view determines the loan disbursement schedule based on time, or event, or both.

36.17.2 IMG Node

SM30 ➤ V_T7INJ5

36.17.3 Screen

HR-IN: Loans Dusbursement Schedule

Loa...	Seq. no.	Start date	End date	Type of t...	Time dur.	Time du...	Event code	Event c...	Disb. sch.
				🖹		🖹			
				🖹		🖹			
				🖹		🖹			

36.17.4 Primary Key

Loan Grouping + Sequence number + End Date

36.17.5 Important Fields

Loan grouping

In this view, the loan grouping includes employee grouping and loan type. It is determined by feature 40LGR.

Sequence number

Here you specify the installment number of loan disbursement.

Start date and end date

Your disbursement schedule could vary with time.

Type of tranche

Depending on your company policy, the loan disbursement may be time-based, or event-based, or both.

Event-based	Where the disbursement amount depends on a particular event. For example, when an employee buys the land, he gets 20% of the approved loan amount.
Time-based	Where the disbursement amount depends on the time period. For example, the employee gets 40% of the loan amount after a period of three months from the date of loan approval.
Both	Where the disbursement amount depends on both, time and event.

Time duration and unit

If the loan disbursement is time-based or both time- and event-based you need to maintain these fields.

Event codes and text

If the loan disbursement is event-based or both time- and event-based you need to maintain these fields. You choose the event from the master list maintained in V_T7INJ6.

Disbursement schedule

Here you specify the percentage of loan to be disbursed.

36.18 EVENT CODES

Functional Consultant	User	Business Process Owner	Senior Management	My Rating	Understanding Level
B	C	C	X		

36.18.1 Purpose

In this view you maintain the master list of events which is shown in view V_T7INJ5.

36.18.2 IMG Node

SM30 ➤ V_T7INJ6.

36.18.3 Screen

HR-IN : Loan Tranche Disbursement Text for Events Code			
Language	Loan grouping	Event code	Text for event code

36.18.4 Primary Key

Language + Loan Grouping + Event Codes

36.18.5 Important Fields

Language

You can maintain the event code text in multiple languages.

Loan grouping

In this view, the loan grouping includes employee grouping and loan type. It is determined by feature 40LGR. The events are maintained for each loan grouping.

Event code and text

The events you define here are shown in the list of value in view V_T7INJ5.

36.19 PENAL INTEREST ON SPECIAL REPAYMENT

Functional Consultant	User	Business Process Owner	Senior Management	My Rating	Understanding Level
B	C	C	X		

36.19.1 Overview

The constant LONPI in view V_T511K is used to store the factor to be multiplied by the special repayment amount, stored in infotype 0045, to arrive at the penal interest amount.

Constant	Info	Payroll constant	Start Date	End Date	Value
LONPI	**i**	% Penal Int. foreclosure loans	01.04.1998	31.03.9999	1.00

If your rules for penal interest are more complex, you can create your custom rules in Payroll ≻ Payroll: India ≻ Company Loans ≻ Master Data ≻ BAdI: Penal Interest Amount.

36.20 PAYMENT TYPES

Functional Consultant	User	Business Process Owner	Senior Management	My Rating	Understanding Level
C	X	X	X		

36.20.1 Overview

Usually the payment types defined by SAP would meet your needs. However, if you want to define your own payment types for infotype 0078, you need to do all the configuration in this chapter.

In the case of special repayment (external), the day you specify as the payment date is not taken into consideration in interest calculation. In the case of complete repayment, this day is taken into consideration in interest calculation.

If you want to enter a repayment for an employee, who leaves the company or changes company code, use the complete repayment payment type. This guarantees that interest is calculated for the loan even for the last day that the employee works in the company or is assigned to the old company code.

36.20.2 Payment Types

You can define payment types in V_T591A (infotype 0078).

Subtype characteristics for Loan Payments	
Subtype	Name
0050	Fees
0100	Loan payment (external)
0120	Third-party payment
0150	Loan payment (payroll)

36.20.3 Country Assignment of Payment Types

You need to maintain country assignment of payment types in VV_T582L_78. This table is explained in infotype properties.

36.20.4 Loan Wage Type Characteristics

You define characteristics of loan wage view in view T506W. Here you specify whether the loan payment is an incoming payment or an outgoing payment, whether it is external or through payroll, whether it is interest relevant or not, and whether it is copied from the previous period (e.g. cumulated interest) or not. Normally you are not required to maintain this view.

	C..	Wa...	Payment direction	Payment method		Interest-rel.	Transfer...
Technical Characteristics of Loan Wage Types							
		/INT	🖹		🖹	☐	☐
		/LBC	🖹		🖹	☐	☑
		/LCI	🖹		🖹	☐	☑
		/LEE	I Inpayment 🖹	E External	🖹	☑	☐
		/LEP	I Inpayment 🖹	P With the payroll run 🖹		☑	☐
		/LER	I Inpayment 🖹	E External	🖹	☑	☐
		/LEX	I Inpayment 🖹	E External	🖹	☑	☐
		/LFP	I Inpayment 🖹	P With the payroll run 🖹		☐	☐

36.20.5 Assignment of Wage Types to Payment Types

For each payment type you specify the wage type and country grouping in view V_T506P.

Payment type		C..	WT	Payment direction		Pmt.met
Assignment of Wage Types to Payment Types						
0050 Fees	🖹		/LFP	I Inpayment	🖹	P With the... 🖹
0100 Loan payment (external)	🖹		/LOE	0 Payment	🖹	E External 🖹
0120 Third-party payment	🖹		/LO3	0 Payment	🖹	E External 🖹
0150 Loan payment (payroll)	🖹		/LOP	0 Payment	🖹	P With the... 🖹
0200 Special repayment (ext...	🖹		/LEE	I Inpayment	🖹	E External 🖹

36.20.6 Payment Types Valid for More than One Interval

Infotype 0078 is used to make loan payments. For repayments, you don't need to make any entry in infotype 0078. Installments and interests are recovered based on information in infotype 0045. However, if the employee wants to make a special repayment, or complete repayment, that data is entered in infotype 0078. Thus, each entry in infotype 0078 has a one-time occurrence on the specified date. This is true for all payment types defined by SAP as well as for most of the customer payment types. However, if you want you can create a customer payment type for repayments, which has multiple occurrences by ticking interval field in view V_506P_B. On ticking this field, you see an end date column in payment tab which is infotype 0078.

Payment type	Name	CGrpg	Interval
Make Payment Type Valid for One Interval			
0050	Fees		☐
0100	Loan payment (external)		☐
0120	Third-party payment		☐
0150	Loan payment (payroll)		☐

36.20.7 Processing Logic for Customer Payment Types

If you define your own payment types, you need to define the processing logic in BAdI HRPY_LOAN_PAYMENTS.

36.21 INTERFACE WITH PAYROLL

Functional Consultant	User	Business Process Owner	Senior Management	My Rating	Understanding Level
A	B	B	X		

36.21.1 Overview

In payroll, the payments/deductions and financial accounting can take place without creating any wage types for loans. You need to create wage types only if you want to post different loans to different accounts, or give them different descriptions.

Your payroll schema would have a subschema for loans.

Since SAP gives you flexibility in deducting installments from employees, and you may not deduct it every month, it creates three wage types for interest: /LIM (Interest for current month), /LIC (Cumulated interest), and /LID (Interest due). It would compute interest for each month, and put in /LIM, cumulate it in /LIC, and when due, transfer it from /LIC to /LID. Same thing is done for interest rate advantage, and interest exemption.

36.21.2 Wage Types Generated

Wage type	Wage type text
/LBC	Cumulated interest advantage
/LBD	Taxed interest advantage
/LBM	Interest rate advantage/current period
/LCI	Interest-bearing capital
/LEE	Special repayment, external
/LEP	Special payroll repayment
/LER	Loan remission
/LEX	Complete repayment
/LFC	Cumulated interest exemption
/LFM	Interest exemption/current period
/LFP	Loan fees
/LIC	Cumulated interest
/LID	Interest due
/LIM	Interest for current period
/LLB	Loan balance
/LO3	Third-party loan payment
/LOE	External loan payment
/LOP	Loan payment—payroll
/LRP	Regular repayment (both installment and annuity loans)
/LTE	Transfer loan balance

Membership Fees

37.1 MEMBERSHIP FEES (INFOTYPE 0057)

Functional Consultant	User	Business Process Owner	Senior Management	My Rating	Understanding Level
A	A	A	A		

37.1.1 Screen

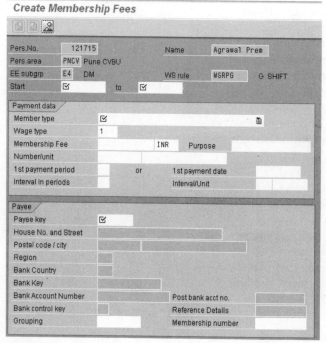

Create Membership Fees

Pers.No.   121715   Name   Agrawal Prem
Pers.area   PNCV Pune CVBU
EE subgrp   E4   DM   WS rule   WSRPG   G SHIFT
Start   ☑   to   ☑

Payment data
Member type   ☑   📋
Wage type   1
Membership Fee   INR   Purpose
Number/unit
1st payment period   or   1st payment date
Interval in periods   Interval/Unit

Payee
Payee key   ☑
House No. and Street
Postal code / city
Region
Bank Country
Bank Key
Bank Account Number   Post bank acct no.
Bank control key   Reference Details
Grouping   Membership number

37.1.2 Purpose

This infotype is for payment of membership fees. It generates a wage type at desired frequency like infotype 0014. In addition you can specify the payee information directly.

37.1.3 Subtypes

Membership types

37.1.4 Time Constraint

T (Time constraint is based on subtype or subtype table)

37.1.5 Important Fields

Member type

You can have different types of membership. These are subtypes of infotype 0057. The master list is maintained in view V_T591A.

Wage type

Here you specify the wage type under which the payment is to be made.

Membership fee and currency

Membership fee can be entered, or it can be indirectly valuated.

Purpose

The purpose entered in this field is indicated on the bank transfer form.

Number/unit

These fields are available for every wage type.

1st payment period and interval in periods

In a yearly cycle, the 1st payment period is the period in which payments happen first time. Then they happen at specified intervals, till the year changes.

1st payment date and interval/unit

This is a more flexible way of specifying recurring payments/deductions for membership.

Payee key

The payees are allowed to receive contributions. For each membership type, there may be one or more payees, from which you can select, when you create a record in infotype 0057. When you specify a payee key, details of the payee, from house number and street to reference details, are displayed from V_T521B.

Grouping

You can use this field to identify institutions.

Membership number

Here you enter the membership number of the institution.

Membership function

A member can be assigned certain functions, e.g. union representative, etc. Infotype 0057 has a field to capture this information, although it is not there on screen 2000.

37.2 MEMBERSHIP TYPES

Functional Consultant	User	Business Process Owner	Senior Management	My Rating	Understanding Level
A	X	X	X		

37.2.1 Purpose

A company's employees may be members of several institutions. The master list of membership types is maintained here.

37.2.2 IMG Node

SM30 ➢ VV_T591A_0057___AL0

37.2.3 Screen

Subtype characteristics for Membership Fees		
Subtype	Name	Time constraint
1	Union	2
2	Works council	2
3	Sports club	3

37.2.4 Primary Key

Infotype + Subtype

37.3 DEFAULT VALUES FOR MEMBERSHIPS

Functional Consultant	User	Business Process Owner	Senior Management	My Rating	Understanding Level
A	B	C	X		

37.3.1 Purpose

When you create an infotype 0057 record, this feature determines the default values for wage type, payee, and grouping.

37.3.2 IMG Node

PE03 ➤ PAYEE

37.3.3 Screen

37.3.4 Fields for Decision-making

Company Code
Personnel Area
Personnel Subarea
Employee Group
Employee Subgroup
Transaction class for data storage
Infotype
Subtype
Country Grouping
Wage type

37.3.5 Return Value

Wage type + payee + grouping

37.4 PAYEE KEYS

Functional Consultant	User	Business Process Owner	Senior Management	My Rating	Understanding Level
B	X	X	X		

37.4.1 Purpose

This view contains master list of payees. One of the users of this information is infotype 0057.

37.4.2 IMG Node

SM30 ➤ V_T521B

37.4.3 Screen

37.4.4 Primary Key

Payee key for bank transfers + End Date

37.4.5 Important Fields

Payee

The payee key is used for bank transfers.

Start and end date

Payee details can change over a period of time.

Payee text, postal code, city, house number/street, region

These fields contain payee's address.   .

Bank country

The bank country identifies the country in which the bank is located. It is used to define the rules according to which bank data, such as the bank and account numbers, is to be validated.

Bank key

Here you specify the bank and branch of the payee.

Bank account

Here you specify the bank account number of the payee.

Reference

If additional data for the bank details is needed for payment transactions in your country, enter the reference information here.

Control key

The bank control key has different uses for different countries. You may see field help for more details.

Payment method

Here you can enter the payment method, e.g. remittance to bank or cash payment, etc.

37.5   ALLOWED PAYEES

Functional Consultant	User	Business Process Owner	Senior Management	My Rating	Understanding Level
B	X	X	X		

37.5.1   Purpose

You can have one or more payee for each membership type, from which you can choose in infotype 0057. These valid combinations are maintained here.

37.5.2   IMG Node

SM30 ➤ VV_T521C_0057_AL0

37.5.3   Screen

	Subtype	Name	Payee key	Payee name
	4075	Dedn Adarsh Nidhi	SBICAPS	SBI Caps
	5705	E.M.B.F. II	SBICAPS	SBI Caps

37.5.4   Primary Key

Country Grouping + Infotype + Subtype + Payee key for bank transfers

37.5.5   Important Fields

Subtype and name

Here you enter the membership type for which you are defining valid payees.

Payee key and name

This field contains valid payees for a membership type.

37.6   MEMBERSHIP FUNCTION

Functional Consultant	User	Business Process Owner	Senior Management	My Rating	Understanding Level
B	X	X	X		

37.6.1   Purpose

A member can be assigned certain function, e.g. union representative, treasurer, etc. Infotype 0057 has a field to capture this information, although it is not there on screen 2000. Here you maintain the master list of membership function for each membership type.

37.6.2   IMG Node

SM30 ➤ V_T557V

37.6.3   Screen

Subtype	Membership function	Description
1	GS	General Secretary
1	PR	President
1	TR	Treasurer
1	UR	Union Representative

37.6.4   Primary Key

Country Grouping + Subtype + Membership function

37.6.5   Important Fields

Subtype

Here you enter the membership type, or subtype of infotype 0057.

Membership function and description

For each type of membership, you can have various functions the members can perform. The master list is maintained here.

Notifications

38.1 NOTIFICATIONS (INFOTYPE 0128)

Functional Consultant	User	Business Process Owner	Senior Management	My Rating	Understanding Level
A	A	A	A		

38.1.1 Purpose

Sometimes a company wants to print messages on employee's remuneration statement. You can use this infotype to specify the messages to be printed. You may print general notifications or personal notifications. The remuneration statement should be designed to print notifications.

38.1.2 General Notifications

When you want to print the same message on the remuneration statement of a large number of employees, you use general notifications. To print general notifications, you first create a standard text using transaction SO10, and enter the notification in that. You then attach the standard text to an employee in infotype 0128, subtype 1.

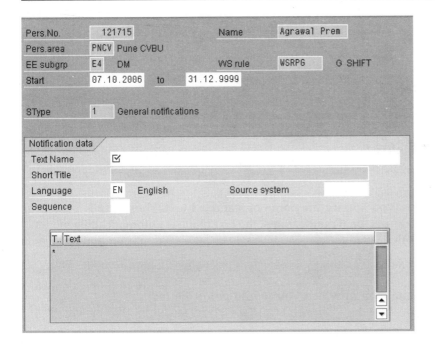

38.1.3   Personal Notifications

To print personal notifications, you directly enter the message in infotype 0128, subtype 2.

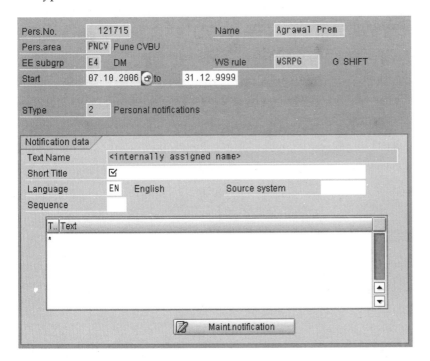

38.1.4 Subtypes

Types of notifications

38.1.5 Time Constraint

T (Time constraint is based on subtype or subtype table)

38.1.6 Important Fields

Text name, short title

For general notifications, you specify the name of standard text. Short title is picked up from the standard text. For personal notifications, the text name is automatically generated. You specify the short title.

Language

Here you specify the language in which you would enter the text.

Source system

Here you can enter either the source system or additional information.

Sequence

In the case of multiple notifications, they are printed in the order of this sequence field. If there are multiple notifications with identical sequence value, they are printed in chronological order of saving the records.

Tag column and text

In the case of general notification, the standard text is displayed. In the case of personal notification, you can enter the text. In tag column you can specify the formatting of text.

38.2 TYPES OF NOTIFICATION

Functional Consultant	User	Business Process Owner	Senior Management	My Rating	Understanding Level
A	X	X	X		

38.2.1 Purpose

You can print notifications on remuneration statement. There are two types of notifications: general notifications and personal notifications. Their use is predefined by SAP. If you create additional type of notification, they will not be used by SAP. In this view you can change the time constraints of general and personal notifications.

38.2.2 IMG Node

SM30 ➤ V_T591A (infotype 0128)

38.2.3 Screen

	Subtype characteristics for Notifications		
	Subtype	Name	Time constraint
	1	General notifications	3
	2	Personal notifications	3

38.2.4 Primary Key

Infotype + Subtype

Additional Off-cycle Payments

39.1 ADDITIONAL OFF-CYCLE PAYMENTS (INFOTYPE 0267)

Functional Consultant	User	Business Process Owner	Senior Management	My Rating	Understanding Level
A	A	A	A		

39.1.1 Screen

Additional Off-Cycle Payments	
Wage type	⬜
Amount	INR
Number/unit	
Payment date	30.04.2005
Default Date	
Assignment number	
Reason for Change	
Off-cycle reas.	
Payroll type	A
Payroll ID	

39.1.2 Purpose

If you want to pay some employee in between the payroll period, SAP allows you to run an off-cycle payroll. One-time payments to be done during off-cycle payrolls are entered in infotype 0267. Thus, it is similar to infotype 0015. You can specify cost assignment of an infotype 0267 record.

39.1.3 Subtypes

Wage type

39.1.4 Time Constraint

T (Time constraint is based on subtype or subtype table)

39.1.5 Important Fields

Wage type

You can select only from those wage types, which are permitted for infotype 0267.

Amount and currency

Here you enter the amount to be paid or deducted. If the wage type is a deduction wage type, an 'A' appears on the left-hand side of the amount field. Also, if a wage type is indirectly valuated, an 'I' is indicated on the right-hand side of the currency field.

Number/unit

Here you can enter the number and its unit. This field can be used to convert number in amount during payroll run, if your system is so designed. It can also be used to keep some related information, which can be printed in the payslip.

Payment date

Like infotype 0015, infotype 0267 is also valid only for a single day and not for a period. The date in this field goes in both start date and end date. This field is defaulted to the last day of the current payroll period and can be changed.

Default date (payroll period and year)

If your payment/deduction is not for the current period, you may enter the payroll period and year here. The system determines the payment date.

Assignment number

You can use this field for reference information. However, this does not enter RT, and cannot be printed in payslip. If you wish to print reference information, you can use number field.

Reason for change

You can maintain a master list of reasons for creating infotype 0267 records in view V_T530E, and assign the reason here.

Off-cycle reason

When you run off-cycle payroll, you can specify the reason. It takes infotype 0267 records only for that off-cycle reason.

Payroll type

This is used by the system to recognize which of the following payroll runs should be executed:

Blank	Regular payroll run
A	Bonus payment
B	Correction accounting
C	Manual check
S	Supplemental payment

Payroll identifier

If you run different off-cycle payroll runs on the same day, you can use this field to determine the payroll run in which this record will be selected.

39.1.6 Menu and Menu Bar

When you click this icon, you get the following dialog box, where you can maintain cost assignment for the current record of infotype 0267. For more details, you may see chapter 45, Cost Assignment.

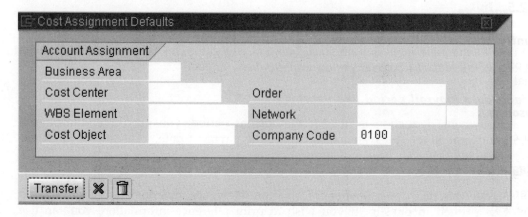

39.2 REASONS FOR OFF-CYCLE PAYROLL RUNS

Functional Consultant	User	Business Process Owner	Senior Management	My Rating	Understanding Level
A	X	X	X		

39.2.1 Purpose

When you run off-cycle payroll, you can specify the reason. It takes infotype 0267 records only for that off-cycle reason. The master list of off-cycle reason is maintained here. Note that this view is cross client.

39.2.2 IMG Node

SM30 ➤ V_T52OCR

39.2.3 Screen

	OC...	Description off-cycle rea...	OC cat.	Name	Pa...	OC reason type
	0001	Advance payment	01	Advance payment		G Payment in Advanc...
	0002	Bonus	02	Bonus	A	B Bonus (Infotyp 02...
	0003	Reimbursement	03	Reimbursement	A	B Bonus (Infotyp 02...
	0005	Regular 'On Demand'	05	Regular		D On-demand Payroll

39.2.4 Primary Key

Country Grouping + Reason for Off-cycle Payroll

39.2.5 Important Fields

Country grouping

The off-cycle reasons can be country-dependent. You specify the country grouping in the initial dialog box.

Reason for off-cycle payroll

You create the master list of the code and description.

Category for off-cycle reason

Several off-cycle reasons can be grouped together in a category, which is processed in the same way during the payroll run.

Payroll type and type of off-cycle reason

Both these fields are attributes of category for off-cycle reason, and picked up from V_T52OCC.

39.3 CATEGORIES FOR OFF-CYCLE REASONS

Functional Consultant	User	Business Process Owner	Senior Management	My Rating	Understanding Level
A	X	X	X		

39.3.1 Purpose

This view contains master list of categories for off-cycle reasons. Each off-cycle reason has a category, through which the payroll type and type of off-cycle reason are determined. Note that this view is cross client.

39.3.2 IMG Node

SM30 ➢ V_T52OCC

39.3.3 Screen

OC cat.	Name	Pay.type	OC reason type
01	Advance payment		G Payment in Advance w…
02	Bonus	A	B Bonus (Infotyp 0267)
03	Reimbursement	A	B Bonus (Infotyp 0267)
05	Regular		D On-demand Payroll

39.3.4 Primary Key

Country Grouping + Category for off-cycle reason

39.3.5 Important Fields

Country grouping

The off-cycle reason categories can be country-dependent. You specify the country grouping in the initial dialog box.

Category for off-cycle reason

Several off-cycle reasons can be grouped together in a category, which is processed in the same way during the payroll run.

Payroll type

The payroll types are predefined by SAP.

Blank	Regular payroll run
A	Bonus payment
B	Correction accounting
C	Manual check
S	Supplemental payment

Type of off-cycle reason

This determines how the payroll processing is done. These are predefined by SAP.

B	Bonus (infotype 0267)
D	On-demand Payroll
E	Payment in advance with original result
G	Payment in Advance with Retroactive Calculations
L	LTI Processing
O	Others
S	Supplemental Payment
V	Absences (vacations)

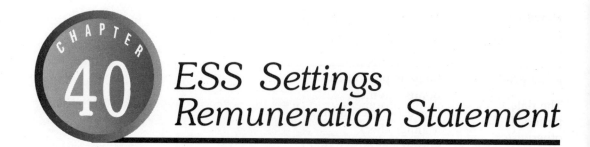

ESS Settings Remuneration Statement

40.1 ESS SETTINGS REMUNERATION STATEMENT (INFOTYPE 0655)

Functional Consultant	User	Business Process Owner	Senior Management	My Rating	Understanding Level
A	A	A	A		

40.1.1 Screen

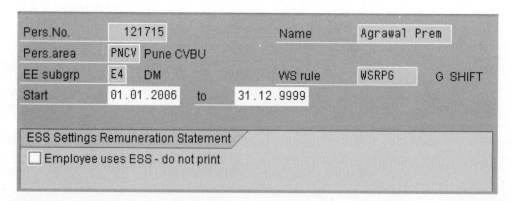

40.1.2 Purpose and Overview

Normally an employee gets a remuneration statement from the employer giving details of salary payments. When the companies implement employee self service, they provide the remuneration statement to the employee online, and do away with printing of the remuneration statement.

However, sometimes it is not possible to discontinue printing of the remuneration statement for all employees. In such cases, you maintain this infotype for those employees whose remuneration statement is not to be printed. While printing remuneration statement, if you mark the field 'Check ESS' in the report selection screen, then remuneration statement is not printed for those employees for whom you have maintained a tick in this infotype.

The date with which this infotype is read depends on the payment date of the payroll period. If the payment date is in future, the infotype is read with the payment date, otherwise it is read with the system date.

Also, for preliminary DME program for Canada and the USA, if the employee is paid by bank transfer then no payment advice note for transfer is created for employees for whom the field 'Employee uses ESS - do not print' is marked in this infotype. But where the payment is through check, the remuneration statement is printed on the check for these countries irrespective of this field.

40.1.3 Subtypes

No subtypes

40.1.4 Time Constraint

3 (Record may include gaps, can exist more than once)

Infotype Properties

41.1 INFOTYPE ATTRIBUTES

Functional Consultant	User	Business Process Owner	Senior Management	My Rating	Understanding Level
A	A	A	A		

41.1.1 Purpose and Overview

This view defines some of the most important properties of infotypes. Changing the properties will change the behaviour of infotypes, which should be done with extreme caution. Change only if you understand the implications, and in consultation with user. Important changeable information is screens, header, sort sequence, time constraint, default start and end date.

41.1.2 IMG Node

SM30 ➤ V_T582A

41.1.3 Primary Key

Infotype

41.1.4 General Attributes

Infotype	0000 Actions		
General attributes			
Time constraint 1	☐ Subtype obligatory	☐ Accntng/log.data	
Time cnstr.tab.	Subtype table	☑ Text allowed	
Maint.aft.leave	Subty.text tab.	☐ Copy infotype	
☑ Access auth.	Subtype field	☐ Propose infotype	

Infotype

Infotype, whose properties are being defined. Technical properties of infotype are also defined in view T777D, which is the check table for this field.

Time constraint

While an employee's information may change with time, some information about him must be unique at a given point of time. For example, an employee must have only one cost center at a given point of time. However, he can have two emergency addresses at the same time. Also, some data must exist without gaps, whereas in some data gaps are allowed. In SAP, this can be controlled through time constraints. Time constraints can also be specified at subtype level. Note that in personnel administration, the time constraint is applied at day level, whereas in time management, the time constraint is applied at time level. In personnel administration there is no interdependence of infotypes whereas in time management the infotypes are interdependent. You cannot say that a person was both present and absent at the same time, just because the data is in two different infotypes.

1	Record must have no gaps, no overlappings
2	Record may include gaps, no overlappings
3	Record may include gaps, can exist more than once
A	Infotype exists just once from Jan. 1, 1800 to Dec. 12, 9999
B	IT exists for maximum of once from Jan. 1, 1800 to Dec. 12, 9999
T	Time constraint is based on subtype or subtype table
Z	Time constraint for time management infotypes → T554Y

Time constraint table

This field contains the name of the time constraint table if the time constraint is dependent on the subtype. In most cases, both the subtype table and time constraint table is T591A. Where the subtype is a wage type, the subtype table is T512Z and time constraint table is T591B.

Maintenance permitted after leaving

This field determines whether you can maintain the infotype after an employee has left. Regardless of the value in this field you can maintain the infotype after running separation action if the system date is before separation date. This field is particularly important for payroll and time management infotypes.

Blank	Maintenance is permissible
E	Maintenance is not permissible
W	Maintenance with warning is permissible

Access authorization

If you are authorized to see data for a certain PA, you can see all employees who belong to that PA. But some of those employees may have been in a different PA earlier, will you see those records? The answer to that depends on this tick. If this indicator is blank you can see all records of a person, provided you can see one record. If it is ticked, you will see only those records where his PA is within the list of PAs you are authorized to see.

Subtype obligatory

If the layout of an infotype screen depends on the subtype, you must tick this so that the user has to enter the subtype when creating a new record.

Subtype table

Usually, subtypes of an infotype are maintained in table T591A. However, where subtype is a wage type, it is in table T512Z. In time management infotypes also, there are some subtype tables.

Subtype text table

This field contains the text table for the subtype table.

Subtype field

This field contains the field name in the subtype table, which identifies the subtypes. When you enter a subtype, the value is checked against this field.

Accounting/logistics data

This field determines whether you can do cost assignment for an infotype. Infotypes 0014, 0015, 0267, and some time management infotypes have this indicator ticked.

Text allowed

If you set this parameter, SAP allows entry of free text associated with a record (Edit ➤ Maintain Text). This text is stored elsewhere and not in the infotype. However, a flag is kept in the infotype, so that the system knows when it needs to fetch that data.

Copy infotype

In some scenarios, one person can have multiple personnel number in SAP. If you are hiring such a person and specify reference personnel number, the infotypes which have this field ticked get copied. Infotypes 0002, 0006 etc. that contain employee's personal data, which is likely to be same for all personnel numbers, should have this checkbox ticked.

Propose infotype

Infotypes that should be proposed by the system if an employee has a cross-country organizational change have this checkbox ticked.

41.1.5 Display and Selection

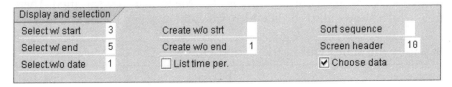

Use of display and selection settings

SAP maintains all infotypes with history. So, when you need to look at data, you need to specify the period for which you want to see the data and only those records are shown which are valid during that period. These date fields are there in the infotype menu you get by running transaction code PA30.

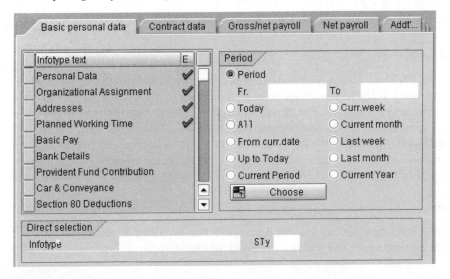

However, it is too much hassle to enter these dates every time and users would like SAP to behave more intelligently. Here you can specify what the system should do, if you omit one or both dates.

Select w/ start

Here you specify what the system should do, if you specify only the from-date and omit the to-date. SAP gives you two options. If you select value 3, it takes to-date to be same as from-date. In this option only those records which are valid on the from-date are shown. If you select value 4, it takes the system date as to-date and all records valid during this period are shown.

3	Records which are valid on Start date
4	Records which are valid between Start date and CPU date

Select w/ end

Here you specify what the system should do, if you specify only the to-date. Obviously, you do not want to see records whose entire validity is after the to-date you specified. There is only one option, 5, which shows all records which are valid anytime before the to-date.

5	Records with valid dates within the period entered

Select w/o date

This is the most common scenario where the user enters neither dates. The options are given below and their descriptions are self-explanatory.

1	Read all records
2	Valid record(s) for CPU date
6	All records from CPU date to 31.12.9999
7	All records from 01.01.1900 to CPU date

List time period

In transaction codes PA20 or PA30, you can also see the records in overview mode. In overview mode, you may want to see all records, or you may want from-date and to-date filter to apply to the overview also. For those infotypes, where you do not expect too many records, you would like to see all records. For these, you leave this field blank. But there are some infotypes, particularly in time management, where there are too many records. There you would like the date filter to apply to overview mode also. For such infotypes, you tick this field.

Create w/o start

If you do not enter a start date on the selection screen when creating a record, the system sets a default date according to the value you enter in this field.

Blank	Infotype dependent, in general no default
1	Hiring date, if no record exists, otherwise blank or 0
2	Start date of the current organizational assignment
3	CPU date

Create w/o end

If you do not enter an end date on the selection screen when creating a record, the system proposes a default date according to the value you enter in this field.

Blank	Infotype dependent, in general no default
1	Default value is 31.12.9999
2	Leaving date
3	Start date of the current record

Sort sequence

When there are multiple records, in what order they should be sorted, is determined by the value in this field.

Field value	First sort by	Then sort by
Blank	subtype ascending	from-date descending
1	from-date descending	subtype ascending
2	subtype ascending	from-date ascending
3	from-date ascending	subtype ascending

Screen header

When you see data in an infotype, you see some header information on the top. This information, e.g. employee's name is useful in understanding the infotype data. The requirement of header is not same for all infotypes. For example, you may want to see employee's work schedule in time infotypes, but not in other infotypes. SAP lets you create different screen headers, and assign them to an infotype here.

Choose data

When you are seeing an infotype record, it is showing data for a validity period. Should the header data be shown for the same period, or should it show the current status? This field determines that. If you set the choose data indicator, the header data is as on the start date of the period, otherwise, it is as on the system date.

41.1.6 Retroactive Accounting Trigger

Retroactive accounting trigger		
☑ Before ERA date	☐ Entry of RA limit time	Past entry all. X
Retr.acct.payr. R	Retr.acct.PDC R	No org.assign. W

If an infotype is changed with retro effect, whether it will trigger retro run for payroll and time management or not is determined by these fields.

Before ERA date

When you enter the master data which can trigger retro payroll, this information is kept in infotype 0003 and triggers retro payroll for the employee from that date. But for each payroll area there is also an earliest retroactive accounting period (transaction PA03) before which payroll cannot run. Therefore, logically you should not be allowed to enter the data for any employee before this period, as retro accounting cannot take place. But if you say that you want to keep the data for information purpose, knowing well that retro accounting will not happen, you may tick this field.

Retroactive accounting relevance for payroll

This field determines whether a change in this infotype for past period triggers retro payroll. If you want to trigger retro payroll only for some fields, but not for others, even that can be done. This field must be carefully set.

Blank	Infotype is not relevant for retroactive accounting
R	Change triggers retroactive accounting
T	Retroactive accounting is field-dependent acc. to T588G

Feature name for payroll recalculation recognition

You can control payroll retro even more finely than at field level. If the value of the earlier field is T, you can enter the name of a feature here. The feature indicated here would return a variable key, which would be used in reading view V_T588G. Therefore, the logic to further determine whether a field triggers retroactive run or not, can be built in the feature specified here.

Entry before time evaluation retroactive accounting limit

For each employee, in infotype 0003 you can maintain 'Earliest personal recalculation date for time evaluation', which prevents retro running of time evaluation before the specified date. It also prevents the entry of time data, which results in retro, prior to this date. But if you say that you want to keep the data for information purpose, knowing fully well that retro accounting will not happen, you may tick this field.

Retroactive accounting relevance for PDC time management

This field determines whether a change in this infotype for past period triggers retro time evaluation. If you want to trigger retro payroll only for some fields but not for the others, even that can be done. This field must be carefully set.

Blank	Infotype is not relevant for PDC retroactive accounting
R	Change triggers retroactive accnt. in PDC time evaluation
T	PDC retroactive accnt. is field-dependent acc. to T588G

Feature name for PDC/time management recalculation recognition

You can control time evaluation retro even more finely than at field level. If the value of the earlier field is T, you can enter the name of a feature here. The feature indicated here would return a variable key, which would be used in reading view V_ T588G. Therefore, the logic to further determine whether a field triggers retroactive run or not, can be built in the feature specified here.

Past entry allowed

The entry in this field determines whether you can enter data in this infotype for a past period.

Blank	Entries in payroll past are permissible: No message
X	Entries in payroll past are permissible: W message
E	Entries in payroll past are not permissible
I	Check for entries in payroll past is infotype-specific. This is valid only for some infotypes.

No organizational assignment

If this infotype is relevant for payroll retro, the system ensures that you are not entering data for a period, prior to the earliest retroactive accounting period of the payroll control record. For this, it needs to find payroll area of the employee from infotype 0001.

However, some payroll-relevant infotypes should also be stored for a time period during which the employee has no organizational assignment (e.g. tax data for the entire year even if the employee entered the company in the middle of the year). In this case, you must specify the indicator 'W' or 'N'.

Blank	Error message if no organizational assignment exists
W	Warning if no organizational assignment exists
N	No message if no organizational assignment exists

41.1.7 Technical Data

Technical data			
Single screen	2000	Dialog module	RP_0000
List screen	3000	Structure	P0000
☐ List entry		Database table	PA0000

Single screen

SAP is used worldwide. The needs of all countries may not be the same. SAP, therefore, provides a number of screens for each infotype. This field specifies which screen the country need to use. Usually SAP takes care to populate this field with the value most suited for your country.

List screen

Same as above for overview screens.

List entry, dialog module, structure, database table

These fields show the technical characteristics of the infotype from view T777D.

41.1.8 Applicant Infotypes

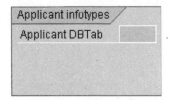

Applicant DB table

This field shows the table name where data for this infotype for applicants is stored.

41.1.9 Other Infotype Properties

Period indicator: key date/interval

Most infotypes are for a period (I), but there are some which are for a single key date (S). Those, which are for a single key date, are:

0015	Additional Payments
0019	Monitoring of Tasks
0028	Internal Medical Service
2010	Employee Remuneration Info
2011	Time Events
2012	Time Transfer Specifications
2013	Quota Corrections

This field is there in the table, but not shown on the screen.

Database name

This field indicates which infotypes are applicable to employee, which to applicant, and which to both. This field is also not shown on the screen.

Technical properties of an infotype

Views T777D and T77ID contain technical properties of an infotype and are maintained automatically when transaction PM01 is used to create the infotype.

41.2 INFOTYPE TEXTS

Functional Consultant	User	Business Process Owner	Senior Management	My Rating	Understanding Level
A	B	B	C		

41.2.1 Purpose

You can create multiple views of an infotype through screen control, you can call them by different names, and you can show different screens when they are called. When an infotype is selected in transaction PA30, etc., the screen control is also selected implicitly. When an infotype record is created, the screen control which was used is also recorded because the record should be displayed or changed using the screen determined through the same screen control.

41.2.2 IMG Node

SM30 ➤ V_T582S

41.2.3 Screen

IType	SC	Infotype text
0216		Garnish. Adjustment
0216	01	Separate Calculation
0216	02	Calculate End Date
0216	03	New Balance
0216	04	Refund

41.2.4 Primary Key

Language Key + Infotype + Infotype Screen Control

41.3   INFOTYPE VALIDITY FOR COUNTRY

Functional Consultant	User	Business Process Owner	Senior Management	My Rating	Understanding Level
A	B	B	C		

41.3.1   Purpose

This view can be used to allow or prevent use of infotypes and subtypes for a country. It does not contain all entries, merely exceptions.

41.3.2   IMG Node

SM30 ➤ V_T582L

41.3.3   Screen

	IType	Infotype text	STyp	Name	CG...	Name of HR ...	Per...	Not p...	Warning
	0006	Addresses	E1		04	Spain	◉	○	○
	0006	Addresses	FPCB		07	Canada	○	◉	○
	0006	Addresses	HKTX		27	Hong Kong	◉	○	○
	0006	Addresses	I1		15	Italy	◉	○	○
	0006	Addresses	J1		22	Japan	◉	○	○

41.3.4   Primary Key

Infotype + Subtype + Country Grouping

41.3.5   Important Fields

Infotype, subtype, and country grouping

You specify whether an infotype and subtype is permitted for a country grouping.

Permitted/not permitted/warning

Specify whether an infotype subtype combination is permitted/not permitted/warning for a country grouping.

41.4 DYNAMIC ACTIONS

Functional Consultant	User	Business Process Owner	Senior Management	My Rating	Understanding Level
A	A	A	A		

41.4.1 Purpose and Overview

This view offers a very powerful set of functionalities, through which you can implement a lot of rules and actions needed by your company.

> You can check data, either with constant values, or with previous values. If the result is 'True', subsequent commands are executed, otherwise they are skipped.
> You can create, copy, modify, or delete another infotype.
> You can set default values for a new record.
> You can call internal, or external routines.
> You can send an e-mail.

These actions are triggered depending on multiple conditions, which you specify; e.g. whether you are creating, changing, or deleting the record, the field in which you entered data, subtype, etc.

This tool is not just powerful, but also complex. It must be used with caution. In skilled hands, with good planning, it can do wonders. Handled carelessly, it can create nightmare.

41.4.2 IMG Node

SM30 ➤ T588Z

41.4.3 Screen

ITy...	STy.	Fi...	F..	No	S	Variable function part
				0	F	GET_NEW_DATES(HBRDYNMS)
0000			04	1		*-- US MODEL: DEFAULT U1/U2 DATES ON NEW HIRE --*
0000			04	2	P	T001P-MOLGA='10'
0000			04	3	P	PSPAR-MASSN='01'
0000			04	4	I	INS,0041,,,(P0000-BEGDA),(P0000-ENDDA)/D
0000			04	5	W	P0041-DAR01='U1'

41.4.4 Primary Key

Infotype + Subtype + Field Name + Function character of step + Sequence Number

41.4.5 Important Fields

Infotype, subtype, field name

Here you specify the infotype, subtype, and field name for which this step is to be executed.

Function character of step

This field determines whether dynamic action is run when an infotype is added, changed, or deleted. Possible values are:

00	for independent of the function being performed
02	for change
04	for create
06	for change and create
08	for delete
10	for change and delete
12	for create and delete

Sequence number

Here you specify the sequence in which the steps are executed.

Indicator for step

This field determines what this step does. It gives meaning to the variable function part.

P	Check conditions
I	Maintain infotype record
W	Set default values when creating a new record
V	Reference to another step
F	Call routine
M	Send mail

Variable function part

Here you define what the step is supposed to do, e.g. which infotype to maintain, or which condition to check. You may see field help for more information.

41.5 MAIL ON CHANGE TO INFOTYPE RECORD

Functional Consultant	User	Business Process Owner	Senior Management	My Rating	Understanding Level
A	C	C	C		

41.5.1 Purpose

When an infotype is created, changed or deleted, you can send a mail through dynamic action. Through this feature you determine the recipients and content of the mail. This feature can be used for all master data infotypes of both employees and applicants.

41.5.2 IMG Node

PE03 ➤ M0001

41.5.3 Screen

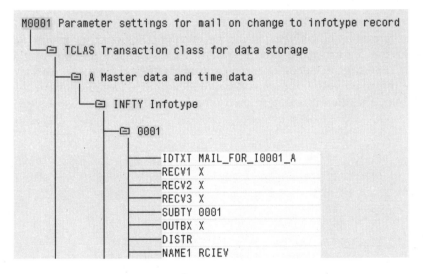

```
M0001 Parameter settings for mail on change to infotype record
   └─⊡ TCLAS Transaction class for data storage
        └─⊡ A Master data and time data
             └─⊡ INFTY Infotype
                  └─⊡ 0001
                       ├──── IDTXT MAIL_FOR_I0001_A
                       ├──── RECV1 X
                       ├──── RECV2 X
                       ├──── RECV3 X
                       ├──── SUBTY 0001
                       ├──── OUTBX X
                       ├──── DISTR
                       └──── NAME1 RCIEV
```

41.5.4 Fields for Decision-making

Company Code
Personnel Area
Personnel Subarea
Employee Group
Employee Subgroup
Infotype
Subtype
Country Grouping
Transaction class for data storage

41.5.5   Return Value

You may see feature help.

41.6   FIELD-SPECIFIC RETROACTIVE ACCOUNTING RECOGNITION

Functional Consultant	User	Business Process Owner	Senior Management	My Rating	Understanding Level
A	B	B	C		

41.6.1   Purpose

In view V_T582A, you specify whether retro accounting for payroll, or time evaluation is triggered if you enter data for past period. If you want retro to be triggered only for some fields of an infotype, but not for the others, you can achieve it through this view. In view V_T582A, you enter T, and here you enter the fields for which past entry is not allowed.

You can achieve even more fine control than that. When a field changes, you can prevent past data entry for one group of employees, while permitting it for another group. To achieve this, you enter the feature name for payroll recalculation recognition, or the feature name for PDC/Time Mgt. recalculation recognition, as the case may be, in view V_T582A. This feature returns a value, which is compared with the variable key in this view, along with the field, and then it is determined whether past data entry is allowed, or not.

41.6.2   IMG Node

SM30 ➤ V_T588G

41.6.3   Screen

Infotype	Infotype text	Var.key	Table	Field	Cat	N...
0000	Actions		P0000	BEGDA	1	☐
0000	Actions		P0000	ENDDA	1	☐
0000	Actions		P0000	MASSN	1	☐
0000	Actions		P0000	PERNR	1	☐

41.6.4   Primary Key

Infotype + Variable key + Table Name + Field Name + Retroactive Accounting Category

41.6.5 Important Fields

Infotype

Infotype for which 'permissibility for past data entry' is to be checked.

Variable key

In view V_T582A, you have two fields: Feature name for payroll recalculation recognition and Feature name for PDC/Time Mgt. recalculation recognition. They return a variable key, which is matched with this field.

Table name and field name

When an infotype is maintained, the screen contains fields from a structure. Although in most cases there is one-to-one correspondence between the two, sometimes, there can be differences. For this reason, you have to specify the structure name and field name of the screen field for which 'permissibility for past data entry' is to be checked.

Retroactive accounting category

You can prevent retro, for payroll, time management, or both (by making two entries).

Data entry not allowed in payroll past

If you tick this field, you cannot enter past data. However, if for an employee, payroll has not been run for a period, you can enter data for that period. Past is defined in this way, and not with respect to the system date.

41.7 RETROACTIVE ACCOUNTING DATE CHANGE

Functional Consultant	User	Business Process Owner	Senior Management	My Rating	Understanding Level
A	X	X	X		

41.7.1 Purpose

When an infotype changes from a past date, and it has impact on payroll or time accounting, this information is recorded in infotype 0003. When payroll or time evaluation runs, these dates are read and these processes start from an appropriate past period or date.

Usually the date on which the infotype changed is the date recorded. However, there may be occasions when you need to set this date further in the past. In some cases, this date has to be one day before the infotype change date. For example, when work schedule in infotype 0007 changes from a certain date, you want time evaluation to start from one day prior to that.

Also in the case of payroll, if there is a time gap between payment date and payroll period, and if infotype change date falls between the two, you may want to run retro for that period also. In that case the earliest master data change date is set to the last day of the payroll period.

41.7.2 IMG Node

PE03 ➤ RETRO

41.7.3 Screen

```
RETRO Different retroactive accounting trigger
   └─🖃 RRTYP Retroactive Accounting Category
        └─🖃 2 Retroactive accounting relevant for time management (PDC)
             └─🖃 MASSN Action Type
                  ├─🖃 10
                  │    └────1
                  └─⊞ otherwise
   └─⊞ otherwise
```

41.7.4 Fields for Decision-making

Country Grouping
Infotype
Subtype
Action Type
Retroactive Accounting Category

41.7.5 Return value

0	No change to the retroactive accounting trigger.
1	Retroactive accounting triggered on the day before the previous specified date. If the employee does not have an active work relationship on the day before, then the retroactive accounting trigger is not changed.
C	The previously specified retroactive accounting date is set to the earliest end date of the payroll periods already calculated and which have a payment date that is later than the retroactive accounting date determined previously. The date is only ever set further in the past and never further in the future. This return value is only meaningful for retroactive accounting category '1', payroll and not time management.

41.8 DEFAULT VALUES FOR INFOTYPES

Functional Consultant	User	Business Process Owner	Senior Management	My Rating	Understanding Level
A	C	C	X		

41.8.1 Purpose

When you copy an infotype, default values are generally taken from the previous record. In certain cases, you may want the values to come from customizing, as they would when you create an infotype. You make that choice here. Note that this feature is only for some infotypes. You should not add any infotype in it.

41.8.2 IMG Node

PE03 ➤ DFINF

41.8.3 Screen

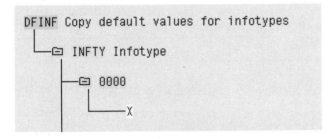

```
DFINF Copy default values for infotypes
   └─🗀 INFTY Infotype
        ├─🗀 0000
        │    └─X
```

41.8.4 Fields for Decision-making

Infotype
Action Type
Reason for Action

41.8.5 Return Value

If the return value is blank, the field is copied from the previous record. If 'X', it is taken from customizing.

Infotype Menus

42.1 INFOTYPE MENU OVERVIEW

Functional Consultant	User	Business Process Owner	Senior Management	My Rating	Understanding Level
A	A	B	C		

42.1.1 Screen

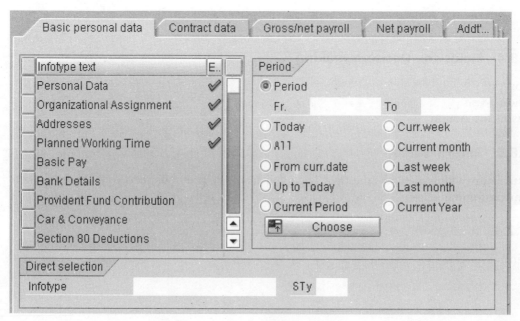

42.1.2 Overview

When you run transaction code PA30 or PA20, you get the screen shown above. There are multiple tabs and several infotypes in each tab. This menu can be set as per user requirement. The menu can depend on user groups. You can specify the tabs in view VV_T588C_I_AL0 and infotypes in the tabs in view V_T588B. While specifying the infotype, you can also specify screen control. With different screen controls, the same infotype can have different names and can give you different screens.

42.2 USER GROUP DEPENDENCY ON MENUS AND INFOGROUPS

Functional Consultant	User	Business Process Owner	Senior Management	My Rating	Understanding Level
A	C	X	X		

42.2.1 Purpose

In this view you define the tabs which you get when you run transaction PA30 or PA20.

42.2.2 IMG Node

SM30 ➤ VV_T588C_I_AL0

42.2.3 Screen

Menu ty.   I

Menu	Text	User-dep.	Reaction	Ref.
01	Basic personal data	✔		01
02	Contract data	✔		01
03	Gross/net payroll	✔		01
04	Net payroll	✔		01
05	Addt'l payroll data	✔		01

42.2.4 Primary Key

Menu Type + Menu

42.2.5 Important Fields

Menu type

View V_T588C is used for five different purposes. For infotypes, the menu type is I.

Menu and text

The menus you see here appear as tab pages when you run transaction PA30 or PA20.

User group dependent

Details of menus are maintained in view V_T588B. If your menus do not depend on user group, you should leave this checkbox blank and define the menu for the reference user group. Otherwise, you should tick this checkbox and maintain menus for each user group for whom you want a different menu, in addition to the menu for the reference user group.

Reaction

If you have not maintained the parameter UGR in the user defaults, the system may show an error (E), use reference user group (blank) or use it with a warning (W).

Reference user group

View V_T588B provides the flexibility to show different menus depending on the user group of the logged on user. If there are many user groups, maintenance of these views could become very complex. Also, if the UGR parameter is not set in user profile, the system does not know what menu to show to the user. This view provides the flexibility to pick up a reference user group, if parameter UGR is not set, or if there is no menu definition in view V_T588B.

42.3 INFOTYPE MENU

Functional Consultant	User	Business Process Owner	Senior Management	My Rating	Understanding Level
A	C	X	X		

42.3.1 Purpose

When you run transaction PA30 or PA20, you get a menu in each tab page. The menus you see in those tab pages is defined here.

42.3.2 IMG Node

SM30 ➤ V_T588B

42.3.3 Screen

	User group	No	Infotype	Scr...	Infotype text	
	01	01	0000		Actions	
	01	02	0001		Organizational Assignment	
	01	03	0002		Personal Data	
	01	04	0006		Addresses	
	01	05	0009		Bank Details	

Menu 01 Basic personal data   ☑ User group-dependent

Reaction

Reference user group 01

42.3.4 Primary Key

Menu type + Infotype menu + User group + Sequence Number

42.3.5 Important Fields

Menu type

Menu type (I); not seen on the screen.

Menu

When you run transaction code PA30 or PA20, you see different tabs. Each tab corresponds to a menu defined in this field. Master list of menu type + menu is maintained in view T588C.

User group

The sequence of infotypes in menu can be varied depending on the user group of the logged on user. User group comes from login (System ≻ User Profile ≻ Own data ≻ Parameters ≻ Parameter ID = UGR). If the user group is blank, or the menu is not defined for your user group, reference user from view T588C is taken.

Sequence number

The sequence in which infotypes are listed in the menu is specified here.

Infotype and screen control

Here you specify the infotypes, which are seen on a tab page. If there are different screen controls maintained in table T588S, you also specify the screen control. When you select an entry in the menu, the screen control value is also known. This is an input to feature Pnnnn, which along with view T588M determines the screen to be shown.

Infotype Screens

43.1 OVERVIEW

Functional Consultant	User	Business Process Owner	Senior Management	My Rating	Understanding Level
A	A	A	C		

43.1.1 Infotype Screen

Multiple screens for an infotype

When you run an action, or maintain an infotype through PA30, you are presented a screen. For each infotype, SAP has created multiple screens, because the requirements may differ from country to country, company to company, and even within a company.

Selecting the screen for an infotype

When you install SAP, it shows you the screen most suitable for your country, which is specified in view V_T582A. However, SAP has kept the system flexible, and you can change the configuration to get a different screen instead.

Getting different screens based on context

You can not only change the screen, but you can use multiple screens if you so require. The requirement can arise either because you want to use different screens for

➢ Different set of employees, or
➢ Different subtypes, or
➢ Different purpose.

Screen control

There are four ways, in which you get an infotype screen. No matter in which way you get your infotype screen, you always get value for a data item called screen control. The following table explains how you get the value of screen control in each case.

Entering the infotype number in PA30, PA20, etc.	If you just enter infotype, screen control is blank. If you want a specific screen control, specify infotype followed by screen control, e.g. 0027/01 (note that 27/01 does not work).
Selecting the infotype from the list of values in the infotype field in PA30, PA20, etc.	The list of values comes from view V_T582S, which contains infotype + screen control.
Selecting from the infotype menu in PA30, PA20, etc.	Infotype menu comes from view V_T588B, which contains infotype + screen control.
Executing an infogroup by running an action	Infogroups are defined in view V_T588D, which contains infotype + screen control.

Different screens for different screen control

The screen control you get from these sources is passed to Pnnnn set of features, which may give you different screen depending on your screen control.

When you create an infotype, the following process is followed.

> For the infotype (without screen control), the default screen is specified in view V_T582A.
> Then the system goes to view T588M. There, for each infotype, a feature is specified.
> The system goes to that feature with details of the employee, infotype, subtype and screen control number.
> Screen control field is available only in certain features. You can either see individual features to see whether this field is available, or query table T549B with Indicator for type of feature = 'F' and Variable key for T549B = 'ITBLD'.
> Depending on the data and decision tree built in the feature, it comes back with a return value.
> The system again goes to view T588M, and depending on the default screen number, and variable key (return value from the feature) determines the screen to show you.

If this sounds too complicated, don't worry. In most cases, you just get the default screen number specified in view V_T582A. But, if need be, SAP has the flexibility to show you different screens for different employees or purpose. To get full flavor of the flexibility available, you may see documentation of feature P0001.

Seeing the screen number

Finally, to see which screen you have, you may see screen number in System > Status.

43.1.2 List Screen

Many infotypes have two screens, a form screen and a list screen. The list screen shows the overview of many records, showing only the important fields. The form screen shows a single record. One can easily switch from one to the other. Like form screen, the list screen can also be customized.

Just as you can get a different single screen, depending on the employee characteristics, subtype, screen control, etc., you can get a different list screen. The data source and access path remain the same.

43.1.3 Screen Header

Infotype screen header

When you see an infotype screen, you see two parts. The top part, screen header, contains general information, e.g. the employee's name. The bottom part, screen detail, contains data items for that infotype either as single screen, or list screen.

Different screen headers for different infotypes

Although one might think that all infotypes require the same header, it is not really so. For example, in time infotypes, you may want to see the employee's work schedule rule, but it is not relevant for other infotypes.

Configuring screen headers

A summary of how you get the header is given below. When you go to 'Personnel Management ➤ Personnel Administration ➤ Customizing User Interfaces ➤ Change Screen Header' node in IMG, it gives the following screen. Here, you understand what they are and how they are related to each other. Detail of each item is covered in following chapters.

Header structure per infotype
Header Modifier
Infotype header definition
Passport photo
Infotype header data selection control
Field names different to DDIC entry

Header structure per infotype

For each infotype, you specify a screen header.

Infotype	Infotype text	Screen header	Choose data
0000	Actions	00	☑
0001	Organizational Assignment	03	☑
0002	Personal Data	01	☐

Header modifier

For a screen header, you can get different header modifiers for employee master data and applicant data.

Screen header	Tr.Class	Header mod.

Infotype header definition

For a header modifier you define which fields from which infotypes appear in which lines and positions of the header.

Header Mod	Line	Column	IT	STy.	Field name	Fldty	Keyword	Lngth	Con.
00	1	01	0001		ENAME	DAT		00	
00	2	01	0001		PERSG	DTX		00	
00	2	30	0001		BUKRS	DTX		00	
00	3	01	0001		PERSK	DTX		00	
00	3	30	0001		WERKS	DTX		00	

Passport photo

This node shows view V_T77S0SC. Here, you specify the document type you use to enter passport photos in the optical archive.

Infotype header data selection control

This node shows view T588H. Here, you can specify whether the header data is for the current date or for the record date, at subtype level. Note that in V_582A_B, you can define it at infotype level.

Field names different to DDIC entry

This node shows view T588L. When you are defining the field description in a header in view T588J, you can use any of the field descriptions defined in the data dictionary. However, if your need is not met through these, SAP lets you enter a keyword in view T588J and enter its description in view T588L, thus giving you total control over field description.

43.1.4 Fast Entry Screen

In view T588C, for menu type I, there are two menus: 07 (Fast entry of master data) and 09 (Fast entry of time data). When you run transaction PA70, the menu is shown from view V_T588B for menu type I, and menu 07. Similarly, when you run transaction PA71, the menu is shown from view V_T588B for menu type I, and menu 09.

When you select a menu item, the system has to determine the screens to show you. These are defined in view T588Q. In this view, you define the screen for default values, screen for fast entry, and report name for employee selection. These are at infotype + screen control level.

View T588R lets you assign multiple selection reports to an infotype, which are available in 'Preselect using report' field for you to choose from.

43.2   FEATURES FOR SCREEN CONTROL

Functional Consultant	User	Business Process Owner	Senior Management	My Rating	Understanding Level
A	C	X	X		

43.2.1   Purpose

You can use these features to determine which screen the user gets depending on the organizational assignment of the employee and other factors. In some features, screen control is also a field for decision-making.

43.2.2   IMG Node

PE03 ➤ Pnnnn where nnnn is infotype number.

43.2.3   Screen

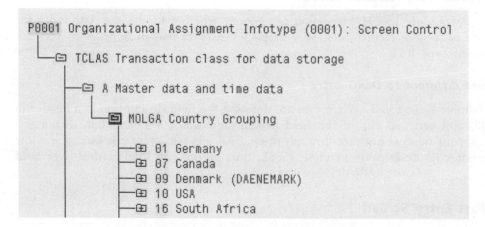

43.2.4   Fields for Decision-making

These features use structure PME04, which has the following fields. In each feature, a subset of these fields is available based on appropriateness.

Employee-related fields

When an infotype is created, the personnel number is available. The following fields can be determined from that: Country Grouping, Company Code, Personnel Area, Personnel Subarea, Employee Group, Employee Subgroup, Work Contract, Personnel subarea grouping for absence and attendance types, Personnel Number.

Infotype-related fields

When an infotype is created, the following fields are available: infotype, subtype, infotype screen control.

Action-related fields

If you are running an action, the following fields are available: infogroup number, action type, reason for action.

Other fields

Transaction class for data storage (determined from transaction), User group (comes from the user parameter), Number of the following screen, Function code (used in flow control, you may see table T185F).

43.2.5 Return Value

In the decision tree, you decide a set of return values. These values are used in view T588M to decide the screen that is shown to the user.

43.3 INFOTYPE SCREEN CONTROL

Functional Consultant	User	Business Process Owner	Senior Management	My Rating	Understanding Level
A	A	A	X		

43.3.1 Purpose

This view determines which screen the user gets, and which fields are standard/required/optional/output/hidden/initial.

43.3.2 IMG Node

SM30 ➤ T588M

43.3.3 Screen

	Mod. pool	Screen	Feature	Variable key	Alt. screen	Next screen
	MP000000	2000			0	0
	MP000100	2000	P0001		2000	0
	MP000100	2000		07	2007	0
	MP000100	2000		09	2000	0

Module pool	MP000000	Variable key	
Standard screen	2000	Feature	
Alternative screen		[Feature]	
Next screen			

Scrn control

Grp	Field name	Field text	Std	RF	OF	Outp	Hide	Init
001	P0000-STAT1	Customer-Specific Status	●	○	○	○	○	○
002	Q0000-RFPNR	Reference personnel number	○	○	○	○	●	○
003	P0000-STAT3	Special Payment Status	●	○	○	○	○	○
004	PSPAR-PLANS	Position	●	○	○	○	○	○
005	P0000-MASSN	Action Type	●	○	○	○	○	○
006	P0000-MASSG	Reason for Action	●	○	○	○	○	○
007	BZPNR		●	○	○	○	○	○

43.3.4 Primary Key

Module pool name + Standard Screen + Variable key

43.3.5 Important Fields

Module pool name

MP followed by infotype name, e.g. MP002100.

Standard screen

This is determined from view V_T582A.

Feature for determining variable key

SAP provides flexibility to show different screens depending on a number of parameters. These parameters are used to build a decision tree in feature Pnnnn. The name of the feature is specified here. The feature name is specified in a row where the variable key is blank. Other entries for that screen have variable key. The feature applies to all these entries, even though the feature column is blank.

Variable key

The above feature provides a return value, which is used here.

Alternative screen

This field contains the screen number, which is shown for the standard screen (picked from view V_T582A) and screen control returned from the feature.

Next screen

Here you specify the screen number which usually follows the screen being processed. Screen number 0 causes the transaction to be terminated or the program/screen to go back one level.

Screen field properties

When you select a line on the screen, and click details, you see the second screenshot. Here, you can see whether a field is standard/required/optional/output/hidden/initial. In the case of initial, the screen field is hidden and the system initializes the corresponding field content if you create or copy an infotype record.

43.4 HEADER STRUCTURE PER INFOTYPE

Functional Consultant	User	Business Process Owner	Senior Management	My Rating	Understanding Level
A	B	B	X		

43.4.1 Purpose

This is a view of table T582A. In this view you specify the screen header for each infotype and whether the header data is for the current date or for the start date of the infotype record.

43.4.2 IMG Node

SM30 ➤ V_582A_B

43.4.3 Screen

Infotype	Infotype text	Screen header	Choose data
0000	Actions	10	☑
0001	Organizational Assignment	03	☑
0002	Personal Data	01	☐

43.5 HEADER MODIFIER

Functional Consultant	User	Business Process Owner	Senior Management	My Rating	Understanding Level
A	B	B	X		

43.5.1 Purpose

In view V_582A_B you define a screen header for an infotype. An infotype is used both for employees and for applicants. If you want to show one screen header for employee and another for applicant, you can define that here. The header modifier selected from here has a definition in view T588J, which is shown on the screen.

43.5.2 IMG Node

SM30 ➤ V_T588I

43.5.3 Screen

Screen header	Tr.class	Header mod.
00	A	06
00	B	04
01	A	04
02	A	04

43.5.4 Primary Key

Key for screen header layout + Country Grouping + Transaction class for data storage

43.5.5 Important Fields

Screen header

For an infotype, this is picked up from V_582A_B.

Transaction class

Here you specify whether the header is for employee or for applicant, as you can have different headers for them.

Header modifier

This is the header you see on the screen. It is defined in view T588J.

43.6 HEADER DEFINITION

Functional Consultant	User	Business Process Owner	Senior Management	My Rating	Understanding Level
A	B	B	X		

43.6.1 Purpose

This view contains the definition of infotype header.

43.6.2 IMG Node

SM30 ➤ T588J

43.6.3 Screen

	Header Mod	Line	Column	IT	STy.	Field name	Fldty	Keyword	Lngth	Con.
	00	1	01	0001		ENAME	DD1			
	00	1	14	0001		ENAME	DAT			
	00	2	01	0001		PERSG	DD2			
	00	2	14	0001		PERSG	DAT			
	00	2	17	0001		PERSG	DTX			

43.6.4 Primary Key

Screen header modifier + Line number of screen header + Column number of screen header

43.6.5 Important Fields

Header modifier

The header modifier for an infotype is determined via V_582A_B and T588I. What fields are shown for the header modifier is defined here.

Line

Here you specify the line of the screen header in which the field will appear.

Column

Here you specify the position of the field in the line in terms of column number.

Infotype, subtype, field name

Here you specify which field from which infotype and subtype is shown.

Field type

When you are creating the header, you need field description, as well as field value. In SAP, for each data element, you have descriptions of different lengths, so that you can use them as per available space. This field lets you decide whether you are showing data, related text, or field description. In the case of field description, you also specify which description. Depending on the field you have chosen, the list of values is appropriately shown.

DAT	field contents
DTX	field content text (if available)
PIC	passport photo
DD1	field short text according to DDIC
DD2	middle field text according to DDIC
DD3	long field text according to DDIC
DD4	field header according to DDIC
TXD	like 'TXT' but with a DDIC interface to the relevant field
TXT	user-defined text according to customizing settings

Note that the field types 'TXT' and 'TXD' are only available for compatibility reasons. It is recommended that you use the field types 'DD1' and 'DD4' instead.

Keyword

DD1 to DD4 give you the flexibility of choosing the field description, which you like most. But what if you don't like any? Normally you choose field description from the field you are displaying, but it is not necessary. For example, if you want to display RUFNM field of infotype 0002, where all the descriptions are 'Known as', but you would like to describe it as 'Name', you can choose any other field of that infotype, or another infotype, and display its description. To show name in the description, you could choose ENAME field of infotype 0001, with field type DD1. Your objective is just to get description; it does not matter where it comes from.

However, if your need is still not met, SAP lets you enter a keyword here (field type must be 'TXT' or 'TXD'), and enter the description in view T588L. Note that these field types are available only for downward compatibility reasons and you can use them only where possible.

Length

Even though the length of the field you specify may be longer, you can specify the display length here. If this field is blank, the length is taken from data dictionary.

Conversion

You can format the data, e.g. displaying leading zeros or concatenating with next field.

43.7 PHOTO

Functional Consultant	User	Business Process Owner	Senior Management	My Rating	Understanding Level
A	X	X	X		

43.7.1 Purpose

Semantic abbreviation PHOTO of the ADMIN group enables you to determine the document type you use to enter passport photos in the optical archive for use in HR.

43.7.2 IMG Node

SM30 ➤ V_T77S0SC

43.7.3 Screen

System Switch (from Table T77S0)			
Group	Sem. abbr.	Value abbr.	Description
ADMIN	PHOTO	HRICOLFOTO	Document type for (passport) photo in HR

43.8 HEADER DATA SELECTION CONTROL

Functional Consultant	User	Business Process Owner	Senior Management	My Rating	Understanding Level
A	C	C	X		

43.8.1 Purpose

When you are seeing an infotype record, you may be seeing data for present, past, or future. If you are seeing data for past, should the header information, e.g. employee's grade or work schedule, also be for that period, or should it be for current period? SAP lets you decide what you would like to see. You can decide this at infotype level and record in view V_582A_B. If you want to make different choices for different subtypes in an infotype, you can decide that and record it here. When you create, change, or display an infotype with a subtype, the system looks at this view and determines whether header data should be for current period, or for the period for which details are being shown.

43.8.2 IMG Node

SM30 ➢ T588H

43.8.3 Screen

Header Mod	IType	STy.	Data sel.
06	0002		☐

43.8.4 Primary Key

Screen header modifier + Infotype + Subtype

43.8.5 Important Fields

Header modifier, Infotype, subtype

The header modifier for an infotype is determined via V_582A_B and T588I. Infotype and subtype is specified by the user who is creating, changing, or displaying infotype data.

Data selection

If you tick this field, the header data is as on the start date of the period, otherwise, it is as on the system date. In the case of clash between this field and choose data field in view V_582A_B, the data in the header is shown as on the system date.

43.9 HEADER FIELD NAMES

Functional Consultant	User	Business Process Owner	Senior Management	My Rating	Understanding Level
A	C	C	X		

43.9.1 Purpose

When you are defining the field description in a header in view T588J, you can use any of the field descriptions defined in the data dictionary. However, if your need is not met through these, SAP lets you enter a keyword in view T588J and enter its description in view T588L, thus giving you total control over field description.

43.9.2 IMG Node

SM30 ➢ T588L

43.9.3 Screen

Key	Different key word from DDIC
AG1	AppGr
AG2	Applicant group
AK1	AppRng.
AK2	Applicant range

43.9.4 Primary Key

Different field names for screens than DDIC entries

43.10 SCREEN TYPES FOR FAST ENTRY

Functional Consultant	User	Business Process Owner	Senior Management	My Rating	Understanding Level
A	X	X	X		

43.10.1 Purpose and Overview

In this view you define the screens for fast entry using transactions PA70 and PA71.

In view T588C, for menu type I, there are two menus:
    07 (Fast entry of master data) and
    09 (Fast entry of time data).

When you run transaction PA70, the menu is shown from view V_T588B for menu type I, and menu 07. Similarly, when you run transaction PA71, the menu is shown from view V_T588B for menu type I, and menu 09.

When you select a menu item, the system has to determine the screens to show you. These are defined in this view.

43.10.2 IMG Node

SM30 ➤ T588Q

43.10.3 Screen

Infotype	Screen control	Default value	Fast data entry	Selection report
0012			5000	RPLFST00
0014		4000	5000	RPLFST00
0015		4000	5000	RPLFST00
0067		5000	5000	

43.10.4 Primary Key

Infotype + Infotype Screen Control

43.10.5 Important Fields

Infotype and screen control

Here you specify the infotype and screen control for which you are defining the screens.

Default value

Here you specify the screen number for entering default values.

Fast data entry

Here you specify the screen number for entering data for fast entry.

Selection report

When you do fast entry using transaction PA70, or PA71, you get a selection screen, where you can give a report name, and the population returned by it is available for fast data entry. You can specify the report name here. Perhaps this field is no longer used. Now you can assign multiple reports to an infotype in view T588R, and choose from them in the menu.

43.11   SELECTION REPORTS FOR FAST DATA ENTRY

Functional Consultant	User	Business Process Owner	Senior Management	My Rating	Understanding Level
A	X	X	X		

43.11.1   Purpose

When you do fast entry using transaction PA70, or PA71, you get a selection screen. In this part ⦿ Preselect using report   RPLFST00   ⟳ you can give a report name, and the population returned by it is available for fast data entry. In this view, you can assign one or more module pool to an infotype. You can use any of these programs to create data for fast entry.

43.11.2   IMG Node

SM30 ≻ T588R

43.11.3   Screen

IType	Mod. pool.	Title
0012	RPLFST00	Personnel Number Selection for Fast Data Entry
0014	RPLFST00	Personnel Number Selection for Fast Data Entry
0015	RPLFST00	Personnel Number Selection for Fast Data Entry
0015	RPLFSTW0	Personnel Number Selection for Fast Data Entry
0024	RPLFST00	Personnel Number Selection for Fast Data Entry

43.11.4   Primary Key

Infotype + Module pool name

Infotype Change Tracking

44.1 INFOTYPES TO BE LOGGED

Functional Consultant	User	Business Process Owner	Senior Management	My Rating	Understanding Level
A	A	A	A		

44.1.1 Overview

Whenever an infotype is created or changed, SAP maintains the date of last change and the user who changed it. However, you don't know what the field values were before change. Also, when a record is deleted, there is no information left.

For some important infotypes, you may want to keep track of changes. SAP lets you do that. You can specify the infotypes that are to be logged automatically when a change is made (deletion, change, insertion).

The changes made to an infotype are logged per field. You are free to choose which fields are to be logged. You can group fields together in field groups that are always logged, i.e. even if you only make a change to one of the fields in the group.

You can specify a supplementary field group for each field group, which is always logged at the same time as the field group. If, however, a field in the supplementary field group changes, this change is not logged.

44.1.2 Purpose

In this view you specify the infotypes to be logged. Unless an infotype is present in this view it is not logged.

44.1.3 IMG Node

SM30 ➤ V_T585A

44.1.4 Screen

	Tr.class	Infotype	Infotype text
	A	0001	Organizational Assignment
	A	0002	Personal Data
	A	0008	Basic Pay
	A	0014	Recurring Payments/Deductions
	A	0015	Additional Payments

44.1.5 Primary Key

Transaction class for data storage + Infotype

44.1.6 Important Fields

Transaction class

Here you specify whether the infotype to be logged is for employees, or for applicants.

Infotype and text

Here you specify the infotype which is to be logged.

44.1.7 Reports

S_AHR_61016380—Logged Changes in Infotype Data

You can use this report to see infotype data change which has been logged. There are rich selection options.

```
Logged Changes in Infotype Data
_____

                    Long-term documents


 _____
| PersNo    Infotype Date       Time      SqNo Changed by   |
|_____|
| 00121715 A 0002   07.07.2006 13:58:35 0001 QHRPKA000137   |
| 00121715 A 0001   07.07.2006 13:59:37 0001 QHRPKA000137   |
| 00121715 A 0001   27.09.2006 11:27:34 0001 QHRPKA000137   |
|_____|
```

44.2   FIELD GROUP DEFINITION

Functional Consultant	User	Business Process Owner	Senior Management	My Rating	Understanding Level
A	X	X	X		

44.2.1   Purpose

In an infotype, there may be certain fields which you want to track, while there may be other fields which you don't want to track. SAP lets you do that. Here you specify the fields you want to track. You can group the fields in field groups. If any field in the group changes, the old and new values of all the fields in the group are recorded. A field can be in more than one field groups.

44.2.2   IMG Node

SM30 ➢ V_T585B

44.2.3   Screen

	Infotype	Infotype text	Field grp	Field Name	A/L
	0001	Organizational Assignment	01	ABKRS	☐
	0001	Organizational Assignment	01	ANSVH	☐
	0001	Organizational Assignment	01	BTRTL	☐
	0001	Organizational Assignment	01	BUKRS	☐
	0001	Organizational Assignment	01	KOSTL	☐

44.2.4   Primary Key

Infotype + Field group for creating IT log + Field Name

44.2.5   Important Fields

Infotype

Here you specify the infotype whose fields are being grouped in field groups.

Field group

A field group consists of multiple fields. If any field in a field group changes, entire field group is logged.

Field name

Here you specify the fields in the field group.

Indicator for entry of additional data

Here you define whether or not one can enter additional controlling objects for the infotype.

44.3 FIELD GROUP CHARACTERISTICS

Functional Consultant	User	Business Process Owner	Senior Management	My Rating	Understanding Level
A	X	X	X		

44.3.1 Purpose

Infotype logging can be used for two purposes: for transferring changed data to other systems (short-term documents) and for keeping track of who changed what and when (long-term documents). Here you specify which type of document is created by a field group. You can also specify that a supplementary field group should be recorded along with a field group.

44.3.2 IMG Node

SM30 ➤ V_T585C

44.3.3 Screen

Tr.class	Infotype	Infotype text	DocFieldGr	Doc.type	SupFldGr.
A	0001	Organizational Assignment	01	L	01
A	0001	Organizational Assignment	01	S	01
A	0002	Personal Data	01	L	02
A	0008	Basic Pay	01	L	03

44.3.4 Primary Key

Transaction class for data storage + Infotype + Document trigger field group + Document relevance (short-term/long-term)

44.3.5 Important Fields

Transaction class

Here you specify whether the infotype to be logged is for employees, or for applicants.

Infotype and document trigger field group

Here you specify the infotype and field group whose document type and supplementary field group you are defining.

Document type

Long-term documents are sorted by personnel number and infotype. They are used for revision purposes, in other words, to find out who changed, deleted or created what and when.

Short-term documents are sorted by the date on which the last change was made. They can be used to link external systems to the SAP. In this way, customer-specific programs can be used to evaluate short-term documents and the modified data can then be transferred to the external system.

Supplementary field group

If you specify a field group here, that field group is also logged whenever a document is created because of change in document trigger field group. But the reverse is not true; i.e. if a field in supplementary field group changes, no document is created.

44.4 REPORT START LOGS

Functional Consultant	User	Business Process Owner	Senior Management	My Rating	Understanding Level
A	A	A	A		

44.4.1 Purpose

You may like to keep track of running of important programs, when they were run, who ran them, and with what parameters. You can do that by specifying them in this view. A record is created, every time these programs are run. You can also specify whether this record should be created only for online reports, or for background reports, or for both. This facility works only if the programs use logical database PNP.

44.4.2 IMG Node

SM30 ➤ V_T599R

44.4.3 Screen

Prog.Name	Record online	Prot batch
ADP_PU12_P00	☐	☐
DBPNPSEQ	☐	☐
H04UP002	☐	☐
HARCALC0	☐	☐

44.4.4 Primary Key

ABAP program name

44.4.5 Important Fields

Program name

Here you specify the program name whose start is recorded.

Record online

Tick this checkbox if you want to record when the program is run online.

Protocol batch

Tick this checkbox if you want to record when the program is run in batch.

44.4.6 Reports

S_AHR_61016381—Log of Report Starts

If you are logging report-starts, you can use this report to see the log.

Maintain log					
Report	Title		User	Date	Time
ZRPA0196	Personal Details in SAP HR		QHRPKA000137	03.12.2006	09.56

S_PH0_48000151—Maintain Log

You can use this report to delete log entries. The report output is similar to that of 'S_AHR_61016381—Log of Report Starts'. You can delete selected logs from this list, or you may delete all logs.

Cost Assignment

Functional Consultant	User	Business Process Owner	Senior Management	My Rating	Understanding Level
A	A	A	A		

45.1.1   Purpose and Overview

Charging personnel costs to cost objects

Personnel costs are determined in payroll and transferred to Controlling. Controlling objects (such as cost centers) are debited with these primary costs in Controlling. Costs can be assigned to various controlling objects. In the case of cost assignment the data is transferred from payroll to FI/CO through cluster table C1.

Master cost center

Personnel costs are most commonly charged to the employee's master cost center, which is maintained in infotype 0001. When payroll is run, this cost center is transferred to table WPBP, from where it is picked up when FI document is created.

However, if an employee is deployed to another cost center, you may like to charge his costs to the cost center where he is deployed. This can be done by changing the cost center in infotype 0001 itself. However, this may not be possible, if the employee's cost center is derived from the position to which he is assigned.

You may not change the cost center in infotype 0001, either because you don't want to change the employee's master cost center (because the deployment is a temporary one), or because you are not allowed to change the cost center (because it is derived from the position).

Cost assignment

In such cases, you may specify that the employee's cost be charged to another cost center in infotype 0027 (cost distribution). Infotype 0027 gives you a number of options:

> ➤ You can specify whether you want to charge wages/salaries, or travel costs to another cost center.
> ➤ You can specify that the cost be born between multiple cost centers, in the proportions you define.
> ➤ You can charge the cost to other cost objects, e.g. purchase order, sales order, WBS element, etc.

Cost assignment of specific costs

SAP provides you even more flexibility. You may want to charge a specific payment, e.g. bonus, or a specific time, e.g. training, to a different cost object. You can achieve that by doing cost assignment of a specific infotype record. You can do cost assignment in payroll infotypes 0014, 0015 and 0267. Similarly, you can specify cost assignments in time management infotypes 2001 (absences), 2002 (attendances), 2003 (substitutions), 2004 (availability), 2005 (overtime) and 2010 (employee remuneration info).

Specifying cost assignment in time recording systems

When employees enter their time data at external time recording systems, they can also record information regarding cost assignment there at the same time. This data can be uploaded to the SAP system and stored in the time events infotype (2011).

Infotypes in which cost assignment is permitted

You can control the infotypes where cost assignment can be done (view V_T582A and T582Z), which fields are available and their properties (view V_T588N), and whether the fields and their properties can differ from employee to employee (view T588O).

Activity allocation

All these methods are for transfer of actual costs. SAP also lets you transfer cost on the basis of activity performed, which is priced, through activity allocation.

Cost assignment screen

If you click Cost assignment , you get the screen shown below, where you can define whom to charge the costs.

45.1.2 Screen

Cost Assignment Defaults

Account Assignment

Business Area		
Cost Center		Order
WBS Element		Network
Cost Object		Company Code	0100

Transfer

45.1.3 Cost Assignment Fields

SAP lets you customize the fields of cost assignment subscreen shown above. If you want the fields to be different for different groups of employees, you create a feature and specify it in view T588O.

The fields which are available for cost assignment are defined in view V_T588N. This definition depends on the variable key returned by the feature. Hence, the fields can be different for different employees.

After the fields available for cost assignment are determined in view V_T588N, the system selects the most appropriate screen from table TCOBL, which is maintained through 'Maintain Subscreens for Controlling Objects'.

45.2 SCREEN MODIFICATION FOR ASSIGNMENT DATA

Functional Consultant	User	Business Process Owner	Senior Management	My Rating	Understanding Level
A	X	X	X		

45.2.1 Purpose and Overview

When you do cost assignment, you get a screen. SAP allows you to customize this screen, so that the users see only those fields, which are implemented. Apart from simplifying the screen, this prevents entry of unwanted data. SAP also allows this screen to differ from one group of employees to another.

SAP has defined function module RP_TIME_COBL_002 for cost Assignment. If the layout of this screen is employee dependent, you can specify a feature in view T588O. If the screen is not employee dependent, you do not specify any feature in view T588O. The value returned by the feature is used in view V_T588N to determine the fields, which are shown on the screen.

45.2.2 IMG Node

SM30 ➤ T588O

45.2.3 Screen

Function Module	Feature
RP_TIME_003	
RP_TIME_COBL_001	
RP_TIME_COBL_002	
RP_TRAVEL_COBL_1200	TRVCO
RP_TRAVEL_COBL_1700	TRVCO

45.2.4 Primary Key

Name of Function Module

45.3 SCREEN MODIFICATION FOR ACCOUNT ASSIGNMENT BLOCK

Functional Consultant	User	Business Process Owner	Senior Management	My Rating	Understanding Level
A	X	X	X		

45.3.1 Purpose and Overview

When you do cost assignment, you get a screen. SAP allows you to customize this screen, so that the users see only those fields, which are implemented. Apart from simplifying the screen, this prevents entry of unwanted data. SAP also allows this screen to differ from one group of employees to another.

SAP has defined function module RP_TIME_COBL_002 for cost Assignment. If the layout of this screen is employee dependent, you can specify a feature in view T588O. If the screen is not employee dependent, you do not specify any feature in view T588O.

In view V_T588N, you specify the list of fields (variables) for cost assignment. If the screen is employee dependent, then you specify the fields for each value the feature might return.

For each field, you specify the field characteristics. When you specify the field attributes, you can hide it, display it in input or output mode, highlight it, etc. You can also specify the field, in which the cursor is placed.

45.3.2 IMG Node

SM30 ➤ V_T588N

45.3.3 Screen

Function Module	RP_TIME_COBL_002	
Variable key	9999	
Variable name	COBL-AUFNR	Order

Field attributes	
Reqd entry	0
Input field	1
Output field	1
Highlighted	0
Invisible	0
Active	1
Cursor pos.	

45.3.4 Primary Key

Name of Function Module + Variable key + Variable name

45.3.5 Important Fields

Name of function module

SAP has defined function module RP_TIME_COBL_002 for cost assignment.

Variable key

If the layout is employee dependent, a feature is specified in view T588O. The return key of the feature is entered here to determine the screen layout. If no feature is specified in view T588O, this field should be blank.

Variable name

This contains the name of the variable (field), which appears on the screen. It should be available in the function module.

Required entry

Here you define whether a field is mandatory or not.

Input field

Here you define whether a field is enterable or not.

Output field

Here you define whether a field is output or not.

Highlighted

Here you define whether a field is highlighted or not.

Invisible

Here you define whether a field is invisible or not.

Active

Here you define whether a field is active or not.

Cursor position

Here you define the field on which the cursor will be positioned.

45.4 SUBSCREENS FOR CONTROLLING OBJECTS

Functional Consultant	User	Business Process Owner	Senior Management	My Rating	Understanding Level
A	X	X	X		

45.4.1 Purpose

Here you can maintain subscreens for controlling objects, from which the most appropriate one is selected for cost assignment. The fields decided in view V_T588N are compared with the screens available in this transaction, and the most suitable screen is selected and shown. When multiple screens meet your requirement, the screen with highest priority is selected.

45.4.2 IMG Node

Transaction OXK1 Maintain Coding Block Subscreens

45.4.3 Screen

Subscreen	1001	BusArea/CCtr
Priority	3	☑ Active

Field Name	Position	With Text	
Accounting Indicator	0	☐	▲
Activity Type	5	☐	▼
Asset	0	☐	
Business Area	1	☐	
Business Process	0	☐	
CRP Calculation	0	☐	
Commitment item	0	☐	
Company Code	0	☐	
Controlling Area	0	☐	
Cost Center	3	☑	

46 Payment Model

46.1 PAYMENT MODEL

Functional Consultant	User	Business Process Owner	Senior Management	My Rating	Understanding Level
B	C	C	X		

46.1.1 Purpose and Overview

You need payment model to take care of complex scenarios, which arise from mismatch in payroll frequency and payment/deduction frequency. Suppose you have a weekly payroll, and monthly deduction. The deduction may be due on 1st of every month, 15th of every month, or last day of every month.

To cater to such situations, you need a payment model. The periodicity of payroll depends on period parameter and date modifier. You define a payment method with same combination of period parameter and date modifier as an employee's payroll area. You also specify the frequency of payment or deduction.

When you select a payment model in V_T549X, you see all the payroll periods. Here you can tick the periods in which payment or deduction should take place.

46.1.2 IMG Node

SM30 ≻ V_T549W

46.1.3 Screen

Paym...	Name	D..	P...	Name per. pa...	C..	Name c...
BB00	Each last period of month	01	04	Bi-Weekly	M	Monthly
BB01	Last pay period of each month	01	04	Bi-Weekly	M	Monthly
BB02	Each last period of month	01	04	Bi-Weekly	Y	Annually
BM00	Each period	01	01	Monthly	M	Monthly

46.1.4 Primary Key

Payment Model

46.1.5 Important Fields

Payment model

Here you specify different payment models you are defining.

Date modifier, period parameter

Here you define the payroll periods of the employees. In SAP, payroll periods are determined from period parameter date modifier combination. This combination should match with the combination for the payroll area.

Cumulation type

This indicates the frequency of payment or deduction.

46.2 PAYMENT PERIODS

Functional Consultant	User	Business Process Owner	Senior Management	My Rating	Understanding Level
B	X	X	X		

46.2.1 Purpose and Overview

Here you specify the payroll periods in which payment or deduction should take place. There is one checkbox for each payroll period. If you tick the checkbox, the payment or deduction takes place.

46.2.2 IMG Node

SM30 ➤ V_T549X

46.2.3 Screen

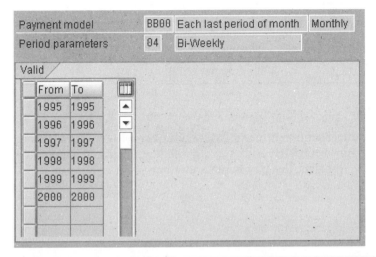

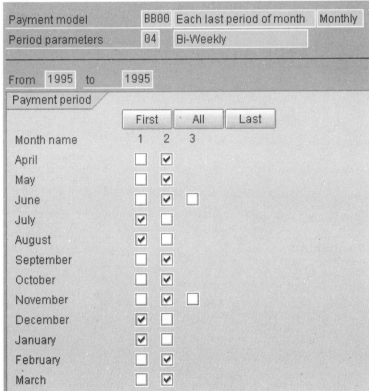

46.2.4 Primary Key

Payment Model + Payroll Year

46.3 EMPLOYEE GROUPING FOR DEFAULT PAYMENT MODEL

Functional Consultant	User	Business Process Owner	Senior Management	My Rating	Understanding Level
B	X	X	X		

46.3.1 Purpose

Default payment model can be different for different categories of employees. Depending on employee characteristics, feature MODDE returns a variable key. That key is matched with the field in view V_T549V to select the payment model based on employee.

46.3.2 IMG Node

PE03 ≻ MODDE

46.3.3 Screen

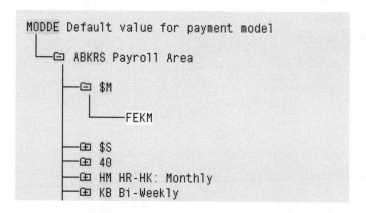

46.3.4 Fields for Decision-making

Company Code
Personnel Area
Personnel Subarea
Employee Group
Employee Subgroup
Payroll Area

46.3.5 Return value

A four-character value, which is used in view V_T549V.

46.4 DEFAULT VALUES FOR PAYMENT MODEL

Functional Consultant	User	Business Process Owner	Senior Management	My Rating	Understanding Level
B	X	X	X		

46.4.1 Purpose

When you enter a wage type in an infotype, depending on employee characteristics (variable key returned by feature MODDE), the system gives you a default payment model.

46.4.2 IMG Node

SM30 ➤ V_T549V

46.4.3 Screen

	VarKey	Wage type	Wage Type Long Text	Payment...	Name
				☑	
				☑	
				☑	
				☑	

46.4.4 Primary Key

Country Grouping + Variable key from feature + Wage type

46.4.5 Important Fields

Variable key

Default payment model can be different for different categories of employees. Depending on employee characteristics, feature MODDE returns a variable key. That key is matched with this field to select the payment model based on employee.

Wage type

You can get different payment models for different wage types. Wage type entered by the user in the infotype is matched with this field to select the payment model based on wage type.

Payment model

Here you enter the payment model proposed by the system as default based on employee characteristics and wage type.

Ad Hoc Query

47.1   AD HOC QUERY

Functional Consultant	User	Business Process Owner	Senior Management	My Rating	Understanding Level
A	A	A	A		

47.1.1   Purpose

Ad hoc query is a powerful means of extracting HR data stored in logical databases. HR has several logical databases, e.g. PNP, PNPCE, PCH, PAP. Logical database PNP and PNPCE store data of all infotypes in personnel administration.

47.1.2   User Menu

S_PH0_48000510—Ad Hoc Query
S_PH0_48000513—Ad Hoc Query

47.1.3 Screen

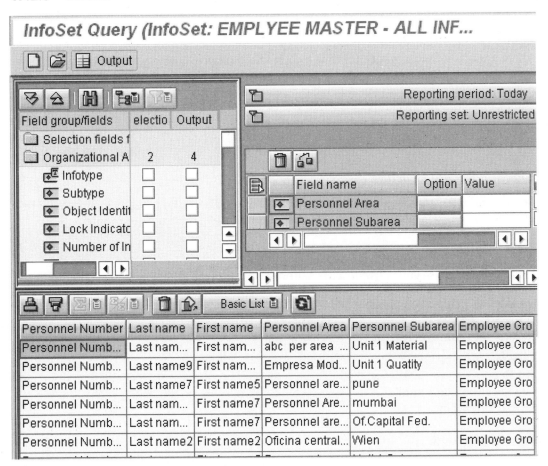

The above screen consists of the following areas:

- ➢ Field selection (top-left quadrant)
- ➢ Record selection (top-right quadrant)
- ➢ Set operations (also in top-right quadrant)
- ➢ Output (bottom half)

47.1.4 Field Selection

This part of the screen contains fields. You can select the fields from
- ➢ Field groups
- ➢ Logical database structure
- ➢ Field catalog

Field groups

Fields are grouped in field groups. You can select the fields, you want to output. You can also select the fields, based on which you want to do record selection.

There are many fields, where there is a code and a description, e.g. employee group. You may want either the code, or description, or both in your output. If you right-click the output checkbox, you can specify what you want in your output. You can make similar choice in selection checkbox.

Field groups can be customized. Your consultant can delete fields you don't want. They can also add more fields, and write code to populate them.

Logical database structure

Logical database structure is similar to field groups. The only difference is that the field groups can be customized, while the logical database structure is standard.

Field catalog

Field catalog gives you all the fields without any grouping.

47.1.5 Record Selection

Record selection consists of the following parts:
- ➢ Reporting period
- ➢ Reporting set
- ➢ Selection conditions
- ➢ Set operations

Reporting period

SAP stores data with history. You therefore need to specify the period for which you want to see the data. You can specify either a date, or a period.

Reporting set

Most of the time, you want to look at relevant data, or data which is filtered according to certain criteria. In ad hoc query, you can define these filters either as Reporting set or as Selection conditions.

When you want to filter data based on field values, you do so through selection conditions. Reporting set caters to more complex filtering scenarios. You can select the persons to be reported on based on organization structure. If you don't find reporting set on your screen, go to 'Extras' and 'Switch on object selection'.

You can also define data sets, and perform set operations to determine the set of employees, you want to report on. This is covered in more detail in 'Set operations' below.

Selection conditions

When you tick the selection checkbox in field group/fields, that field is transferred to this section. You can specify one or more values of that field. The data selected is then restricted only to those records where the data matches the selection condition. You can also specify a range of values. If you want you can specify list or range of values to be excluded.

Set operations

The right-top quadrant of ad hoc query is for specifying the data selection. In this area, you will always see 'Reporting period' and 'Selections'. If you have ticked the fields for selection, they will appear there. You can enhance the data selection by switching on object selection (Extras ➤ Switch on object selection).

If you want the ad hoc query to report for persons, who belong to one or more organizational units, you can do so by selecting the organizational units here. You can also maintain budget allocation using relationship B003, and report based on that structure.

SAP also provides for determination of reporting set in more complex ways. To use this feature, you switch on set operations (Extras ➤ Show set operations). When you do that, the screen changes to show two tabs, 'Selection' and 'Set operations', as shown below.

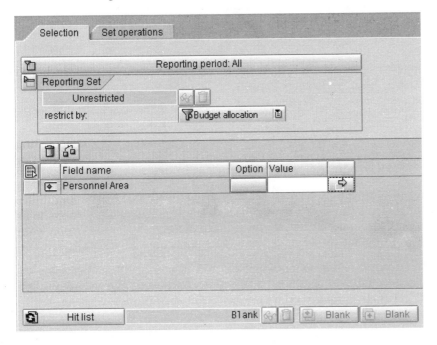

For the purpose of set operations, there are two sets in ad hoc query; set A and set B. When the set operations are switched on, you can add the result of your query in set A by clicking push button ⊞ Blank or in set B by clicking push button ⊞ Blank . If you don't see these push buttons, change the screen resolution to more pixels. In order to perform set operations, you populate both set A, as well as set B. Then you go to 'Set operations' tab page. You will see the following screen.

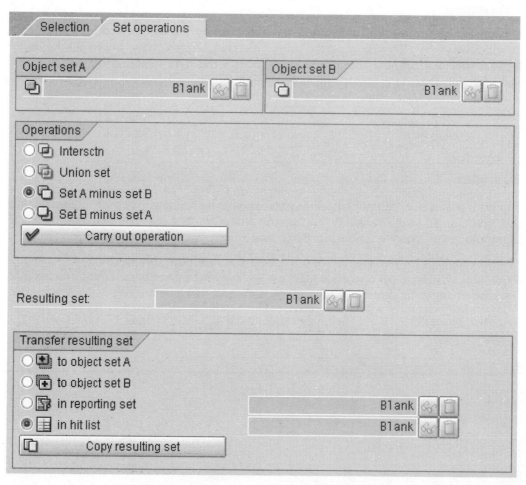

On this tab page, you can perform the desired set operations (intersection, union, minus), and transfer the result to a resulting set. If the desired result is achieved, you copy the resulting set to the reporting set and hit list. If you want to perform further set operations, you can transfer the resulting set to set A or set B, and continue.

After you have got the desired result, and transferred it to the reporting set and hit list, you come back to 'Selection' tab and remove the selection condition. If you don't do this, the reporting set will get further restricted as per selection conditions.

47.1.6   Output

When you tick the output checkbox in field group/fields, that field is transferred to this section. You can do the following things to the output.

> Select a field, and drag and drop to left or right.
> Decide whether you want the normal report (basic list), or statistics, or ranked list.
> Convert your output in various formats, e.g. Excel, Word, etc.
> Sort the data on a column of your choice, and perform totals and subtotals.
> Call a standard report from ad hoc query.

47.1.7   Saving a Query

You can save the queries that you perform in ad hoc query. Your queries are visible to other users of your user group. They can even modify or delete your queries, if they have change authorization for ad hoc queries. Unless you use a good naming convention, finding the queries may become a difficult task. You can also save variants of a query.

47.1.8   Tracking Query Use

You can track the use of a query by activating log. To activate the log, run transaction SQ02, and select Extras ➤ Set Logs. You can specify the infosets for which you want the log to be activated.

If you want to see the logs, go to global query area. SAP delivers the user group/ SAPQUERY/SQ and the Infoset/SAPQUERY_LOGGING as well as some queries with which you can analyze log data. You can also create queries of your own for analyzing the log data if you want. Alternatively, you can look at the log data in table AQPROT.

If you want to delete log data, you go to Extras ➤ Manage log.

47.1.9   Settings

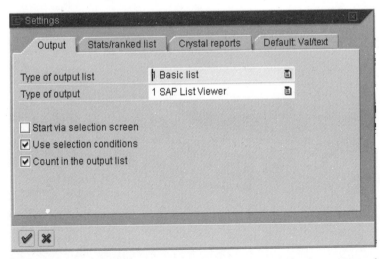

You can go to Edit ➤ Settings to maintain default settings for ad hoc query.

Type of output list

Here you can specify whether you want the normal report (basic list), or statistics, or ranked list.

Type of output

Here you can specify the default output formats, e.g. spreadsheet, word processing, etc.

Start via selection screen

If you tick this checkbox, when you run the query, the selection screen is shown first. The selections you specify here are in addition to the selections given by you in selection conditions, which are also transferred to the selection screen.

Use selection conditions

Usually you will have this checkbox ticked, so that you can specify selection conditions. However, if you have ticked 'Start via selection screen', you may untick this and operate only through selection screen.

Count in the output list

If you tick this checkbox, a count is displayed in your output list.

Statistics/ranked list

In this tab apart from other things, you can specify the number of rankings.

Default for selection

Usually the default for selection will be value, and not text.

Default for output

Your default for output may be either value or text, depending on your personal preference.

47.1.10   Selection Screen

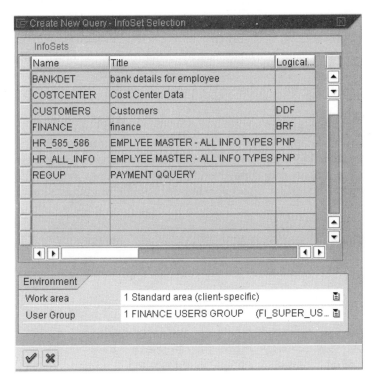

While explaining the ad hoc query screen, the selection screen was deliberately skipped. In the selection screen, you see work area, user group and infosets. These are briefly explained below.

Work area

When you execute ad hoc query first time in a session, it lets you choose from standard work area and global work area. Queries in standard work area are only for that client while queries in global work area are available in all clients.

Queries in global area can be transported using normal transport method, while those in standard area are usually not transported, but if need be they can be transported through Environment ➤ Transport. SAP provides a number of queries in global work area. There are two transactions for ad hoc query, the only difference between them is the work area you get by default.

User group

You may see chapter 47.3.

InfoSets

You may see chapter 47.2.

47.2 INFOSETS

Functional Consultant	User	Business Process Owner	Senior Management	My Rating	Understanding Level
A	X	X	X		

47.2.1 Purpose and Overview

SAP stores employee data in logical database PNP or PNPCE. In logical database PNP or PNPCE, infotypes are joined on their key fields. Therefore, you do not have to perform table joining operations if you have to extract data from multiple infotypes in a query. Apart from table fields, the logical database also contains additional fields, as shown below. These are derived fields.

Data fields	Technical name	Fie...
▽ ☐ Actions	P0000	
▷ ▦ Actions	P0000	
▽ ▤ Additional fields		
◈ Counter field	SYHR_A_P0000_AF_COUNTFLD	
◈ Leaving date	SYHR_A_P0000_AF_FIREDATE	01
◈ Entry date	SYHR_A_P0000_AF_HIREDATE	01
◈ ID Without Leading Zeros	SYHR_A_P0000_AF_IDNOZERO	
◈ Length of service (in days)	SYHR_A_P0000_AF_NODYS	01
◈ Length of service (in months)	SYHR_A_P0000_AF_NOMNS	01
◈ Length of service (in years)	SYHR_A_P0000_AF_NOYRS	01
▨ RECRUIT	SYHR_A_P0000_AF_RECRUIT	
▨ TECAT	SYHR_A_P0000_AF_TECAT	
▨ TERMINATION	SYHR_A_P0000_AF_TERMINATI	

Since each infotype contains a large number of fields, particularly key fields and control fields, the user may find it inconvenient. SAP, therefore, provides a concept of field groups. Usually there is a field group for each infotype, which contains fields of that infotype. You can add or delete fields from field group. Also, you can add any field to any field group. There is no constraint that all fields in a field group must belong to the same infotype.

You can also create or delete field groups. You can also create your own fields. For more advanced facilities on creating field groups and fields, you may see IMG nodes under Personnel Management ➢ Human Resources Information System ➢ HR Settings for SAP Query ➢ Additional Information on InfoSet Maintenance.

Both global and standard query areas have a number of infosets. While maintaining infosets, you can change the query area through menu path Environment ➢ Query areas. While using SAP query, or ad hoc query, the user decides the query area in which he wants to work.

All infosets are not available to all users. Infosets are linked to user groups, and users belonging to those user groups can use them. If you use role based authorization, you can assign a role to a user group. Then all users who are assigned that role, can use the infoset.

47.2.2 Menu Path

SQ02—InfoSets

47.2.3 Screen

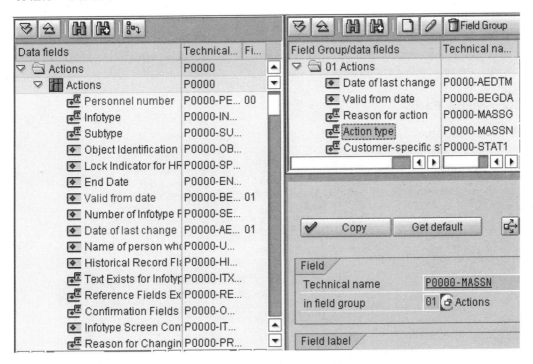

47.3 USER GROUPS FOR SAP QUERY

Functional Consultant	User	Business Process Owner	Senior Management	My Rating	Understanding Level
A	X	X	X		

47.3.1 Purpose and Overview

For ad hoc query, you can define various user groups. Note that these user groups are different from the user groups, whose value comes from the parameter UGR. These are also distinct from the user groups of HIS.

First you select the query area in which you want to create user group. By default, you get standard query area. You can change it by going to Environment ➢ Query area.

SAP provides you predefined user groups in global query area. You can assign users to user groups. A user can be assigned to multiple user groups. It is also possible to assign a role to a user group, thereby indirectly assigning users to user groups.

The queries saved by a user, are visible to other users in his user group. They can even change or delete the query created by their colleague. You should therefore be careful in designing user groups.

Authorization of a user to create or change query is determined by authorization object S_QUERY. However, if you want you can revoke that authorization for the user when he belongs to a user group.

You also assign infosets to user groups. This limits the infosets, which are available to a user when he selects a user group.

47.3.2   Menu Path

SQ03—User Groups

47.3.3   Screen

User group		✎ Change	🗋 Create
		𝖔𝖞 Display	🗈 Description
		Assign users and InfoSets	

User group assignment

User		✎ Change
InfoSet		✎ Change

HIS

48.1 HIS

Functional Consultant	User	Business Process Owner	Senior Management	My Rating	Understanding Level
A	A	A	A		

48.1.1 Starting HIS

HIS is a tool for reporting based on the organization structure. You can take-up any part of the organization structure and generate various reports for it. However, the reporting is not structured in the manner of the organization structure. It is like any other report except that the objects, e.g. positions or persons, come from the selected organizational units. When you run transaction PPIS to run HIS, the system asks you to select the plan version. You would normally select current plan.

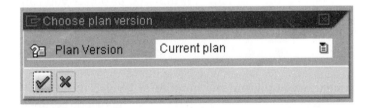

Once you do that, the system displays an initial screen.

48.1.2 Initial Screen

View	STANDARD Standard view 🗐

Graphical display
- ⦿ Organizational units
- ◯ With positions
- ◯ With persons

Access object

Organizational unit	
Display depth	
Date	Period indicator D

View

HIS can be used not only for reporting based on organization structure, but also for reporting of training, etc. These are created as views by SAP.

Graphical display

SAP offers different views of the organization structure. One view of the organization structure would be a tree-like structure of organizational units. In another view, you can also see positions linked to the tree-like structure of organizational units. In yet another view, you can also see persons who fill those positions. The view you select determines what you see in the window 'HIS: Access Object'. For example, if you select 'Organizational units' in graphical display, you see only organizational units in 'HIS: Access Object' window. But if you select 'With persons' in graphical display, you see the persons in 'HIS: Access Object' window. Note that you cannot select specific persons and run the 'Birthdays' report only for them. For each radio button here, the type of object you can select is defined in configuration, and it is organizational unit for all three radio buttons in this case. It is only the display in 'HIS: Access Object' window which is different.

Access object

Here you specify the starting organizational unit and the number of levels you want to go down. Also specify the period for which you want the data to be reported, because SAP not only keeps current data, but also past data. You can either specify the period indicator, or from-date and to-date.

48.1.3 Defaults

When you click the 'Defaults' icon on the HIS initial screen, the following window is displayed.

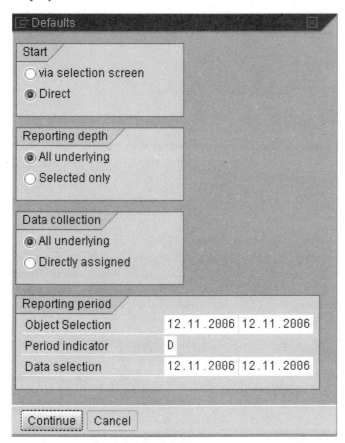

Direct or via selection screen

When you run a report, normally you first get a selection screen. In HIS, objects have already been selected based on the organization structure. Therefore, you may not need the selection screen, in which case you can select the radio button 'Direct'. However, if you want, you can go via the selection screen and further restrict the objects selected.

Reporting depth

You also specify whether reporting should be for selected organizational units only, or for all organizational units under them. Note that you cannot specify depth for reporting. Reporting depth is for object selection.

Data collection depth

Here you specify the depth of data collection for the selected objects.

Distinction between object selection period and data selection period

It is important to understand the distinction between object selection period and data selection period. Suppose you want past history of organizational assignment of all employees who are active today. The objects, employees in this case, are selected based on their employment status on a given date, the system date in this case. But their data is selected from 01.01.1900 till the system date.

Object selection period

Here you specify the period for which objects should be selected.

Period indicator and data selection period

Here you specify the period for which data should be selected. If you specify the period indicator, the system determines the data selection period. Alternatively, you can directly specify the data selection period.

48.1.4 Selected Objects

When you execute, you see two windows. The first window 'HIS: Access Object' shows the objects. In the initial screen you selected starting object and display depth. In choosing the graphical display radio button, you selected the evaluation path which determines how to select objects related to the starting object. These objects are shown in this window. You can select some or all of these objects in this window. The reporting takes place based on the objects selected in this window.

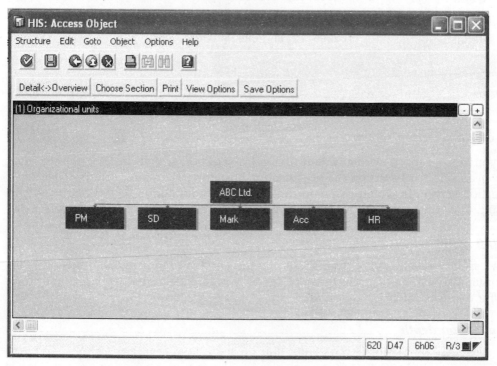

You can change the look and feel of this window according to your liking. You need to explore the options in this window. The important ones are described below.

Detail<->Overview You can switch between a detail view which shows the object with full text and an overview.

Choose Section When you are in overview, you can click on this icon. The system gives you a window, which you position at the desired place in the overview. The system then shows you detailed view of that part in the overview.

Print You can print this window on local printer, or create a spool in the system, or print to a file.

View Options You can change the display of the organization structure from top-to-bottom to left-to-right.

Save Options Click this icon to see save options of the current user.

Substructure If you select an object and click this icon, you would see substructure of only that object.

Whole Structure If your display is for substructure of an object, you can click on this icon to see the whole structure.

48.1.5 Reporting

When you run HIS you see areas in the top part of the reporting window. These are the areas of business activity.

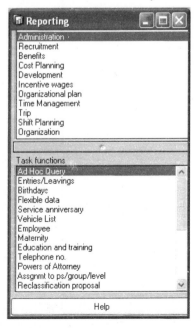

Task functions

Each area has a set of reports. Once you select an area, in the top part of the reporting window, the system shows you the reports you can run in 'Task functions'. You can run a report by double-clicking it. The report is run for the objects selected in 'HIS: Access Object' window.

48.2   DATA VIEWS

Functional Consultant	User	Business Process Owner	Senior Management	My Rating	Understanding Level
A	X	X	X		

48.2.1   Purpose

Master list of data views is defined here. The system contains predefined views, which are generally adequate. You specify the view in the initial screen, when you run HIS.

48.2.2   IMG Node

SM30 ➢ T77I6

48.2.3   Screen

View	Text for view
MDT	Manager's Desktop
PM_BUDGE	PM: Budget
PM_ORGAN	PM: Organization
STANDARD	Standard view
TRAINING	Training and Event Mgmt

48.2.4   Primary Key

View for Start

48.3 GROUPINGS FOR DATA VIEWS

Functional Consultant	User	Business Process Owner	Senior Management	My Rating	Understanding Level
A	X	X	X		

48.3.1 Purpose

When you are looking at the organization chart in 'HIS: Access Object' window, you may want to see only organizational units, or organizational units with positions, or organizational units with positions and persons. These are defined as groupings for a data view and are seen as radio buttons in the initial screen of HIS. Depending on the radio button you select, the system uses an evaluation path which is defined here.

48.3.2 IMG Node

SM30 ➤ V_T77IC

48.3.3 Screen

View	STANDARD	Standard view

	No.	Classification
	10	Organizational units
	20	With positions
	30	With persons

View	STANDARD	Standard view

Number	10
Classification	Organizational units
Object type	O
Evaluation Path	ORGEH
Status vector	1
☑ Status Overlap	

48.3.4 Primary Key

View for Start + Sequential Number within View

48.3.5 Important Fields

The fields in this view determine the initial screen you see when you run HIS.

View

Depending on the view you select in the initial screen of HIS, the radio buttons in graphical area change. This field contains the view for which you are defining radio buttons.

Number

The radio buttons appear in the order of this field.

Classification

This field contains the text of radio buttons.

Object type

In 'Access object' in the initial screen above, you can select objects only of this type.

Evaluation path

When you run HIS, you get a window 'HIS: Access Object'. This window shows the starting object, and objects under it. The evaluation path specified here determines the objects that are shown under the starting object.

Status vector and status overlap

If your organization structure undergoes a change, you can go through an approval process in SAP. You can make the changes in structure as planned. You can then submit it for approval, which may then be either approved or rejected. Finally, you would change the status of approved structure to active.

Normally, you would want a report based on active organization structure. However, SAP gives you a facility to simulate how the report would look if you activated the organization structure in different stages of planning, viz. planned (2), submitted (3), approved (4) and if you want even rejected (5). If you want to use this functionality, you specify the statuses to be activated in status vector field and tick the status overlap field. The simulation activates all relationship infotypes with the statuses listed in the status vector field. The change in status is only for reporting purpose and your structure remains unchanged.

48.4 AREAS

Functional Consultant	User	Business Process Owner	Senior Management	My Rating	Understanding Level
A	X	X	X		

48.4.1 Purpose and Overview

Areas are usually sub-modules of SAP HR. They represent the area of business activity. The system contains predefined areas, which are generally adequate. Although shown on the screen, you cannot specify evaluation paths here.

48.4.2 IMG Node

SM34 ➤ T77IB (Areas).

48.4.3 Screen

Area	Single	Struct.	Text for area
ADHOC_BU			Ad-hoc query regarding budget
ADHOC_O			Ad-hoc query regarding organization
COURSES			Business Events
EMPLOYEE			Employee data

48.4.4 Primary Key

Area

48.5 AREAS FOR A VIEW

Functional Consultant	User	Business Process Owner	Senior Management	My Rating	Understanding Level
A	X	X	X		

48.5.1 Purpose

Depending on the view you select, you get certain areas in the top part of the reporting window. The areas for each view are specified here. You can maintain this table either from view-cluster or from area-cluster.

48.5.2 IMG Nodes

SM34 ➤ T77I6 (view V_T77IA)
SM34 ➤ T77IB (view V_T77IA_2)

48.5.3 Screen

View	STANDARD	Standard view

Area	Text for area
EMPLOYEE	Employee data
HRADM	Administration
HRAPL	Recruitment

48.5.4 Primary Key

View for Start + Area

48.6 TASK FUNCTIONS

Functional Consultant	User	Business Process Owner	Senior Management	My Rating	Understanding Level
A	X	X	X		

48.6.1 Purpose

When you run HIS, you see two windows, viz. HIS: Access Object and Reporting. Reporting window consists of two parts. The top part shows areas and the bottom part shows task functions. Task functions are the reports which can run from HIS. If you want to add a report in HIS, you add it here.

48.6.2 IMG Node

SM30 ➤ T77I3

48.6.3 Screen

User group	****
Area	ADHOC_O Ad-hoc query regarding organi...
FctMenuEntryNo.	10
Function text	Ad Hoc Query
Program Name	RHADHOC0
Object type	*
Variant Name	
Depth 0 path	
Depth 1 path	
Data collection	O_ADHOC
Selected obj.	2

48.6.4 Primary Key

User group + Area + Function Menu Entry Number

48.6.5 Important Fields

User group

The task functions you see in HIS can be different for different users. If you want to use this feature, you create user groups in view T77I9. Then you assign users to user groups in view T77I8. For each user group you define task functions here.

Area

Task functions are defined for an area.

Function menu entry number

Task functions shown at the bottom of the reporting window are sorted by this field.

Function text

This is the task function name, which appears in the 'Task functions' pane of the reporting window.

Program name

This is the program, which runs when you double-click a task function.

Object type

When you select a view, a radio button and execute, you see the organization chart in 'HIS: Access Object'. There you select the objects for which you want to generate the report. There you can select objects only of this type, although you may see other objects depending on the evaluation path specified. Thus, this is the type of object based on which reporting takes place.

Variant name

If you want to use a specific variant of the program, you can specify that here.

Depth 0 path, depth 1 path

When you run a report, your default settings determine whether the report is for all objects underlying the selected object, or only those objects, which are directly assigned to it.

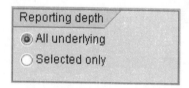

In depth 0 path, you specify the evaluation path which is used for identifying all underlying objects. Similarly, in depth 1 path you specify the evaluation path which is used for identifying directly assigned objects.

Data collection

Here you specify the data collection method. Data collection methods are maintained in view T77I4, where you specify the evaluation paths for accessing data, and type of object to be selected.

Selected objects

Here you specify the number of objects to be selected in 'HIS: Access Object' window. The choices are:

0	No object may be marked, i.e. no objects are processed.
1	Only one object must be marked, i.e. one object is processed.
2	One or more objects must be marked.

48.7 DATA COLLECTION

Functional Consultant	User	Business Process Owner	Senior Management	My Rating	Understanding Level
A	X	X	X		

48.7.1 Purpose

Here you maintain the parameters for data retrieval. These data collection methods are used in task functions.

48.7.2 IMG Node

SM30 ➤ T77I4

48.7.3 Screen

	Data coll.	Program	D0 path	D1 path	Obj. type
	APPLICAN	RHGRIN23	O-S-AP	O-AP	AP
	BU_ADHOC	RHGRIN23	BU-BU-SP	BU-SP	P
	D_COURSE	RHGRIN23	D-E	D-E	E
	JOBS	RHGRIN23	O_O_S_C	O_S_C	C
	L_D	RHGRIN23	L-D	L-D-ONE	D
	O_ADHOC	RHGRIN23	O-O-S-P	O-P	P
	PERSONS	RHGRIN23	O-S-P	O-P	P
	POSITION	RHGRIN23	PLSTE	PLSTE-S	S
	QUALIS	RHGRIN23	QUALIALL	QUALIALL	Q

48.7.4 Primary Key

Data Collection

48.7.5 Important Fields

Data collection

Here you enter the data collection method being defined.

Program

Here you specify the program which is used for data collection.

D0 path, D1 path

When you run a report, the system first selects a set of objects and then collects data about those objects. Here you specify the evaluation paths for data collection.

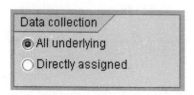

In D0 path, you specify the evaluation path which is used for collecting data from all underlying objects. In D1 path, you specify the evaluation path which is used for collecting data only from directly assigned objects.

Object type

Here you specify the type of objects which come in the report.

48.8 USER GROUPS

Functional Consultant	User	Business Process Owner	Senior Management	My Rating	Understanding Level
A	X	X	X		

48.8.1 Purpose

HIS can work differently for different groups of users. Task functions are defined at user group level. You define the master list of user groups here.

48.8.2 IMG Node

SM34 ➤ T77I9 (view T77I9)

48.8.3 Screen

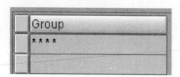

48.8.4 Primary Key

User group

48.9 USERS IN USER GROUPS

Functional Consultant	User	Business Process Owner	Senior Management	My Rating	Understanding Level
A	X	X	X		

48.9.1 Purpose

Here you assign users to user groups for the purpose of HIS. A user can be assigned to only one user group.

48.9.2 IMG Node

SM34 ➤ T77I9 (view T77I8)

48.9.3 Screen

User	Group
SAP*	****

48.9.4 Primary Key

User Name

Authorizations

49.1 AUTHORIZATION CONCEPTS

Functional Consultant	User	Business Process Owner	Senior Management	My Rating	Understanding Level
A	A	A	A		

49.1.1 Authorization Objects

Creating a test role

The best way to understand how SAP controls authorizations is to create a test role using transaction PFCG. After creating a role, you go to 'menu' tab, and add a transaction, e.g. PA20. You then go to 'Authorizations' tab, and click 'Change Authorization Data'. You will see the following screen.

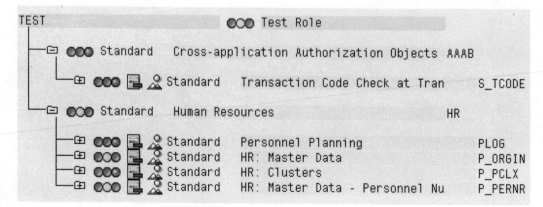

Object classes

The screenshot above shows two object classes, AAAB and HR.

Authorization objects

The screenshot above shows five authorization objects. Expand the authorization object P_ORGIN.

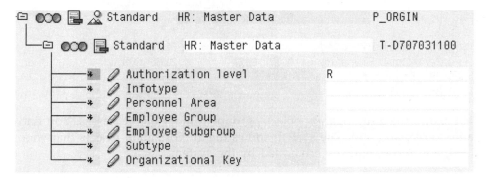

Authorization fields

The screenshot above shows authorization fields in one authorization object. An authorization object groups up to ten authorization fields that are checked in an AND relationship. In this object you specify the authorization given to a role (or profile), which will become the authorization for one or more users through assignment of the role to users. In this object, you specify the following:

> ➢ The infotype and subtype, for which the user has authorization.
> ➢ The personnel area, employee group and employee subgroup, for which the user has authorization.
> ➢ If you use organizational key, the organizational key, for which the user has authorization.
> ➢ The level of authorization, e.g. display or change.

If a user tries to create an infotype 0001 record for a person, the system will check whether the user has authorization for each of the fields above. If any of the tests fail, the user will not be able to carry out the action. In other words, the final result is determined by applying AND operation to the result of all tests within an authorization object.

Multiple copies of the same authorization object

But, what would you do if you want to give display authorization for infotype 0001 and change authorization for infotype 0002? You can do that by creating two authorization objects in the same role, one for each infotype. If the user satisfies any one authorization object fully, he will be able to perform the transaction.

Adding an authorization object manually

You can add an authorization object manually. If you don't know the technical name of the organization object, you click ⚏ Selection criteria . It opens the following screen.

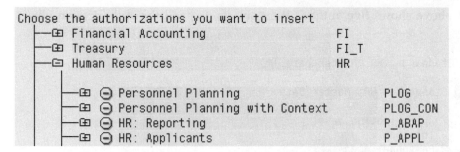

```
Choose the authorizations you want to insert
  ├──⊞ Financial Accounting              FI
  ├──⊞ Treasury                          FI_T
  ├──▭ Human Resources                   HR

      ├──⊞ ⊝ Personnel Planning                   PLOG
      ├──⊞ ⊝ Personnel Planning with Context      PLOG_CON
      ├──⊞ ⊝ HR: Reporting                        P_ABAP
      ├──⊞ ⊝ HR: Applicants                       P_APPL
```

This screenshot shows the authorization objects, grouped under object classes. You find the authorization object and add. The system shows the authorization objects that were manually added, and those, which were added by the system.

Default authorization objects and values

When you generated authorization profile, the system automatically added certain authorization objects, and in some cases, it also put values for the fields. SAP has created these defaults, but you can change the defaults if you want. You are advised not to do so, unless you have adequate mastery over the subject.

Authorization objects for infotypes

You have seen an authorization object of type P_ORGIN. This can be used to control authorization for infotypes. There are also other authorization objects, e.g. P_ORGXX, which can be used to control authorization for infotypes. If you wish to give infotype authorization based on administrator, rather than PA, EG and ESG, you can use authorization object P_ORGXX. Similarly, if you want to use structural authorization, you can use authorization object P_ORGINCON. SAP provides a large number of authorization objects, which you can use to control different activities in SAP.

Authorization objects for personnel planning

For personnel planning infotypes you use authorization objects PLOG or PLOG_CON.

49.1.2   Structural Authorizations

For infotypes, you can control authorizations based on personnel area, employee group and employee subgroup in authorization object P_ORGIN. However, there is often a need to control authorization based on organizational structure. SAP meets this requirement through structural authorizations.

To maintain structural authorizations, you first maintain authorization profiles. This topic is discussed in detail, latter in this chapter. Then, you use authorization object

P_ORGINCON, in place of P_ORGIN. In P_ORGINCON, there is an additional field, 'Authorization Profile'. You attach the authorization profile created earlier to this field. In this way you will give authorization only for a specified part of organizational structure. If you are using structural authorizations, review whether you still want to restrict based on personnel area, employee group and employee subgroup.

49.1.3 Authorizations for User's Own Data

In Employee Self-Service (ESS), an employee may see, or update his own data, but he should not see data of other employees. To meet this requirement, SAP provides an authorization object P_PERNR. Also, you may want that while HR administrators update data for everyone else, they should not be able to update their own data. Even this requirement can be met through authorization object P_PERNR. The link between a user and his personnel number is maintained in infotype 0105, subtype 0001.

49.1.4 Roles and Profiles

You can create a role using transaction PFCG. You can also create a menu for a role. This is displayed in user menu of all users, who are assigned that role.

If you go to authorizations tab, and click 'Change authorization data', SAP proposes a set of authorization objects, along with their default values. You fill up the missing values, and check whether the proposed values are okay. If necessary, you may change them. Finally when you save them, all authorization objects should be green, as only those authorization objects are effective.

You can also see all users who have been granted the role. If 'User comparison' icon on the user tab is not green, click it. Otherwise, the authorizations may not work correctly.

49.1.5 Authorization for User

You can use transaction SU01 to assign roles to users. You can assign him one or more roles, which govern user authorization in SAP. You can also specify a reference user, whose authorizations will be available to the current user. You can also assign a user one or more profiles, which also grant him authorization in SAP.

49.1.6 Double Verification

There is often a need that the data is entered in the system by one person, and verified by another. SAP provides a lock indicator in infotype record to meet this requirement. However, if a user creates a locked record and unlocks it himself, then the purpose is defeated. Therefore, you should be able to provide authorizations in such a way that this cannot be done. SAP provides the following methods of doing it.

Asymmetrical double verification

In Asymmetrical double verification, one user does data entry (Authorization levels E, R and M) and another approves it (Authorization levels D, R and M).

Symmetrical double verification

In Symmetrical double verification, both users have same authorizations (Authorization levels S, R and M). But the record locked by one user cannot be unlocked by him. Also, none of the two users given these authorizations can delete a record; that authorization must be given to a third user.

49.1.7 Preventing Change of Checked Data

SAP also has a concept of checking and locking the data. Here, you can have multiple users doing decentralized data entry. This data is checked by an approving user. He then freezes the data by creating an entry in infotype 0130. After that, only the approving users can change the data.

49.1.8 Troubleshooting Authorization Problems

When a user faces authorization failure, you need to know what authorization did he need, and what authorization did he have. This is displayed by executing transaction SU53 immediately after authorization failure.

49.1.9 Customer-Specific Authorization Check

You can use BAdI HRPAD00AUTH_CHECK to replace the SAP standard authorization check for HR master data and infotypes with a customer-specific check.

49.2 AUTHORIZATION MAIN SWITCHES

Functional Consultant	User	Business Process Owner	Senior Management	My Rating	Understanding Level
A	B	B	X		

49.2.1 Purpose

SAP provides you a lot of choices in authorization control. These are exercised through the switches explained in this chapter.

49.2.2 IMG Node

SM30 ➤ V_T77S0 (Group name AUTSW)

49.2.3 Screen

System Switch (from Table T77S0)			
Group	Sem. abbr.	Value abbr.	Description
AUTSW	ADAYS	15	HR: tolerance time for authorization check
AUTSW	APPRO	0	HR: Test procedures
AUTSW	DFCON	1	HR: Default Position (Context)
AUTSW	INCON	0	HR: Master Data (Context)
AUTSW	NNCON	0	HR:Customer-Specific Authorization Check (Context)
AUTSW	NNNNN	0	HR: Customer-specific authorization check
AUTSW	ORGIN	1	HR: Master data
AUTSW	ORGPD	0	HR: Structural authorization check
AUTSW	ORGXX	0	HR: Master data - Extended check
AUTSW	PERNR	1	HR: Master data - Personnel number check
AUTSW	XXCON	0	HR: Master Data - Enhanced Check (Context)

49.2.4 Authorization Switches

Switch	Explanation
ADAYS	If an HR administrator changes the organizational assignment of a person, and he has no authorization for the new area where the employee now belongs, he will not be able to see the record he has created. This can cause problems. Here you can specify the number of calendar days, for which the administrator can see the record he created, even though he does not have authorization for employee's new area.
APPRO	You set this switch to 1 if you want to implement infotype 0130, test procedures. Test procedures can be used if certain entries are to be checked centrally and should not be changeable after the check without further action.
DFCON	See the explanation in switch ORGPD.
INCON	This switch determines whether authorization object P_ORGINCON is used in the authorization check.
NNCON	This switch determines whether customer-specific authorization object P_NNNNNCON is used for authorization check. Note that this is not a standard authorization object.
NNNNN	This switch determines whether customer-specific authorization object P_NNNNN is used for authorization check. Note that this is not a standard authorization object. You have to create the authorization object first.

(Contd.)

Switch	*Explanation*
ORGIN	This switch determines whether authorization object P_ORGIN is used for authorization check. Alternatively, you could use P_ORGXX, or P_ORGINCON.
ORGPD	Structural authorizations can be implemented in two ways; by using P_ORGINCON object, or by assigning a profile to user in table T77UA. If you are using P_ORGINCON method, you use switch DFCON. If you are using T77UA method, you use switch ORGPD. These switches determine whether structural authorization check is on, and what is its behaviour.
	In structural authorization, a user has authorization for an organizational unit. The organizational unit has positions. The positions are linked to persons in infotype 0001. This is the link to determine whether a user has authorization for a personnel number or not.
	However, sometimes you use default positions. In that case the above link will not work. You have the following options:
	1. Org Unit Checked (Initial → No Authorization) 2. Org Unit Not Checked (No Authorization) 3. Org Unit Checked (Initial → Authorization) 4. Org Unit Not Checked (Authorization)
	In options 1 and 3, employee's organizational unit in infotype 0001 is checked. If the organizational unit exists, it determines whether the user is authorized or not. However, if the organizational unit does not exist, in option 3, user is authorized, in option 1, he is not authorized.
	In options 2 and 4, the employee's organizational unit is not checked at all. In option 4, user is authorized, in option 2, he is not authorized.
ORGXX	This switch determines whether authorization object P_ORGXX is used for authorization check. You use this object if you want to check authorization by administrators.
PERNR	This switch determines whether authorization object P_PERNR is used for authorization check. You can use this object to permit, or deny, the user to see/change his own data.
XXCON	This switch determines whether authorization object P_ORGXXCON is used in the authorization check.

49.3 AUTHORIZATION OBJECTS FOR TRANSACTIONS

Functional Consultant	User	Business Process Owner	Senior Management	My Rating	Understanding Level
A	X	X	X		

49.3.1 Purpose and Overview

When you add a transaction code in menu of a role and generate authorization profile, the system proposes the authorization objects, and in some cases default values. These are defined here, and you can change them if you wish. The objects shown under column C are checked, and objects shown under column CM are both checked and maintained, i.e. inserted in the profile when you add the transaction to a role. You can add or delete an object. You can change between columns U, N, C and CM, simply by clicking the point of your choice. These are just like radio buttons. You can maintain default values of the fields, which will appear when the object is inserted.

49.3.2 IMG Node

Transaction SU24—Authorization Object Check under Transactions

49.3.3 Screen

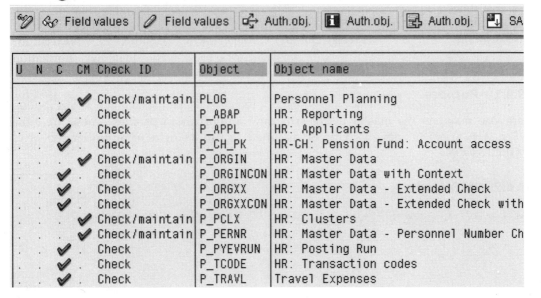

U	N	C	CM	Check ID	Object	Object name
.	.	.	✔	Check/maintain	PLOG	Personnel Planning
.	.	✔	.	Check	P_ABAP	HR: Reporting
.	.	✔	.	Check	P_APPL	HR: Applicants
.	.	✔	.	Check	P_CH_PK	HR-CH: Pension Fund: Account access
.	.	.	✔	Check/maintain	P_ORGIN	HR: Master Data
.	.	✔	.	Check	P_ORGINCON	HR: Master Data with Context
.	.	✔	.	Check	P_ORGXX	HR: Master Data - Extended Check
.	.	✔	.	Check	P_ORGXXCON	HR: Master Data - Extended Check with
.	.	.	✔	Check/maintain	P_PCLX	HR: Clusters
.	.	.	✔	Check/maintain	P_PERNR	HR: Master Data - Personnel Number Ch
.	.	✔	.	Check	P_PYEVRUN	HR: Posting Run
.	.	✔	.	Check	P_TCODE	HR: Transaction codes
.	.	✔	.	Check	P_TRAVL	Travel Expenses

Change Field Values for PA30

`⊘` `⊡↓ SAP defaults` `⊡↓ Object descr.` `ℹ Auth.obj.`

Object	Field		Value (interval)
PLOG	INFOTYP	⊘	1001
	ISTAT	⊘	*
	OTYPE	⊘	C
		⊘	O
		⊘	P
		⊘	Q
		⊘	S
	PLVAR		$PLVAR
	PPFCODE	⊘	*
	SUBTYP	⊘	*
P_ORGIN	AUTHC	⊘	R
	INFTY	⊘	
	PERSA	⊘	
	PERSG	⊘	
	PERSK	⊘	
	SUBTY	⊘	
	VDSK1	⊘	

49.4 AUTHORIZATION PROFILES

Functional Consultant	User	Business Process Owner	Senior Management	My Rating	Understanding Level
A	X	X	X		

49.4.1 Purpose

Here you maintain the master list of structural authorization profiles. These are either assigned to users in view T77UA, or assigned to profile field in authorization object P_ORGINCON.

49.4.2 IMG Node

SM34 ➤ T77PQ (view T77PQ)

49.4.3 Screen

Authoriz. profile	Auth.profile name	Info
ALL	ALL	ℹ
ALL_01	ALL_01	ℹ
ALL_02	ALL_02	ℹ
ALL_03	ALL_03	ℹ
ALL_04	ALL_04	ℹ

49.4.4 Primary Key

Authorization Profile

49.5 AUTHORIZATION PROFILE DEFINITION

Functional Consultant	User	Business Process Owner	Senior Management	My Rating	Understanding Level
A	C	C	X		

49.5.1 Purpose

You can give authorization to a user for a part of the organization structure, which is identified by a starting object and an evaluation path. These parts of the organization structure are defined as authorization profiles.

49.5.2 IMG Node

SM34 ➤ T77PQ (view T77PR)

49.5.3 Screen

Auth.profile	No.	O...	Object I	Maint.	Eval.path	S..	Depth	Sign	Period	Function module
PUC_TRG_SUPE	1	0	10000056	✔	OS-CP	1				
PUC_TRG_SUPE	2	0	10000499	✔	OS-CP	1				
PUC_TRG_SUPE	3	0	10001341	✔	OS-CP	1				
PUC_TRG_SUPE	4	F	50012926	✔	KURSORT	1				

49.5.4 Primary Key

Authorization Profile + Sequence Number

49.5.5 Important Fields

Authorization profile

Here you enter the authorization profile being defined.

Sequence number

An authorization profile may consist of several structures or subtrees. Each structure is identified by a sequence number.

Plan version

Here you specify the plan version for which the defined profile is valid. Note that plan version 01 is generally the active plan version.

Object type and object ID

Here you specify the start object for the evaluation path.

Maintenance

If you tick this field, user can maintain (create/change) data. If this field is not ticked, he can only display data. This can further restrict the authorization granted to the user in activity field.

Evaluation path

In structural authorizations, the authorization is for a part of structure. The part of structure is defined by a starting object and an evaluation path, which determines the structure. The evaluation path is specified here.

Status vector

Status vector determines whether you want to take into account only active relationships, or planned relationships as well.

Depth

When you go down the evaluation path, there can be multiple levels. If you do not want to go beyond certain depth, you can specify that here.

Sign

Your evaluation path takes you in a certain direction of structure. If you want to go in reverse direction, you enter a '−' here.

Period

The structures have a validity period. If you want to see the structure as on a certain date, or period, you can specify that here.

Function module

Although you can explicitly specify a starting object in structural profiles, you will end up creating one profile for each user, just because the starting object is different. SAP lets you specify a function module where you can logically determine the starting object for each user.

If a position is manager of an organizational unit (A012), you can use RH_GET_MANAGER_ASSIGNMENT. In this way, you need only one profile for all managers, instead of one profile for each manager.

SAP also provides a function module, RH_GET_ORG_ASSIGNMENT. If you specify this function module in a profile, the starting object for a person is the organizational unit to which he belongs. For both these functionalities to work, user to person relationship must be maintained in infotype 0105.

49.6 AUTHORIZATION PROFILES TO USER ASSIGNMENT

Functional Consultant	User	Business Process Owner	Senior Management	My Rating	Understanding Level
A	X	X	X		

49.6.1 Purpose and Overview

Here you can assign structural authorization profiles to users. A user's authorization is limited to the objects (ultimately employees) selected by these profiles. These profiles restrict the authorization a user is granted otherwise. A user can be assigned multiple authorization profiles, thereby giving him authorization for multiple groups of employees. However, his authorization for all the employees will be same. If you want a user to have different authorization for different groups of employees, e.g. display of organizational assignment for all employees but change of organizational assignment for his subordinates, this method cannot support it.

SAP has therefore introduced an authorization object P_ORGINCON, where you can assign an authorization profile to an authorization object, and thereby provide different authorizations to a user for different groups of employees. To enable that method, you do appropriate coding in HRBAS00_GET_PROFL Business Add-In (BAdI). Alternatively, you grant unrestricted authorization to the user in this view by giving him authorization profile 'ALL' and restrict him in authorization object P_ORGINCON as appropriate.

If there is no entry in this view for a user, he is granted authorization profile which is linked to the user SAP*. Thus, if you maintain an entry with 'SAP*' in user name field and 'ALL' in authorization profile field (This entry is there in the view by default), all users who are not present in this view will have unrestricted authorization. Their authorization will then be restricted only by the authorization object P_ORGINCON.

49.6.2 IMG Node

SM30 ➤ T77UA

49.6.3 Screen

	User Name		Auth.profile	Start date	End date
	ABA251718	ℹ	ORG_MAVAL	01.04.2003	31.12.9999
	AHZ126134	ℹ	ORG_PUNE_CVD	01.01.2001	31.12.9999
	AKG432068	ℹ	ALL	01.01.2001	31.12.9999
	AKG432068	ℹ	ORG_MUM_D	01.01.2001	31.12.9999

49.6.4 Primary Key

User Name + Authorization Profile + Start Date

49.7 TEST PROCEDURES (INFOTYPE 0130)

Functional Consultant	User	Business Process Owner	Senior Management	My Rating	Understanding Level
A	B	B	B		

49.7.1 Screen

Pers.No.	121715		Name	Agrawal Prem
Pers.area	PNCV	Pune CVBU		
EE subgrp	E4	DM	WS rule	WSRPG	G SHIFT
Start	01.01.1800	To	31.12.9999	

Test Procedures

Test for	☑	
Released by		
Tested by		Tested on	
Tested using		Tested at	00:00:00

49.7.2 Purpose and Overview

You may have a scenario, where multiple users enter the data. This data is then checked by a privileged user and he freezes it up to a certain date. Normal users then cannot enter/modify data up to that date. Only a privileged user can do so. SAP supports such a scenario through test procedures.

You can define different test procedures. Each test procedure refers to an infotype, and if you want, a specific subtype. A privileged user is given authorization for a test procedure (i.e. infotype 0130, subtype specific test procedure).

He checks the data entered by other users for the specific infotype and subtype, which refer to a test procedure, and decides the date till when the data is frozen. He creates an infotype 0130 record, specifying the test procedure and release date. After that, normal users cannot create/modify the data till that date; only a privileged user can do that.

Usually the privileged users do not enter data in infotype 0130 directly. They release the data using a program, e.g. RPTAPPU0. The program creates appropriate infotype 0130 entry automatically.

Other fields of this infotype are change information, which are automatically maintained by the system.

49.7.3 Subtypes

Test procedure

49.7.4 Time Constraint

B (IT exists for maximum of once from Jan. 1, 1800 to Dec. 12, 9999)

49.8 TEST PROCEDURES MASTER

Functional Consultant	User	Business Process Owner	Senior Management	My Rating	Understanding Level
A	X	X	X		

49.8.1 Purpose

Here you maintain master list of test procedures. These are subtypes of infotype 0130.

49.8.2 IMG Node

SM30 ➤ VV_T591A_0130___AL0

49.8.3 Screen

Subtype characteristics for Test Procedures	
Subtype	Name
001	Org. Assignment
008	Basic Pay
014	Recurring Payments
015	One Time Payments
0151	One Time Payments - LIC
201	Absences
202	Attendances

49.8.4 Primary Key

Infotype + Subtype

49.9 INFOTYPES TO TEST PROCEDURES ASSIGNMENT

Functional Consultant	User	Business Process Owner	Senior Management	My Rating	Understanding Level
A	X	X	X		

49.9.1 Purpose

Here you define which infotype, and subtype, will have what test procedure.

49.9.2 IMG Node

SM30 ➤ V_T584A

49.9.3 Screen

Infotype	0015 Additional Payments		
STy.	Name	Test	Name
5005	LIC Premium	0151	One Time Payments - LIC

49.9.4 Primary Key

Infotype + Subtype + Infotypes to be tested

49.10   PREFIX FOR BATCH INPUT SESSIONS

Functional Consultant	User	Business Process Owner	Senior Management	My Rating	Understanding Level
A	B	B	X		

49.10.1   Purpose

When you run batch jobs, you may want to prevent users from seeing each other's job and printing their output. SAP provides an authorization object, S_BDC_MONI, where you can give authorization based on session name. You then need to name your sessions correctly so that unauthorized persons cannot view your session. In feature BIMAP, you can define a prefix based on program name, and thus control unauthorized viewing of batch jobs.

49.10.2   IMG Node

PE03 ➢ BIMAP

49.10.3   Screen

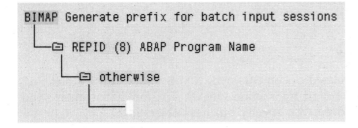

49.10.4   Fields for Decision-making

Transaction Code
Function code
ABAP Program Name
User Name
Company Code
Personnel Area
Personnel Subarea
Country Grouping
Employee Time Management Status

49.10.5   Return Value

A prefix, which is inserted in front of the session name.

Optical Archiving

50.1 OPTICAL ARCHIVING

Functional Consultant	User	Business Process Owner	Senior Management	My Rating	Understanding Level
A	B	B	C		

50.1.1 Purpose and Overview

You may have various employee related documents, which you may want to store. SAP lets you store document images through transaction OAAD. To store a document, you click 'Store and Assign'. For employee, you specify business object PREL.

For an employee, you can maintain various types of documents. These are identified by document type. For example, the document type for a photograph is HRICOLFOTO. After specifying the business object and document type, you click create icon. You are presented the following dialog box.

Key for SAP document	
Personnel Number	
Infotype	
Subtype	
Object ID	
Date of Origin	

✓ &⃝ Object ✗

Depending on the type of document, you would like to maintain contextual information. For all employee related documents, you need to specify the personnel number. If you are storing an employee's child's photograph, in order to identify the child, you need to specify infotype 0022, subtype and object id. If you maintain multiple photographs of the child, you may like to specify the date.

After entering the contextual information, you click the green tick. You are then presented a dialog box, where you specify the file to be loaded and load it by clicking 'Open'. The data you enter in this dialog box forms the object key. If any fields are blank, the key has blanks in corresponding positions. The link between object id and document id is maintained in table TOAHR.

SAP also lets you maintain the following configuration view, so that depending on document type, it can interpret field values.

In transaction PA30, you can go to Extras, and see all attachments. If you are in a specific infotype, you can see attachments pertaining to that infotype only.

50.1.2 IMG Node

SM30 ≻ V_T585O

50.1.3 Screen

Obj. type	Document type	Description	Infotype	Subtype	Obj.ID	Date	Authoriz
PAPL	HRIAPPLICA	Written application	4001	-	-	+	☐
PAPL	HRICERTAPL	Qualifications of applicant		-	-	+	☐
PAPL	HRIDIPLAPL	Training certificate for ap...	0022	+	-	+	✔
PAPL	HRIREFEAPL	Reference for applicant		-	-	+	☐
PAPL	HRIRESUAPL	Applicant's resume		-	-	+	☐
PREL	HRIBENEFIT	Retirement Pension Plan	0053	-	-	+	☐
PREL	HRIBESCHKI	Certificate for child	0021	2	-	+	☐
PREL	HRICERTIFI	Qualifications	0024	-	-	+	☐
PREL	HRICOLFOTO	Color photos	0002	-	-	-	☐

50.1.4 Primary Key

Object type + Document type

50.1.5 Important Fields

Object type

For employee, the object type is PREL, for applicant it is PAPL.

Document type and description

For an employee, you may maintain different types of documents. You specify the type of document here.

Infotype

If you want the document to be assigned to a specific infotype, you enter that here.

Subtype

+	The subtype must be entered when allocating the original.
–	The subtype must not be specified.
Constant	The subtype has already been predefined when allocating the original and cannot be overwritten.

Object ID

+	The object ID must be entered when allocating the original.
–	The object ID must not be specified.
Constant	The object ID has already been predefined when allocating the original and cannot be overwritten. This will generally not be the case since the object ID represents a free sub-structure of the subtypes.

Date

The date of origin of the original is used for the time-dependent authorization check for the display or allocation of an original.

+	When allocating the original, the date of origin must be entered.
–	When allocating the original, the specification of the date of origin is not allowed.

Authorization

This field controls access to infotype data and is used when documents are scanned in and assigned types. Mark this checkbox to check if the employee has an authorization for the infotype.

Concurrent Employment

51.1 OVERVIEW

Functional Consultant	User	Business Process Owner	Senior Management	My Rating	Understanding Level
A	A	A	A		

Concurrent employment

There may be situations, where the same person has multiple employment relationships with the company at the same time. This is called concurrent employment. If a person is hired, separated, and rehired, it is not concurrent employment. You can rehire the person under the same personnel number.

Requirements in case of concurrent employment

Concurrent employment presents a new set of requirements, e.g.

➢ Identification of all personnel numbers, who are in fact the same person.
➢ Ensuring consistency of data that must remain same across all personnel numbers of the same person.
➢ Reduction in effort when hiring a person again, as part of the data is already available in the system.
➢ Ability to view multiple assignments of a person together.
➢ If the same person has multiple assignments with the company, is he eligible for Benefits multiple times?
➢ Even though a person has multiple assignments, you may want to process his payroll for all assignments together, give him a single remuneration statement and cheque, and deduct taxes considering income from all assignments.

> You have to ensure that time data is consistent across various assignments, and may want to have some time balances for each assignment, and some for all assignments taken together.

Concurrent employment activation

SAP supports concurrent employment. If you have concurrent employment in your company, you have to activate it in SAP. There are several switches, which you activate depending on your requirements. For personnel administration, you need to activate CCURE + PAUIX switch in view T77S0. On activating this switch, you get additional information on the initial screen of transaction PA30/ PA40. You can customize the layouts of this additional information. These are covered in this chapter.

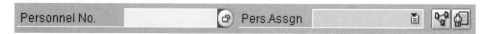

Finding if the employee is hired before

When concurrent employment is active, and you run a hiring action, the system helps you find whether the person has been hired before. The search is based on name, date of birth, etc.

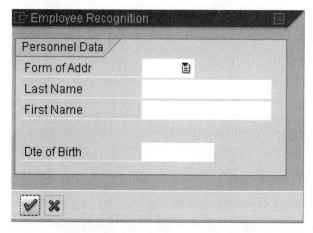

If the search does not yield a result, you are perhaps hiring a new person. If the search finds some personnel numbers, you examine them to see whether they are for the same person you are hiring. If not, you hire him as a new employee. If you find that the person you are hiring already exists in your database, there are two possibilities.

> The employee is not active any more. In this case, you can hire him under his old personnel number. Alternatively, you can hire him under a new personnel number, creating personnel assignment.
> The employee is still active. In this case, you are probably hiring him for an additional assignment. You can do so by giving him a new personnel number.

Linking all personnel numbers of a person

While hiring an employee, if you enter a reference personnel number, infotype 0031 automatically gets updated for all personnel numbers. Also, certain infotypes, e.g. personal data, challenge, bank details, family member/dependents, etc. get copied. Which infotypes get copied depends on 'Copy infotype' field of view V_T582A.

When you edit these infotypes for a personnel number, all relevant infotype records for all related personnel numbers are also updated. Other infotypes can be maintained independently for each personnel number.

You only need to maintain infotype 0031 manually, if you want to retrospectively create a relationship between two personnel numbers that already exist, or if you want to delete a link between two personnel numbers. Otherwise, it is automatically maintained by hiring action.

Person id

SAP also maintains a person id, which is common for all personnel numbers of the same person. There are four ways in which you can maintain external person id. You make your choice in switch CCURE + PIDGN.

System Switch (from Table T77S0)			
Group	Sem. abbr.	Value abbr.	Description
CCURE	PIDGN		Generation Rule RESONID
CCURE	PIDSL		Selection with PERSONID

External person ids can be

Gen. Rule	Short text
	Generation Rule for External Person ID
1	Number of Central Person (Object CP)
2	Number of First Personnel Assignment (Pernr)
3	Personal Identification Number (P0002-PERID)
4	HR_CE_GEN_PERSONID BAdI

Where you want selection to be through external person id, it can be set in CCURE + PIDSL. This activates the external person id in the initial screen.

Personnel number priority

For the purpose of concurrent payroll, you maintain infotype 0121. If you have reference personnel numbers in infotype 0031, you can maintain their priority in infotype 0121. You cannot enter a personnel number in infotype 0121, which does not exist in infotype 0031. Also, all reference personnel numbers must be in the same payroll area and legal person.

Multiple payroll

If payroll is run for an employee who has more than one personnel number, it is called multiple payroll. Payroll is not run for reference personnel numbers that have not been entered in the infotype 0121. Payroll considers the personnel numbers in the sequence in which they are entered in infotype 0121. You can also specify a main personnel number in infotype 0121, which can be used in payroll and reporting.

51.2 CONCURRENT EMPLOYMENT ACTIVATION

Functional Consultant	User	Business Process Owner	Senior Management	My Rating	Understanding Level
B	X	X	X		

51.2.1 Purpose and Overview

If you want to use concurrent employment functionality in personnel administration, you activate this switch (CCURE + PAUIX = 'X') in view T77S0.

System Switch (from Table T77S0)			
Group	Sem. abbr.	Value abbr.	Description
CCURE	PAUIX		CE Master Data User Interface Enhancements

Upon activating this switch, you see personnel assignment details in PA20/PA30.

Personnel No.	121715		Pers.Assgn	00121715		
Name	Prem Kumar Agrawal					
Pers.area	PNCV	EE group	1	ID number	21715	
Subarea	CV9Z	EE subgrp	E4	Emp Status	3	

You also see personnel assignment details in PA40.

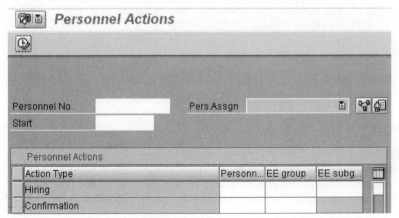

There are also other switches for concurrent employment. If you maintain view T77S0 for group CCURE, you can see these switches. You find them gray even in maintenance mode, because activation of concurrent employment, except for personnel administration, requires activities like modifying the tables, etc. However, personnel administration can be activated.

System Switch (from Table T77S0)			
Group	Sem. abbr.	Value abbr.	Description
CCURE	MAINS		Concurrent Employment Main Switch
CCURE	PAY99		Pers. Country Grouping 99: Start Date CE Payroll
CCURE	PAYCA		Canada: Start Date CE Payroll
CCURE	PAYUS		USA: Start Date CE Payroll

51.3 LAYOUT OF PERSONNEL ASSIGNMENT

Functional Consultant	User	Business Process Owner	Senior Management	My Rating	Understanding Level
B	X	X	X		

51.3.1 Purpose

Personnel assignment appears in three places, as shown below.

Personnel assignment

Pers.Assgn	00121715	🗐

Personnel assignment overview

Per.Assign	Pers.area	Subarea	EE group	EE subgrp
00121715	PNCV	CV9Z	1	E4
00121714	PNCV	CV23	1	M1

Personnel assignment details

	00121715	00121714
📄 Hire date	01.01.2005	29.09.1978
▽ 🗀 Organizational Assignment		
📄 CoCode	0100	0100
📄 Pers.area	Pune CVBU	Pune CVBU
📄 Subarea	CV9Z	CV23
📄 EE group	Permanent	Permanent
📄 EE subgrp	E4	M1
📄 Cost Ctr		1112467
▽ 🗀 Work Schedule		
📄 WS rule	WSRPG	WSRPG
📄 TM status	0	1

Default personnel assignment

By default, personnel assignment is personnel number. If you want to see some more information in this, you can enhance it in this node. All the information appears as a concatenated string.

Personnel assignment text

The personnel assignment text can vary depending on country grouping. If no personnel assignment text is specified for a country grouping, the system takes it from country grouping 99.

51.3.2 IMG Node

SM30 ➤ V_T587C_T

51.3.3 Screen

Ctry Grouping	40						

	Seq...	IType	Subtype	Field Name	Conversion	Dis.Length	Key/Text
					📄		Display 📄
					Display key		
					1 Display description		
					2 Display description and key		
					📄		Displa... 📄

51.3.4 Primary Key

Country Grouping + Description of Personnel Assignments – View + Detail View: Personnel Assignments – Categories + Sequence Number

51.3.5 Important Fields

Sequence number

Here you specify the sequence in which fields are concatenated.

Infotype, subtype, field name

Here you specify the field which is to be displayed.

Conversion

Here you specify whether the field is to be displayed for all personnel numbers, or only for active personnel numbers, or only for non-active personnel numbers.

Display length

Here you specify the maximum display length.

Key/text

In case the field has a key and a text, specify whether key is to be displayed, or text, or both.

51.4 LAYOUT OF PERSONNEL ASSIGNMENT OVERVIEW

Functional Consultant	User	Business Process Owner	Senior Management	My Rating	Understanding Level
B	X	X	X		

51.4.1 Purpose

When you click personnel assignment overview, you see important user details. You decide that layout here. A sample layout is shown below.

Per.Assign	Pers.area	Subarea	EE group	EE subgrp
00121715	PNCV	CV9Z	1	E4
00121714	PNCV	CV23	1	M1

51.4.2 IMG Node

SM30 ➤ V_T587C_O

51.4.3 Screen

Ctry Grouping	40

	S..	IType	Subtype	Field Name	KeyText	
	1	0001		WERKS	Display key	🗎
	2	0001		BTRTL	Display key	🗎
	3	0001		PERSG	Display key	🗎
	4	0001		PERSK	Display key	🗎

Personnel Assignment Overview

51.4.4 Primary Key

Country Grouping + Description of Personnel Assignments – View + Detail View: Personnel Assignments – Categories + Sequence Number

51.4.5 Important Fields

Sequence number

Here you specify the sequence in which fields appear.

Infotype, subtype, field name

Here you specify the field which is to be displayed.

Key/text

In case the field has a key and a text, specify whether key is to be displayed, or text, or both.

51.5 CATEGORIES FOR PERSONNEL ASSIGNMENT DETAILS

Functional Consultant	User	Business Process Owner	Senior Management	My Rating	Understanding Level
B	X	X	X		

51.5.1 Purpose and Overview

In personnel assignment details, you can organize the information in categories.

	00121715	00121714
📄 Hire date	01.01.2005	29.09.1978
▽ 🗀 Organizational Assignment		
📄 CoCode	0100	0100
📄 Pers.area	Pune CVBU	Pune CVBU
📄 Subarea	CV9Z	CV23
📄 EE group	Permanent	Permanent
📄 EE subgrp	E4	M1
📄 Cost Ctr		1112467
▽ 🗀 Work Schedule		
📄 WS rule	WSRPG	WSRPG
📄 TM status	0	1

Here you maintain the list of categories, and the sequence in which they should appear. If settings for personnel assignment details are not maintained for employee's country, they are taken from country grouping 99.

51.5.2 IMG Node

SM30 ➢ V_T587A

51.5.3 Screen

Ctry Grouping	99

Detail View: Personnel Assignments - Categories		
Category	Seq. no.	Cat Text
1	1	Organizational Assignment
7	2	Work Schedule
8	3	Basic Pay

51.5.4 Primary Key

Country Grouping + Detail View: Personnel Assignments – Categories

51.6 LAYOUT OF PERSONNEL ASSIGNMENT DETAILS

Functional Consultant	User	Business Process Owner	Senior Management	My Rating	Understanding Level
B	X	X	X		

51.6.1 Purpose

Here you define the layout of personnel assignment details.

51.6.2 IMG Node

SM30 ➢ V_T587C_D

51.6.3 Screen

Ctry Grouping 99

Personnel Assignment Details

Category	S...	IType	Subtype	Field Name	KeyText	
1	1	0001		BUKRS	Display key	📄
1	2	0001		WERKS	1 Display description	📄
1	3	0001		BTRTL	Display key	📄
1	4	0001		PERSG	1 Display description	📄
1	5	0001		PERSK	Display key	📄
1	6	0001		KOSTL	Display key	📄
7	1	0007		SCHKZ	Display key	📄
7	2	0007		ZTERF	Display key	📄

51.6.4 Primary Key

Country Grouping + Description of Personnel Assignments – View + Detail View: Personnel Assignments – Categories + Sequence Number

51.6.5 Important Fields

Category

Personnel assignment details are grouped in categories. Layout is defined for each category.

Sequence number

Here you specify the sequence in which fields appear.

Infotype, subtype, field name

Here you specify the field which is to be displayed.

Key/text

In case the field has a key and a text, specify whether key is to be displayed, or text, or both.

51.7 ACTIONS FOR CONCURRENT EMPLOYMENT

Functional Consultant	User	Business Process Owner	Senior Management	My Rating	Understanding Level
B	X	X	X		

51.7.1 Purpose

You can use this feature to determine how the system should react when you perform hiring actions for employees for whom a personnel relationship exists (employee recognition). When identifying employees you can choose whether the system should, for example, create an additional personnel assignment for an existing employee or perform a rehiring action for an employee who has left. So that the system can determine the accompanying action types, carry out an assignment between logical keys and action types using this feature.

51.7.2 IMG Node

PE03 ≻ ACTCE

51.7.3 Screen

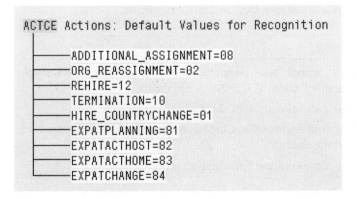

```
ACTCE Actions: Default Values for Recognition
     ├──── ADDITIONAL_ASSIGNMENT=08
     ├──── ORG_REASSIGNMENT=02
     ├──── REHIRE=12
     ├──── TERMINATION=10
     ├──── HIRE_COUNTRYCHANGE=01
     ├──── EXPATPLANNING=81
     ├──── EXPATACTHOST=82
     ├──── EXPATACTHOME=83
     └──── EXPATCHANGE=84
```

51.7.4 Fields for Decision-making

Company Code
Personnel Area
Personnel Subarea
Employee Group
Employee Subgroup
Country Grouping
Personnel Number
Work Contract
Reason for Action

51.7.5 Return Value

Table of action types

51.8 CONSISTENCY IN INFOTYPE DATA

Functional Consultant	User	Business Process Owner	Senior Management	My Rating	Understanding Level
B	X	X	X		

51.8.1 Purpose and Overview

For implementing concurrent employment, SAP had to create a new infotype framework. The new framework supports data sharing. In each infotype, there is a field, 'Grouping Value for Personnel Assignments'. If data sharing is applicable, this field should be same for all personnel numbers of a person. When that happens, the infotype information for all personnel numbers is the same. In the new framework, infotype properties are maintained in view V_T582ITVCLAS. Infotypes are categorized in four categories:

Category	Data sharing
Not Permitted	Infotypes cannot take part in data sharing. For them, copy mechanism of view V_T582A is applicable.
Central Services	Infotypes can take part in data sharing.
Permitted in Certain Circumstances	Only the country versions listed in view V_T582ITD can take part in data sharing
Permitted in All Circumstances	Infotypes can take part in data sharing.

In the new framework, grouping value is determined based on grouping reason. You assign grouping reason to an infotype here. You also specify whether the information is copied before the personnel assignment starts or from the point when the current personnel assignment exists.

51.8.2 IMG Node

SM30 ≻ V_T582G

51.8.3 Screen

IType	Type	IT Text	GrpRsn	+	Group Before...
0002		Personal Data	0002	Personal Data (I...	X Before … 🗎
0006		Addresses	0006	Addresses (Infot...	X Before … 🗎
0009	0	Bank Details	0009	Bank Details (Inf...	From Ass… 🗎
0048	US01	Residence Status	XMOL	Country Grouping	X Before … 🗎
0048	US02	Residence Status	XMOL	Country Grouping	X Before … 🗎

Infotype/Subtype Assignment - Grouping Reason

51.8.4 Primary Key

Infotype + Subtype

51.8.5 Important Fields

Infotype, subtype

Here you specify the infotype and subtype to which grouping reason is assigned.

Grouping reason

For each infotype and subtype you specify the grouping reasons.

Group before/from assignment start

This field determines whether the information is copied before the personnel assignment starts (X) or from the point when the current personnel assignment exists (blank).

51.8.6 Repairing Data Sharing Inconsistencies

You can run report RPUFIXDS to check and repair data sharing inconsistencies. Business Add-In (BAdI) HRPA_SHARING_REPOR enables you to determine the sequence of personnel numbers that should be repaired by report RPUFIXDS (Repairing Data Sharing Inconsistencies). The sequence of personnel numbers plays a decisive role in the result of the repair since the data comparison that takes place via the report always runs according to the previous personnel numbers.

51.9 GROUPING REASONS FOR PERSONNEL ASSIGNMENTS

Functional Consultant	User	Business Process Owner	Senior Management	My Rating	Understanding Level
B	X	X	X		

51.9.1 Purpose

This view contains master list of grouping reasons. Each program that must group the personnel assignments for certain processes is assigned a grouping reason. In customizing, the grouping reason is assigned a grouping rule. The grouping rule defines how the personnel assignments are grouped.

Each grouping reason for personnel assignments is assigned at least one grouping rule. Grouping rules are assigned to grouping reason at country + grouping reason + SAP/ customer entry level. Thus, a grouping reason can be assigned several grouping rules simultaneously. The following types of assignment exist:

➢ Customer-specific country-specific assignment
➢ Customer-specific cross-country assignment
➢ Country-specific standard assignment
➢ Cross-country standard assignment

Only one of these assignments is valid for a given period. To determine which grouping rule it must use, SAP checks the assignments in the sequence specified above.

In infotype 0712, you can maintain main personnel number for each person. The main personnel number can be different for different grouping reason. Grouping reason is subtype of infotype 0712.

51.9.2 IMG Node

SM30 ➢ T7CCE_GPREASON

51.9.3 Screen

51.9.4 Primary Key

Grouping Reason for Personnel Assignments

51.9.5 Important Fields

Grouping reason and name

Here you maintain master list of grouping reasons.

Changeability of assignment

Grouping rules are assigned to grouping reasons. Here you can determine whether they can be changed or not.

Grouping context

In a grouping context, a program provides additional data on a certain grouping reason that can be evaluated by a grouping rule. Note that a grouping reason is valid only in a specified context (since grouping reason is primary key of this view).

51.10 GROUPING RULES FOR PERSONNEL ASSIGNMENTS

Functional Consultant	User	Business Process Owner	Senior Management	My Rating	Understanding Level
B	X	X	X		

51.10.1 Purpose

This view contains master list of grouping rules.

51.10.2 IMG Node

SM30 ➤ T7CCE_GPRULE

51.10.3 Screen

Gr...	Name	Grouping Rule Class	Grouping Context	Do...	Cla...
0002	Personal Data (Infotype 0002)	CL_HRPA_GPRULE_...			
0004	Impairment (Infotype 0004)	CL_HRPA_GPRULE_...			
0006	Addresses (Infotype 0006)	CL_HRPA_GPRULE_...			
0009	Bank details (infotype 0009)	CL_HRPA_GPRULE_...			

Grouping Rules for Personnel Assignments

51.10.4 Primary Key

Grouping Rule for Personnel Assignments

51.10.5 Important Fields

Grouping rule and name

Here you maintain master list of grouping rules.

Grouping rule class

Grouping rules are implemented in grouping rule class.

Grouping context

In a grouping context, a program provides additional data on a certain grouping reason that can be evaluated by a grouping rule.

51.11 ASSIGNMENT OF GROUPING RULE TO GROUPING REASON

Functional Consultant	User	Business Process Owner	Senior Management	My Rating	Understanding Level
B	X	X	X		

51.11.1 Purpose

This view contains grouping rule for every grouping reason. These are cross-country assignments. Country-specific assignments are maintained in V_T7CCE_GPASG.

Grouping rules are assigned to grouping reason at country + grouping reason + SAP/ customer entry level. Thus, a grouping reason can be assigned several grouping rules simultaneously. The following types of assignment exist:

➢ Customer-specific country-specific assignment
➢ Customer-specific cross-country assignment
➢ Country-specific standard assignment
➢ Cross-country standard assignment

Only one of these assignments is valid for a given period. To determine which grouping rule it must use, SAP checks the assignments in the sequence specified above.

51.11.2 IMG Node

SM30 ➢ V_T7CCE_GPASGM

51.11.3   Screen

Assignment of Grouping Rule to Grouping Reason				
Grp...	Name	Status	Grp ...	Name
0002	Personal Data (Infotype 0002)	SAP ... 📄	0002	Personal Data (Infotype 0002)
0006	Addresses (Infotype 0006)	SAP ... 📄	0006	Addresses (Infotype 0006)
0009	Bank Details (Infotype 0009)	SAP ... 📄	XMOL	Country Grouping
TITO	Grouping According to Featu...	SAP ... 📄	TITO	Feature TIROG

51.11.4   Primary Key

Grouping Reason for Personnel Assignments + Flag: Customer entry or SAP entry

51.11.5   Important Fields

Grouping reason and name

Here you specify the grouping reason to which grouping rule is being assigned.

Status

SAP provides grouping rules for grouping reasons. If you want to specify your own grouping rule, you create your own entry, instead of overwriting SAP entry.

Grouping rule and name

Here you specify the grouping rule which is assigned to grouping reason.

51.12   COUNTRY-SPECIFIC ASSIGNMENT OF GROUPING RULE TO GROUPING REASON

Functional Consultant	User	Business Process Owner	Senior Management	My Rating	Understanding Level
B	X	X	X		

51.12.1   Purpose

This view contains grouping rule for every grouping reason. These are country-specific assignments. Cross-country assignments are maintained in V_T7CCE_GPASGM.

Grouping rules are assigned to grouping reason at country + grouping reason + SAP/customer entry level. Thus, a grouping reason can be assigned several grouping rules simultaneously. The following types of assignment exist:

> ➤ Customer-specific country-specific assignment
> ➤ Customer-specific cross-country assignment
> ➤ Country-specific standard assignment
> ➤ Cross-country standard assignment

Only one of these assignments is valid for a given period. To determine which grouping rule it must use, SAP checks the assignments in the sequence specified above.

51.12.2 IMG Node

SM30 ➤ V_T7CCE_GPASG

51.12.3 Screen

Assignment of Grouping Rule to Grouping Reason				
GrpRsn	Name	Status	Grp Rule	Name
		Customer en...▤		
		Customer en...▤		
		Customer en...▤		
		Customer en...▤		

51.12.4 Primary Key

Country Grouping + Grouping Reason for Personnel Assignments + Flag: Customer entry or SAP entry

51.12.5 Important Fields

Country grouping

Assignment of grouping rule to grouping reason can be country dependent.

Grouping reason and name

Here you specify the grouping reason to which grouping rule is being assigned.

Status

SAP provides grouping rules for grouping reasons. If you want to specify your own grouping rule, you create your own entry, instead of overwriting SAP entry.

Grouping rule and name

Here you specify the grouping rule which is assigned to grouping reason.

51.13 REFERENCE PERSONNEL NUMBERS (INFOTYPE 0031)

Functional Consultant	User	Business Process Owner	Senior Management	My Rating	Understanding Level
B	λ	X	X		

51.13.1 Screen

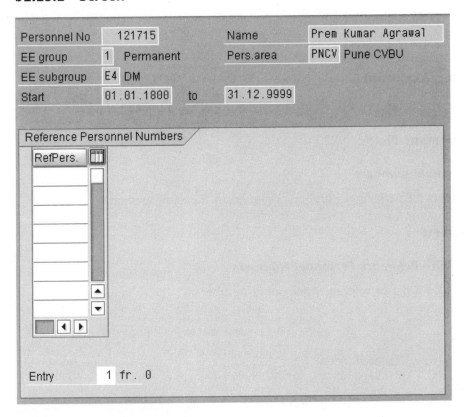

51.13.2 Purpose and Overview

If you have multiple employment relationships with a person at the same time, you have to assign him multiple personnel numbers. You would like to know all the personnel numbers assigned to the same person, so that you can maintain consistency in data, e.g. name, date of birth, etc. You may also use this information while running his payroll.

Infotype 0031 is used to maintain all related personnel numbers. While hiring an employee, if you enter a reference personnel number, infotype 0031 automatically gets updated for all personnel numbers. Also, certain infotypes, e.g. personal data, challenge, bank details, family member/dependents, etc. get copied. Which infotypes get copied depends on 'Copy infotype' field of view V_T582A.

When you edit these infotypes for a personnel number, all relevant infotype records for all related personnel numbers are also updated. Other infotypes can be maintained independently for each personnel number.

You only need to maintain infotype 0031 manually if you want to retrospectively create a relationship between two personnel numbers that already exist, or if you want to delete a link between two personnel numbers. Otherwise, it is automatically maintained by hiring action.

51.13.3   Subtypes

No subtypes

51.13.4   Time Constraint

B (IT exists for maximum of once from Jan. 1, 1800 to Dec. 12, 9999)

51.13.5   Important Fields

Reference personnel numbers

This field contains all personnel numbers assigned to the same person.

51.13.6   Reports

S_AHR_61016358—Reference Personnel Numbers

This report creates a list of reference personnel numbers.

```
                              Reference personnel numbers overview

Name              Agrawal Prem
Reporting period  01.01.2005 to  31.12.9999

Sort:      in ascending order by pers.no.

PerNo.    StaffStatus   Company code        Personnel area        EmplGroup

Data in period from   01.01.2005 to  31.12.9999:

00121714  3 Active      0100 Tata Motors Lim  PNCV Pune CVBU       1 Permane
00121715  3 Active      0100 Tata Motors Lim  PNCV Pune CVBU       1 Permane
```

51.14 REFERENCE PERSONNEL NUMBER PRIORITY (INFOTYPE 0121)

Functional Consultant	User	Business Process Owner	Senior Management	My Rating	Understanding Level
B	X	X	X		

51.14.1 Screen

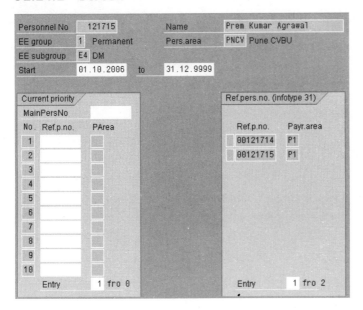

51.14.2 Purpose and Overview

If you have maintained reference personnel numbers in infotype 0031, you can maintain their priority in infotype 0121. You cannot enter a personnel number in infotype 0121, which does not exist in infotype 0031. Also, all reference personnel numbers must be in the same payroll area and legal person.

If payroll is run for an employee who has more than one personnel number, it is called multiple payroll. Payroll is not run for reference personnel numbers that have not been entered in infotype 0121. Payroll considers the personnel numbers in the sequence in which they are entered in infotype 0121. You can also specify a main personnel number in infotype 0121, which can be used in payroll and reporting.

51.14.3 Subtypes

No subtypes

51.14.4 Time Constraint

1 (Record must have no gaps, no overlappings)

Recruitment

Recruitment Process

52.1 KEY CONCEPTS

Functional Consultant	User	Business Process Owner	Senior Management	My Rating	Understanding Level
A	A	A	A		

Position

An organization has positions, which are occupied by persons. The person occupying a position does the work assigned to that position.

Vacancy

If a position is not occupied, it would be deemed vacant and should be filled up by recruitment. However, sometimes companies would like to review unoccupied positions and declare them vacant or obsolete. Also, sometimes they may want to create vacancy even for occupied position, so that a successor is in place before the position falls vacant. For these reasons, a distinction is made between non-occupancy and vacancy.

Advertisement

In order to fill vacancies, you would advertise them and seek applications. An advertisement can be for one or more vacancies.

Application

In response to the advertisement, you receive applications. Usually the applicants specify the vacancy for which they are applying, but sometimes you may get unsolicited applications which are not in response to your advertisement. Although uncommon, sometimes an application may be for more than one vacancy, or you may like to consider it for more than one vacancy.

Applicant

You should make a distinction between an applicant and an application. If the same person applies a second time, you should consider it as second application from the same applicant. By doing so you are able to relate your earlier experience with that applicant to his current application. You also save data entry effort.

There are two categories of applicants: external and internal. Internal applicants are your employees who are looking for a change in their existing position.

Components of recruitment process

You can visualize the recruitment process to be interplay of the following:

➤ Applicant data
➤ Activities
➤ Decisions
➤ Internal correspondence
➤ Applicant correspondence

Applicant data

You can keep a lot of applicant data in SAP. It is organized into logical groups called infotypes.

Activity

The process of selecting an applicant consists of a number of activities. These activities need to be created in the system so that people know that they are required to perform them. In most cases, SAP creates these activities for you. You can also create activities manually. You can also change or delete activities. Usually the activities are created as 'planned'. After you perform them, you change their status to 'completed'. As you perform activities and make decisions, you create more activities. This goes on until the recruitment process is completed.

Decisions/applicant status

When an application is received, the applicant is in 'In process' status. As an applicant goes through the selection process, and you make decisions, his status would change.

An applicant may be considered for a single vacancy, or for multiple vacancies. In the latter case, he can have different statuses for different vacancies and an overall status which is consistent with his vacancy statuses. In the former case, his vacancy status and overall status would be the same.

Internal correspondence

As you create activities pertaining to the recruitment process, you need to inform people that they are required to perform it. The system supports this by sending internal mails, which you can access through SAP business workplace.

Applicant correspondence

SAP supports multiple methods of applicant correspondence including e-mail. It also lets you handle applicant correspondence in bulk.

Action

SAP provides a composite mechanism called actions, through which you can deal with data entry, activities and decisions together. An applicant action does the following:

➢ Changes the overall status of an applicant and hence usually creates further activities.
➢ Runs an infogroup, which presents multiple infotypes one by one for capturing applicant data.
➢ Records the action in infotype 4000.

52.2 MANAGING POSITIONS

Functional Consultant	User	Business Process Owner	Senior Management	My Rating	Understanding Level
A	A	A	B		

52.2.1 Creating a Position

Purpose

In your company, you have an organization chart, which has different positions. These positions are occupied by persons who do the work assigned to their respective positions. The objective of recruitment module is to fill vacant positions with suitable persons either from inside or from outside the organization.

You create the organization chart containing positions in the Organizational Management (OM) module of SAP. If you have not implemented the OM module, but are implementing the recruitment module, you can create positions using transaction S_AHR_61011490 as described in chapter 4.16.

If you want to find applicants suitable for a position, you should maintain competencies for the position.

Transaction

PPOME—Organization and Staffing Change

Screen

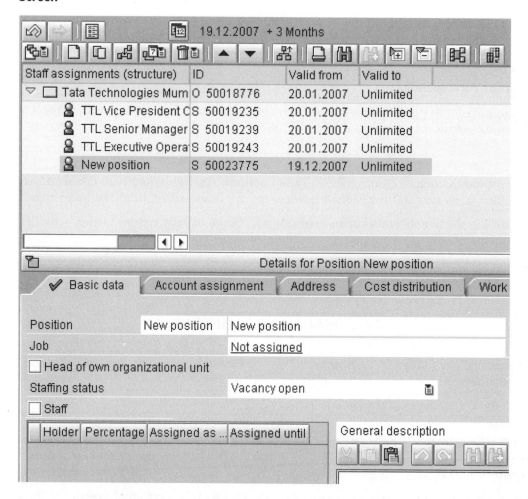

52.2.2 Delimiting a Position

When you no longer need a position, you can delimit it, provided it is unoccupied.

52.2.3 Making a Position Obsolete

If you recognize that a position is not required in the future, but it is occupied, you can't delimit the position. It may so happen that when it becomes unoccupied, someone may declare it vacant and fill it up not realizing that the position is obsolete. To prevent such a contingency, SAP provides infotype 1014, through which you can declare a position obsolete. Once a position is declared obsolete, it can't be made vacant. Also, if a vacancy already exists for that position that is also delimited. You can make a position obsolete using transaction PO13. Select the position you want to make obsolete, and create obsolete infotype for the period you want.

52.2.4 Identifying Unoccupied Positions

If there are unoccupied positions in your organization, you would probably like to fill them, or declare them obsolete. SAP provides transaction S_AHR_61018869 for identifying positions which are unoccupied in an organizational unit and all organizational units below it. If you want to see unoccupied positions only in an organizational unit and not in organizational units below it, use program RHFILLPOS with transaction code SA38. You should ensure that all unoccupied positions are either delimited, or made vacant.

52.3 CREATING A VACANCY

Functional Consultant	User	Business Process Owner	Senior Management	My Rating	Understanding Level
A	A	A	B		

52.3.1 Maintaining Vacancy Infotype

Positions are occupied by persons. Although one could infer that every unoccupied position is a vacant position, many organizations like to review before declaring a position vacant. Sometimes organizations also like to declare a position vacant so that they can do recruitment, even though the position is still occupied. This happens when you want to appoint successor for a position, while the incumbent is still occupying the position. Therefore, SAP treats non-occupancy distinct from vacancy and provides infotype 1007 in which you can declare a position vacant. Positions declared vacant are automatically transferred to recruitment module table T750X, where you maintain other information, e.g. personnel officer and line manager. You can create a vacancy for a position by specifying 'Vacancy open' in the 'Staffing status' field in transaction PPOME. You can also use transaction PO13 to create vacancy for a position.

Position	GM - HR	General Manager - Human Resource
Planning Status	Active	
Validity	06.12.2007 to 31.12.9999	⚭ Change Information

Vacancy

◉ Open   ☐ Historical rec.

○ Vacancy filled

52.4 ASSIGNING A PERSONNEL OFFICER

Functional Consultant	User	Business Process Owner	Senior Management	My Rating	Understanding Level
A	A	A	B		

52.4.1 Purpose

If integration with OM is active, and you create vacancy infotype 1007 in OM, a record is inserted in table T750X. Any vacancies that you create in organizational management are marked with a P in the 'Maintained in OM' field of view V_T750X. You cannot edit these vacancies in recruitment except personnel officer, line manager and percent reserved fields.

If integration with OM is not active, you first create positions in table T528B using transaction S_AHR_61011490 (refer to chapter 4.16), and then you can create, change, or delete a vacancy using transaction PBAY.

In recruitment only vacant positions can be assigned to applicants. If you have multiple persons doing recruitment, you can assign a personnel officer who looks after the administrative aspects of filling a vacancy and a line manager who is responsible for the selection of applicant. This is recorded using transaction PBAY (PBAZ for display). You should also determine the PA, PSA, applicant group and applicant range for a vacancy, which would be used during initial data entry.

52.4.2 Transactions

PBAY—Maintain Vacancy
PBAZ—Display Vacancy

52.4.3 Screen

Vacancy	Activity	from	to	Line manager	POf	St	OM	Req.profi
20000117	Deputy General Manager (Law)	20.08.2007	31.12.9999	Gill Nirmala		occ.	P	
20000134	SENIOR OFFICER(INTERNAL AUDIT)	01.01.2001	31.12.9999			vac.	P	
20000237	DEPUTY MANAGER (GEAR CX)	31.12.9999	31.12.9999	Gupta Rajeev		vac.	P	

Evaluation period: 26.11.2007 to 31.12.9999

Vacancy	05010001	Senior manager	Validity	
		Created in OM	Start Date	30.11.2007
			End Date	31.12.9999

Vacancy

Personnel Officer	
Line manager	
Pct.approved	100.00
Pct.reserved	
Staffing pct.	0.00 Staffing status 0 vacant

If the vacancy is created in recruitment all the fields can be maintained.

	Validity	
	Start Date	☑
Vacancy ☑	End Date	☑

Vacancy

Personnel Officer	
Line manager	
Pct.approved	
Pct.reserved	
Staffing pct.	Staffing status

52.4.4   Important Fields

Vacancy

Here you enter or choose the vacancy for which you are defining details.

Start and end date

By maintaining the validity period of the vacancy record you know when the vacancy was created and when it was filled, or the requirement dropped.

Personnel officer

The personnel officer you specify here is proposed as default during initial data entry of applicants.

Line manager

The line manager is responsible for deciding on an applicant's suitability for the vacancy. Any person who is an employee of the company in personnel administration can be defined as a line manager. A line manager can also perform activities pertaining to recruitment from manager self-service in SAP.

Percent approved

In SAP you can create positions which do not require a full-time person. They may be filled with part time employees, or a full time employee who is assigned to the position only partly. You can also have a position which requires multiple full-time persons. These percentages are specified in relationships between organizational unit and position and shown here.

Percent reserved

If you have identified an applicant for a vacancy, you may update this field. This is particularly important if multiple personnel officers are trying to fill the same vacancy.

Staffing percentage

The system determines staffing percentage as percent occupied divided by percent approved. Percent reserved is not considered in staffing percentage.

Staffing status

The system determines the staffing status of a vacancy automatically on the basis of the percentage of the vacancy which is approved, reserved and occupied.

Vacant	At least part of the vacancy is neither occupied nor reserved.
Reserved	The vacancy is either completely reserved or partially reserved and partially occupied (100% altogether).
Occupied	The entire vacancy is occupied.

52.5 SEARCHING APPLICANT POOL

Functional Consultant	User	Business Process Owner	Senior Management	My Rating	Understanding Level
A	A	A	B		

After a personnel officer is assigned a vacancy, he would like to see whether he has suitable applicants in his applicant pool (applicants having overall status 'On hold'). There are three ways of doing it.

52.5.1 Searching based on Applicant Characteristics

You can search for a suitable applicant based on unsolicited application group, applicant group and applicant range. You can use transaction PBAE to locate such applicants. You can see their short profiles and facsimiles. If an applicant is found suitable, you can change his overall status and assign vacancy. You may then contact him to see if he is interested in the vacancy you have. If he is, you may proceed in the normal way.

App.no.	Name	Action	Ov.status	POf
06000158	Pratap Rudra	Put applicant on hold	On hold	VM
06000161	Chand Gopal	Additional Data - Hold	On hold	AJ

Short profile

Applicants by action

Evaluation period 01.01.2007 to 23.01.2008

52.5.2 Searching based on Competencies of Position

You can search based on competencies provided you have defined competencies required for the vacant position and competencies are also maintained in your applicant database. You can use transaction PBAG for this purpose.

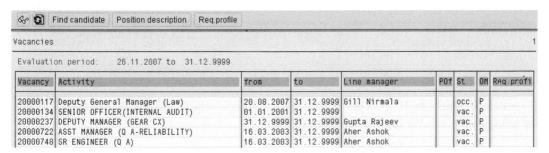

Vacancy	Activity	from	to	Line manager	POf	St.	OM	Req.profi
20000117	Deputy General Manager (Law)	20.08.2007	31.12.9999	Gill Nirmala		occ.	P	
20000134	SENIOR OFFICER(INTERNAL AUDIT)	01.01.2001	31.12.9999			vac.	P	
20000237	DEPUTY MANAGER (GEAR CX)	31.12.9999	31.12.9999	Gupta Rajeev		vac.	P	
20000722	ASST MANAGER (Q A-RELIABILITY)	16.03.2003	31.12.9999	Aher Ashok		vac.	P	
20000748	SR ENGINEER (Q A)	16.03.2003	31.12.9999	Aher Ashok		vac.	P	

Find candidate Position description Req.profile

Vacancies   1

Evaluation period: 26.11.2007 to 31.12.9999

You can select a vacancy and see its position description and requirement profile. If you click 'Find candidate', it shows the competencies required for the position.

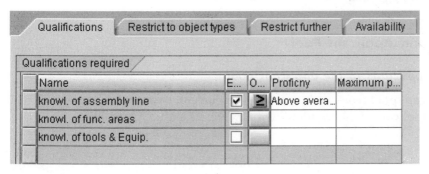

Name	E...	O...	Proficny	Maximum p...
knowl. of assembly line	☑	≥	Above avera...	
knowl. of func. areas	☐			
knowl. of tools & Equip.	☐			

Qualifications | Restrict to object types | Restrict further | Availability

Qualifications required

You can add or delete competencies if you wish. To add competencies, get qualifications in object manager, select the qualification you want to add and double-click.

The tab 'Restrict to object types' has external and internal applicants selected. If you want to consider only external or only internal applicants, deselect the other. If you want to consider only certain applicants, you can specify them in 'Restrict further'. When you click execute, the system suggests suitable applicants in the format given below.

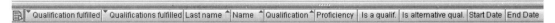

| Qualification fulfilled | Qualifications fulfilled | Last name | Name | Qualification | Proficiency | Is a qualif. | Is alternative qual. | Start Date | End Date |

If competencies for position are not maintained, you can use transaction PBAP, PBAQ, or PBAI. To add competencies, get qualifications in object manager, select the qualification you want to add and double-click.

52.5.3 Searching based on Education

You can search based on education of the applicants using transaction S_AHR_61015511.

Name	Educ. est. text	Institute/location	Valid From	End Date	Name	Cert.Text	Educ./train. text	Dur.	Unit
sharma ajay	CBSE		26.08.2000	26.08.2004	India	Full Time	BE	0	
Kumar Ravi	Other Mgmt Inst	Bharti Vidyapeeth	19.11.2006	31.12.9999	India	Full Time	MBA	2	Years

You can summarize the list in two ways. If you click 'Statistics I' you get the following screen where the list is summarized by educational establishment, certificate, branches of study and education.

Number	Educ. est. text	Cert.Text	Branch of study text	Branch of study text	Educ./train. text
1	CBSE	Full Time			BE
1	Other Mgmt Inst	Full Time	HR Management	HR Management	MBA

If you click 'Statistics II' you get the following screen where the list is summarized only by educational establishment and certificate.

Number	Educ. est. text	Cert.Text
1	CBSE	Full Time
1	Other Mgmt Inst	Full Time

52.5.4 Maintaining Applicant Pool

Identification of applicants in the applicant pool

If you use the applicant pool, you need to maintain it current, relevant and easy to search. Applicants in the applicant pool are identified by overall status 'On-hold'.

Adding an applicant to the applicant pool

You must not add all unwanted applications in the applicant pool. If you do that you would fill it with junk and finding an applicant when you are looking for one would become difficult. Also, when you are adding an applicant to the applicant pool, you need to enter data needed for performing the search in future. This data depends on the method of search you are going to use. If you use all three methods described above, you need to enter unsolicited application group, applicant group, applicant range, competencies and education.

Using an applicant from the applicant pool

If your search shows that an applicant from the applicant pool may be suitable for some vacancy, you should invite fresh application from that applicant for the vacancy you have. By doing this you will know whether the applicant is interested in the vacancy or not, and you will also get updated information on the applicant. You should then enter the new application, which will bring him from the applicant pool into active consideration.

52.6 ADVERTISING

Functional Consultant	User	Business Process Owner	Senior Management	My Rating	Understanding Level
A	A	A	B		

52.6.1 Displaying/Creating Recruitment Instruments

In case you decide to seek fresh applications for a vacancy, you can advertise it in various media including portal, employment agencies and head hunting. An advertisement is published in a recruitment instrument. You would like to know which recruitment instruments are available to you for advertising your vacancy. You can display the list of recruitment instruments using transaction PBAV. You can also change a recruitment instrument, or create a new one in the same transaction.

Instrument	Instrument	Medium	Name of medium	Address	Contact
00000001	Times Of India	01	Press	A	
00000002	Indian Express	01	Press		
00000003	Hindustan Times	01	Press		

You can also maintain address of a recruitment instrument.

```
┌─ Maintain address ─────────────────────────────────[×]─┐
│                                                        │
│  Var.key for address      │ TOI │                      │
│                                                        │
│  Last name          ┌──────────────────────────────┐  │
│  Affix              ├──────────────────────────────┤  │
│  Street/PO box      ├──────────────────────────────┤  │
│  Postal code/city   ├──────────────────────────────┤  │
│  District           ├──────────────────────────────┤  │
│  Country            ├──────────────────────────────┤  │
│  Telephone number   ├──────────────────────────────┤  │
│  Fax number         ├──────────────────────────────┤  │
│  Department         └──────────────────────────────┘  │
│                                                        │
│  [ Save address ]  [ Delete address ]                  │
└────────────────────────────────────────────────────────┘
```

52.6.2   Evaluating Recruitment Instruments

When you look at the list of recruitment instruments, you may wonder which recruitment instrument to choose. You may want to evaluate their past performance. This can be done using transaction PBAA or S_AHR_61015518. You can see total cost and cost per application of different recruitment instruments.

👓 Instrument	Evaluate advert	Applicant statistics	Applicant list

Evaluate Recruitment Instruments

Instrument	Number of adverts	Number of applications	Total cost		Cost per application	
Times Of India	15	25	20,676.00	INR	827.04	INR
Indian Express	1	2	200.00	INR	100.00	INR
Job Street.com	1	6	500.00	INR	83.33	INR

Displaying recruitment instrument

You can select a recruitment instrument and display its details.

	Instrument	Instrument	Medium	Name of medium	Address	Contact
	00000001	Times Of India	01	Press	A	

Evaluating advertisement

You can select a recruitment instrument and see the details of all advertisements in it.

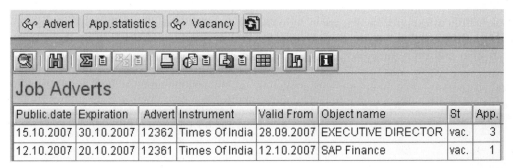

Public.date	Expiration	Advert	Instrument	Valid From	Object name	St	App.
15.10.2007	30.10.2007	12362	Times Of India	28.09.2007	EXECUTIVE DIRECTOR	vac.	3
12.10.2007	20.10.2007	12361	Times Of India	12.10.2007	SAP Finance	vac.	1

You can also get this screen by using transaction PBA0 or S_AHR_61015517. After selecting an advertisement, you can display it, see applicant statistics, or display vacancies in the advertisement.

Applicant statistics

You can select a recruitment instrument and see the applicant statistics.

Applicant status (overall)	Number
In process	10
On hold	0
Rejected	4
To be hired	7
Contract offered	0
Offer rejected	0
Invite	2
Total	23

Applicant list

You can select a recruitment instrument and see the list of applicants.

Pers.No.	Employee/app.name	App.status	Valid From
6000005	sharma ajay	In process	26.08.2006
6000011	SHARMA K K	In process	18.11.2006
6000013	SHARMA GAJENDRA	Invite	27.11.2006

52.6.3 Creating Advertisement

Purpose

To seek applications for a vacancy, you need to advertise it. Advertisements are created/modified/deleted using transaction PBAW and displayed using transaction PBAX. You can also maintain an advertisement through configuration view V_T750B.

Screen

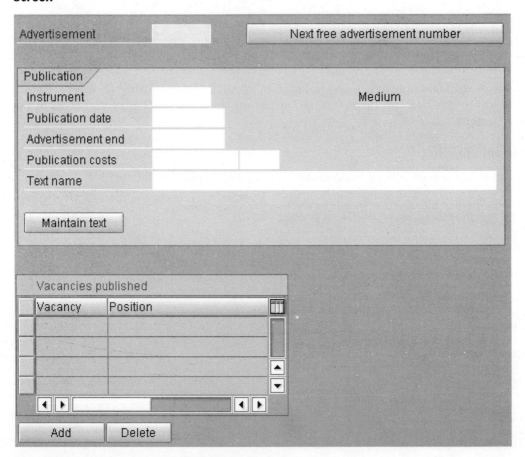

Publication date and advertisement end

An advertisement is published in a recruitment instrument on a certain date. If an advertisement is repeated, the advertisement end date can also be maintained.

Publication costs

You can maintain publication costs of an advertisement, which is used in comparing effectiveness of different advertisements and recruitment instruments.

Text name, maintain text

You can give the advertisement a name, and maintain its text.

Vacancies published

An advertisement can contain one or more vacancies. It is possible that the same vacancy may be published in more than one advertisement. Vacancy assignment is optional.

52.7 RECEIVING APPLICATION

Functional Consultant	User	Business Process Owner	Senior Management	My Rating	Understanding Level
A	A	A	B		

After you advertise your requirement, you start receiving applications. You should sort the applications by vacancy to facilitate data entry. If you receive any unsolicited applications, you should assign each application an unsolicited application group. You should let the system generate applicant numbers. Assigning applicant numbers externally is not recommended, but in case you are doing it, you should stamp the applicant number on the application.

52.8 ENTERING APPLICATION IN THE SYSTEM

Functional Consultant	User	Business Process Owner	Senior Management	My Rating	Understanding Level
A	A	A	B		

52.8.1 Purpose

After you receive applications, you would enter the data in SAP using transaction PB10. The data you enter in this screen goes into infotypes 4000, 0001, 0002, 0006 (subtype 1), 0105 (subtype 0010), 4001, 4004 and 4005. You should also do vacancy assignment, which would normally be mentioned in the application. If you scrutinize the applications before initial data entry, you can enter the decisions during initial data entry itself. You can also enter additional data for those applications in which you are interested. If you receive an application, which is not suitable for your requirement, you should still enter his data, if you want to send him a rejection/regret letter. If you receive any unsolicited applications you should do initial data entry of those also. In case your system is configured to generate applicant number automatically, you should write the applicant number on the application and file it. You can also create facsimiles during initial data entry. The system ensures that an applicant is not given multiple applicant number.

52.8.2 Transaction

PB10–Initial data entry

52.8.3 Screen

Initial data entry

| 🔓 Former applicant/former employee | 🖉 Save+add.data | In process | Put on hold | Reject | 🗋 |

Appl.no.		Start	22.11.2007
Status	In process	☐ Reference available
Reason		
Pers.no.		☐ Assign facsimiles

Organizational assignment

Per.area	☑	Subarea	
Ap.group	☑	Appl.range		🖺
Pers.off			☐ Further data

Personal data / Address

Title	🖺	Title	🖺
F. name		Last name	
Birth dt		Comm.lang.	English	🖺
		National.	🖺	☐ Further data
Street			
PCd/city			
Tel. no.		Country	🖺	☐ Further data
Email			

Application

| Advert | | Pub.date | |
| Unsol.AG | | 🖺 | ☐ Further data |

52.8.4 Important Fields

Applicant number

You can either let the system determine the applicant number from an internal number range, or enter the applicant number yourself, depending on your configuration. In the former case, you should leave this field blank. The system generates the applicant number automatically. In the latter case, you should give an applicant number, which does not exist in the system. In case the system determines that the applicant already exists, and you confirm it, this field is populated by the system, and you enter a new application for the existing applicant.

Start date

Here you maintain the application date. You should decide on a convention that your company would follow, e.g. the date of entering the application in the system, or the date of receiving the application, or the date written by the applicant in the application. When you enter the data in this screen, it gets saved in various infotypes. Each infotype record has a start and end date. The following table gives the start date and end date of all infotypes created from this screen.

Infotype	Infotype description	Start date	End date
0001	Organizational Assignment	Date in start date field	31.12.9999
0002	Personal Data	Date of birth	31.12.9999
0006	Addresses	Date in start date field	31.12.9999
0105	Communication	Date in start date field	31.12.9999
4000	Applicant Actions	Date in start date field	31.12.9999
4001	Applications	Date in start date field	Date in start date field
4004	Applicant Activity Status	01.01.1800	31.12.9999
4005	Applicant's Personnel Number	01.01.1800	31.12.9999

Status

Each applicant has an overall status. Normally, when you enter the data in this screen, the applicant is assigned 'In process' status. But if you choose to reject him, or put him on hold, the status is changed accordingly.

Reason

Here you can specify the reason for assigning a particular status.

Personnel number

This field is used only for internal applicants who are still with the company. Do not specify the personnel number of a former employee (employment status 0) here. If you specify the personnel number, and the employee has never been an applicant before, his personal data and address data infotypes are copied, so that you do not have to enter it again. You can, however, modify them. The system also creates infotype 4005 maintaining the link between the applicant number and the personnel number. If the employee has been an applicant before, the applicant number field is populated by the system, and you enter a new application for him. The system also ensures that you enter the personnel number if the applicant group is for internal applicants. Similarly, you cannot specify the personnel number if the applicant group is for external applicants.

Reference available

If you tick this checkbox, the system asks you to enter the reference employee. A reference employee is an employee who is able to provide information on the quality of the applicant's work and recommend that the applicant be hired.

Assign facsimiles

When you are entering the applicant information, you may want to store facsimiles of the applicant's application and other documents so that during further processing you can view the facsimiles rather than the original documents. This topic is covered in detail in chapter 52.8.8, 'Applicant Document Storage'.

Personnel area, personnel subarea

Personnel area and personnel subarea are locations of the organization where the applicant is expected to work if hired. Personnel area can be used to restrict authorizations.

Applicant group, applicant range

Applicant group and applicant range are two parameters for classifying applicants. These can be used for searching a suitable applicant in applicant pool. They can also be used to restrict authorizations.

Personnel officer

Personnel officer is responsible for processing an application. He gets a mail whenever an activity is created in the applicant's selection process. The personnel officer is defaulted either from the vacancy assigned to an advertisement or from the unsolicited application group. Personnel officer of an applicant can be used to restrict authorizations of persons accessing applicant data.

Personal data

Here you can enter personal data of the applicant. In case of an internal applicant, this data is copied from the employee data. For details of fields, see chapter 5.1.

Address

Here you can enter permanent address of the applicant which is stored in subtype 1 of infotype 0006. In case of an internal applicant, this data is copied from the employee data.

Advertisement

Here you specify the advertisement against which the application has been made. This is used to determine the number of applications received against an advertisement and thereby determine the effectiveness of advertisement and recruitment instrument. When you are assigning vacancies to an application, the vacancies published in the advertisement are available by default.

Unsolicited application group

Sometimes you may receive applications which are not for any specific vacancies. You may like to retain them for future use. You can group these unsolicited applications, so that when you have to search among these applications in future, you can search only in appropriate unsolicited application groups.

Further data

The data you enter in this screen goes into different infotypes. These infotypes have many more fields. What have been shown on this screen are only important fields of that infotype. If you want to enter more data for an infotype than what is shown on the screen, you can tick on 'Further data' checkbox of that infotype. After you click save, the system displays all fields of that infotype, where you can enter data in other fields of that infotype.

52.8.5 Menu

| Former applicant/former employee | When you enter an applicant's data, the system checks whether the applicant is a former applicant or a former employee. This check is performed automatically. You can also perform this check manually by clicking this icon.

| Save+add.data | If the person entering an applicant's data is in a position to decide whether the applicant is of interest to the company, he may want to finish entering all the data for him, so that the application does not need to be handled again. By clicking this icon, you can enter data for vacancy, education, other/previous employers and competencies. It is recommended that you at least enter the vacancy mentioned in the application. If you enter additional data, the action type recorded is 14, 15 or 16, instead of 11, 12 or 13.

| In process | This icon is to set the applicant's overall status to 'In process'.

| Put on hold | If you want to put an applicant on hold, you can do so by clicking this icon.

| Reject | If you want to reject an applicant, you can do so by clicking this icon.

When you are entering data for many applications, it saves effort if the field values you entered last are proposed as default values. SAP supports this. But while doing so, it also copies personal data and address. Since these are most likely to change, SAP has given this icon to clear the fields of personal data and address.

52.8.6 Unsolicited Applications

When you receive an unsolicited application, you should check whether there is a suitable vacancy. If there is, you should assign it to the applicant and put him in process. If there is no suitable vacancy, you should consider whether to add it to the applicant pool for future use (click 'Put on hold') or to reject it (click 'Reject'). If you are adding an applicant to applicant pool, you should carefully choose the values of applicant group, applicant range and unsolicited application group. If you use competencies and education for searching your applicant pool, you should also enter them in the system.

52.8.7 Multiple Applications from an Applicant

Unique applicant number

If a person, who had applied for a job in your company earlier, applies again, should he be given a new applicant number? The answer is no for two reasons. First, you have previous experience with the applicant, which you would like to consider before further processing his application. Second, you can save on data entry effort, as most of the data about him would be already available in your system, which you can update if required. The same applies to former employee. In the case of former employee, you would also like to maintain a link between his applicant number and personnel number. SAP allows you to do all this. When you enter an applicant's data and save, the system checks whether he is a former applicant or a former employee. The check is based on last name. If you specify first name and/or date of birth, the search is refined further. The match of first and last name may not be exact, as can be seen from the following screenshot.

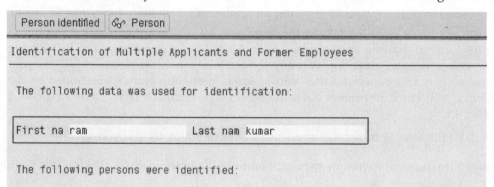

| Person identified | &5° Person |

Identification of Multiple Applicants and Former Employees

The following data was used for identification:

| First na ram | Last nam kumar |

The following persons were identified:

Applicant

Name	Init.entry	Overall status	Status reason
ram kumar	10.11.2003	In process	New application
ram kumar	03.12.2007	In process	
Ram Kumar	03.07.2003	In process	New application
RAMASWAMI RAJ KUMAR	23.08.2003	Rejected	
RAMASWAMI RAJ KUMAR	23.08.2003	Rejected	
ramesh kumar	04.08.2003	Rejected	Not Suitable
Ramesh Kumar	07.08.2003	In process	New application
Ramesh Kumar	07.08.2003	In process	New application
RAMESH KUMAR	21.09.2003	In process	New application

Former employees

Name	Leaving da	Personnel action	Action reason
RAMAN KUMAR	04.06.2007	Separation	Temp. Services Termi
Ramendra Kumar	12.10.2006	Resignation	Resignation better J
RAMESH KUMAR	30.05.2007	Separation	Temp. Services Termi
RAMESH KUMAR	31.05.2007	Separation	Temp. Services Termi

However, if the date of birth is specified, it is matched exactly, as can be seen from the following screenshot.

```
┌──────────────────────┬─────────────────┐
│ Person identified    │ &ᵧ Person       │
└──────────────────────┴─────────────────┘
═══════════════════════════════════════════
Identification of Multiple Applicants and Former Employees
───────────────────────────────────────────

  The following data was used for identification:

┌─────────────────────────────────────────────────────────┐
│ First na ram               Last nam kumar                │
│ DoB       26.10.1979                                     │
└─────────────────────────────────────────────────────────┘

  The following persons were identified:

┌───────────────────────────────────────────────────────────┐
│ Applicant                                                   │
├──────────────────┬───────────┬───────────────┬─────────────┤
│ Name             │ Init.entry│ Overall status│ Status reason│
├──────────────────┼───────────┼───────────────┼─────────────┤
│ ram kumar        │ 10.11.2003│ In process    │ New application│
└──────────────────┴───────────┴───────────────┴─────────────┘

┌───────────────────────────────────────────────────────────┐
│ Former employees                                            │
├───────────────────────────────────────────────────────────┤
│ No persons found with same data                            │
└───────────────────────────────────────────────────────────┘
```

If you select an applicant or a former employee, and click 'Person identified' icon, the system copies the applicant number in initial entry screen. You then no longer create a new applicant, only a new application.

Similarly, when an existing employee applies for a position, you would like to know that for considering your existing knowledge about that person, as well as to save data entry effort. When an existing employee makes an application, you enter his personnel number in the initial entry screen. For an existing employee, the applicant number check is based on this personnel number, and not on name and date of birth as in the case of external applicants and former employees. The system checks whether the employee is applying for the first time. If he is, his data is copied into the applicant data base. If he applies again, he is assigned his old applicant number; only a new application is created.

Distinction between an applicant and an application

What are the implications of receiving multiple applications from an applicant? From a business perspective, you may have rules to allow or disallow the application. You may also want to consider your earlier experience with the applicant. From a process/system perspective, an application is merely data about an applicant and his interest in certain vacancies. Usually you would receive another application from an applicant when you are no longer actively considering him. The new application brings him back in consideration and you update his data. If you receive another application from an applicant when you are still actively considering him, the new application can only result in assignment of a new vacancy and change in his overall status.

Processing of an application has two perspectives—the decision perspective and the activities perspective. From a decision perspective there is no difference between the application and the applicant. Your decisions are either for the applicant as a whole (overall status), or his suitability for certain vacancy (vacancy status). In both these decisions, application has no role.

Activities, on the other hand, are carried out with respect to an application. When you receive an application, you start performing activities. Finally, you close the application and the activities cease.

Another significance of an application is in evaluating effectiveness of advertisement and effectiveness of recruitment instrument. The information in the system for an application is stored in infotype 4001 which contains the advertisement through which the applicant came to know of the vacancy, and therefore helps to determine the effectiveness of advertisement and the effectiveness of recruitment instrument.

When a new applicant is created through initial data entry, the system runs infogroup 47 and records actions 11 (Initial data entry), 12 (Initial data entry—Hold) or 13 (Initial data entry—Reject). When a new application is created for an existing applicant, the system runs infogroup 43 and records actions 21 (New Application), 22 (New Application—Hold) or 23 (New Application—Reject).

52.8.8 Applicant Document Storage

If you select the checkbox to assign facsimiles to an applicant during initial data entry, on saving the application you get the following window:

Doc.type	Description
HRIRESUAPL	Applicant's resume
HRICERTAPL	Qualifications of applicant
HRIREFEAPL	Reference for applicant
HRIDIPLAPL	Training certificate for applicant
HRIAPPLICA	Written application

This shows all the document types you can store in the system. This is a flexible list which is created based on your requirements, and can be changed. Once you select a document type, you get the following window:

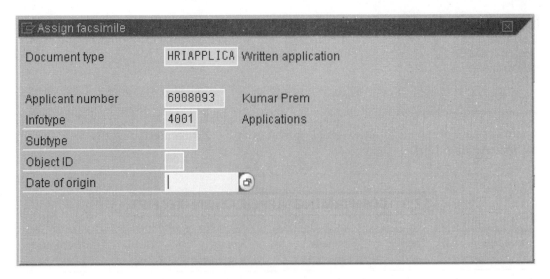

After you specify the date, you get the following window:

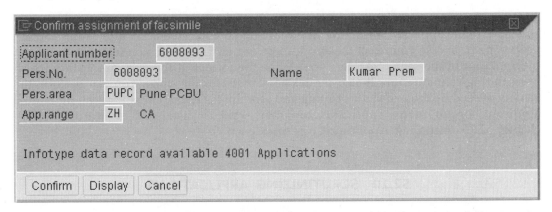

Once you confirm, the system prompts you to enter a bar code as shown below:

Enter a bar code for the facsimile and click the green tick icon. You can use this bar code to record the application document. You get the following window through which you can continue assigning more facsimiles.

Documents are archived in an external optical archive and connected to the SAP system via SAP Archive Link.

52.9   CONFIRMING APPLICATION RECEIPT

Functional Consultant	User	Business Process Owner	Senior Management	My Rating	Understanding Level
A	A	A	B		

After you have entered an application in the system, you may want to send a letter or an e-mail to the applicant informing him that you have received the application and are processing it. In case you reject the application, or put it on-hold, you may like to inform the applicant of the same. SAP lets you define the format of this communication which is set during configuration. It also creates an activity for the same. You can perform the activity of sending the e-mail, or printing and sending the letter, either for each individual applicant, or for many applicants together. This is discussed in more detail in chapter 52.15, 'Handling Applicant Correspondence'.

52.10   SCRUTINIZING APPLICATIONS

Functional Consultant	User	Business Process Owner	Senior Management	My Rating	Understanding Level
A	A	A	B		

Manual application scrutiny

You may scrutinize applications either before initial data entry or after. You would compare the applicant's details with the requirements of the vacancy he has applied for to determine his suitability. If you find that the applicant is not suitable for the vacancy he has applied for, you may examine the application to see if he is suitable for any other vacancy you have. If he is not suitable for any existing vacancy, you would decide either to keep his application in the applicant pool for future use, or to reject it. You may also consider an application for multiple vacancies. You should do application scrutiny of unsolicited applications also and take the same decisions. You would then update the decision and vacancy assignment in the system.

System supported application scrutiny

SAP can also help you to find suitable vacancy for an applicant through profile match up. In order to use this facility, you need to maintain competencies for positions and enter competencies of an applicant. You run transaction PPPD and select the applicant.

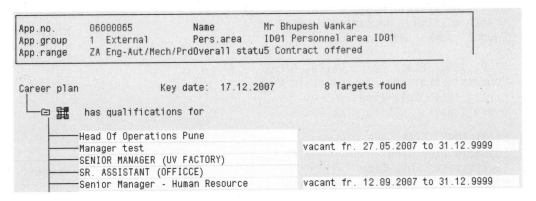

You then select Goto ≻ Career planning, and select 'Qualifications'. The system shows you the positions for which the applicant is suitable, including vacancies.

```
App.no.       06000065      Name       Mr Bhupesh Wankar
App.group     1  External   Pers.area  ID01 Personnel area ID01
App.range     ZA Eng-Aut/Mech/PrdOverall statu5 Contract offered


Career plan              Key date:  17.12.2007       8 Targets found

 └─⊟ ▦   has qualifications for

      ├──── Head Of Operations Pune
      ├──── Manager test                  vacant fr. 27.05.2007 to 31.12.9999
      ├──── SENIOR MANAGER (UV FACTORY)
      ├──── SR. ASSISTANT (OFFICCE)
      └──── Senior Manager - Human Resource   vacant fr. 12.09.2007 to 31.12.9999
```

52.11 VIEWING APPLICANT PROFILE

Functional Consultant	User	Business Process Owner	Senior Management	My Rating	Understanding Level
A	A	A	B		

You need to see the data you enter for an applicant in a structured format. You can do that by clicking Short profile , which can be accessed from many transactions. SAP lets you customize the short profile to your requirements. It supplies a standard text,

APPLICANT_SHORT_PROFILE, which you can copy and modify. You can also have different formats of short profiles for different categories of applicants. Which short profile is used for which applicant is determined by feature SHPRO.

```
Mr RAO VENKATESHWAR H. NO. 9-8-443
GOURI GANESH NILAYA
KALIDAS NAGAR

BIDAR

Cell Phone:

Date of Birth: 10.12.1980
Birthplace: BIDAR , Karnataka , India
Gender: Male
Marital status: Single
Nationality: Indian
Mother Tongue: Kannada

Education :
01.01.2002: Other Colleges/Unive S.J.C.E MYSORE
Education/training: BE
Certificate: Full Time
Branch of study: Mechanical
Overall marks: 60% to <75%

01.01.1998: State Board GNIPUC BIDAR
Education/training: Intermediate/HSC
Certificate: Full Time
Overall marks: 60% to <75%

01.01.1996: CBSE GNPS BIDAR
Education/training: High School/SSC
Certificate: Full Time
Overall marks: 60% to <75%


Events:
Event: Recr - Data Upload, valid from 19.06.2003
Status: In process , New application

Aplication(Action):
on 19.06.2003 , unsolicited application group Fresh Graduate
```

52.12 FLEXIBLE SELECTION PROCESS

Functional Consultant	User	Business Process Owner	Senior Management	My Rating	Understanding Level
A	A	A	B		

Recruitment process can be visualized to be interplay of data, activities and decisions, apart from correspondence. There are a number of ways through which you can update data, activities and decisions in SAP. Here is a list of transactions, their capability, when best to use them and advantages and disadvantages if any. You can select the transaction best suited for your purpose.

52.12.1 Applicant Data

Transaction	Comments
PB10-Initial data entry	All applications should be entered through this transaction first.
PB30-Maintain applicant master data PB20-Display applicant master data	This is the basic transaction for entering applicant master data in all infotypes except 4000, 4003 and 4004. When you click 'Master data' icon on any screen, this transaction is called.
PB40-Applicant actions	This is the basic transaction for running actions. When you click 'Actions' icon on any screen, this transaction is called.

52.12.2 Applicant Activities

Transaction	Comments
PB60-Maintain applicant activity PB50-Display applicant activity	This is the basic transaction for maintaining applicant activity. When you click 'Activity' icon on any screen, this transaction is called.
PBA9-Planned activities	This transaction can be used to see activities pending with a person.
PBAL-Bulk processing	This transaction can be used to create activities for multiple applicants.

52.12.3 Applicant Decisions

Transaction	Comments
PBA1-Applicants by name PBA4-Receipt of application PBAE-List applicant pool	**Applicant** All these transactions are similar. It shows applicants. You can call 'Additional data', 'Activity', 'Master data', and 'Actions'. You can also do 'Bulk processing', see 'Short profile', and change 'Overall status'. Only problem is that you don't know if an applicant is assigned to multiple vacancies. Also, vacancy is not a field on selection screen. Hence, if you want to update decisions about all applicants for a vacancy together, you may use transaction PBA3. Even if you were to operate applicant by applicant, PBA3 is better because it shows all vacancies of the applicant.
PBAC-Applicant statistics	This transaction shows overall-status wise summary. You can also see activity statistics for an overall status. You can't see applicant statistics for a vacancy as the vacancy field is not there on the selection screen.
PBA2-Application	**Applications** This transaction shows applications. You can update data, but you cannot change status.
PBA3-Vacancy Assignments PBAF-Administration	**Vacancies** Both these transactions call the same program. These transactions show vacancies of applicants. You cannot change vacancy status in these transactions but you can change overall status. These transactions are suitable if you want to see whether an applicant has multiple vacancies and what is their status, before updating overall status.
PBAB-Maintain Vacancy Assignments	This transaction shows vacancies of applicants. You should use this transaction to change vacancy status of an applicant. You can also assign a new vacancy to an applicant, see vacancy details and delimit vacancy assignment.
PBAH-Decision	You can change vacancy status through this transaction also. The only advantage of this transaction over PBAB is that there is an icon for each vacancy status, which you can click directly. But you cannot enter status reason. Transaction PBAB offers more facilities and is recommended instead of this transaction.

52.13   ENTERING APPLICANT MASTER DATA

Functional Consultant	User	Business Process Owner	Senior Management	My Rating	Understanding Level
A	A	A	B		

52.13.1   Initial Data Entry

When you receive an application, you enter data in the system using initial data entry, which has already been discussed in detail.

52.13.2   Maintaining Applicant Master Data

You may not enter all the data about all the applicants in initial data entry. You may restrict it only to those applicants who appear promising. If you scrutinize the applications before initial data entry, you can enter most of the data using transaction PB10 itself. Otherwise, you can enter applicant data using transaction PB30 and display the data using transaction PB20. You can also access this transaction from many screens by clicking

icons   Master data   and   Additional data .

Applicant data is stored in the following infotypes. You can use transaction PB30 to enter data in all infotypes except 4000, 4003 and 4004.

Infotype	Infotype text	Chapter
0001	Organizational Assignment	60.1
0002	Personal Data	5.1
0006	Addresses	8.1
0007	Planned Working Time	9.1
0008	Basic Pay	30.1
0009	Bank Details	31.1
0014	Recurring Payments/Deductions	33.1
0015	Additional Payments	34.1
0016	Contract Elements	61.1
0022	Education	13.1
0023	Other/Previous Employers	14.1
0024	Skills	15.1
0028	Internal Medical Service	16.1
0041	Date Specifications	23.1
0105	Communication	26.1
4000	Applicant Actions	56.1
4001	Applications	54.1
4002	Vacancy Assignment	55.1
4003	Applicant Activities	52.14.2
4004	Applicant Activity Status	58.1
4005	Applicant's Personnel Number	59.1

52.13.3 Applicant Actions

You can run applicant actions using transaction PB40. Applicant actions operate at applicant level, e.g. reject applicant, offer contract, etc. They cannot be used for activities pertaining to a vacancy. For each action, an overall status is defined. Whenever the action is run, the overall status gets updated to this predefined value. When you run an applicant action, you get the following screen. As you run the action, infotypes in the associated infogroups are presented in predefined sequence.

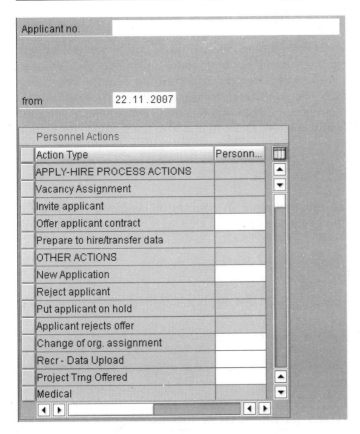

Unlike personnel administration where actions are run only using transaction PA40; in recruitment, actions are run from various transactions. These are discussed below.

Initial data entry

When you do initial data entry using transaction PB10, actions recorded are 11, 12 or 13 depending on whether the applicant is in-process, on-hold, or rejected. If you enter additional data, actions recorded are 14, 15 or 16. If the applicant exists and you are entering a new application, actions recorded are 21, 22 or 23.

Decision recording

There are a large number of transactions which let you change the overall status of the applicant. If you change the overall status of the applicant using any of these transactions, actions recorded are 01 to 07 depending on the value of the overall status. If there is an associated infogroup, that is also run.

Data transfer to PA

When you transfer data to PA using transaction PBA7, action 06 is run.

Actions

All actions can be run from transaction PB40 but actions 10 and 51 can be run exclusively from it. Both these actions change the applicant's overall status to 'In process'. You can do without these actions. You can change the overall status through decision recording. If you want to enter any data, you may do so through transaction PB30. You can thus do without transaction PB40 altogether. However, if your organization's processes are designed in terms of actions, these are specifically created, and you may run them using transaction PB40.

52.13.4 Applicant Training

Training module of SAP extends all functionalities to applicants. He can be booked for a training program, attend a training program, appraise a training program and acquire a qualification.

52.13.5 Applicant Appraisal

You can create an applicant's appraisal in SAP. An applicant can also be an appraiser.

52.13.6 Applicant in Organization Chart

SAP lets you put an applicant in the organization chart, e.g. successor for a position.

52.14 ACTIVITIES IN SELECTION PROCESS

Functional Consultant	User	Business Process Owner	Senior Management	My Rating	Understanding Level
A	A	A	B		

52.14.1 Activity Basics

Activities

Applicant selection may consist of a number of steps or activities, e.g. forming interview panel, calling an applicant for an interview, conducting one or more tests, discussions and interviews, conducting medical fitness test, getting approval for making an offer, making an offer, getting acceptance or rejection of the offer from the applicant, etc.

Planned and completed activities

The activities which need to be performed during the selection process, first need to be planned. SAP lets you do that. You specify the person who would perform an activity and the date by which that activity would be performed. The system would inform the people concerned. When the activity is performed, its status would be changed in the system from 'planned' to 'completed'. Completed activities are not deleted and provide a log of the selection process.

Methods of activity creation

SAP supports three methods of activity creation, viz. Automatic, Semi-automatic (follow-up) and Manual. You would usually create planned activity, but you can also create completed activity.

Automatic activity creation

Every organization follows certain procedures in applicant selection. These procedures may be different for different category of applicants being hired and may involve different steps or activities. Even within a procedure, the activities may depend on the decisions you make during the selection process; the activities for a rejected applicant would be different from those for an applicant who is selected to be hired. SAP lets you model these procedures in the system and automatically create the activities for you. During the study of your recruitment process, your consultant determines the logic by which the activities should be created automatically. The logic can depend on the overall status, status reason and applicant action. It can also depend on the fields in the organizational assignment infotype.

Follow-up activity creation

SAP also supports semi-automatic activity creation in the form of follow-up activities. If you can think of what activities are likely to follow an activity, your consultant can set them up as follow-up activities. When you select an activity and click 'Follow-up activities' icon the system proposes those activities. You can select the activities you want to create.

Manual activity creation

You need the flexibility of manual activity creation to deal with contingencies. In transaction PB60, you can create either a planned activity or a completed activity manually.

Bulk activity creation

There are occasions when the same activity is to be created for a large number of applicants. You may use transaction PBAL to select multiple applicants and create an activity, which is created for all selected applicants.

Activity change or deletion

You can change an activity. You can also delete an activity. For this reason, the activity log does not provide an audit trail.

52.14.2 Creating a Manual Activity

Activities are maintained through transaction PB60 and stored in infotype 4003. If you select an applicant in transaction PB60 and execute, you would see all his applications.

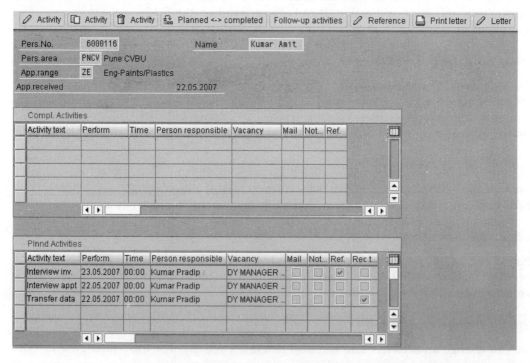

	Start Date	Advert	Instrument	UnsAp	Unsol.app.group	SeqNo
	15.10.2007	00012362	Times Of India	000		0
	15.10.2007	00012362	Times Of India	000		1
	12.10.2007	00012361	Times Of India	000		0

If an applicant has only one application, the above screen is skipped. This shows that activities are linked to applications. If you double-click any application, you see the following screen.

The above screen shows all activities for an applicant, both planned and completed. Everything pertaining to an applicant's activities, e.g. creation, deletion, changing planned to completed, bringing in follow-up activities, printing letters, etc. can be done through this screen. This data is saved in infotype 4003.

You can create an activity through Edit ≻ Create planned activity or Edit ≻ Create completed activity. You can also create an activity through Edit ≻ Copy activity.

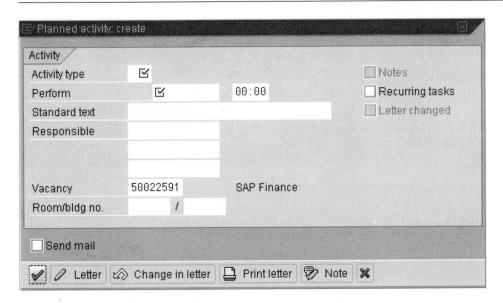

Planned activity or completed activity

An activity is usually first planned, then completed. But you can create a completed activity as well. When you create an activity you specify whether you are creating a planned activity or a completed activity. When you copy an activity, you create a planned activity if you copy from a planned activity and a completed activity if you copy from a completed activity.

Activity type

You perform different types of activities during applicant selection. Here you specify the type of activity which is to be performed.

Performance date and time

Here you specify the planned performance date. Activity type determines whether the activity has to be performed on that specific date, or whether it can be performed by that date.

Standard text

Certain activities involve correspondence with applicant. This is specified at activity type level. If the activity involves correspondence, you specify the standard text here. By assigning standard text to an activity, you can create letters and documents for applicants which may be printed or sent through e-mail. If the activity does not involve correspondence, this field must be left blank.

Person responsible

Here you specify the person who is responsible for this activity along with two more persons who are involved in performing it. The mail goes to all the persons. This activity then shows against the person responsible in transaction PBA9 and he knows that he is supposed to perform it. It does not show against the other two persons in transaction PBA9. If the person responsible field is blank for an activity, then the personnel officer is responsible for it.

Vacancy

There may be certain activities which are not related to any specific vacancy, e.g. acknowledging receipt of application. But there may be some activities which are performed for a specific vacancy, e.g. interview. You can choose only from vacancies which are assigned to the applicant. If only one vacancy is assigned to the applicant, it comes by default.

Room number, building number

Here you specify the room and the building in which the activity is to be performed.

Notes

You can maintain notes for an activity. If you do so, this checkbox is ticked by the system.

Recurring task

SAP lets you perform two categories of activities in bulk, applicant correspondence and data transfer to PA. If an activity is from these two categories and you want to perform it with other activities of the same category, you tick this checkbox. When you create completed activities, you cannot select the recurring tasks field.

Letter changed

SAP can generate a letter which you can print or e-mail. The content of this letter comes from the standard text. If you want to make change in the letter to a specific applicant, you may do so. In that case this checkbox is ticked by the system. You can also undo the change in the letter. Changed letters are not saved in SAP if you are using Microsoft Word as the editor.

Send mail

If you tick this checkbox an internal mail is sent to the following persons.

> Personnel officer
> Person responsible for the activity
> Person responsible for the reference activity
> Other persons involved in performance of the activity

For each of these persons, their SAP user code is determined. For the personnel officer it is determined from table T526. For others it is determined from infotype 0105 (subtype 0001) of their personnel number. When you save the activity, the mail goes to the Inbox in their SAP Business Workplace which can be accessed from SAP menu.

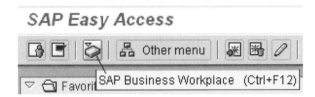

The content of the mail is determined by feature MAILS and can depend on activity type. It can also depend on the fields of infotype 0001 of the applicant.

52.14.3 Reference Activity

You can have a referencing activity, which refers to a referenced activity. When creating letters or mails for a referencing activity, you can include details of the referenced activity. Only one referenced activity can be assigned to a referencing activity.

Creating a reference

To create a reference, select the referencing activity and click 'Maintain reference'. Then select the referenced activity and click ✔ Reference activity . The reference is created. If you double-click the referencing activity now, you would see the referenced activity in it.

```
Planned activity: change                                                    ▣

                                              Chngd 22.05.2007   16:54 QHRBWW004...
  ┌ Activity
  │ Activity type        015    Transfer applicant data        ☐ Notes
  │ Perform To            22.05.2007    00:00                   ☑ Recurring tasks
  │ Standard text        [                              ]       ☐ Letter changed
  │ Responsible          197892         Kumar Pradip
  │
  │
  │ Vacancy              20000224       DY MANAGER (INFORMATION T
  │ Room/bldg no.              /

  ┌ Reference activity
  │ Activity type        Selection Process Date
  │ Perform on               22.05.2007    00:00
  │ Responsible          Kumar Pradip

  ☐ Send mail

  ✔  ✐ Letter  ⟳ Change in letter  ⊟ Print letter  ⊟ Fax letter  ⛃ E-mail letter  ✎ Note  ✖
```

Deleting reference

To delete reference, select the referencing activity and click 'Maintain reference'. Then click 🗑 Reference .

Changing reference

To change reference, select the referencing activity and click 'Maintain reference'. Then select the referenced activity and click ✔ Reference activity . You get a message that the existing reference will be overwritten, which you accept by pressing Enter. The reference is changed.

52.14.4 Creating a Follow-up Activity

If you select an activity and click Follow-up activities , you get the following window.

```
┌─ Select Follow-up Activities ──────────── ⊠ ─┐
│                                               │
│  Follow.activ.for        Mail confirmation of receipt │
│                                               │
│  ┌────────┬─────────┬──────────────┬──────┬──┐│
│  │planned │complete │Activity      │Ref.  │🔲││
│  │  ☐     │   ☐     │Receipt       │ ☐    │  ││
│  │  ☐     │   ☐     │Interview inv.│ ☐    │  ││
│  │        │         │              │      │  ││
│  │        │         │              │      │▲ ││
│  │        │         │              │      │▼ ││
│  └────────┴─────────┴──────────────┴──────┴──┘│
│  ◀ ▶ [           ]              ◀ ▶            │
│                                               │
│  ✔ ✖                                          │
└───────────────────────────────────────────────┘
```

The activities shown in this window are defined during configuration and can depend on the activity whose follow-up activity you are creating and other applicant information. Here you can create a planned or completed activity. You can also make the original activity as reference of the follow-up activities you have created.

52.14.5 Creating Activities in Bulk Processing

You receive a large number of applications in response to an advertisement. You enter them in the system. You reject some and put some on hold. You would like to call the remaining for interview. Should you create this activity for each applicant? SAP lets you create an activity for all the applicants in one shot. You run transaction PBAL, enter appropriate selection parameters and execute. The system shows you all applicants meeting the selection criteria.

	App.no.	Name of applicant	Receipt of ...	Activity created	Error message text	Personnel Area Text
	06000060	Bambani Shekhar	20.01.2007			Head Office India
	06000062	Sharma Anil	20.01.2007			Head Office India
	06000063	Jain Adish	20.01.2007			Head Office India
	06000064	Ghosh Aurobindo	20.01.2007			Head Office India

You can select them all, or exclude some, and click one of the following icons.

Planned indiv.activities	Completed indiv.activities	Planned mass activities	Completed mass activitie

After you click the appropriate icon, you get a window for entering activity details. If you selected a mass activities icon, after you enter the activity detail and press Enter, the activity gets created for all applicants. However, if you select individual activities icons, the activity is created for one applicant at a time. For the first applicant you enter the activity detail and press Enter. This creates the activity for the first applicant. You see the applicant number change. The activity details which you entered for the earlier applicant remain in the activity window. If you want to create the same activity, you can press Enter. If you want to change the activity, you can change it and then press Enter. You can even cancel activity creation for an applicant. Thus, if you are sure that you want to create same activity for all applicants you should use mass activities icons. If the activities are not identical, or if you want to make last minute decision before creating an activity for an applicant, you should choose individual activities icons.

After you have created the activities, it is shown in 'Activity created' column. If for some reason an activity could not be created for an applicant, it is shown in 'Error message text' column.

52.14.6   Performing the Activities

Which activities are pending?

In a business there are a large number of activities going on at any point of time. In order to ensure that activities are performed on time, activity performers need to know which activities are pending with them, the supervisors need to know which activities are pending with their subordinates and personnel officers need to know all the activities which are pending with anyone for the vacancies for which they are responsible. All of them can use transaction PBA9 to see the planned activities, applying filters as per their need.

Changing activity status

You can not only see the planned activities but also change their status to 'completed'. You can do so for a number of activities together. You cannot create or delete an activity here. Nor can you print letters. Do not remove the date in the data selection period, otherwise you only see data but the activity buttons are missing. Transaction S_AHR_61015514 is display version of transaction PBA9.

```
The following appls. have planned activities:

  POf Name of applicant              Activity txt      Date        Mail on

User respons. for the following activitiesMenon Sasidharan
  AJ  Rao Krisna                     Receipt           04.12.2007
  VM  Pratap Rudra                   Receipt           04.12.2007
```

Changing activity details

When an activity's status is changed to 'completed' should you be also changing activity details, e.g. performers, date of performance, etc.? If you do, you would have accurate information on activity performance, but it also means extra work. You need to decide this as a company policy, so that the data is consistent and everyone knows what it is. If you decide to change the activity details along with activity status, you should click the Activity icon, which takes you to the screen of transaction PB60 where you can change the activity details as well as its status.

52.15 HANDLING APPLICANT CORRESPONDENCE

Functional Consultant	User	Business Process Owner	Senior Management	My Rating	Understanding Level
A	A	A	B		

```
Planned activity: change                                                         ☒

                                              Chngd 21.12.2007    09:24 QHRPKA0001...

 Activity
 Activity type        001    Mail confirmation of receipt        ☐ Notes
 Perform To           22.12.2007    00:00                         ☐ Recurring tasks
 Mail sent        on  21.12.2007
 Standard text        RECEIPT                                     ☐ Letter changed
 Responsible


 Vacancy              50022591            SAP Finance
 Room/bldg no.                  /

 ☐ Send mail

 ✓  ✎ Letter  ✐ Change in letter  🖶 Print letter  🖶 Fax letter  📠 E-mail letter  📝 Note  ✖
```

There are certain activities where you need to correspond with applicants. For these activities you specify the standard text, which contains fixed content, applicant information, information from the activity, and information from reference activity if applicable. The standard text can be either in SAPscript or in Microsoft Word. You can assign standard text to an activity, only for certain activity types. This property is defined at activity type level.

Once a standard text is defined for an activity, the letter can be printed and sent, or faxed, or e-mailed. Before sending the letter, you can change it. If the standard text is in SAPscript, the change is saved in SAP and is available for viewing later. You can also undo the change in the letter. If the standard text is in Microsoft Word, the changed letter is saved on your PC and not in the SAP system.

If you e-mail a letter, it uses the applicant's e-mail id which was entered at the time of initial data entry and saved in infotype 0105, subtype 0010.

SAP supports printing of individual letters as well as bulk printing of letters. If you want to print the letters in bulk, you should use a SAPscript standard text and tick on the recurring tasks field. This field is stored as P in 'Status of recurring task: Print letter' field of table PB4003. You can use transaction PBAT to print letters, or send e-mails, which identifies the letters to be printed based on recurring task status P. After the letters are printed, this status is changed to 3. Letters can also be reprinted if necessary. You can also print labels using transaction PBAK. Once the letters are printed, you can change the status of activities to 'completed' using transaction PBA6, which identifies the activities based on recurring task status value 3. After changing the status of the activities to 'completed', it sets their recurring task statuses to blank.

SAP sends mail to outside world through SAPconnect, which you can run using transaction SCOT. This job should be scheduled to send the mail periodically. The checkbox 'Send mail' is for internal correspondence and not for applicant correspondence.

52.16 UPDATING DECISIONS

Functional Consultant	User	Business Process Owner	Senior Management	My Rating	Understanding Level
A	A	A	B		

52.16.1 Decision Recording Scenarios

Company policy

As a company you may decide to process an applicant one vacancy at a time (he may be considered for multiple vacancies but not at the same time), or you may decide that you would process an applicant for multiple vacancies at a time. The former scenario is simpler from an operational perspective, while the latter may be more cost effective if you often consider an applicant for multiple vacancies at the same time.

Single vacancy for an applicant scenario

If you process an applicant for a single vacancy at a time, the overall status and vacancy status should be maintained in synch. You should always update overall status and the system should change the vacancy status. SAP can be configured to achieve this. If there is one-to-one correspondence between overall status and vacancy status, it should be enforced by feature STATU. Also, your configuration should ensure that on any given day an applicant cannot be assigned to more than one vacancy. This can be done by keeping only priority 1 in view VV_T591A_4002___AL0, and deleting all other priorities. Further, you should always use transaction PBA3 and ensure that there is no mismatch between overall status and vacancy status. If need be, maintain vacancy status using transaction PBAB.

Multiple vacancies for an applicant scenario

Even in multiple vacancies for an applicant scenario, many applicants would be considered for a single vacancy. You should check out if that is the case using transaction PBA3. In the selection screen specify the applicant and not the vacancy; otherwise, you will not know if the applicant is assigned to multiple vacancies. If the applicant is assigned to a single vacancy, update the overall status. If need be, maintain vacancy status such that it is in synch with the overall status using transaction PBAB.

Even if the applicant is assigned to multiple vacancies, sometimes the decision may be at applicant level. For example, while interviewing an applicant for one vacancy, you may decide that he has an attitude problem and is not fit for the company. In this case the decision is at applicant level, and you can choose from transactions PBA1, PBA4, PBA3 and PBAF to update it.

If an applicant is assigned to multiple vacancies, and the decision is applicable to only one vacancy, you can update the vacancy level decision using transaction PBAB and overall status using transactions PBA1, PBA4, PBA3 or PBAF.

52.16.2 Consistency of Overall Status with Vacancy Statuses

Feature STATU ensures consistency of overall status with vacancy assignment statuses. For each overall status, it specifies the possible values of vacancy statuses.

What happens to vacancy assignment status if overall status is changed?

If overall status is changed and vacancy status is from permitted values, vacancy status does not change. If it is not from permitted values, it is changed to overall status value. Dynamic action of infotype 4000 may sometimes bring up infotype 4002, which contains vacancy assignment status, for change.

What happens to overall status if vacancy assignment status is changed?

Vacancy assignment status can be changed only within permitted values for an overall status.

52.16.3 Recommended Transactions to Update Decisions

To update decisions you may use the following transactions. It is recommended that you should use transaction PBA3 to update overall status and transaction PBAB to update vacancy status. These transactions are discussed in chapter 52.16.4 in more detail.

Transaction	Comments
PBA1-Applicants by name PBA4-Receipt of application PBAE-List applicant pool	**Applicant** All these transactions are similar. It shows applicants. You can call 'Additional data', 'Activity', 'Master data', and 'Actions'. You can also do 'Bulk processing', see 'Short profile', and change 'Overall status'. Only problem is that you don't know if an applicant is assigned to multiple vacancies. Also, vacancy is not a field on selection screen. Hence, if you want to update decisions about all applicants for a vacancy together, you may use transaction PBA3. Even if you were to operate applicant by applicant, PBA3 is better because it shows all vacancies of the applicant.
PBAC-Applicant statistics	This transaction shows overall-status wise summary. You can also see activity statistics for an overall status. You can't see applicant statistics for a vacancy as the vacancy field is not there on the selection screen.
PBA2-Application	**Applications** This transaction shows applications. You can update data, but you cannot change status.
PBA3-Vacancy Assignments PBAF-Administration	**Vacancies** Both these transactions call the same program. These transactions show vacancies of applicants. You cannot change vacancy status in these transactions but you can change overall status. These transactions are suitable for seeing if an applicant has multiple vacancies and what is their status, before updating overall status.
PBAB-Maintain Vacancy Assignments	This transaction shows vacancies of applicants. You should use this transaction to change vacancy status of an applicant. You can also assign a new vacancy to an applicant, see vacancy details and delimit vacancy assignment.
PBAH-Decision	You can change vacancy status through this transaction also. The only advantage of this transaction over transaction PBAB is that there is an icon for each vacancy status, which you can click directly. But you cannot enter status reason. Transaction PBAB offers more facilities and is recommended instead of this transaction.

52.16.4 Applicant Lists

Applicants by name

You can use transaction PBA1 to see all applicants meeting the selection criteria specified by you.

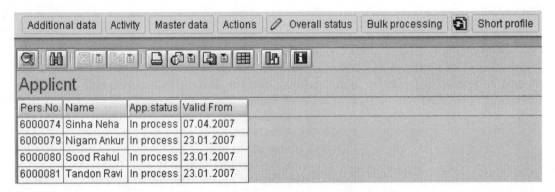

The program shows the applicants, their overall status and the date when the status was changed to the current status. You can select an applicant and see and maintain his additional data, activities, and master data. You can run actions for him. You can also change his overall status and see his short profile and facsimiles. If you want to change the overall status of several applicants at the same time, you can click 'Bulk processing' icon. You can then select multiple applicants and reject them or put them on hold. This changes their overall status. Transaction S_AHR_61015509 is display version of the same program.

Applicants by action

Transaction PBA4 is very similar to transaction PBA1. It has two extra columns: Action and Personnel Officer, but does not have the date of overall status. You can do the same things as in PBA1.

Additional data	Activity	Master data	Actions	Overall status	Bulk processing	Short profile

Applicants by action

Key date: 25.01.2008

App.no.	Name	Action	Ov.status	POf
06000074	Sinha Neha	New Application	In process	AJ
06000079	Nigam Ankur	Initial data entry	In process	AJ
06000080	Sood Rahul	Initial data entry	In process	AJ
06000081	Tandon Ravi	Initial data entry	In process	AJ

Transaction PBAE is same as transaction PBA4. Only the default status in selection screen is different. Transaction S_AHR_61015510 is display version of transaction PBA4.

52.16.5 Application List

Applications

You can use transaction PBA2 to see all applications meeting the selection criteria specified by you. You see application details, e.g. date received, advertisement, recruitment instrument and unsolicited application group. You can select an application and see and maintain applicant's additional data, activities, and master data. You can run actions for him. You can also see his short profile and facsimiles. Transaction S_AHR_61015512 is display version of transaction PBA2.

	Additional data	Activity	Master data	Actions	🔁	Short profile

Applications

No.	App.no.	Name	Date rec'd	Advertisement	Instrument	Unsol.app.group
1	6000074	Sinha Neha	23.01.2007	12349	Times Of India	
2	6000074	Sinha Neha	07.04.2007	12354	Times Of India	
3	6000074	Sinha Neha	18.04.2007			Sales & Marketing
4	6000079	Nigam Ankur	23.01.2007	12351	Job Street.com	
5	6000080	Sood Rahul	23.01.2007	12351	Job Street.com	
6	6000081	Tandon Ravi	23.01.2007	12351	Job Street.com	

52.16.6 Vacancy Lists

Vacancy assignments

You can use transaction PBA3 or PBAF to see vacancies assigned to applicants meeting the selection criteria specified by you. This report is particularly useful if you want to see the status of all applicants for a vacancy or the status of all vacancies for an applicant.

	Additional data	Activity	Master data	Actions	✏ Overall status	Bulk processing	🔁 Short profile

Vacancy Assignments

Key date: 25.01.2008

Name	Overall status	Vacancy	Vac.status
Sinha Neha	In process	Executive VP	To be hired
Nigam Ankur	In process	Head Of Operations Pune	On hold
Sood Rahul	In process	Head Of Operations Pune	On hold
Tandon Ravi	In process	DY. MANAGER(FRONT AXLE BEAM)	In process
>		SENIOR OFFICER(INTERNAL AUDIT)	In process

The program shows the applicants, their overall status and the vacancies assigned to them with vacancy status. You can select an applicant and see and maintain his additional data, activities, and master data. You can run actions for him. You can also change his overall status and see his short profile and facsimiles. If you want to change the overall status of several applicants at the same time, you can click 'Bulk processing' icon. You can then select multiple applicants and reject them or put them on hold. This changes their overall status. However, you cannot change vacancy status in this transaction. Transaction S_AHR_61015515 is display version of transaction PBA3.

Maintaining vacancy assignments

You can use transaction PBAB to maintain vacancy assignments. When you perform a process step for a vacancy, e.g. conducting interview, you would like to update the result by changing vacancy status. You can change the status of one or more applicants. The changed status is shown in the 'New status' column. You can also assign a new vacancy to an applicant, see vacancy details and delimit vacancy assignment.

| | Status (vacancy) | Assign vacancy | Evaluate vacancy | Delimit assignment |

Maintain vacancy assignments

Key date: 25.01.2008

App.no.	Name	Pr	Vacancy	Status (vac.)	New status
06000074	Sinha Neha	01	50019383	To be hired	
06000079	Nigam Ankur	01	50019394	On hold	
06000080	Sood Rahul	01	50019394	On hold	
06000081	Tandon Ravi	01	20002517	In process	
>		02	20000134	In process	

If you select a vacancy and click 'Evaluate vacancy', you get full details of the vacancy.

| | Find candidate | App.statistics | App.list | Position description | Req.profile |

Vacancies

Evaluation period: 25.01.2008 to 31.12.9999

Vacancy	Activity	from	to	Line manager	POf	St	OM	Req.profi
50019383	Executive VP	23.01.2007	31.12.9999		AJ	occ.	P	maintaine

From here you can find candidates by competencies from applicant database, see applicant statistics, applicant list, details of position and competencies required for position.

Applicant selection decision

Transaction PBAH is another transaction through which you can change vacancy status to update a decision in selection process.

| &ℓ° Facsimiles | Short profile | Invite | Offer contract | Put on hold | Reject | Set to 'In process' | ⟳ |

Applicant Selection

Key date: 25.01.2008

Name	Pr	Vacancy		Vac.status
Sinha Neha	01	50019383	Executive VP	To be hired
Nigam Ankur	01	50019394	Head Of Operations Pune	On hold
Sood Rahul	01	50019394	Head Of Operations Pune	On hold
Tandon Ravi	01	20002517	DY. MANAGER(FRONT AXLE BEAM)	In process
>	02	20000134	SENIOR OFFICER(INTERNAL AUDIT)	In process

52.17   OFFERING CONTRACT

Functional Consultant	User	Business Process Owner	Senior Management	My Rating	Understanding Level
A	A	A	B		

Unlike other decisions, offering contract to an applicant for a vacancy means putting him on hold for other vacancies, and putting other applicants on hold for that vacancy. SAP prompts you to do this.

52.18   MONITORING OF RECRUITMENT PROCESS

Functional Consultant	User	Business Process Owner	Senior Management	My Rating	Understanding Level
A	A	A	B		

Monitoring of vacancies

You would like to review the status of vacancies periodically and see whether the recruitment process is working properly. You can use transaction PB80 or S_AHR_61015516 to do that. When you run transaction PB80, you get the following selection screen.

Period
Data selection period   17.12.2007   to   31.12.9999

Selection			
Vacancy		to	⇨
Personnel officer		to	⇨
Line manager		to	⇨
Staffing status		to	⇨

Through this selection screen, you can monitor a specific vacancy, or all vacancies with a personnel officer, or all vacancies with a line manager, or all vacancies in the organization. You can specify the staffing status to exclude filled vacancies. When you execute, you get the following screen.

| 👓 🖫 | Find candidate | App.statistics | App.list | Position description | Req.profile |

Vacancies

Evaluation period: 25.01.2008 to 31.12.9999

Vacancy	Activity	from	to	Line manager	POf	St	OM	Req.profi
20000134	SENIOR OFFICER(INTERNAL AUDIT)	01.04.2004	31.12.9999	Pandey Rajnish	AJ	vac.	P	maintaine
20002517	DY. MANAGER(FRONT AXLE BEAM)	01.04.2003	31.12.9999			vac.	P	
50019383	Executive VP	23.01.2007	31.12.9999		AJ	occ.	P	maintaine
50019394	Head Of Operations Pune	23.01.2007	31.12.9999		AJ	occ.	P	maintaine

For a vacancy, you can see position description and requirement profile. During initial stages of selection process, you can also find candidate, which is described in 'Search Applicant Pool'. You can see applicant list and applicant statistics which would give you a fair picture of the status of the vacancy. In the applicant list, you can see short profile of applicants and in applicant statistics, you can see activity statistics. In this transaction you cannot select multiple vacancies and see global applicant statistics.

Monitoring of vacancies in an organizational unit

If you are interested in seeing vacancies only in an organizational unit and organizational units below it, you can use transaction S_AHR_61016509. If you want to see vacancies in an organizational unit, but not in the organizational units below it, change the evaluation path from PLSTE to PLSTE-S.

Overall applicant statistics

You can use transaction PBAC or S_AHR_61015513 to see summary of applicants based on selection criteria, e.g. vacancy. Here you can see summarized picture of multiple vacancies. For each overall status, it shows count of applicants.

Applicant Statistics

🔍	Activity statistics

Applicant Statistics

Key date 05.12.2007

Applicant status (overall)	Number
In process	29
On hold	0
Rejected	4
To be hired	12
Contract offered	1
Offer rejected	0
Invite	10
Total	56

You can select any line of overall status and click magnifying glass to see the list of applicants having that status. If you select a line and click 'Activity statistics', the system lets you select the activities, and shows activity statistics.

Activity statistics for applicant status: In process

31 Applications from 29 applicants selected

of which per activity type:	at least one completed activity	at least one planned activity	no corr.activity	total
001 Receipt	0	4	27	31
004 Interview inv.	1	0	30	31
005 Interview appt	0	0	31	31

Occupied vacancies

If you see the vacancy using transaction PBAZ, it shows that position 20005224 is vacant from 01.01.2002 to 31.12.9999.

Vacancy	Activity	from	to	St	OM	Req.profi
20005224	SR MANAGER (TESTING) ERC	01.01.2002	31.12.9999	vac.	P	

If you see position details, it shows that the position was occupied from 15.01.1974 to 03.07.2003.

Task assignment	Assigned as...	Assigned until
▽ 🚹 SR MANAGER (TESTING)		
🖬 ✉ SENIOR MANAGER	01.01.2002	Unlimited
☐ ✉ ERC - PRODUCT E	01.01.2002	Unlimited
👥 ✉ Srivastava Radhey	01.04.2002	03.07.2003

The above two records are inconsistent for the period 01.04.2002 to 03.07.2003, where position is occupied as well as vacant. SAP provides transaction S_AHR_61016510 through which you can identify vacancies which are occupied. The above inconsistency is shown by this report.

Ob	ObjectID	Start Date	End Date	H	V	Object name
☐ S	20005224	01.04.2002	03.07.2003	X	X	SR MANAGER (TESTING) ERC

You can select the records you want to correct. When you click save, the system corrects the vacancy data to remove inconsistency. After you do that for the above position, vacancy data is corrected as shown below:

Vacancy	Activity	from	to	St	OM	Req.profi
20005224	SR MANAGER (TESTING) ERC	01.01.2002	31.03.2002	vac.	P	
>		01.04.2002	03.07.2003	occ.	P	
>		04.07.2003	31.12.9999	vac.	P	

This report does not show unfilled positions which are not vacant.

52.19 HANDLING APPLICANT ENQUIRY

Functional Consultant	User	Business Process Owner	Senior Management	My Rating	Understanding Level
A	A	A	B		

If you receive an enquiry from an applicant who does not know his applicant number, you can search it using transaction PBA1. You can search by first name, last name, etc.

52.20 TRANSFERRING DATA TO PA

Functional Consultant	User	Business Process Owner	Senior Management	My Rating	Understanding Level
A	A	A	B		

Data transfer from recruitment to PA can be initiated either in recruitment module, or in PA module. For initiating data transfer in PA module, you would choose an action whose FC field in view T529A is 7 (Initial hiring and transfer of data from Recruitment). While running this action, the system asks you for applicant number and then copies the data from that applicant.

The method of initiating data transfer in recruitment module is described here. An applicant's data can only be transferred to personnel administration if the applicant's overall status is 'To be hired' and if he has been assigned the 'Hire applicant' action and the reference activity 'Transfer applicant data'. You can fulfill these criteria by carrying out the applicant action 'Prepare for hiring'.

In recruitment, you would mark the activity pertaining to data transfer as recurring task. This would get stored in the database as status D. You would run transaction PBA7 to transfer data from recruitment to PA. SAP would do the data transfer one applicant at a time. It would first present you a list of personnel actions, so that you can choose which personnel action to run.

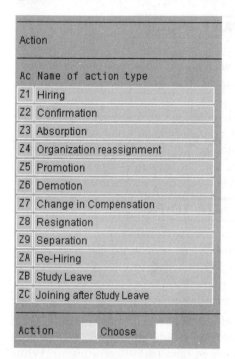

You enter the action type you want to run in the field 'Choose'. The system runs the infogroup, transferring the data which is available and asking you for missing data. After the data is transferred, the value of recurring task status changes from D to 1. This is used to identify the activities whose status is to be changed from 'planned' to 'completed' when you run transaction PBA8. When you run transaction PBA8, the system shows you all the activities where the value of the recurring task status is 1.

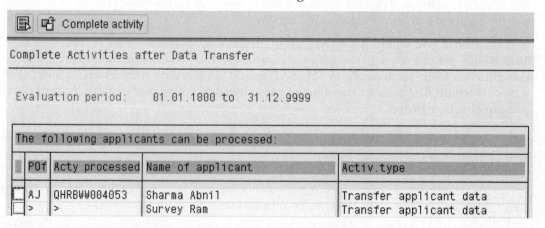

You can select the activities for which you want to change the status to 'completed', and click 'Complete activity' icon. Apart from changing the status of the activity, the system blanks out its recurring task status.

52.21 CLOSING THE VACANCY

Functional Consultant	User	Business Process Owner	Senior Management	My Rating	Understanding Level
A	A	A	B		

When you hire an applicant in PA, the system prompts you to delimit the vacancy. You accept that. Thereafter the staffing status of vacancy is 'Vacancy occupied or put on hold'. The vacancy record in infotype 1007 is delimited. A new record is created, which shows the status of vacancy as filled. In table T750X also, a new record is created showing the vacancy as occupied, delimiting the earlier record. The vacancy can also be viewed using transaction PBAZ.

52.22 REPORTING

Functional Consultant	User	Business Process Owner	Senior Management	My Rating	Understanding Level
A	A	A	B		

52.22.1 Ad Hoc Query

You can use transaction S_PH0_48000512 to perform ad hoc query on the applicant data base. For more information on ad hoc query, see chapter 47.

52.22.2 Variable Applicant List

Transaction S_AHR_61015508 lets you enter the selection criteria and choose up to 20 fields from a large number of applicant fields.

Applicant ...	Application...	Age ...	Personnel officer...	Applican...	Applicant range	Last Name	First Name
06000005	26.08.2006	31	Vishwas Muthyala	External	Others	sharma	ajay
06000011	18.11.2006	32	Anjali Joshi	Internal	CA	SHARMA	K K
06000013	18.11.2006	35	Anjali Joshi	Internal	CA	SHARMA	GAJENDRA
06000016	19.11.2006	32	Anjali Joshi	External	CA	KUMAR2	RAVI
06000047	26.11.2006	31	Anjali Joshi	External	CA	KUMAR003	RAVI
06000048	26.11.2006	31	Anjali Joshi	External	CA	KUMAR004	RAVI
06000049	26.11.2006	32	Anjali Joshi	External	CA	KUMAR005	RAVI

52.23 DELETING APPLICANT

Functional Consultant	User	Business Process Owner	Senior Management	My Rating	Understanding Level
A	A	A	B		

Deleting applicant

There may be occasions when you want to delete an applicant. If you haven't used an applicant number further you can delete it by navigating from the menu in transaction PU90.

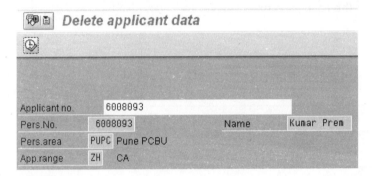

When you enter the applicant number and execute, all infotypes for the applicant are shown.

Delete Applicant Data

Pers.No.	6008093		Name	Kumar Prem
Pers.area	PUPC	Pune PCBU		
App.range	ZH	CA		

Infotype Records

Infotype	IT text	Subtype	Name
0001	Organizational Assignment		
0002	Personal Data		
0006	Addresses	1	Permanent residence
4000	Applicant Actions		
4001	Applications		
4004	Applicant Activity Status		

Select all infotypes and click the delete icon. If all infotypes are not selected, infotypes 0001, 0002, 4000 and 4004 cannot be deleted, as they have time constraint 1. If you are using internal number assignment, the applicant number cannot be used again.

Applicant

53.1 APPLICANT NUMBER RANGES

Functional Consultant	User	Business Process Owner	Senior Management	My Rating	Understanding Level
A	B	C	C		

53.1.1 Purpose

Each applicant is identified by a unique applicant number. If a person makes another application, he will not be given another applicant number. He is still identified by his old applicant number. When you create an applicant, you have to assign him an applicant number. If you do not want to give applicant numbers to all persons in a running serial, you can create multiple intervals of applicant numbers and decide which ones are system generated and which are externally assigned. The next step is to decide which person gets applicant number from which interval. That is determined by feature NUMAP.

53.1.2 IMG Node

Transaction PB04 – Number Ranges for Applicant Administration

53.1.3 Screen

| Number Range Obj. | Applicant Admin. | | | | |

Ranges

No	From number	To number	Current number	Ext	
01	06000000	99999999	6000154		▲
02	00100000	00299999		✓	▼
03	00300000	00399999		✓	
04	00400000	00499999		✓	
05	00500000	00599999		✓	

53.2 APPLICANT NUMBER RANGE DETERMINATION

Functional Consultant	User	Business Process Owner	Senior Management	My Rating	Understanding Level
A	B	C	C		

53.2.1 Purpose

When you create an applicant, you have to assign him an applicant number. If you do not want to give applicant numbers to all persons in a running serial, you can create multiple intervals of applicant numbers and decide which set of applicants are going to be given applicants numbers from which range. In this feature you build a decision tree to determine the applicant number interval for an applicant.

53.2.2 IMG node

PE03 ≻ NUMAP

53.2.3 Screen

```
NUMAP Applicant number ranges
  └─▭ WERKS Personnel Area
      └─▭ HVAL HV Axles Ltd.
          └─▭ PERSG Applicant group
              ├─▭ 6 Temporary worker
              └─▭ otherwise
                     └──01
```

53.2.4 Fields for Decision-making

Company Code
Personnel Area
Applicant group
Applicant range

53.2.5 Return Value

Number range interval for applicant numbers.

53.3 APPLICANT INFOTYPES

Functional Consultant	User	Business Process Owner	Senior Management	My Rating	Understanding Level
A	A	A	B		

53.3.1 Purpose

SAP lets you keep a lot of data about applicants. This data is logically grouped in infotypes. For an applicant you can maintain the following infotypes, apart from some country-specific infotypes. Applicant infotypes are stored in PBnnnn tables where nnnn is infotype number.

Infotype	Infotype text	Chapter
0001	Organizational Assignment	60.1
0002	Personal Data	5.1
0006	Addresses	8.1
0007	Planned Working Time	9.1
0008	Basic Pay	30.1
0009	Bank Details	31.1
0014	Recurring Payments/Deductions	33.1
0015	Additional Payments	34.1
0016	Contract Elements	61.1
0022	Education	13.1
0023	Other/Previous Employers	14.1
0024	Skills	15.1
0028	Internal Medical Service	16.1
0041	Date Specifications	23.1
0105	Communication	26.1
4000	Applicant Actions	56.1
4001	Applications	54.1
4002	Vacancy Assignment	55.1
4003	Applicant Activities	52.14.2
4004	Applicant Activity Status	58.1
4005	Applicant's Personnel Number	59.1

You can use transaction PB30 to maintain all applicant infotypes except 4000, 4003 and 4004. When you run transaction PB30, you get the following screen. You can either select the infotype from menu, or enter the infotype number. Transaction PB20 can be used to display the infotypes.

53.3.2 Screen

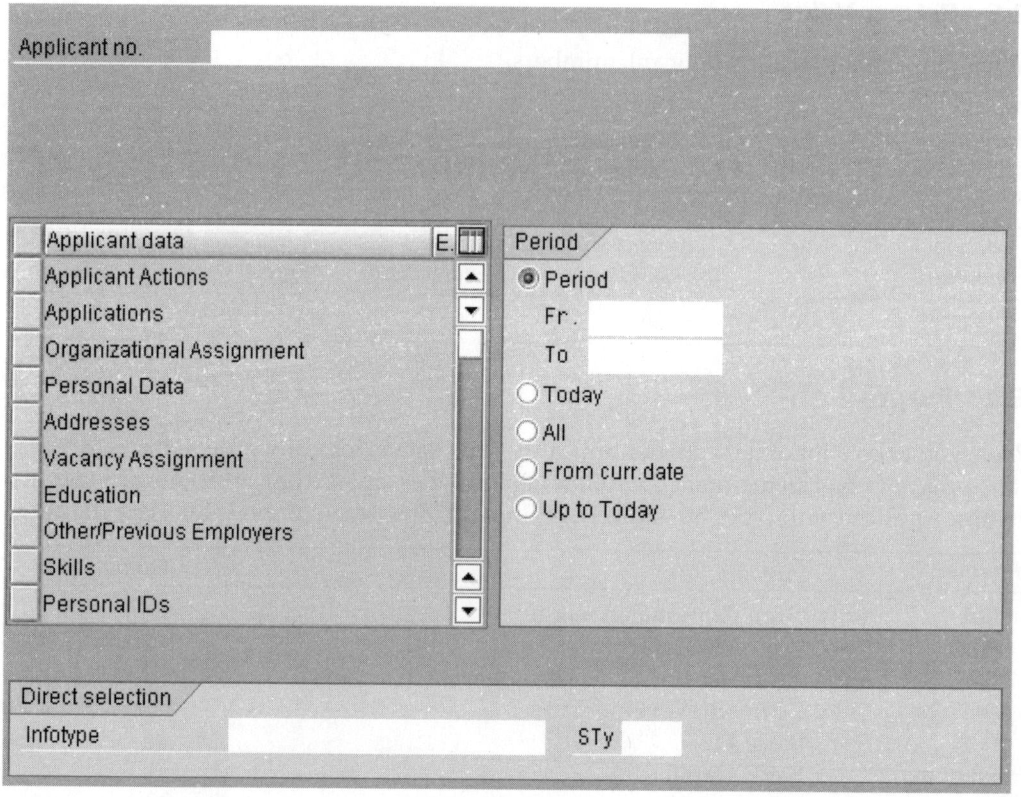

Applicant no.	

Applicant data	E.
Applicant Actions	▲
Applications	▼
Organizational Assignment	
Personal Data	
Addresses	
Vacancy Assignment	
Education	
Other/Previous Employers	
Skills	▲
Personal IDs	▼

Period
- ◉ Period
  - Fr .
  - To
- ○ Today
- ○ All
- ○ From curr.date
- ○ Up to Today

Direct selection

Infotype		STy	

53.4 APPLICANT INFOTYPE MENU

Functional Consultant	User	Business Process Owner	Senior Management	My Rating	Understanding Level
A	B	C	C		

53.4.1 Purpose

When you run transaction PB30 or PB20, you get a menu of infotypes. This menu can be set as per user requirement. It can also be different for different user groups. While specifying the infotype, you can also specify screen control. With different screen controls, the same infotype can have different names and can give you different screens.

53.4.2 IMG Node

SM30 ➤ VV_T588B_IAP____AL0

53.4.3 Screen

	User group	No	Infotype	Screen control	Infotype text
Menu	AP				Applicant data
					User group-dependent
					Reaction
					Reference user group 00
	00	01	4000		Applicant Actions
	00	02	4001		Applications
	00	03	0001		Organizational Assignment
	00	04	0002		Personal Data
	00	65	0006		Addresses
	00	06	4002		Vacancy Assignment
	00	07	0022		Education
	00	08	0023		Other/Previous Employers
	00	09	0024		Skills
	00	10	0185		Personal IDs
	00	11	0016		Contract Elements
	00	12	0007		Planned Working Time
	00	13	0008		Basic Pay

53.4.4 Primary Key

Menu type + Infotype menu + User group + Sequence Number

53.4.5 Important Fields

Menu type

Menu type (I); not seen on the screen.

Menu

This table is used for both personnel administration and recruitment. For recruitment, menu is 'AP'.

User group

The sequence of infotypes in menu can be varied depending on the user group of the logged on user. User group comes from login (System ≻ User Profile ≻ Own data ≻ Parameters ≻ Parameter ID = 'UGR').

Sequence number

The sequence in which infotypes are listed in the menu is specified here.

Infotype and screen control

Here you specify the infotypes, which are seen in transactions PB30 and PB20. If there are different screen controls maintained in T588S, you also specify the screen control. When you select an entry in the menu, the screen control value is also known. This is an input to feature Pnnnn, which along with view T588M determines the screen to be shown.

Application

54.1 APPLICATIONS (INFOTYPE 4001)

Functional Consultant	User	Business Process Owner	Senior Management	My Rating	Understanding Level
A	A	B	C		

54.1.1 Screen

Pers.No.	6000116	Name	Kumar Amit	
Pers.area	PNCV Pune CVBU			
App.range	ZE Eng-Paints/Plastics			
Start	22.05.2007		Chng 22.05.2007	QHRBWW004053

Job advertisement

Advertisement		Publ.date	

Unsolicited applicant

Unsol.app.gp	Design	📄
Contact medium		📄
Contact employee		

54.1.2 Purpose

In recruitment process your interest is basically in an applicant and the information pertaining to him. If an applicant were to make several applications either at the same time or at different times, all applications represent the same applicant. He may apply for different vacancies, which is recorded in vacancy assignment. Main significance of an application in SAP recruitment process is that it helps you to determine the effectiveness of advertisement, recruitment instrument and medium. Another significance of an application is that activities are performed for an application.

54.1.3 Subtypes

No subtypes

54.1.4 Time Constraint

3 (Record may include gaps, can exist more than once)

54.1.5 Important Fields

Advertisement

When an applicant makes an application, he usually specifies the advertisement through which he learnt about your requirement. This information is recorded in this infotype and it can be used to determine the effectiveness of advertisement and recruitment instrument.

Unsolicited application group

In case of unsolicited applications, which are not in response to a specific advertisement, you group the applications in unsolicited application groups. You create unsolicited application groups in such a way that when you are trying to find an applicant from your database, you can look at applications in an unsolicited application group, rather than look at all applicants.

Medium

You can also record the medium through which the applicant making the unsolicited application came to know of your requirement.

Contact employee

In case the applicant came to know of your requirement through one of your employees, you can also record the contact employee number.

54.2 ADVERTISEMENT

Functional Consultant	User	Business Process Owner	Senior Management	My Rating	Understanding Level
A	A	B	C		

54.2.1 Purpose

An advertisement is used to publicize one or more vacancies to inform potential applicants of your requirement.

54.2.2 IMG Node

SM30 ➤ V_T750B

54.2.3 Screen

54.2.4 Primary Key

Advertisement

54.2.5 Important Fields

Advertisement

Each advertisement has a unique advertisement number.

Instrument and medium

An advertisement is published in a recruitment instrument which belongs to a medium.

Publication date and advertisement end

An advertisement is published on the publication date for the first time. In case it is published more than once, you also maintain an advertisement end date.

Publication costs and currency

Here you can maintain the publication cost. This is used to determine the effectiveness of advertisement and recruitment instrument from cost perspective.

Text name

Here you maintain the title of advertisement.

Maintain text

By clicking this icon, you can maintain the text of the advertisement.

Vacancy and choose vacancy

You can assign one or more vacancies to an advertisement by clicking 'Choose vacancy', which is then shown under vacancies column along with position name. It is possible that the same vacancy may be published in more than one advertisement. Vacancy assignment is optional. When you are doing vacancy assignment for an applicant, vacancies assigned to an advertisement are available by default if you have specified advertisement for the applicant.

54.3 RECRUITMENT INSTRUMENT

Functional Consultant	User	Business Process Owner	Senior Management	My Rating	Understanding Level
A	B	C	C		

54.3.1 Purpose

Every job advertisement is published in a recruitment instrument. Here you specify the medium to which a recruitment instrument belongs.

54.3.2 IMG Node

SM30 ➤ V_T750C

54.3.3 Screen

	Instrument	Instrument	Medium	Name of medium	Address	Contact
	00000001	Times Of India	01	Press	A	
	00000002	Indian Express	01	Press		
	00000003	Hindustan Times	01	Press		

54.3.4 Primary Key

Recruitment instrument

54.3.5 Important Fields

Recruitment instrument and name of instrument

You can create several recruitment instruments in which you publish your advertisements.

Medium and name of medium

Each recruitment instrument belongs to a medium.

Address

You can assign an address to a recruitment instrument. You can maintain it by clicking 'Maintain address' icon. You can also maintain addresses through view VV_536A_B__P_AL0.

Maintain address	
Var.key for address	TOI
Last name	
Affix	
Street/PO box	
Postal code/city	
District	
Country	
Telephone number	
Fax number	
Department	

Save address   Delete address

Contact

Here you can maintain the name of a contact for the recruitment instrument.

54.4 MEDIUM

Functional Consultant	User	Business Process Owner	Senior Management	My Rating	Understanding Level
A	B	C	C		

54.4.1 Purpose

The applicants come to know of your company and the job opportunities you offer from a medium, e.g. newspapers, job portals, etc. You would like to know the effectiveness of various media, so that you can find most suitable applicant at the lowest cost. You usually receive applications in response to advertisements which are published in different recruitment instruments which use different media. Sometimes you also receive unsolicited applications which do not refer to a specific recruitment instrument. In such cases, the applicant can specify the media through which he learnt of your requirement, and you can capture it in infotype 4001. Whether an applicant is internal or external is determined from applicant group and not from medium. If a medium can be used by both external and internal applicants, you need not create two separate media, just create one medium and specify the dominant application class.

54.4.2 IMG Node

SM30 ➤ T750D

54.4.3 Screen

Medium	Name of medium	Applicant class	Applicant class text
01	Press	AP	External applicant
02	Internet	AP	External applicant
03	Campus	AP	External applicant
04	Consultants	AP	External applicant
05	Employee Referral	AP	External applicant
06	Internal Adverts	P	Internal applicant
07	Employment Exchange	AP	External applicant
15	Internet	P	Internal applicant

54.4.4 Primary Key

Medium

54.5 UNSOLICITED APPLICATION GROUP

Functional Consultant	User	Business Process Owner	Senior Management	My Rating	Understanding Level
A	B	C	C		

54.5.1 Purpose

In case of unsolicited applications, which are not in response to a specific advertisement, you group the applications in unsolicited application groups in infotype 4001. You create unsolicited application groups in such a way that when you are trying to find an applicant from your database, you can look at applicants in an unsolicited application group, rather than look at all applicants. You can assign an administrator to an unsolicited application group. While designing unsolicited application groups, you should note the fact that it is a decision-making field in the following features:

PACTV	Automatic Creation of Applicant Activities
PACPP	Default for follow-up actions
PACPA	Parameter settings for follow-up activities

54.5.2 IMG Node

SM30 ➤ T750G

54.5.3 Screen

Unsol.application gp	Unsolicited application group	Administrator	Administrator name
001	Sales & Marketing	VM	Vishwas Muthyala
002	After SS/Dealer Devm	VM	Vishwas Muthyala
003	Spare Parts	VM	Vishwas Muthyala
004	Design	VM	Vishwas Muthyala

54.5.4 Primary Key

Unsolicited application group

Vacancy Assignment

55.1 VACANCY ASSIGNMENT (INFOTYPE 4002)

Functional Consultant	User	Business Process Owner	Senior Management	My Rating	Understanding Level
A	A	B	C		

55.1.1 Screen

Pers.No.	6000116	Name	Kumar Amit
Pers.area	PNCV Pune CVBU		
App.range	ZE Eng-Paints/Plastics		
Start	22.05.2007 To 31.12.9999	Chng 22.05.2007 QHRBWW004053	

Vacancy assignment

Priority	Priority 1
Vacancy	20000224 DY MANAGER (INFORMATION T
Vac.assign.stat	2 To be hired
Status reason	08 Good Academics/Experience

55.1.2 Purpose

SAP lets you consider an applicant for one or more vacancies. In this infotype you record all the vacancies assigned to an applicant. If the status of a vacancy changes, the existing vacancy record is delimited and a new vacancy record is created showing new status of the vacancy. You can do vacancy assignment during initial data entry (transaction PB10). You can also do vacancy assignment in transaction PBAB.

55.1.3 Subtypes

Priority of vacancy assignment

55.1.4 Time Constraint

2 (Record may include gaps, no overlappings)

55.1.5 Important Fields

Priority and vacancy

In this infotype you maintain the vacancies for which an applicant has applied, or is considered suitable. If an applicant is assigned to more than one vacancy, for each vacancy he is assigned a priority. No two vacancies can be assigned the same priority for an applicant on a given day. If an applicant is only assigned to one vacancy that vacancy is automatically assigned priority 1.

Vacancy assignment status

An applicant goes through the selection process for each vacancy. His status for the vacancy is stored here.

Status reason

This field contains the reason why an applicant got the status for the vacancy.

55.2   PRIORITIES FOR VACANCY ASSIGNMENT

Functional Consultant	User	Business Process Owner	Senior Management	My Rating	Understanding Level
A	B	C	X		

55.2.1   Purpose

When you assign multiple vacancies to an applicant, you can give different priorities to different vacancies. If your company's policy is to consider an applicant for only one vacancy at a time, you should only retain subtype 01 and delete all other subtypes. This would ensure that no one can assign multiple vacancies to an applicant at the same time by mistake.

55.2.2   IMG Node

SM30 ➤ VV_T591A_4002___AL0

55.2.3   Screen

Subtype characteristics for Vacancy Assignment	
Subtype	Name
01	Priority 1
02	Priority 2
03	Priority 3

55.2.4   Primary Key

Infotype + Subtype

Applicant Action

56.1 APPLICANT EVENTS (INFOTYPE 4000)

Functional Consultant	User	Business Process Owner	Senior Management	My Rating	Understanding Level
A	B	C	C		

56.1.1 Screen

App.no.	6000116			
Pers.No.	6000116	Name	Kumar Amit	
Pers.area	PNCV Pune CVBU			
App.range	ZE Eng-Paints/Plastics			
Valid	22.05.2007 To 31.12.9999	Chgd	22.05.2007 QHRBWY004053	

Applicant action and status

Applicant action ty.	Prepare to hire/transfer data	
Overall status	2	To be hired
Status reason	08	Good Academics/Experience

Reference

☐ Reference available

Reference employee

Organizational assignment

Personnel area	PNCV	Pune CVBU
Applicant group	1	External
Applicant range	Eng-Paints/Plastics	

56.1.2 Purpose

Infotype 4000 stores overall status of an applicant. On any given day, an applicant can have only one overall status. If his overall status changes more than once on the same day, his last overall status is retained and earlier changes in overall status are deleted.

56.1.3 Subtypes

Applicant action type

56.1.4 Time Constraint

1 (Record must have no gaps, no overlappings)

56.1.5 Important Fields

Applicant action type

An infotype 4000 record is created when an applicant action is run. This field contains the type of applicant action which was run.

Overall status

An applicant may be considered for multiple vacancies. As he goes through the selection process for each vacancy, his status for that vacancy changes. But, apart from a vacancy-wise status, an applicant also has an overall status. That status is stored in this field. The overall status should not be inconsistent with vacancy-wise statuses. This check is defined in feature STATU.

Status reason

Here you define the reason for the overall status of the applicant.

Reference available

This checkbox denotes that the applicant has been recommended by an employee of the company. You can save reference information in Edit ➤ Maintain Text.

Reference employee

A reference employee is an employee who is able to provide information on the quality of the applicant's work. A reference employee usually recommends that an applicant be hired.

56.2 APPLICANT STATUS

Functional Consultant	User	Business Process Owner	Senior Management	My Rating	Understanding Level
A	A	A	B		

56.2.1 Purpose

An applicant can have an overall status which is stored in infotype 4000, and vacancy-wise statuses which are stored in infotype 4002. These status values are from the master list of applicant status defined in this view. Whenever an action is run for an applicant, the action type determines his overall status, which is defined in table T751E.

56.2.2 IMG Node

SM30 ➤ T751A

56.2.3 Screen

Status	Text for applicant s
1	In process
2	To be hired
3	On hold
4	Rejected
5	Contract offered
6	Offer rejected
7	Invite

56.2.4 Primary Key

Status of applicant

56.3 STATUS REASON

Functional Consultant	User	Business Process Owner	Senior Management	My Rating	Understanding Level
A	B	C	X		

56.3.1 Purpose

When you change the status of an applicant, you can specify a reason. This view contains the master list of status reasons. In infotype 4000, along with overall status, you can have status reason. In infotype 4002, along with vacancy-wise status, you can have status reason.

56.3.2 IMG Node

SM30 ➤ V_T751C

56.3.3 Screen

Status reason	Text for status reason
01	Insufficient qualifications
02	Formal error
03	Overqualified
04	New application

56.3.4 Primary Key

Applicant status reason

56.4 ADMISSIBLE COMBINATION OF STATUS AND REASON

Functional Consultant	User	Business Process Owner	Senior Management	My Rating	Understanding Level
A	B	C	X		

56.4.1 Purpose

All status reasons may not be valid for each applicant status. This view contains valid combinations of applicant status and status reasons.

56.4.2 IMG Node

SM30 ➤ V_T751D

56.4.3 Screen

	Status	Text for applicant status	Status reason	Text for status reason
	1	In process	00	
	1	In process	04	New application
	2	To be hired	00	
	2	To be hired	08	Good Academics/Experience
	2	To be hired	09	Good Potential

56.4.4 Primary Key

Status of applicant + Applicant status reason

56.5   PERMISSIBLE VACANCY ASSIGNMENT STATUSES

Functional Consultant	User	Business Process Owner	Senior Management	My Rating	Understanding Level
A	B	C	X		

56.5.1 Purpose

This feature ensures consistency of overall status with vacancy assignment statuses. For each overall status, it specifies the possible values of vacancy statuses.

56.5.2 IMG Node

PE03 ➤ STATU

56.5.3 Screen

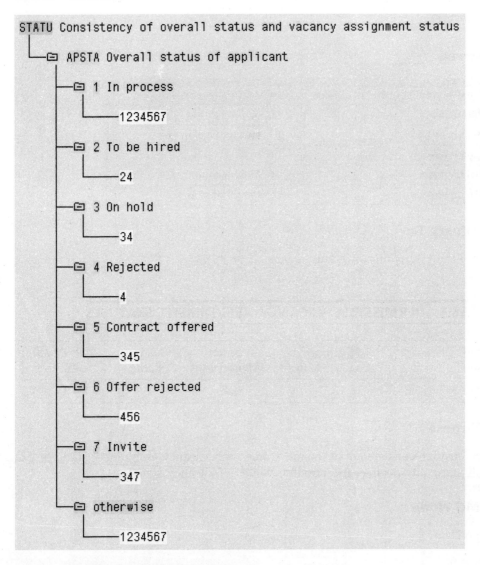

```
STATU Consistency of overall status and vacancy assignment status
   └── APSTA Overall status of applicant
         ├── 1 In process
         │      └── 1234567
         ├── 2 To be hired
         │      └── 24
         ├── 3 On hold
         │      └── 34
         ├── 4 Rejected
         │      └── 4
         ├── 5 Contract offered
         │      └── 345
         ├── 6 Offer rejected
         │      └── 456
         ├── 7 Invite
         │      └── 347
         └── otherwise
                └── 1234567
```

56.5.4 Fields for Decision-making

Overall status of applicant

56.5.5 Return Value

Possible values of vacancy status for an overall status.

56.6 APPLICANT ACTION TYPE

Functional Consultant	User	Business Process Owner	Senior Management	My Rating	Understanding Level
A	B	C	X		

56.6.1 Purpose

This view defines the properties of applicant action types including the overall status that is set for an applicant and infogroup that is executed when an action is run. Applicant actions can be run from various transactions.

56.6.2 IMG Node

SM30 ➤ V_T751E

56.6.3 Screen

App...	Name of action type	Status	Applicant status	Ent...	Ent...	Ent...	Info...	Func...	Upd...
01	Process applicant	1	In process	☐	☐	☐		☐	☑
02	Put applicant on hold	3	On hold	☐	☐	☐		☐	☑
03	Reject applicant	4	Rejected	☐	☐	☐		☐	☑
04	Offer applicant contract	5	Contract offered	☑	☐	☐	Y4	☐	☑

56.6.4 Primary Key

Applicant action type

56.6.5 Important Fields

Applicant action type and name

These fields contain the type and name of applicant action whose properties are being defined.

Applicant status and text

When you run an applicant action, it changes the overall status of the applicant to the value defined here.

Enter personnel area

If you tick this field, you can change personnel area of an applicant only through an action.

Enter applicant group

If you tick this field, you can change applicant group of an applicant only through an action.

Enter applicant range

If you tick this field, you can change applicant range of an applicant only through an action.

Infogroup

When you run an action, the system presents you a set of infotypes, which are defined in the infogroup entered here.

Function character

In recruitment, new applicants are created through initial data entry. This field identifies the actions which create a new applicant. Normally, you do not include these actions in the menu of transaction PB40. But, if you do, the system calls transaction PB10 even when you run it from transaction PB40.

Update infotype 4000

If you do not tick this checkbox, no data record is created in infotype 4000 when you run that action. This field must be ticked for the actions where the overall status is to be changed.

56.7 APPLICANT ACTIONS MENU

Functional Consultant	User	Business Process Owner	Senior Management	My Rating	Understanding Level
B	C	X	X		

56.7.1 Purpose

When you run transaction PB40, you get a menu which is defined here.

56.7.2 IMG Node

SM30 ➤ VV_588B_B_B40__AL0

56.7.3 Screen

Menu 40 Applicant action	User group-dependent ☐
	Reaction ☐
	Reference user group 00

	User group	No	Action	Name of action type
	00	01	X1	APPLY-HIRE PROCESS ACTIONS
	00	02	X4	Vacancy Assignment
	00	03	07	Invite applicant
	00	04	04	Offer applicant contract

56.7.4 Primary Key

Menu type + Infotype menu + User group + Sequence Number

56.7.5 Important Fields

Menu type

Menu type (B), is not seen on the screen.

Menu

Menu 40 is for applicant actions.

User group

The sequence of actions in menu can be varied depending on the user group of the logged on user. User group comes from login (System ➢ User Profile ➢ Own data ➢ Parameters ➢ Parameter ID = 'UGR'). If the user group is not defined for that user, reference user from view T588C is taken.

Sequence number

Here you specify the sequence in which actions are presented in menu.

Action type and name

Here you specify the applicant action type which is run if you select this item from the menu.

56.8 USER GROUP DEPENDENCY ON MENUS AND INFOGROUPS

Functional Consultant	User	Business Process Owner	Senior Management	My Rating	Understanding Level
A	C	X	X		

56.8.1 Purpose

When you run transaction PB40, you see a set of applicant actions you can perform. This set depends on user group and is defined in view V_T588B. If your applicant action sets are fewer than the number of user groups, you can reduce your maintenance effort by specifying a reference user group in this view.

56.8.2 IMG Node

SM30 ➤ VV_T588C_B_AL0

56.8.3 Screen

Menu ty.	B				

Menu	Text	User-dep.	Reaction	Ref.
40	Applicant action	☐		00

56.8.4 Primary Key

Menu Type + Menu

56.8.5 Important Fields

Menu type

View T588C is used for five different purposes. For applicant actions, the menu type is B.

Menu

For menu type B, menu 40 is for applicant actions, and is used in transaction PB40.

User group dependent

Details of menus are maintained in view V_T588B. If your menus do not depend on user group, you should leave this checkbox blank and define the menu for only one user group. Otherwise, you should tick this checkbox and maintain menus, for each user group, or reference user group.

Reaction

If you have not maintained the parameter 'UGR' in the user defaults, the system can give an error (E), use reference user group (blank) or use it with a warning (W).

Reference user group

View V_T588B provides the flexibility to show different sequence of actions depending on the logged on user. If there are many user groups, maintenance of these views could become very complex. This view provides the flexibility to pick up a reference user group, thereby making that maintenance simpler.

Applicant Activities

57.1 APPLICANT ACTIVITY TYPE

Functional Consultant	User	Business Process Owner	Senior Management	My Rating	Understanding Level
A	A	A	B		

57.1.1 Purpose

During the recruitment process, from the time an application is received till a final decision is made, several activities take place, e.g. calling the applicant for interview, conducting interview, offering appointment, etc. This view contains the master list of all activities that take place in recruitment.

57.1.2 IMG Node

SM30 ➤ T750J

57.1.3 Screen

	Activity	Act.type short text	Act.type long text	S	System function text	Date indicator
	001	Receipt	Mail confirmation of receipt	P	Applicant corre…	☐
	002	Transfer file	Transfer applicant file			☐
	003	File returned	File returned			☐
	004	Interview inv.	Selection Process Invitation			☐
	005	Interview appt	Selection Process Date	P	Applicant corre…	☑

57.1.4 Primary Key

Applicant activity type

57.1.5 Important Fields

Activity type, short text, long text

Here you specify the master list of activities in recruitment.

System function and text

If the activity involves applicant correspondence or data transfer to employee database, you specify that here. When you create an activity, you can specify a standard text only if the activity type created has a value P in this field.

Date indicator

Usually an activity is scheduled to be completed by a certain date. But certain activities, e.g. interview, have to be performed on a specific date. For activities which need to be performed on a specific date, you tick this field.

57.2 AUTOMATIC CREATION OF APPLICANT ACTIVITIES

Functional Consultant	User	Business Process Owner	Senior Management	My Rating	Understanding Level
A	A	A	B		

57.2.1 Purpose

Recruitment process requires a lot of activity creation. SAP lets you automate this process to save effort. Here you can specify the activities that are created automatically and when that happens. You can also specify the values that are filled in different fields of an automatically created activity. You can specify when an activity is created in foreground, which permits you to enter/change field values before the activity is created. You can also cancel the activity being created in foreground. During automatic activity creation if an essential parameter is missing, the system has no choice but to create the activity in foreground.

57.2.2 IMG Node

PE03 ≻ PACTV

57.2.3 Screen

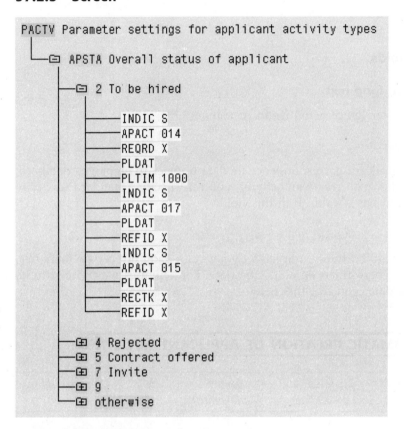

```
PACTV Parameter settings for applicant activity types
   │
   └─▭ APSTA Overall status of applicant
        │
        ├─▭ 2 To be hired
        │    │
        │    ├────── INDIC S
        │    ├────── APACT 014
        │    ├────── REQRD X
        │    ├────── PLDAT
        │    ├────── PLTIM 1000
        │    ├────── INDIC S
        │    ├────── APACT 017
        │    ├────── PLDAT
        │    ├────── REFID X
        │    ├────── INDIC S
        │    ├────── APACT 015
        │    ├────── PLDAT
        │    ├────── RECTK X
        │    └────── REFID X
        │
        ├─⊞ 4 Rejected
        ├─⊞ 5 Contract offered
        ├─⊞ 7 Invite
        ├─⊞ 9
        └─⊞ otherwise
```

57.2.4 Fields for Decision-making

Company Code
Personnel Area
Personnel Subarea
Country Grouping
Applicant group
Applicant range
Applicant action type
Overall status of applicant
Applicant status reason
Advertisement
Unsolicited application group

57.2.5 Return Value

The return matrix of the feature has the following structure: XXXXX ZZZZZ, where XXXXX is field name for activity and ZZZZZ is 20-character value to be entered in the field.

57.3 FOLLOW-UP ACTIVITIES

Functional Consultant	User	Business Process Owner	Senior Management	My Rating	Understanding Level
A	B	C	X		

57.3.1 Purpose

This feature determines the activities that are proposed when you click 'Follow-up activities' icon in transaction PB60.

57.3.2 IMG Node

PE03 ➤ PACPP

57.3.3 Screen

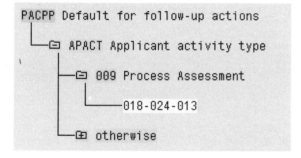

57.3.4 Fields for Decision-making

Company Code
Personnel Area
Personnel Subarea
Country Grouping
Applicant group
Applicant range
Overall status of applicant
Advertisement
Unsolicited application group
Object type (vacancy)
Vacancy
Applicant activity type
Indicator

57.3.5 Return Value

This feature returns up to nine three-character activity types from table T750J, separated by hyphens. If you want the system to propose more than 9 activities, you can define these in additional lines. The next line in the feature is accessed by means of operation NEXTR. The last line in an action ends with a comma (not NEXTR).

57.4 PARAMETERS FOR FOLLOW-UP ACTIVITIES

Functional Consultant	User	Business Process Owner	Senior Management	My Rating	Understanding Level
A	B	C	X		

57.4.1 Purpose

This feature defines how the parameters are to be set for activities proposed as follow-up activities in transaction PB60. Follow-up activities are defined using feature PACPP.

57.4.2 IMG Node

PE03 ≻ PACPA

57.4.3 Screen

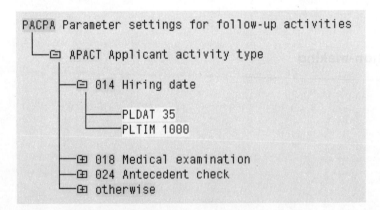

57.4.4 Fields for Decision-making

Company Code
Personnel Area
Personnel Subarea
Country Grouping
Applicant group

Applicant range
Overall status of applicant
Advertisement
Unsolicited application group
Object type (vacancy)
Vacancy
Applicant activity type

57.4.5 Return Value

The return matrix of the feature has the following structure: XXXXX ZZZZZ, where XXXXX is field name for an activity and ZZZZZ is 20-character value to be entered in the field.

57.5 VARIABLES FOR CREATING TEXT

Functional Consultant	User	Business Process Owner	Senior Management	My Rating	Understanding Level
B	X	X	X		

57.5.1 Purpose

You can use this feature to hide variables that are required for creating employment contracts. In the standard system, the VARIA feature is set up so that text variables are available for creating texts.

57.5.2 IMG Node

PE03 ➤ VARIA

57.5.3 Screen

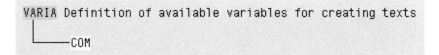

```
VARIA Definition of available variables for creating texts
   |
   |————COM
```

57.5.4 Fields for Decision-making

None

57.5.5 Return Value

If return value is blank, you cannot use text variables to create employment contract.

57.6 PARAMETERS FOR MAIL CONNECTION

Functional Consultant	User	Business Process Owner	Senior Management	My Rating	Understanding Level
A	C	X	X		

57.6.1 Purpose

Whenever a planned or a completed activity is created, you can tick ☐ Send mail . After creating the activity, when you save, the system sends a SAP internal mail to the personnel officer, the person responsible for the activity, persons involved in the activity and the person responsible for the reference activity. This mail comes in the inbox of SAP business workplace of the user, which you access as shown below.

In feature MAILS you determine the title, contents and recipient of a mail. The title and contents are specified in the standard text. The standard text is specified in variable IDTXT in feature MAILS. The recipients can be the personnel officer (RECV1), the person responsible for the activity (RECV2) and the person responsible for the reference activity (RECV3).

For a personnel officer the user id is maintained in table T526. For other categories, personnel number is available, which is linked to user ids in infotype 0105 subtype 0001. The mail goes in the user's SAP Office.

57.6.2 IMG Node

PE03 ≻ MAILS

57.6.3 Screen

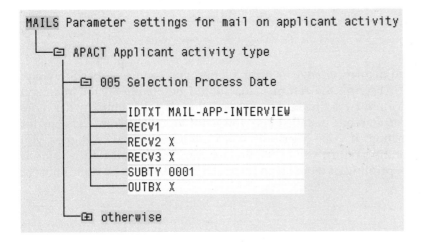

```
MAILS Parameter settings for mail on applicant activity
   └─⊟ APACT Applicant activity type
        └─⊟ 005 Selection Process Date
             ├────IDTXT MAIL-APP-INTERVIEW
             ├────RECV1
             ├────RECV2 X
             ├────RECV3 X
             ├────SUBTY 0001
             └────OUTBX X
        └─⊞ otherwise
```

57.6.4 Fields for Decision-making

Company Code
Personnel Area
Personnel Subarea
Country Grouping
Applicant group
Applicant range
Applicant activity type

57.6.5 Return Value

The return matrix of the feature has the structure XXXXX ZZZZZ, where XXXXX is Mail Attribute and ZZZZZ is 30-character value to be written to the field.

57.7   WORD PROCESSING SYSTEM

Functional Consultant	User	Business Process Owner	Senior Management	My Rating	Understanding Level
B	X	X	X		

57.7.1   Purpose

In transaction PB60, if you display, change or print a letter, you can use either SAPscript or Microsoft Word. For SAPscript, the return value should be blank and for Microsoft Word, it should be RTF. You must define several return values if your company has more than one version of Microsoft Word installed and you want to use different versions for the letters and notes function. If your Microsoft Word versions are 8.0 or higher, you must define the corresponding return values for the feature. The default return value is SAPscript. Note that bulk printing of letters using transaction PBAT can be done only for SAPscript.

57.7.2   IMG Node

PE03 ➢ WPROC

57.7.3   Screen

```
WPROC Specify word processing system
   |___
       ▮
```

57.7.4   Fields for Decision-making

None

57.7.5   Return Value

Blank, RTF, or version numbers of Microsoft Word.

Applicant Activity Status

58.1 APPLICANT ACTIVITY STATUS (INFOTYPE 4004)

Functional Consultant	User	Business Process Owner	Senior Management	My Rating	Understanding Level
A	B	X	X		

58.1.1 Screen

Pers.No.	6000116	Name	Kumar Amit
Pers.area	PNCV Pune CVBU		
App.range	ZE Eng-Paints/Plastics		

Chgd 22.05.2007 QHRBWW004053

Status of actions

☑ Planned activities

☑ PREL data transfer
☐ Send mail
☐ Print letter
☐ Travel Expense Acct.

58.1.2 Purpose

When an applicant is created, the system automatically creates an infotype 4004 record for him. As you plan and perform activities for him, the system automatically maintains certain status values for him which you can view but not change. Table PB4004 is the check table for applicant number field in all applicant infotype tables.

58.1.3 Subtypes

No subtypes

58.1.4 Time Constraint

A (Infotype exists just once from Jan. 1, 1800 to Dec. 12, 9999)

58.1.5 Important Fields

Planned activities

If this checkbox is blank it means that there is no planned activity for this applicant.

PREL data transfer

If this checkbox is ticked, it means that the applicant has a planned activity from which applicant data can be transferred to PREL, and for which the 'Recurring tasks' checkbox has been set.

Send mail

If this checkbox is ticked, it means that the applicant has at least one planned activity from which messages can be sent, and for which the 'Recurring tasks' checkbox has been set.

Print letter

If this checkbox is ticked, it means that the applicant has at least one planned activity from which letters can be printed out, and for which the 'Recurring tasks' checkbox has been set.

Travel expense accounting

CHAPTER 59

Applicant's Personnel Number

59.1 APPLICANT'S PERSONNEL NUMBER (INFOTYPE 4005)

Functional Consultant	User	Business Process Owner	Senior Management	My Rating	Understanding Level
A	B	C	X		

59.1.1 Screen

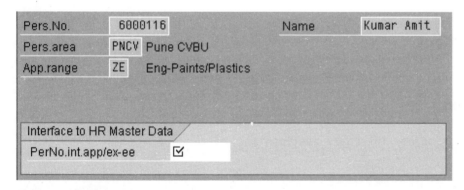

59.1.2 Purpose

When you enter an internal applicant's application in transaction PB10, you would enter his personnel number. The system stores that personnel number in infotype 4005. Depending on the settings in feature PRELI, it also checks the personnel number in personnel administration and copies infotypes 0002 and 0006 from personnel administration to recruitment.

59.1.3 Subtypes

No subtypes

59.1.4 Time Constraint

B (IT exists for maximum of once from Jan. 1, 1800 to Dec. 12, 9999)

59.2 INTEGRATION OF INTERNAL APPLICANTS WITH PA

Functional Consultant	User	Business Process Owner	Senior Management	My Rating	Understanding Level
B	X	X	X		

59.2.1 Purpose

When you enter an internal applicant's application in transaction PB10, you would enter his personnel number. The system stores that personnel number in infotype 4005. If you have implemented personnel administration, you would want this personnel number to be validated. You would also want the employee's personal data (infotype 0002) and address (infotype 0006) to be copied to save effort. This can be done by returning a '*' from this feature. On the other hand, if you have not implemented the personnel administration, you would not want the personnel number to be validated and it would not be possible to copy personal data and address. In that case you would return an 'N' from this feature.

59.2.2 IMG Node

PE03 ➤ PRELI

59.2.3 Screen

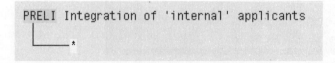

```
PRELI Integration of 'internal' applicants
    └── *
```

59.2.4 Fields for Decision-making

None

59.2.5 Return Value

* for validating the personnel number of internal applicant; N for not validating.

Applicant's Organizational Assignment

60.1 ORGANIZATIONAL ASSIGNMENT (INFOTYPE 0001)

Functional Consultant	User	Business Process Owner	Senior Management	My Rating	Understanding Level
A	A	A	A		

60.1.1 Screen

Personnel No	6000157	Name		
Applicant gr	1 External	Pers.area	MBCO	Mumbai Corporate
Applicant ra	ZH CA			
Start	04.12.2007	To 31.12.9999	Chng 12.12.2007 QHRPKA000137	

Enterprise structure

Company Code	040	Tata Motors Limited
Personnel area	MBCO	Mumbai Corporate
Personnel subarea	BANG	Bangalore

Applicant structure

Applicant group	1	External
Applicant range	ZH	CA
Organizational key	MBCO	

Personnel Officer

Personnel Officer	AJ	Anjali Joshi

60.1.2 Purpose and Overview

Infotype 0001 for applicants is similar to infotype 0001 for employees. The main difference is that instead of employee group and employee subgroup, you have applicant group and applicant range fields. Also instead of personnel, time, and payroll administrators you have a personnel officer who interacts with the applicant.

60.1.3 Subtypes

No subtypes

60.1.4 Time Constraint

1 (Record must have no gaps, no overlappings)

60.1.5 Important Fields

Company code, personnel area and personnel subarea

Here you maintain the company code, personnel area and personnel subarea where the applicant is likely to be posted if hired. Personnel area can be used for authorization control.

Applicant group and applicant range

Applicant group and applicant range are two important applicant characteristics. They should be designed considering their uses which are the following:

> Searching applicant pool
> Authorization control
> Decision making in the following features

NUMAP	Applicant Number Range Determination
PACTV	Automatic Creation of Applicant Activities
PACPP	Default for Follow-up Actions
PACPA	Parameter Settings for Follow-up Activities
SHPRO	Standard Text Assignment for Short Profile
MAILS	Parameters for mail connection

> Determination of internal or external applicant (Applicant group only)

Organizational key

In SAP, you can restrict authorization of a user based on personnel area, applicant group, applicant range, and personnel officer of the applicant. However, if your company wants to restrict authorization in some other way, you can use the organizational key.

Personnel officer

Each applicant is assigned a personnel officer, who interacts with the applicant. You can also control authorization based on this field.

60.2 APPLICANT GROUP

Functional Consultant	User	Business Process Owner	Senior Management	My Rating	Understanding Level
A	A	A	B		

60.2.1 Purpose

Applicant group is an important applicant characteristic. It should be designed considering its uses which are the following:

➤ Searching applicant pool
➤ Authorization control
➤ Decision making in the following features

NUMAP	Applicant Number Range Determination
PACTV	Automatic Creation of Applicant Activities
PACPP	Default for Follow-up Actions
PACPA	Parameter Settings for Follow-up Activities
SHPRO	Standard Text Assignment for Short Profile
MAILS	Parameters for mail connection

➤ Determination of internal or external applicant

60.2.2 IMG Node

SM30 ➤ T750K

60.2.3 Screen

Applicant group	Applicant group text	Applicant class	Applicant class text
1	External	AP	External applicant
2	Internal	P	Internal applicant
3	Grad Engg Trainee	AP	External applicant
4	Wards	AP	External applicant

60.2.4 Primary Key

Applicant group

60.3 APPLICANT RANGE

Functional Consultant	User	Business Process Owner	Senior Management	My Rating	Understanding Level
A	A	A	B		

60.3.1 Purpose

Applicant range is an important applicant characteristic. It should be designed considering its uses which are the following:

➢ Searching applicant pool
➢ Authorization control
➢ Decision making in the following features

NUMAP	Applicant Number Range Determination
PACTV	Automatic Creation of Applicant Activities
PACPP	Default for Follow-up Actions
PACPA	Parameter Settings for Follow-up Activities
SHPRO	Standard Text Assignment for Short Profile
MAILS	Parameters for mail connection

60.3.2 IMG Node

SM30 ➢ V_T750F

60.3.3 Screen

Applicant range	Applicant range text
ZA	Eng-Aut/Mech/Prd/Ind
ZB	Eng-Civil/Arch
ZC	Eng-Elect/Electronic
ZD	Eng-Aero/Others

60.3.4 Primary Key

Applicant range

60.4 PERSONNEL OFFICER

Functional Consultant	User	Business Process Owner	Senior Management	My Rating	Understanding Level
A	B	C	X		

60.4.1 Purpose

You can maintain the master list of personnel officers in this view under group 'APPL'. If you want to print the name, form of address and telephone number of the personnel officer in a letter to an applicant, you must maintain the corresponding fields using the format desired for correspondence.

SAP user ids of personnel officers are maintained for two purposes: for sending internal mail when an activity is created and send mail checkbox is ticked, and for creating signature lines in applicant correspondence.

The system uses the specified unsolicited application group or advertisement to automatically assign a personnel officer to an applicant during initial data entry. This can only be done if every unsolicited application group and every vacancy (published in an advertisement) has been assigned a personnel officer.

60.4.2 IMG Node

SM30 ➤ T526

60.4.3 Screen

Group	Administrator	Administrator name	Title	Telephone no.	SAP name
APPL	AJ	Anjali Jaywant	Ms		PHRANJALI
APPL	DR	Deepali Rao	Ms		MHRDEEPIKA
APPL	EB	Edrina Boyce	Ms		LHREDRINA

60.4.4 Primary Key

Administrator Group + Administrator

60.5 SIGNATURE LINE FOR LETTERS TO APPLICANTS

Functional Consultant	User	Business Process Owner	Senior Management	My Rating	Understanding Level
B	X	X	X		

60.5.1 Purpose

In applicant correspondence you may want the letters to be signed by your personnel officers or other employees who are responsible for applicant activity. You need to determine their SAP user ids and using the link between the user id and signature line in this view, determine their signature line. These signature lines can be included in standard text. SAP user ids of personnel officers are maintained in table T526. SAP user ids of other employees are determined from their personnel numbers using infotype 0105, subtype 0001.

60.5.2 IMG Node

SM30 ➢ V_513A_C

60.5.3 Screen

Name	Signature

60.5.4 Primary Key

Object type (program class) 'APPLIC' + Object name (parameter) 'SIGNA' + User Name

Applicant's Contract Elements

61.1 CONTRACT ELEMENTS (INFOTYPE 0016)

Functional Consultant	User	Business Process Owner	Senior Management	My Rating	Understanding Level
A	A	A	A		

61.1.1 Screen

Pers.No.	6000116		Name	Kumar Amit
Pers.area	PNCV Pune CVBU			
App.range	ZE Eng-Paints/Plastics			
Start	22.05.2007 To	31.12.9999		

Contractual regulations

Contract type	Probationary 🗒
Start of contract	
Work location	

Deadlines

Probationary period	6 Months 🗒
Notice period for ER	1 month/month's end 🗒
Notice period for EE	1 month/month's end 🗒

Planned organizational assignment according to settings

Employee group	
EE subgroup	

61.1.2 Purpose and Overview

You can use infotype 0016 to maintain the applicant's contractual relations with the company. When you create an infotype 0016 record, the contract type, notice period and probationary period can be populated by default using feature CONTR. When an applicant from recruitment module is hired in personnel administration, the relevant data is transferred; this infotype is one of them.

61.1.3 Subtypes

No subtypes

61.1.4 Time Constraint

1 (Record must have no gaps, no overlappings)

61.1.5 Important Fields

Contract type

In your company, you may have different types of contract for applicants. Here you specify the contract type applicable to the applicant.

Start of contract

Here you specify the date from which the contract is effective.

Work location

Here you specify the place where the applicant will work when hired.

Probationary period: number and unit

The applicant will be on probation for this period when he is hired.

Notice period for employer

If the employer needs to give a notice to the employee before terminating his contract, that period is specified here.

Notice period for employee

If the employee needs to give a notice to the employer before resigning his job, that period is specified here.

Employee group and employee subgroup

When you create an infotype 0008 record for an applicant, the system needs to do indirect valuation of wage types. For indirect valuation of wage types the system needs pay scale type, area, group, level and ESG for CAP. The first four are available in infotype 0008, but employee group and employee subgroup which are required for determining ESG for CAP are not available in infotype 0001 for applicants. You specify the employee group and employee subgroup for an applicant here. These are used for indirect valuation of wage types for applicants in all the infotypes.

Other Recruitment Configuration

62.1 STANDARD TEXTS

Functional Consultant	User	Business Process Owner	Senior Management	My Rating	Understanding Level
A	B	C	C		

62.1.1 Purpose

You can create standard texts with embedded variables which can be used for various purposes in recruitment, e.g. applicant's short profile (PASP), internal correspondence (PAML), applicant correspondence (PALT) and internet status tracking (PAWW). Standard texts provided by SAP are given below, which you can copy and modify. Standard texts may contain fixed text, applicant data, activity data, reference activity data, etc. Standard texts are created using transaction SO10.

Text ID	Text Name	Purpose
PASP	APPLICANT_SHORT_PROFILE	This standard text can be used for creating an applicant's short profile.
PAML	MAIL-APPLICANT	This standard text can be used for sending internal mail when an applicant activity is created.
PAML	MAIL-APP-INTERVIEW	This standard text can be used for sending internal mail when an applicant is called for interview.

(Contd.)

Text ID	Text Name	Purpose
PALT	RECEIPT	This standard text can be used for informing applicant that his application has been received.
PALT	ON-HOLD	This standard text can be used for informing applicant that his application has been put on hold.
PALT	REJECTION	This standard text can be used for informing applicant that his application has been rejected.
PALT	INVITATION	This standard text can be used to invite the applicant for an interview.
PALT	PRELIMINARY-RECEIPT	This standard text can be used to send an interim reply to the applicant.
PALT	OFFER-CONTRACT	This standard text can be used to offer contract to the applicant.
PALT PAWW	CONTRACT	

Standard Text	
Text Name	APPLICANT_SHORT_PROFILE
Text ID	PASP Short portrait of applicant
Language	EN

62.2 STANDARD TEXT ASSIGNMENT FOR SHORT PROFILE

Functional Consultant	User	Business Process Owner	Senior Management	My Rating	Understanding Level
A	B	C	X		

62.2.1 Purpose

You can create short profile of an applicant using standard text with embedded applicant data. Using this feature you can format short profiles differently for different locations, groups of applicants, etc. This feature returns the name of the standard text module used to edit the applicant short profile. In the standard system, the standard text APPLICANT_SHORT_PROFILE is assigned.

62.2.2 IMG Node

PE03 ≻ SHPRO

62.2.3 Screen

```
SHPRO Text module for brief applicant description
  |
  |——————APPLICANT_SHORT_PROFILE
```

62.2.4 Fields for Decision-making

Company Code
Personnel Area
Personnel Subarea
Country Grouping
Applicant group
Applicant range
User group

62.2.5 Return Value

Name of the standard text module used to edit the applicant short profile.

62.3 DEFAULT VALUE FOR INTERNET MEDIUM

Functional Consultant	User	Business Process Owner	Senior Management	My Rating	Understanding Level
B	X	X	X		

62.3.1 Purpose

This feature determines the value of medium for external internet applicants and internal applicants through employee self-service. It also determines the default value of country for showing the address screen.

62.3.2 IMG Node

PE03 ≻ INTDF

62.3.3 Screen

```
INTDF Default value for Internet medium
  |
  |——————MEDEX 15
  |——————MEDIN 15
  └——————LAND1 IN
```

62.3.4 Fields for Decision-making

None

62.3.5 Return Value

Medium for external and internal internet applicants and the default value of country.

62.4 DEFAULT VALUES FOR INTERNET APPLICATIONS

Functional Consultant	User	Business Process Owner	Senior Management	My Rating	Understanding Level
B	X	X	X		

62.4.1 Purpose

When a company officer enters an applicant's data, he enters several data items which are not provided by the applicant. When an applicant enters his data on the internet, how to determine these values? SAP provides this feature where you can default the values of the following fields.

PERSG	Applicant group
PERSK	Applicant range
WERKS	Personnel area
BTRTL	Personnel subarea
SACHP	Personnel officer responsible
SPAPL	Unsolicited application group
DYNNR	Screen number

62.4.2 IMG Node

PE03 ≻ INTDY

62.4.3 Screen

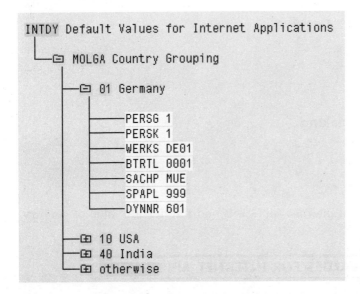

```
INTDY Default Values for Internet Applications
  |
  └─🗁 MOLGA Country Grouping
        |
        ├─🗁 01 Germany
        |    |
        |    ├─────PERSG 1
        |    ├─────PERSK 1
        |    ├─────WERKS DE01
        |    ├─────BTRTL 0001
        |    ├─────SACHP MUE
        |    ├─────SPAPL 999
        |    └─────DYNNR 601
        |
        ├─⊞ 10 USA
        ├─⊞ 40 India
        └─⊞ otherwise
```

62.4.4 Fields for Decision-making

Country Grouping
Advertisement

62.4.5 Return Value

Default values of various fields.

62.5 PERMITTED DOCUMENT FORMATS FOR INTERNET APPLICATIONS

Functional Consultant	User	Business Process Owner	Senior Management	My Rating	Understanding Level
B	X	X	X		

62.5.1 Purpose

In this view you define the types of documents which an applicant can load in the archive link when he makes an application on the internet or through employee self-service.

62.5.2 IMG Node

SM30 ➤ T750R

62.5.3 Screen

Permitted document formats for internet applications	
Doc.class	MIME typ
DOC	
HTM	
HTML	
JPG	
TXT	
XML	

62.5.4 Primary Key

SAP Archive Link: Document class + HTML content type

62.6 CHECK FOR PERSONNEL NUMBERS

Functional Consultant	User	Business Process Owner	Senior Management	My Rating	Understanding Level
B	X	X	X		

62.6.1 Purpose

You can use this feature to determine whether the system checks the personnel numbers of reference employees, contact employees, and line managers against the employee master data file at the time of entry, and to specify how the system should react. If recruitment is implemented but PA is not, then the return value should be blank. If PA is implemented, then the first character should be *, and second character can be E (Error), W (Warning) or I (Information message).

62.6.2 IMG Node

PE03 ➤ PRELR

62.6.3 Screen

```
PRELR Integration applicant/employee
   |
   |_____ * W
```

62.6.4   Fields for Decision-making

None

62.6.5   Return Value

See Purpose.

62.7   SWITCH FOR DEFINING A VACANCY

Functional Consultant	User	Business Process Owner	Senior Management	My Rating	Understanding Level
B	X	X	X		

62.7.1   Purpose

For implementing recruitment module, you need to create vacancies for positions in infotype 1007, for which you must set the switch for defining a vacancy.

62.7.2   Screen

System Switch (from Table T77S0)			
Group	Sem. abbr.	Value abbr.	Description
PPVAC	PPVAC	1	Switch for defining a vacancy

Utilities

63.1 FUNCTIONALITY

Functional Consultant	User	Business Process Owner	Senior Management	My Rating	Understanding Level
A	A	A	B		

63.1.1 Users

Logging on

If you are going to work in SAP, your system administrator creates a SAP log on pad on your desktop/laptop. The log on pad can be accessed either through a shortcut on your desktop, or through the Windows Start icon. When you open the SAP log on pad, you find one or more entries in it.

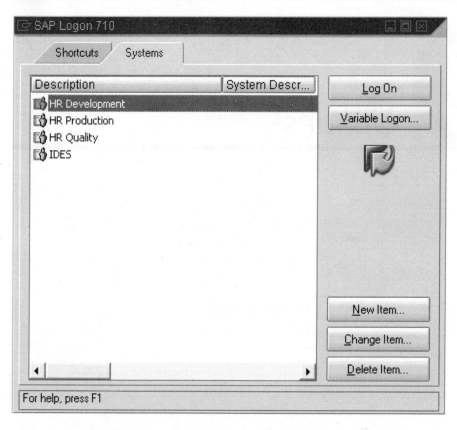

Each entry represents a server. Your system administrator tells you the purpose for which each server is to be used. You select the server you want to work on, and click the 'Log On' icon. The system gives you the log on screen.

SAP

New password

Client		Information
		ℹ️ Welcome to IDES ECC 6.0
User	☑	
Password	★★★★★★★★★★★★	
Language		

You enter the details given to you by your system administrator. You can change your password or press Enter to log on. The system gives you the SAP menu.

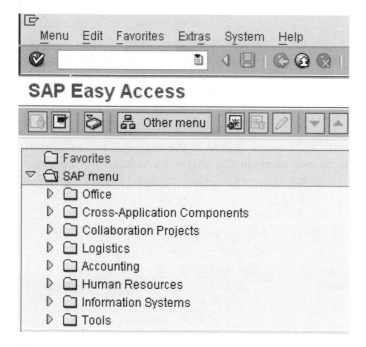

You can open the tree-like structure of the SAP menu to reach the transaction you want to carry out. You can switch to user menu, if one has been set up for you. You can add transactions to the Favorites folder, which can have sub-folders.

Executing a transaction in the command field

An important part of all SAP screens is the command field, located in the top left corner of the screen. Here, you can enter a transaction directly, instead of going through a menu. If you are already in some transaction which you want to leave, prefix the transaction with /n, e.g. /nPA30. If you want to run the new transaction in a new session, prefix the transaction with /o, e.g. /oPA30.

Aborting the current transaction

You can abort the current transaction by entering /n in the command field.

Opening multiple sessions

You can open another session of SAP (same server and client) by clicking ▒ icon, or by entering /o in the command field.

Closing a session

You can close a session by entering /i in the command line or by closing the window. If the session you are closing is the only session on a client, you are logged off. The system asks you to confirm that you want to log off.

Logging off

You can log off by entering /nend or /nex in the command line. In the former case, the system asks you to confirm that you want to log off. All the sessions on the client are closed.

Displaying transactions

You work in SAP either through menu, or through transactions. Experienced users often prefer the latter method. Therefore, they need to know the transactions of various transactions. You can display the transactions in the menu by ticking the checkbox ☑ Display technical names in Extras ➤ Settings. The menu display changes as shown below.

▽ 🗂 Time Management	▽ 🗂 Time Management
▷ 🗀 Shift Planning	▷ 🗀 Shift Planning
▽ 🗂 Administration	▽ 🗂 Administration
◈ Time Manager's Workplace	◈ PTMW - Time Manager's Workplace
▽ 🗂 Time Data	▽ 🗂 Time Data
◈ Maintain	◈ PA61 - Maintain
◈ Display	◈ PA51 - Display
◈ Fast Entry	◈ PA71 - Fast Entry
◈ Maintain Additional Data	◈ PA62 - Maintain Additional Data
◈ Quota Overview	◈ PT50 - Quota Overview
▷ 🗀 Time Evaluation	▷ 🗀 Time Evaluation

Displaying keys in drop down lists

In many fields, SAP provides a dropdown list from which you can choose a value. These list of values usually have a key and a description. Users who like to see the key in addition to the description can tick ☑ Show Keys in All Dropdown Lists . They can even sort the dropdown list by the key by ticking ☑ Sort Items by Key . You access these checkboxes by clicking 📇 ➤ Options ➤ Expert.

Quick copy and paste

SAP provides a method of quick copy and quick paste. You enable this by ticking ✔ Quick Cut and Paste in 📇. After that, if you press the left button of the mouse, move the mouse on some text, and release it, the text gets copied to the clipboard. The text is not selected, as would be the case, if this feature is not enabled. Also, if you press the right button of the mouse in any field of SAP, the text is pasted from the clipboard. The text may have been copied on the clipboard from any application, e.g. Microsoft Word.

Business workplace

SAP provides a wide range of office functionality, e.g. mail, workflow, etc. in business workplace. You can access it using transaction SBWP, or by clicking the icon as shown.

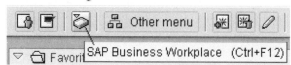

You can create document and send by selecting 'New message' from business workplace, or by running transaction SO00, or through menu (System ➢ Short Message).

Maintaining own data

You can maintain your own data using transaction SU3 (System ➢ User Profile ➢ Own Data).

Running ABAP programs

You can run ABAP programs using transaction SA38 (System ➢ Services ➢ Reporting). It is recommended to avoid doing this by creating a transaction for every program.

Quick viewer

You can run quick viewer using transaction SQVI (System ➢ Services ➢ QuickViewer).

Output control

You can run transaction SP01 (System ➢ Services ➢ Output Control) to list the spool requests and output requests for a user id in a specific period. You can display their contents, print them and delete them. You can run transaction SP02 (System ➢ Own Spool Requests) to list your own spool requests.

Batch input

You can run transaction SM35 (System ➢ Services ➢ Batch Input ➢ Sessions) to monitor, process and analyze the batch input sessions. You can see the logs using transaction SM35P (System ➢ Services ➢ Batch Input ➢ Logs). You can do recording for batch input using transaction SHDB (System ➢ Services ➢ Batch Input ➢ Recorder).

Computer aided test tool

You can use transaction SECATT (System ➢ Services ➢ ECATT ➢ Record) to perform computer aided testing.

Background jobs

You can use transaction SM36 to define and schedule a background job (System ≻ Services ≻ Jobs ≻ Define Job). You can use transaction SM37 (System ≻ Services ≻ Jobs ≻ Job Overview) to monitor and manage jobs. You can release a job, stop an active job, delete a job, display spool list, display job log and display step list. You can also check status, change status from released to scheduled, copy job, change job, repeat scheduling and move the job to a different server. You can also run transaction SMX to see your own jobs (System ≻ Own Jobs).

Queue

You can use transaction SM38 (System ≻ Services ≻ Queue) to display queue.

Reporting authorization problems

You can use transaction SU53 (System ≻ Utilities ≻ Display Authorization Check) to see details of authorization problems and to report to the Basis team for resolution. Immediately after you encounter the authorization problem, enter /nSU53. The system shows a comparison between authorization available and authorization required.

Archived documents

You can use transaction OAAD to store and assign a new document in the content server. The transaction also provides a facility to search the archived documents.

Downloading file

You can use transaction CG3Y to download a file from the application server to your desktop.

Uploading file

You can use transaction CG3Z to upload a file from your desktop to the application server.

SAP query

You can start SAP queries using transaction SQ00.

63.1.2 Functional Consultants

Customizing

Transaction SPRO is used for accessing the customizing environment. You can customize the SAP system using the SAP Reference IMG or you can define projects for customization, e.g. adapting the SAP Reference IMG to the needs of your company and/or subdivide the customization task into different subprojects.

View maintenance

Transactions SM30 (System ≻ Services ≻ Table Maintenance ≻ Extended Table Maintenance) and SM31 are used for maintaining data in one or more tables through a maintenance view. This transaction also provides a facility to navigate to the underlying IMG node for a particular maintenance view. Transaction SM34 (System ≻ Services ≻ Table Maintenance ≻ View Cluster Maintenance) is used for maintaining view clusters.

Customizing comparison

You can compare customizing of two systems or two clients in the same system by using transaction SCMP. You can also create comparison runs involving multiple objects using transaction SCU0 or OY19.

Transport Management

You can use transactions SE09 and SE10 for creating and releasing a customizing or workbench transport request.

Data migration, computer aided testing, BDC

You can use transaction LSMW to migrate legacy data to SAP. You can use transaction SCAT or SECATT for creating a test case by recording a transaction and creating and loading test data. You can record or modify a BDC and run it using transaction SHDB.

Viewing data in tables

You can view data in a table using transaction SE11, SE16, SE16N or SE17.

Logging on to OSS

You can use transaction OSS1 (System ≻ Services ≻ SAP Service) to log on to OSS. It is generally used to import and apply SAP notes.

Searching string in programs

You can use program RPR_ABAP_SOURCE_SCAN to search strings in programs.

Searching in SAP menu

You can use transaction SEARCH_SAP_MENU to search in SAP menu.

Searching in user menu

You can use transaction SEARCH_USER_MENU to search in user menu.

SAP query

You can use transaction SQ01 to maintain SAP queries, transaction SQ02 to maintain infoset and SQ03 to maintain user groups. You can start SAP queries using transaction SQ00.

Workflow builder

You can use transaction SWDD for creating and editing workflows.

System status

You can see SAP version, operating system and the database by clicking System ➤ Status. You can also see the transaction, program and screen number.

Translation

You can use transaction SE63 to translate texts for various ABAP and non-ABAP objects.

63.1.3 ABAP

ABAP programs

You can create, modify, delete, and display source code of ABAP programs using transaction SE38. You can also execute ABAP programs using transaction SA38 or SE38. You can compare ABAP programs using transaction SE39.

Function modules

You can create, modify, delete, display and test function modules using transaction SE37. You can also maintain a function group.

Dialog modules

You can create, modify, delete, display and test dialog modules using transaction SE35. You can create menus using transaction SE41. Screens can be painted using transaction SE51 and its underlying flow logic defined.

Classes

You can create, modify, delete, display and test classes using transaction SE24.

Logical databases

You can create, modify, delete, display and test logical databases using transaction SE36. SAP provides several logical databases for HR, e.g. PAP, PCH, PNP, PNPCE. If you use logical databases in your ABAP programs, authorization checks are automatically taken care of; otherwise you must explicitly build authorization checks in your programs.

Enhancements

You can create enhancements through transaction CMOD. Enhancements are created in projects, which are logical groups of enhancements. You can test the enhancements using transaction SMOD.

BAdIs

You can use transaction SE19, to implement a Business Add-In. SAP provides predefined BAdIs for use by the customers. If you want to define your own BAdI, you can use transaction SE18.

Area menus

You can create area menus using transaction SE43. Area menus can be used in creating role menus in transaction PFCG.

Tables and views

You can create, modify, delete and display tables and table fields using transaction SE11. You can view data in a table using transaction SE11, SE16, SE16N or SE17. You can display/change technical settings of a table in transaction SE13.

Documentation

You can create documentation using transaction SE61.

SAP scripts

You can create SAP scripts using transaction SE71. Other transactions related to SAP script are SE72, SE73, SE74, SE75, SE75TTDTGC, SE75TTDTGD, SE76, SE77 and SO10.

Messages

You can maintain messages using transaction SE91. You can then call them in your own programs. You can also use SAP defined messages in your own programs.

Transactions

You can maintain transactions using transaction SE93. It is recommended that you have a transaction for every program so that the users are not required to run programs using transaction SA38 or SE38. This provides better control on authorizations. It is also recommended that you keep the transaction same as the program name.

Repository information

SAP has created lot of software objects. You can use transaction SE15/SE85/SE84 to find them.

HR form editor

You can create/change/delete HR forms, e.g. remuneration statements, payroll account, wage type statement or payroll journal using transaction PE51. Alternatively, you may use HR Forms Workplace, transaction HRFORMS. You can also use transaction SMARTFORMS to create and maintain forms in the SAP system.

BAPIs

You can see the BAPIs provided by SAP using transaction BAPI.

Object navigator

You use the transaction SE80 to organize your programming in an integrated development environment. Development objects are arranged together in object lists. Each object list contains all of the objects in a certain category, such as package, program and global class. From the object list, you can select an object by double-clicking it. When you open an object, the workbench calls up the development tool with which the object was created.

ABAP dump analysis

You can use transaction ST22 to see details of any runtime error or short dump. This helps in analyzing the root cause of the dump and finding its solution.

63.1.4   Basis

System administration

You can use transaction S002 to get the menu for system administration.

Users

You can maintain users using transaction SU01. You can get a variety of information about users, roles and authorizations using transaction SUIM. You can view users' log on dates and password changes using transaction RSUSR200. You can use transaction SM04 to check the status of the users; for example, how many users have logged on and how many sessions a user is working on.

Roles

You can maintain roles using transaction PFCG. The system automatically inserts authorization objects based on transactions selected by you (These can be maintained using transaction SU22 or SU24). You update them with appropriate values. You can see change documents for roles using transaction RSSCD100_PFCG. The same program is called by transaction RSSCD100_PFCG_USER. Transaction S_BCE_68001403 gives the list of critical authorizations.

Transport Management

You can manage transports using transactions SE01, SE03, SE09 and SE10.

SAP connect

You can use transaction SCOT for monitoring the status of the inbound and outbound traffic through SAPconnect.

ALE

Customizing of ALE can be done using transaction SALE. You can monitor ALE messages using transaction BD87.

Displaying and deleting locks

Transaction SM12 is used for checking and releasing lock entries.

Locking/unlocking transactions

You can use transaction SM01 to lock/unlock transactions.

63.2 TABLES AND VIEWS

Functional Consultant	User	Business Process Owner	Senior Management	My Rating	Understanding Level
A	B	C	C		

63.2.1 Data Dictionary

Domains

View DD01V contains the list of domains. View DD07V contains values for domains.

Data elements

View DD04V contains data elements and their descriptions.

Tables

View DD02V contains the list of tables.

Table fields

Table DD03L contains table fields and DD03T their descriptions. Table DD03M contains table fields with data elements, text, and domains. View DDVAL contains fixed values for table fields.

Foreign key fields

View DD08V contains foreign key relationship definitions.

Pool/cluster structures

View DD06V contains pool/cluster structures.

Technical settings of tables

Table DD09L contains technical settings of tables.

Matchcode objects

View DD20V contains matchcode objects. Table DD24S contains fields of a matchcode id.

Views

Table TVDIR contains directory of views. Table DD25T contains views, matchcode objects and lock objects. Table DD27S contains fields in a view, matchcode object or lock object.

63.2.2 Software Repository

Packages

All objects are developed under Packages (earlier called Development Classes), which are logical grouping of objects. Table TDEVC contains list of Packages. Packages of SAP HR can be identified by selecting entries from table TDEVC where software component is SAP_HR. Some of the important Packages are:

P40C	HR customizing: India
PB40	HR master data: India
PBAC	Customizing HR master data
PBAS	SAP HR Master Data Application Development
PC40	HR payroll accounting: India
PCAC	Customizing HR Payroll
PCAL	SAP HR Payroll Application Development
PCCC	HR accounting: Company Car
PCLM	Claims processing: Asia
PCLO	HR-PY: International Loan Functions

Repository objects

Table TADIR contains the directory of repository objects, along with their development class. Tables and structures are identified by object type TABL.

Objects

Objects are stored in OBJ series of tables.

ABAP programs

Table TRDIR contains list of ABAP programs. Table D010TAB contains the tables used by ABAP programs.

Transactions

View TSTCV contains list of transactions and programs associated with them.

63.2.3 Users, Roles and Authorization

User data

User data is stored in USR series of tables. Table USR01 stores the master list of users. Table USR04 contains the profiles attached to a user. A user's parameter IDs and their values are stored in table USR05.

Role maintenance

You can create, delete, or modify roles using transaction PFCG. Role related data is stored in tables starting with AGR.

Authorization objects

Authorization objects and their field names are in table TOBJ.

Authorization objects for roles

Table AGR_1250 contains authorization objects for a role which you see in transaction PFCG.

Master list of roles

Table AGR_DEFINE contains master list of roles.

Transactions for a role

Table AGR_TCODES contains transactions for roles.

Users having a role

Table AGR_USERS contains users for roles. Also see table AGR_USERT.

63.2.4 IMG Menu

Table CUS_IMGACH contains master list of IMG activities including documentation object and transaction.

63.2.5 Forms and SAP Scripts

Forms

Master list of forms is in table T514D. Details of forms are stored in T514 series of tables.

SAP scripts

SAP scripts are stored in STX series of tables.

63.2.6 Others

Documentation

Documentation header is stored in table DOKHL and text in table DOKTL.

Reserved Names

Reserved Names for Customizing Tables/Objects are stored in table TRESC.

63.2.7 Delivery Classes of Tables

SAP stores data in tables. The tables are classified in delivery classes that determine which tables are controlled by SAP and which tables are controlled by customers.

Code	Delivery class	Explanation
A	Application table (master and transaction data)	A Support Pack of SAP is not expected to update these tables in any client.
L	Table for storing temporary data, delivered empty	A Support Pack of SAP is not expected to update these tables in any client.
G	Customizing table, protected against SAP Upd., only INS all.	A Support Pack of SAP is not expected to update these tables in any client.
C	Customizing table, maintenance only by cust., not SAP import	A Support Pack of SAP updates these tables in client 000 only. In other clients, these tables have to be adjusted from client 000 to get these entries.
E	Control table, SAP and customer have separate key areas	A Support Pack of SAP updates these tables in all clients.
S	System table, maint. only by SAP, change = modification	A Support Pack of SAP updates these tables in all clients.
W	System table, contents transportable via separate TR objects	A Support Pack of SAP updates these tables in all clients.

63.2.8 Search Help

When SAP designs tables, for each column it tries to provide search help. If search help is provided, you can choose a value from it. By assigning search help to table columns, the help becomes standardized. There are different types of search help. In transaction SE11, if you go to tab 'Entry help/check', you can see which columns have got entry help and of which type in the column 'Origin of the Input Help'. Different types of search help are listed below.

Code	Search help	Explanation
T	Input help based on data type	For example Date (Calendar), Time.
D	Explicit search help attachment to data element	Attachment of a search help to the data element assigned to the field.
X	Explicit search help attachment to field	Data integrity is checked against search help. There is no check table.
P	Input help implemented with check table	Data integrity is checked using a check table.
F	Input help with fixed values	The field can take values only from a fixed list, which is defined in the Domain.
Blank	No input help	There is no input help.

63.3 IMPLEMENTATION GUIDE

Functional Consultant	User	Business Process Owner	Senior Management	My Rating	Understanding Level
A	C	X	X		

When a consultant implements SAP HR Personnel Administration or Recruitment for a client, how does the consultant determine the client requirement and do configuration, and how does the client know that the right configuration is done for him? The answers to these twin questions lie in the methodology you follow.

The consultant can use the structure of this book to guide the implementation. He can ask specific questions to the users, record their answers and use the answers to do the configuration. Having done the configuration, he can explain it to the users and get it approved. If the users do not have enough SAP knowledge to confirm the configuration, the consultant should record the user input and get it signed off. An auditor should then confirm that the configuration reflects the user input. The source of all configuration should be user input.

Whereas many factual inputs can come from a knowledgeable power user, policy inputs should come from senior management. In large companies, senior management is often surprised at the diversity of practices followed in different parts of the company. Implementation of SAP provides an opportunity to senior management to either commonize the practice, or approve diversity. Even when there is no diversity, decisions on policy should be approved by management.

Both user inputs and corresponding configuration should be recorded in a configuration manual. The configuration manual should explain what has been configured and, if necessary, why. If you use the following table as the Table of Content of your configuration manual, your configuration manual will be easy to understand. Apart from what you configure, you should also indicate what is not implemented (NR) and what is SAP standard (SS). You should also add all Z developments done by you in respective chapters. Feel free to add chapters in the table of contents, but don't delete any line which has configuration in it. The support team needs to know if something is not implemented. If some configuration is not implemented, you can keep the chapter number blank, instead of creating empty chapters in the configuration manual. The Reference column contains the chapter number in the book.

In the 'Approved by' column you should record the name of the person who has approved that particular configuration. The entries in the table below show the suggested approving level: SM—Senior Management/Steering Committee, PO—Business Process Owner, US—Power User, FC—Functional Consultant. If users are not knowledgeable enough to sign off the configuration, the users should sign off their input, and the auditor should sign off the configuration.

63.3.1   Implementation Guide Personnel Administration

Chapter	Description	Configuration	NR/SS/ Done	Reference	Approved by
1	**Infotypes**			**1**	
1.1	Infotypes Implemented			1.7	
2	**Common Infotype Structure**			**2**	
2.1	Number Range Intervals for Personnel Numbers	Transaction PA04		2.4	
2.2	Number Range Interval Determination	Feature NUMKR		2.5	
2.3	Personnel Number Check	V_T77S0SC		2.6	
2.4	Entry Values for Subtypes	BAdI HR_F4_ GET_SUBTYPE		2.7.1	
2.5	Reason for Change	V_T530E		2.8	
2.6	Personnel Number Help Tabs	Feature NSHLP		2.9.2	
2.7	Hiding Free Search in Personnel Number Help	T77S0		2.9.3	
2.8	Adding Your Own Search Help	Maintain search helps		2.9.4	
3	**Actions**			**3**	
3.1	Customizing Tool for Action Fast Entry	Transaction OG42		3.1.3	
3.2	Default Values and Checks For Transaction PA42	BAdI HR_FAST_ ACTION_CHECK		3.1.3	
3.3	Additional Actions Activation	T77S0		3.4	
3.4	Action Type	T529A		3.5	

(Contd.)

Chapter	Description	Configuration	NR/SS/ Done	Reference	Approved by
3.5	Action Type Priority	V_529A_B		3.6	
3.6	Action Reasons	V_T530		3.7	
3.7	Customer-specific Status	V_T529U		3.8.3	
3.8	Employment Status	V_T529U	SS	3.8.4	
3.9	Special Payment Status	V_T529U	SS	3.8.5	
3.10	Infogroup	V_T588D		3.9	
3.11	Employee-dependent Infogroup Definition	Feature IGMOD		3.10	
3.12	User Groups			3.11	PO
3.13	User Group Dependency of Infogroup	VV_T588C_G_AL0		3.12	
3.14	User Group Dependency of Personnel Action Menu	VV_T588C_M_AL0		3.13	
3.15	Action Sequence in Menu	V_588B_M		3.14	
4	**Organizational Assignment**			**4**	
4.1	Organizational Assignment (Infotype 0001) Layout, Default Values and Validation	T588M+[a]		4.1	
4.2	Personnel Area	T500P		4.2	
4.3	Personnel Area to Company Code Assignment	V_T500P		4.3	
4.4	Personnel Subarea	V_T001P		4.4	
4.5	Personnel Subarea Groupings	V_001P_ALL		4.5	
4.6	Employee Group	T501		4.6	
4.7	Employee Subgroup	T503K		4.7	
4.8	Employee Group/Subgroup to Country Assignment	V_T503Z		4.8	
4.9	Employee Subgroup Groupings	V_503_ALL		4.9	
4.10	Employee Subgroup Grouping for Work Schedules	V_T508T		4.10	
4.11	Payroll Area	V_T549A		4.11	
4.12	Default Payroll Area	Feature ABKRS		4.12	
4.13	Work Contract	V_T542A		4.13	
4.14	Organizational Key			4.14	
4.14.1	Employee Grouping for Authorization Control	Feature VDSK1		4.14.2	
4.14.2	Organizational Key Rules	T527		4.14.3	
4.14.3	Organizational Key Creation Rules	T527A		4.14.4	
4.14.4	Organizational Key Master	T527O		4.14.5	
4.15	Administrator Groups	Feature PINCH		4.15.2	
4.16	Administrators	T526		4.15.3	

(Contd.)

Chapter	Description	Configuration	NR/SS/ Done	Reference	Approved by
4.17	Positions	V_528B_C		4.16	
4.18	Position-based Payments	V_T528C_B		4.17	
4.19	Indirect Valuation of Position-based Payments	V_528B_D		4.18	
4.20	Jobs	T513		4.19.3	
4.21	Job Titles	V_T513S		4.19.4	
4.22	Organizational Units	V_T527X		4.20	
4.23	OM-PA Integration	V_T77S0		4.21	
4.24	Partial OM-PA Integration	Feature PLOGI		4.22	
5	**Personal Data**			**5**	
5.1	Personal Data (Infotype 0002) Layout, Default Values and Validation	T588M+[a]		5.1	
5.2	Name Affixes	V_T535N		5.2	
5.3	Form of Address	T522G		5.3	
5.4	Name Formatting: Program to Name Type Link	T522F		5.5	
5.5	Name Formatting: HR Name Format	V_T522N		5.6	
5.6	Marital Status	V_T502T		5.7	
5.7	Longer Description of Marital Status	V_T7BRE1		5.7.6	
5.8	Religious Denominations	V_T516T		5.8	
5.9	Consistency of Form-of-address and Gender	Feature 27GMS		5.9	
6	**Payroll Status**			**6**	
6.1	Payroll Status (Infotype 0003) Layout, Default Values and Validation	T588M+[a]		6.1	
7	**Challenge**			**7**	
7.1	Challenge (Infotype 0004) Layout, Default Values and Validation	T588M+[a]		7.1	
7.2	Challenge Groups	T543		7.2	
7.3	Challenge Types	V_T523T		7.3	
8	**Addresses**			**8**	
8.1	Addresses (Infotype 0006) Layout, Default Values and Validation	T588M+[a]		8.1	
8.2	Address Type	VV_T591A_0006 ___AL0		8.2	

(Contd.)

Chapter	Description	Configuration	NR/SS/ Done	Reference	Approved by
8.3	Countries	V_T005		8.3	
8.4	Country Field Checks	V_005_B		8.4	
8.5	Regions/States	V_T005S		8.5	
8.6	Counties	V_T005E		8.6	
8.7	Screens for Foreign Addresses	Feature CSSCR		8.7	
9	**Planned Working Time**			**9**	
9.1	Planned Working Time (Infotype 0007) Layout, Default Values and Validation	T588M+[a]		9.1	
10	**Contract Elements**			**10**	
10.1	Contract Elements (Infotype 0016) Layout, Default Values and Validation	T588M+[a]		10.1	
10.2	Contract Types	V_T547V		10.2	
10.3	Periods of Notice	V_T547T		10.3	
10.4	Corporations	T545T		10.4	
10.5	Default Values for Contract Elements	Feature CONTR		10.5	
11	**Monitoring of Tasks**			**11**	
11.1	Monitoring of Tasks (Infotype 0019) Layout, Default Values and Validation	T588M+[a]		11.1	
11.2	Task Types	V_T531		11.2	
12	**Family Member/Dependents**			**12**	
12.1	Family Member/Dependents (Infotype 0021) Layout, Default Values and Validation	T588M+[a]		12.1	
12.2	Family Members	VV_T591A_0021 ___AL0		12.2	
12.3	Family Characteristics	V_T577		12.3	
12.4	Default Values in Family Members	Feature NLNAM		12.4	
13	**Education**			**13**	
13.1	Education (Infotype 0022) Layout, Default Values and Validation	T588M+[a]		13.1	
13.2	Education/Training	T518A		13.2	
13.3	Education/Training Categories	T518D		13.3	
13.4	Education/Training Linkage to Categories	V_T518E		13.4	
13.5	Educational Establishment	V_T517T		13.5	

(Contd.)

Chapter	Description	Configuration	NR/SS/ Done	Reference	Approved by
13.6	Institutes/Schools	V_T5J65		13.6	
13.7	Institute/School Type	V_T5J66		13.7	
13.8	Faculty	V_T5J68		13.8	
13.9	Branch of Study	T517Y		13.9	
13.10	Branches of Study in an Educational Establishment	V_T517Z		13.10	
13.11	Certificates	V_T519T		13.11	
13.12	Certificates Given by an Educational Establishment	V_T517A		13.12	
14	**Other/Previous Employers**			**14**	
14.1	Other/Previous Employers (Infotype 0023) Layout, Default Values and Validation	T588M+[a]		14.1	
14.2	Industry Sectors	V_T016		14.2	
14.3	Jobs with Previous Employers	V_T513C		14.3	
14.4	Work Contracts with Previous Employers	T542C		14.4	
15	**Skills**			**15**	
15.1	Skills (Infotype 0024) Layout, Default Values and Validation	T588M+[a]		15.1	
15.2	Qualifications/Skills/ Competencies	T574A		15.2	
15.3	Integration with PD	T77S0		15.3.6	
16	**Internal Medical Service**			**16**	
16.1	Internal Medical Service (Infotype 0028) Layout, Default Values and Validation	T588M+[a]		16.1	
16.2	Examination Type	VV_T591A_0028 ___AL0		16.2	
16.3	Examination Area	V_T578Z		16.3	
16.4	Examination Area: Permissible Values	V_T578X		16.4	
16.5	Examination Results	V_T578Y		16.5	
17	**Powers of Attorney**			**17**	
17.1	Powers of Attorney (Infotype 0030) Layout, Default Values and Validation	T588M+[a]		17.1	
17.2	Power of Attorney Type	VV_T591A_0030 ___AL0		17.2	

(Contd.)

Chapter	Description	Configuration	NR/SS/ Done	Reference	Approved by
18	**Internal Data**			**18**	
18.1	Internal Data (Infotype 0032) Layout, Default Values and Validation	T588M+[a]		18.1	
18.2	Car Rule for Tax	V_T544A		18.2	
18.3	Asset Number Check against Asset Master	Feature ANLAC		18.3	
19	**Corporate Functions**			**19**	
19.1	Corporate Functions (Infotype 0034) Layout, Default Values and Validation	T588M+[a]		19.1	
19.2	Corporate Function	VV_T591A_0034 ___AL0		19.2	
20	**Company Instructions**			**20**	
20.1	Company Instructions (Infotype 0035) Layout, Default Values and Validation	T588M+[a]		20.1	
20.2	Instruction Types	VV_T591A_0035 ___AL0		20.2	
21	**Insurance**			**21**	
21.1	Insurance (Infotype 0037) Layout, Default Values and Validation	T588M+[a]		21.1	
21.2	Insurance Types	VV_T591A_0037 ___AL0		21.2	
21.3	Insurance Companies	V_T564T		21.3	
22	**Objects on Loan**			**22**	
22.1	Objects on Loan (Infotype 0040) Layout, Default Values and Validation	T588M+[a]		22.1	
22.2	Types of Objects on Loan	VV_T591A_0040 ___AL0		22.2	
22.3	Asset Number Check against Asset Master	Feature ANLAC		22.3	
23	**Date Specifications**			**23**	
23.1	Date Specifications (Infotype 0041) Layout, Default Values and Validation	T588M+[a]		23.1	
23.2	Date Types	V_T548Y		23.2	
23.3	Default Value for Date Specifications	Feature DATAR		23.3	

(Contd.)

Chapter	Description	Configuration	NR/SS/ Done	Reference	Approved by
24	**Works Councils**			**24**	
24.1	Works Councils (Infotype 0054) Layout, Default Values and Validation	T588M+[a]		24.1	
25	**Disciplinary Action and Grievances**			**25**	
25.1	Disciplinary Action & Grievances (Infotype 0102) Layout, Default Values and Validation	T588M+[a]		25.1	
25.2	Disciplinary Action/Grievance Type	VV_T591A_0102 ___AL0		25.2	
25.3	Grievance Reasons	V_T505O		25.3	
25.4	Grievance Levels	V_T505K		25.4	
26	**Communication**			**26**	
26.1	Communication (Infotype 0105) Layout, Default Values and Validation	T588M+[a]		26.1	
26.2	Communication Type	VV_T591A_0105 ___AL0		26.2	
27	**Employee's Applicant Number**			**27**	
27.1	Employee's Applicant Number (Infotype 0139) Layout, Default Values and Validation	T588M+[a]		27.1	
27.2	Recruitment to PA Integration	Feature PAPLI		27.2	
28	**Calculation of Employment Period**			**28**	
28.1	Selection Rule	V_T525A_A		28.2	
28.2	Rule for determining entry date	Feature ENTRY		28.2.2	
28.3	Determining Entry/Leaving Dates	BAdI HRPAD00_ ENTRY_LEAVE		28.2.2	
28.4	Permitted Infotypes for Selection Rule	V_T525Z		28.2.4	
28.5	Selection Condition	VC_T525I_A		28.2.4	
28.6	Selection Exit	T525V		28.2.5	
28.7	Selection Class	T525N		28.3.1	
28.8	Selection Rules in a Selection Class	V_T525M_A		28.3.2	
28.9	Indicator for Selection Class	VC_T525NI		28.3.3	
28.10	Legal Regulations	T525OL		28.3.4	
28.11	Valuation Model	V_T525L		28.4.2	

(Contd.)

Chapter	Description	Configuration	NR/SS/ Done	Reference	Approved by
28.12	Assignment of Selection Classes to Valuation Model	V_T525O_A		28.4.3	
28.13	Valuation Model for Add-On HR-VADM	VC_T525L		28.4.4	
28.14	Calculation Process	V_T525P		28.5.1	
28.15	Override Attributes for Calculation Process	V_T525Q		28.5.2	
28.16	Process Step	V_T525R		28.5.3	
28.17	Assignment of Valuation Model to Process Step	V_T525S		28.5.4	
28.18	Employee Grouping for Valuation Model Determination	Feature SENOR		28.5.5	
28.19	Conversion Rule	T525U		28.6.1	
28.20	Conversion Rule for Infotype 0552	Feature CRULE		28.6.2	
28.21	Rounding Rule	V_T525E		28.7	
28.22	Calculation of Service (Infotype 0553) Layout, Default Values and Validation	T588M+[a]		28.8	
28.23	Time Specifications for Employment Period (Infotype 0552) Layout, Default Values and Validation	T588M+[a]		28.9	
28.24	Time Specification Types	T525T		28.10	
28.25	Approval of Time Specification Types	V_T525TD		28.11	
28.26	Occasions for Time Specification Type	T525TR		28.12.1	
28.27	Consideration of the Occasion for Time Specification Type	V_T7DEPBS25TR		28.12.2	
28.28	Occasion to Time Types Assignment	T525TRP		28.12.3	
28.29	Display Settings for Employment Period Calculation	Transaction PSEN_ IMG_XX_CUST		28.1.2	
28.30	Test Utility for Employment Period Calculation	Transaction S_PH9_ 46000454		28.1.2	
29	**Wage Type**			**29**	
29.1	Wage Type Creation	Transaction OH11		29.1	
29.2	Wage Type Characteristics	V_T511		29.2	
29.3	Wage Type Texts	V_T512T		29.3	
29.4	Permissibility of Wage Types in Infotypes	V_T512Z		29.4	

(Contd.)

Chapter	Description	Configuration	NR/SS/ Done	Reference	Approved by
29.5	Permissibility of Wage Type Entry in the Past	V_T591B		29.5	
29.6	Permissibility of Wage Types for Employees	V_511_B		29.6	
29.7	Assignment of Wage Types to Wage Type Groups	V_T52D7		29.7	
29.8	Base Wage Type Valuation	V_T539J		29.8	
30	**Basic Pay**			**30**	
30.1	Basic Pay (Infotype 0008) Layout, Default Values and Validation	T588M+[a]		30.1	
30.2	Payment Type	V_T591A		30.2	
30.3	Pay Scale Type	V_T510A		30.3	
30.4	Pay Scale Area	V_T510G		30.4	
30.5	Default Pay Scale Type and Area	Feature TARIF		30.5	
30.6	Pay Scale Groups and Levels	V_T510		30.6	
30.7	Setting the Indirect Valuation Period	T77S0		30.7	
30.8	Default Wage Types for Basic Pay	Feature LGMST		30.8	
30.9	Wage Type Model for Basic Pay	V_T539A		30.9	
30.10	Pay Scale Conversion for Basic Pay	T546		30.10	
30.11	Simulation Variant for the Payroll Program	Feature PM004		30.11	
30.12	Pay Scales for Annual Salaries	V_T510N		30.12	
30.13	Standard Working Hours	V_T510I		30.13	
31	**Bank Details**			**31**	
31.1	Bank Details (Infotype 0009) Layout, Default Values and Validation	T588M+[a]		31.1	
31.2	Bank Details Type	VV_T591A_0009 ___AL0		31.2	
31.3	Default Payment Method	Feature ZLSCH		31.3	
32	**External Bank Transfers**			**32**	
32.1	External Bank Transfers (Infotype 0011) Layout, Default Values and Validation	T588M+[a]		32.1	
33	**Recurring Payments/Deductions**			**33**	
33.1	Recurring Payments/Deductions (Infotype 0014) Layout, Default Values and Validation	T588M+[a]		33.1	
33.2	Wage Type Model	V_T511M		33.2	

(Contd.)

Chapter	Description	Configuration	NR/SS/ Done	Reference	Approved by
34	**Additional Payments**			**34**	
34.1	Additional Payments (Infotype 0015) Layout, Default Values and Validation	T588M+[a]		34.1	
35	**Cost Distribution**			**35**	
35.1	Cost Distribution (Infotype 0027) Layout, Default Values and Validation	T588M+[a]		35.1	
35.2	Costs to be Distributed	V_T591A		35.2	
36	**Loans**			**36**	
36.1	Loans (Infotype 0045) Layout, Default Values and Validation	T588M+[a]		36.1	
36.2	Loan Payments (Infotype 0078) Layout, Default Values and Validation	T588M+[a]		36.2	
36.3	Loan Types	VV_T591A_0045 ___AL0		36.3	
36.4	Loan Categories	V_T506A		36.4	
36.5	Loan Conditions	V_T506D		36.5	
36.6	Default Interest Calculation Method	Feature INTLO		36.6	
36.7	Loan Value Dates	V_T506S		36.7	
36.8	Loan Allocation Control (International)	T506C		36.8	
36.9	Loan Grouping (International)	Feature ALOAN		36.9	
36.10	Loan Approval			36.10	
36.11	Allowance Grouping	V_T7INA1		36.11	
36.12	Allowance Grouping Assignment	V_T7INA3		36.12	
36.13	Loan Grouping	Feature 40LGR		36.13	
36.14	Loans Eligibility Checks and Limits	V_T7INJ3		36.14	
36.15	Salary Components for Loan Eligibility	Feature 40LSL		36.15	
36.16	BAdI: Loans Eligibility	BAdI HR_IN_ LOANS_VALID		36.16	
36.17	Loans Disbursement Schedule	V_T7INJ5		36.17	
36.18	Event Codes	V_T7INJ6		36.18	
36.19	Penal Interest on Special Repayment	T511K		36.19	
36.20	BAdI: Penal Interest Amount	BAdI HR_IN_ PENAL_INTER		36.19	

(Contd.)

Chapter	Description	Configuration	NR/SS/ Done	Reference	Approved by
36.21	Payment Types	V_T591A		36.20	
36.22	Assignment of Wage Types to Payment Types	V_T506P		36.20.5	
36.23	Payment Types Valid for More than One Interval	V_506P_B		36.20.6	
36.24	Processing Logic for Customer Payment Types	BAdI HRPY_LOAN_ PAYMENTS		36.20.7	
37	**Membership Fees**			**37**	
37.1	Membership Fees (Infotype 0057) Layout, Default Values and Validation	T588M+[a]		37.1	
37.2	Membership Types	VV_T591A_0057 ___AL0		37.2	
37.3	Default Values for Memberships	Feature PAYEE		37.3	
37.4	Payee Keys	V_T521B		37.4	
37.5	Allowed Payees	VV_T521C_0057 _AL0		37.5	
37.6	Membership Function	V_T557V		37.6	
38	**Notifications**			**38**	
38.1	Notifications (Infotype 0128) Layout, Default Values and Validation	T588M+[a]		38.1	
38.2	Types of Notification	V_T591A		38.2	
39	**Additional Off-cycle Payments**			**39**	
39.1	Additional Off-cycle Payments (Infotype 0267) Layout, Default Values and Validation	T588M+[a]		39.1	
39.2	Reasons for Off-cycle Payroll Runs	V_T52OCR		39.2	
39.3	Categories for Off-cycle Reasons	V_T52OCC		39.3	
40	**ESS Settings Remuneration Statement**			**40**	
40.1	ESS Settings Remuneration Statement (Infotype 0655) Layout, Default Values and Validation	T588M+[a]		40.1	
41	**Infotype Properties**			**41**	
41.1	Infotype Attributes	V_T582A		41.1	
41.2	Infotype Texts	V_T582S		41.2	
41.3	Infotype Validity for Country	V_T582L		41.3	

(Contd.)

Chapter	Description	Configuration	NR/SS/ Done	Reference	Approved by
41.4	Dynamic Actions	T588Z		41.4	
41.5	Mail on Change to Infotype Record	Feature M0001		41.5	
41.6	Field-specific Retroactive Accounting Recognition	V_T588G		41.6	
41.7	Retroactive Accounting Date Change	Feature RETRO		41.7	
41.8	Default Values for Infotypes	Feature DFINF		41.8	
42	**Infotype Menus**			**42**	
42.1	User Group Dependency on Menus and Infogroups	VV_T588C_I_AL0		42.2	
42.2	Infotype Menu	V_T588B		42.3	
43	**Infotype Screens**			**43**	
43.1	Features for Screen Control	Features Pnnnn		43.2	
43.2	Infotype Screen Control	T588M+[a]		43.3	
43.3	Header Structure per Infotype	V_582A_B		43.4	
43.4	Header Modifier	V_T588I		43.5	
43.5	Header Definition	T588J		43.6	
43.6	Photo	V_T77S0SC	SS	43.7	
43.7	Header Data Selection Control	T588H		43.8	
43.8	Header Field Names	T588L		43.9	
43.9	Screen Types for Fast Entry	T588Q		43.10	
43.10	Selection Reports for Fast Data Entry	T588R		43.11	
44	**Infotype Change Tracking**			**44**	
44.1	Infotypes to be Logged	V_T585A		44.1	
44.2	Field Group Definition	V_T585B		44.2	
44.3	Field Group Characteristics	V_T585C		44.3	
44.4	Report Start Logs	V_T599R		44.4	
45	**Cost Assignment**			**45**	
45.1	Screen Modification for Assignment Data	T588O		45.2	
45.2	Screen Modification for Account Assignment Block	V_T588N		45.3	
45.3	Subscreens for Controlling Objects	Transaction OXK1		45.4	
46	**Payment Model**			**46**	
46.1	Payment Model	V_T549W		46.1	
46.2	Payment Periods	V_T549X		46.2	
46.3	Employee Grouping for Default Payment Model	Feature MODDE		46.3	

(Contd.)

(Contd.)

Chapter	Description	Configuration	NR/SS/ Done	Reference	Approved by
51.3	Layout of Personnel Assignment	V_T587C_T		51.3	
51.4	Layout of Personnel Assignment Overview	V_T587C_O		51.4	
51.5	Categories for Personnel Assignment Details	V_T587A		51.5	
51.6	Layout of Personnel Assignment Details	V_T587C_D		51.6	
51.7	Actions for Concurrent Employment	Feature ACTCE		51.7	
51.8	Consistency in Infotype Data	V_T582G		51.8	
51.9	Repairing Data Sharing Inconsistencies	BAdI HRPA_SHARING _REPOR		51.8.6	
51.10	Grouping Reasons for Personnel Assignments	T7CCE _GPREASON		51.9	
51.11	Grouping Rules for Personnel Assignments	T7CCE_GPRULE		51.10	
51.12	Assignment of Grouping Rule to Grouping Reason	V_T7CCE_GPA SGM		51.11	
51.13	Country-specific Assignment of Grouping Rule to Grouping Reason	V_T7CCE_GPASG		51.12	
51.14	Reference Personnel Numbers (Infotype 0031) Layout, Default Values and Validation	T588M+[a]		51.13	
51.15	Reference Personnel Number Priority (Infotype 0121) Layout, Default Values and Validation	T588M+[a]		51.14	

[a] T588M+ includes view T588M, features Pnnnn, function exits EXIT_SAPFP50M_001 & EXIT_SAPFP50M_002, and transaction PM01.

63.3.2 Implementation Guide Recruitment

Chapter	Description	Configuration	NR/SS/ Done	Reference	Approved by
1	**Applicant**			**53**	
1.1	Applicant Number Ranges	Transaction PB04		53.1	
1.2	Applicant Number Range Determination	Feature NUMAP		53.2	
1.3	Applicant Infotypes			53.3	
1.4	Applicant Infotype Menu	VV_T588B_IAP ____AL0		53.4	

Chapter	Description	Configuration	NR/SS/ Done	Reference	Approved by
2	**Application**			**54**	
2.1	Applications (infotype 4001) Layout, Default Values and Validation	T588M+[a]		54.1	
2.2	Advertisement	V_T750B		54.2	
2.3	Recruitment Instrument	V_T750C		54.3	
2.4	Addresses for recruitment instruments	VV_536A_B__P _AL0		54.3.5	
2.5	Medium	T750D		54.4	
2.6	Unsolicited Application Group	T750G		54.5	
3	**Vacancy Assignment**			**55**	
3.1	Vacancy Assignment (Infotype 4002) Layout, Default Values and Validation	T588M+[a]		55.1	
3.2	Priorities for Vacancy Assignment	VV_T591A_4002 ___AL0		55.2	
4	**Applicant Action**			**56**	
4.1	Applicant Events (Infotype 4000) Layout, Default Values and Validation	T588M+[a]		56.1	
4.2	Applicant Status	T751A		56.2	
4.3	Status Reason	V_T751C		56.3	
4.4	Admissible Combination of Status and Reason	V_T751D		56.4	
4.5	Permissible Vacancy Assignment Statuses	Feature STATU		56.5	
4.6	Applicant Action Type	V_T751E		56.6	
4.7	Applicant Actions Menu	VV_588B_B_B40 __AL0		56.7	
4.8	User Group Dependency on Menu and Infogroups	VV_T588C_B_AL0		56.8	
5	**Applicant Activities**			**57**	
5.1	Applicant Activity Type	T750J		57.1	
5.2	Automatic Creation of Applicant Activities	Feature PACTV		57.2	
5.3	Follow-up activities	Feature PACPP		57.3	
5.4	Parameters for Follow-up Activities	Feature PACPA		57.4	
5.5	Variables for Creating Text	Feature VARIA		57.5	
5.6	Parameters for Mail Connection	Feature MAILS		57.6	
5.7	Word Processing System	Feature WPROC		57.7	

(Contd.)

Chapter	Description	Configuration	NR/SS/ Done	Reference	Approved by
6	**Applicant Activity Status**			**58**	
6.1	Applicant Activity Status (Infotype 4004) Layout, Default Values and Validation	T588M+[a]		58.1	
7	**Applicant's Personnel Number**			**59**	
7.1	Applicant's Personnel Number (Infotype 4005) Layout, Default Values and Validation	T588M+[a]		59.1	
7.2	Integration of Internal Applicants with PA	Feature PRELI		59.2	
8	**Applicant's Organizational Assignment**			**60**	
8.1	Organizational Assignment (Infotype 0001) Layout, Default Values and Validation	T588M+[a]		60.1	
8.2	Applicant Group	T750K		60.2	
8.3	Applicant Range	V_T750F		60.3	
8.4	Personnel Officer	T526		60.4	
8.5	Signature Line for Letters to Applicants	V_513A_C		60.5	
9	**Applicant's Contract Elements**			**61**	
9.1	Contract Elements (Infotype 0016) Layout, Default Values and Validation	T588M+[a]		61.1	
10	**Other Recruitment Configuration**			**62**	
10.1	Standard Texts	Transaction SO10		62.1	
10.2	Standard Text Assignment for Short Profile	Feature SHPRO		62.2	
10.3	Default Value for Internet Medium	Feature INTDF		62.3	
10.4	Default Values for Internet Applications	Feature INTDY		62.4	
10.5	Permitted Document Formats for Internet Applications	T750R		62.5	
10.6	Check for Personnel Numbers	Feature PRELR		62.6	
10.7	Switch for Defining a Vacancy	T77S0		62.7	

[a] T588M+ includes view T588M, features Pnnnn, function exits EXIT_SAPFP50M_001 & EXIT_SAPFP50M_002, and transaction PM01.

63.4 TRANSACTIONS

Functional Consultant	User	Business Process Owner	Senior Management	My Rating	Understanding Level
A	C	X	X		

63.4.1 Personnel Administration

Category	Transaction	Description
User	HRRSM00FBA	External Human Resources Master Data
Customizing	OG42	Customizing Tool for PA42
Customizing	OH11	Copy Wage Types
Customizing	OXK1	Coding Block: Maintain Subscreens
Customizing	PA04	Maintain PA Number Ranges
User	PA10	Personnel File
User	PA20	Display HR Master Data
User	PA30	Maintain HR Master Data
User	PA40	Personnel Actions
User	PA42	Fast Entry for Actions
User	PA70	Fast Entry
Customizing	PFCG	Role Maintenance
Customizing	PM01	Enhance Infotypes
Customizing	PSEN_IMG_XX_CUST	Display settings
User	S_AHR_61010818	Assign residence tax collector number (JP)
User	S_AHR_61011132	Define school information (JP)
User	S_AHR_61011133	Define faculty information (JP)
User	S_AHR_61011474	Define Organizational Units
User	S_AHR_61011475	Define Jobs
User	S_AHR_61011476	Define Jobs (Canada)
User	S_AHR_61011490	Define Positions
User	S_AHR_61011491	Define Jobs (USA)
User	S_AHR_61016354	Telephone Directory
User	S_AHR_61016356	Time Spent in Each Pay Scale Area/ Type/Group/Level
User	S_AHR_61016357	Defaults for Pay Scale Reclassification
User	S_AHR_61016358	Reference Personnel Numbers
User	S_AHR_61016359	Severely Challenged
User	S_AHR_61016360	HR Master Data Sheet
User	S_AHR_61016362	Flexible Employee Data
User	S_AHR_61016369	Employee List
User	S_AHR_61016370	List of Maternity Data
User	S_AHR_61016373	Headcount Development

(Contd.)

Category	Transaction	Description
User	S_AHR_61016374	Nationalities
User	S_AHR_61016376	Salary According to Seniority
User	S_AHR_61016378	Assignment to Wage Level
User	S_AHR_61016380	Logged Changes in Infotype Data
User	S_AHR_61016381	Log of Report Starts
User	S_L7D_24000324	Define Shukko Partners
User	S_L9C_94000095	Headcount Changes
User	S_PH0_48000450	Date Monitoring
User	S_PH0_48000510	Ad Hoc Query
User	S_PH9_46000216	Service Anniversaries
User	S_PH9_46000217	Statistics: Gender Sorted by Seniority
User	S_PH9_46000218	Statistics: Gender Sorted by Age
User	S_PH9_46000220	Vehicle Search List
User	S_PH9_46000221	Birthday List
User	S_PH9_46000222	Family Members
User	S_PH9_46000223	Employees Entered and Left
User	S_PH9_46000224	Education and Training
User	S_PH9_46000225	Powers of Attorney
User	S_PH9_46000454	Test Utility for Employment Period Calculation
Customizing	SQ02	SAP Query: Maintain InfoSet
Customizing	SQ03	SAP Query: Maintain user groups
Customizing	SU24	Auth. Obj. Check Under Transactions

63.4.2 Recruitment

Category	Transaction	Description
Customizing	PB04	Number Range Maintenance: RP_PAPL
User	PB10	Initial entry of applicant master data
User	PB20	Display applicant master data
User	PB30	Maintain applicant master data
User	PB40	Applicant actions
User	PB50	Display Applicant Activities
User	PB60	Maintain Applicant Activities
User	PB80	Evaluate vacancies
User	PBA0	Evaluate advertisements
User	PBA1	Applicants by name
User	PBA2	List of applications
User	PBA3	Applicant vacancy assignment list
User	PBA4	Receipt of application
User	PBA6	Recurring tasks: Print letters
User	PBA7	Recurring tasks: Data transfer
User	PBA8	Recurring tasks: Transfer data

(Contd.)

Category	Transaction	Description
User	PBA9	List of planned actions
User	PBAA	Evaluate recruitment instrument
User	PBAB	Maintain vacancy assignments
User	PBAC	Applicant statistics
User	PBAE	Applicant pool
User	PBAF	Vacancy assignment list
User	PBAG	Screening
User	PBAH	Decision
User	PBAI	All applicants via qualifications
User	PBAK	Recurring Tasks: Print Labels
User	PBAL	Bulk processing
User	PBAP	Internal Applicants Via Quals
User	PBAQ	External Applicants Via Quals
User	PBAT	Choose SAPscript or WinWord
User	PBAV	Display T750C
User	PBAW	Maintain T750B
User	PBAX	Display T750B
User	PBAY	Maintain T750X
User	PBAZ	Display T750X
User	PU90	Delete applicant data
User	S_AHR_61015508	Variable Applicant List
User	S_AHR_61015509	Applicants by Name
User	S_AHR_61015510	Applicants by Action
User	S_AHR_61015511	Applicants' Education and Training
User	S_AHR_61015512	Applications
User	S_AHR_61015513	Applicant Statistics
User	S_AHR_61015514	Planned Activities for Personnel Officer
User	S_AHR_61015515	Vacancy Assignments
User	S_AHR_61015516	Vacancies
User	S_AHR_61015517	Job Advertisements
User	S_AHR_61015518	Evaluate Recruitment Instruments
User	S_PH0_48000512	Ad Hoc Query
Customizing	SO10	SAPscript: Standard Texts

63.4.3 Utility

Category	Transaction	Description
ABAP	BAPI	Bapi explorer
Basis	BD87	Status monitor for ALE messages
User	CG3Y	Download file
User	CG3Z	Upload file
ABAP	CMOD	Enhancements

(Contd.)

Category	Transaction	Description
ABAP	HRFORMS	HR forms workplace
Consultant	LSMW	Legacy system migration workbench
User	OAAD	Archivelink administration documents
Consultant	OSS1	Log on to SAPNet
Consultant	OY19	Customizing cross-system viewer
ABAP	PE51	HR form editor
Basis	PFCG	Role maintenance
Basis	RSSCD100_PFCG	Change documents for role admin.
Basis	RSSCD100_PFCG_USER	For role assignment
Basis	RSUSR200	List of users per login date
Basis	S_BCE_68001403	With critical authorizations
Basis	S002	Menu administration
User	SA38	ABAP reporting
Basis	SALE	Display ALE customizing
User	SBWP	SAP business workplace
Consultant	SCAT	Computer aided test tool
Consultant	SCMP	View/table comparison
Basis	SCOT	SAPconnect - administration
Consultant	SCU0	Customizing cross-system viewer
Basis	SE01	Transport organizer (extended)
Basis	SE03	Transport organizer tools
Consultant, Basis	SE09	Transport organizer
Consultant, Basis	SE10	Transport organizer
Consultant, ABAP	SE11	ABAP dictionary maintenance
ABAP	SE13	Maintain technical settings (tables)
ABAP	SE15	ABAP/4 repository information system
Consultant, ABAP	SE16	Data browser
Consultant, ABAP	SE16N	General table display
Consultant, ABAP	SE17	General table display
ABAP	SE18	Business add-ins: definitions
ABAP	SE19	Business add-ins: implementations
ABAP	SE24	Class builder
ABAP	SE35	ABAP/4 dialog modules
ABAP	SE36	Logical database builder
ABAP	SE37	ABAP function modules
ABAP	SE38	ABAP editor
ABAP	SE39	Splitscreen editor: (new)
ABAP	SE41	Menu painter
ABAP	SE43	Maintain area menu
ABAP	SE51	Screen painter
ABAP	SE61	SAP documentation
Consultant	SE63	Translation: initial screen
ABAP	SE71	SAPscript form

(Contd.)

Category	Transaction	Description
ABAP	SE72	SAPscript styles
ABAP	SE73	SAPscript font maintenance
ABAP	SE74	SAPscript format conversion
ABAP	SE75	SAPscript settings
ABAP	SE75TTDTGC	SAPscript: change standard symbols
ABAP	SE75TTDTGD	SAPscript: display standard symbols
ABAP	SE76	SAPscript: form translation
ABAP	SE77	SAPscript styles translation
ABAP	SE80	Object navigator
ABAP	SE84	Repository information system
ABAP	SE85	ABAP/4 repository information system
ABAP	SE91	Message maintenance
ABAP	SE93	Maintain transaction
Consultant	SEARCH_SAP_MENU	Find in SAP menu
Consultant	SEARCH_USER_MENU	Find in user menu
User, Consultant	SECATT	Extended computer aided test tool
User, Consultant	SHDB	Batch input transaction recorder
Consultant	SLG1	Application log: display logs
Basis	SM01	Lock transactions
Basis	SM04	User list
Basis	SM12	Display and delete locks
Consultant	SM30	Call view maintenance
Consultant	SM31	Call view maintenance like SM30
Consultant	SM34	Viewcluster maintenance call
User	SM35	Batch input monitoring
User	SM35P	Batch input: log monitoring
User	SM36	Schedule background job
User	SM37	Job overview
User	SM38	Queue maintenance transaction
ABAP	SMARTFORMS	SAP smart forms
ABAP	SMOD	SAP enhancement management
User	SMX	Display own jobs
User	SO00	SAPoffice: short message
ABAP	SO10	SAPscript: standard texts
User	SP01	Output controller
User	SP02	Display spool requests
Consultant	SP11	TemSe directory
Consultant	SPRO	Customizing—edit project
User, Consultant	SQ00	SAP query: start queries
Consultant	SQ01	SAP query: maintain queries
Consultant	SQ02	SAP query: maintain infoset
Consultant	SQ03	SAP query: maintain user groups
User	SQVI	Quickviewer

(Contd.)

Category	Transaction	Description
ABAP	ST22	ABAP dump analysis
Basis	SU01	User maintenance
Basis	SU21	Maintain the Authorization Objects
Basis	SU22	Auth. object usage in transactions
Basis	SU24	Auth. object check under transactions
User	SU3	Maintain users own data
User	SU53	Display authorization check
Basis	SUIM	User information system
Consultant	SWDD	Workflow builder

Index

World Government
For a World Free from War, Terrorism and Poverty

Facts

- The world spends trillions of dollars every year on military and war equipment, while its people go hungry.
- Today the world is incapable of resolving any dispute through military actions.
- Terrorism thrives because of covert support of country governments.
- Enormous expenditure on militaries all over the world is not only a waste, but also extremely dangerous as it increases the destructive power of country governments.

We want

- A world free from war, terrorism and poverty.

How can it be done?

- Establish a world parliament, a world government and a world court.
- Disband militaries of all countries simultaneously.
- Use the savings to alleviate poverty.

Will all countries agree?

- Yes! When people of the countries want it.
- We have to awaken the people of the whole world.

How will it work?

- The world parliament will be formed through direct election of members of parliament all over the world. These members of parliament will form the world government.
- The world government will have limited but sufficient power to provide security to all countries, manage global environment and combat terrorism all over the world.
- The world government will secure the borders of all countries to ensure that there is no unauthorized entry or exit.
- The country governments will continue to manage their affairs.
- Disputes between countries will be resolved with the help of the world parliament and the world court.
- No country will disband its military first. All countries will disband their militaries simultaneously in a phased manner,

under the supervision of the world government, which will verify that the militaries are actually disbanded.

- Countries will retain their police to maintain law and order.
- Countries may have special forces to deal with terrorism and to provide relief in the event of natural disasters.

Is it possible?

- Many people say that this is an impossible task because other people will not agree.
- This task is possible if we talk only about ourselves, and not about others. This task is big but not impossible.
- We have only one world, we can't give up on it.
- We can succeed only if we try.

What should I do?

- Level 1: Register with WIII and become a world citizen. Even children can join.
- Level 2: Spread the message to your family, friends and neighbours. Convince five persons to join.

- Level 3: Convince five persons that each one of them would enroll five more persons.
- Level 4: Become an active volunteer.

Act now

- Act now. Don't give up because of enormity of the task.

You have nothing to lose

- There is no membership fee.
- You are not required to work unless you want to. But if you want, there is a lot of work to do.
- You are not required to follow any person or any belief.

Contact

World Integration and Improvement Initiative (WIII)
L/A-4/303, Ajmera Housing Complex, Pune 411018 India.
E-mail: agrawal.prem@gmail.com
Phone: 91(20)27462635

World Language

Need for a World Language

Perhaps the most important gift of nature to mankind is the ability to communicate using a language. However, this gift is not unmitigated, because we have got too much of it. We do not have a single language, but a large number of them, which sometimes is as bad as not having any language.

Lack of a common world language can greatly handicap a person, as more and more people travelling around the world discover to their dismay. With the world becoming smaller and smaller, as a result of advances in transportation and communication, the need for a common world language is felt more and more acutely. One option to overcome this hadicap is for a person to learn multiple languages, which is not only wasteful, but can be done only to a limited extent. Another way to overcome this handicap is through translation and inter-pretation, for which we pay a heavy price in terms of cost, time, and timeliness, and achieve at best partial communication. Scientific and technical literature available in one language cannot be used by people who do not know that language.

There is probably no one, who does not agree with the need for a world language. Only, people do not want to discuss it, fearing that accepting any language, other than their own, as world language will put them at a disadvantage. Also, people are strongly attached to their mother tongue, often considering it as revered as their mother, and feel a sense of guilt in accepting another language.

While there are some, who do not want to discuss this issue fearing that they may have to accept another language, there are others who do the same hoping that their language may become world language by default. This may well happen, but is it desirable even for them?

Importance of a good world language

A language is a tool for communication, and we must evaluate it as we would evaluate any other tool. How effective is it in meeting its objective; and how much resources does it consume in doing so? People who hope that their language may become world language, should think again. Do we just want a common language, or do we want a really good world language—a language which provides effective, unambiguous communication with minimum effort.

This article shows that existing languages score quite badly in a rational evaluation. Let us remember that many of us use almost our entire non-sleeping time in reading, writing, and thinking—activities which depend on the efficiency of language. If we can design a language, which is more efficient than our existing language, we will gain that much extra time, which can be used for productive or recreational purposes. It has also been well accepted that languages influence our thinking, making the role of language even more important.

We must, therefore, consider ourselves lucky that we do not have a single language in the world. This gives us a choice. It is possible for us to have a well designed world language. If we had only one language, we would not have this choice, as we have no choice today in numbering system, computer keyboard, etc. We must not squander this choice away, by letting an existing language become the world language. It will be like losing a fortune, just because we refused to decide. It is also important that we decide to develop a world language as early as possible. The more time we lose, the more will be the backlog of translation, which must necessarily be done.

Should an existing natural language be world language?

Some of the existing natural languages, particularly English, aspire to become world language. Their claim is based primarily on their widespread use in dominant segments of society all over the world, e.g. science, law, business, industry, government, etc. However, if we objectively examine their effectiveness and efficiency, they do not perform too well. Let us take a look at 'English'.

Let us start from the alphabet. English does not have a phonetic alphabet. The same letter is associated with different sounds in different words. This puts tremendous load on people learning the language. They have

to learn both the pronunciation as well as the spelling. Many languages of the world have this problem, while many are free from it.

The length of the words in a language determines the effort in communication to a large extent. If the words are long, the communication time and effort is more. Natural languages being product of evolution, have not paid much attention to length of words. Consequently, the words tend to be long. The best proof of this defect in a language is the existence of short forms for long words. 'Info' for information, and 'ad' for advertisement, amply demonstrate that words can be shorter.

All languages use prefixes and suffixes to add additional meaning to the meaning of a word. By doing so, they avoid the need to define and learn a word. This practice is very good, but often there are exceptions, which are not desirable. Also, usually this concept is not utilized fully. We do not need separate words for boy and girl. We need only one word with a prefix or a suffix for gender.

The meanings of words is another area of concern. Many times the words have contextual meanings. This increases the learning effort, as all the meanings of the words have to be learnt. Also, the words often suffer from overprecision, and underprecision. There are many words which mean exactly, or nearly, the same. On the other hand there are some words, whose meaning is not precise enough.

Grammars of natural languages are usually quite complex. Agreement of number and gender between noun and verb is a case in point. Really speaking, there is no need to alter the verb for number and gender; they should be attributes of noun alone. If that was done, the language will become simpler. By unnecessarily modifying the verb for number and gender, we make the language complex, and introduce the possibility of making mistakes. Needless complexity of grammar is best understood by learners of a foreign language, who constantly compare the grammar of the new language with that of their mother tongues.

Ambiguity or lack of clarity in the meaning of a sentence also exists.

It might be argued that the defects of English may be removed to prepare it for the role of world language. However, the changes may be so many, that we may not recognise it as English at all. Also, however much we improve it, it can never be as good as a language designed from scratch. We are going to build the world language only once, and it must be the best. Evaluation of other natural languages is likely to bring us to the same conclusion.

Also, we must remember that adopting an existing language as world language will be more repugnant to the rest of the world, than adopting a newly designed language.

Should Esperanto be world language?

If natural languages do not qualify to be the world language, what about Esperanto? After all it was created precisely for this purpose. There is no doubt that Esperanto is better suited to be the world language, than any other natural language. However, the question remains: is it possible to design a language better than Esperanto? The answer would be in affirmative, primarily because even Esperanto is based on some natural languages, and has not exercised freedom of choice in design to the fullest. However, Esperanto has definitely proved a major point—that it is possible to design a language.

How to develop a world language?

Designing a language is not a very difficult job, but designing a good language is. Designing a language involves making a large number of decisions. How much effort is put in arriving at these decisions will determine the quality of language. Also, the process should involve wide ranging cosultations with experts in various fields. After an initial decision is made based on expert opinion, it should be widely publicized, and feedback and comments of all the people should be considered, before finalizing the decision. Even then, if there is a good reason to alter a decision previously made, it should be done. In no case should we compromise on the quality of the world language. Some ideas are discussed here to illustrate the kind of improvements possible. Obviously, they are at best the tip of the iceberg.

Objectives of the world language

Some of the objectives of the world language would be as under. These need to be debated and enlarged. They also need to be interpreted for each sub-activity.

1. Achieve effective and unambiguous communication
    1.1 Between humans
    1.2 Between humans and machines
2. Minimize effort in communication
    2.1 Minimize effort in speaking and hearing
    2.2 Minimize effort in writing and reading
3. Minimize effort in learning the language
    3.1 Minimize the length and number of words
    3.2 Maximize the use of rules to form words and sentences. Have no exceptions.

Designing alphabet and script

One of the most fundamental components of a language is its alphabet. The alphabet is in two forms—written and spoken. While designing the alphabet, the spoken alphabet should be designed first. The sounds produced by human beings are not discrete. From a continous spectrum, we have to select a set of sounds. If we select too few sounds, the alphabet will be small and words will be longer. On the other hand, too many sounds may cause problems in distinguishing between them. Fortunately, this science, called phonetics, is well developed, and can be used for selecting a set of sounds. The sounds should be selected in such a way that we get the maximum distinction between sounds, and the effort required in production of sound is minimum. In addition, pleasant-ness of sound in hearing may also be considered. The ability of machines to produce these sounds, and distinguish between them on hearing may also be considered.

In order to minimize learning effort, each sound should be assigned a character. Frequently occurring sound combinations may also be assigned an additional character, as in shorthand. The language should be phonetic. We already have natural languages which are phonetic, and they demonstrate the advantages offered by a phonetic language.

The script for the world language should be designed keeping in mind the ability of human hand for writing, and human eye for reading. In writing, the script should provide continuity. There should be no dotting the 'i', or cutting the 't'. This will minimize the movement of hand, and save effort. Each character should be independent, and combined sequentially. In some scripts, a part of the character is outside the main writing area, e.g. a part of 'g' is below the main line of writing. This should be avoided

to conserve space. Characters should be as uniform in size as possible. Each character should be written in only one way. There should be no concept of upper and lower case, wherein the same character is written in two ways.

The effort in writing can be greatly reduced, if natural movements of body are used in the design of characters. Research should be conducted to determine which movements are easy for human hands, and which are not. For example, it is common experience that people find it easier to write 'u' than to write 'n'. So much so, that often 'n' looks like 'u'. This is not accidental, because its opposit never happens. This is an interesting example, because the two characters are mirror images of one another. It can perhaps be said that human hand can turn in quickly, but cannot turn out as quickly. Perhaps it has a natural tendency to move towards the chest as observed in case of an electric shock. Similarly, research should be conducted to determine if the human eye has any preferences in pattern recognition. We should also consider, whether the writing will be from left to right, right to left, top to bottom, or bottom to top. The suitability of the script for machine production and recognition should also be considered.

Designing words

Words, even in natural languages, consist of parts which have independent meaning. For example, both 'un' and 'well' in unwell have independent meanings, which determine the meaning of unwell. These parts are called morphemes by linguists; we may call them roots. All languages use the concepts of roots, prefixes, suffixes, etc. But they do not use it to the fullest. For example, the word 'bad' is not needed; 'ungood' could be used in its place.

We should design word roots in such a way that their meanings are, as far as possible, independent of each other. For the same meaning there should not be more than one word root. If word roots are well defined, the learning effort will greatly reduce. Let me illustrate.

We need word roots to indicate the number and the gender. We may decide that there will be three genders—masculine, feminine, and unknown or unspecified. Similarly, we may decide that there will be three numbers—singular, plural, and unknown or unspecified. We may combine both these attributes, and assign a vowel to each of the nine combinations. We then use these vowels to suffix nouns and pronouns. Let us see the power of this simple design. We now need only one word for father, mother, and parent. Similarly, only one word will be needed for brother, sister, and sibling. Not only that the number of words will be reduced, some new words will become available, e.g. a word for either son or daughter. Speakers of Hindi, will find new words like parent and sibling, which they never had before. Also, we do not often know the sex of a bird, and use masculine, feminine, or neuter gender, depending on convention. In the new scheme, we can use the unspecified gender most of the time, and can specify it if we know the gender. Also, legal documents often use words like person(s). This is because there is no concept of unknown, or unspecified, number. We can, thus, see the power of a simple well-defined word root.

The above example is not an isolated one. By defining just three morphemes, for parent, child, and spouse, hundreds of existing and non-existing words for family relations can be eliminated. A large number of words describing young members of a species can be eliminated by using a single prefix with the word for species. Also, we

can have a prefix each for first half, second half, first quarter, second quarter etc. of age, and so on. Thus, the communicator can choose the precision with which he wants to convey the age.

Word roots will be formed by assigning a sequence of characters to each concept. This should be done, using principles of classification and codification. In many branches of science, e.g. zoology and botany, such classification already exists. These should be used, so that there is no need to have a separate scientific name. Also, the frequency of their use should be considered. Highly used roots should be identified by few characters, so that the words are short.

Rules should be defined to combine roots into words. Where classification and codification gives a large word, but the frequency of use requires a small word, a synonym may be defined. Thus, synonyms will exist only for the purpose of making the language more efficient.

Designing grammar

Grammar defines how to combine words into sentences. These rules should be as simple as possible, and there should be no exceptions. The sequence of words in a sentence should not affect its meaning. Also, preferably the sequence of words should not change, as it happens in English, where changing a sentence from affirmative to inquisitive requires a change in the sequence of words.

In many existing languages, attributes which should affect only words, are defined at the level of sentence. Number and gender are attributes of noun, and they have nothing to do with verb. Similarly, tense is an attribute of verb, and should not affect the noun. We think that a sentence is affirmative, or inquisitive (asks a question). Let us consider a simple sentence, "Are you going?". This may be interpreted as, "Are you going? (or not going)", or as "Are you? (or someone else) going". Here we can see that the question is an attribute of word, and not of sentence. Research will be needed to determine whether enquiry is always at word level, or sometimes at word level, and sometimes at sentence level.

What do we do next?

There is no doubt that it is possible to develop a language, which is far superior to existing languages. The development of such a language will be an iterative process. It will go through several cycles of improvement, before it becomes reasonably good. If we can assign even 1% of resources being spent in linguistic research, we can easily build such a language. Then it can be improved, and compared with existing languages. Only after its superiority is clearly demonstrated, do we have to think of adopting it. This project is definitely worthy of research, and I call upon the world community to take it up.

Good Governance

Many countries of the world face a number of problems. Are there any solutions? I believe that there are. Here are some ideas that could be helpful in solving some of our problems. There could be a structured public debate on these, and those which meet public approval could be implemented.

Minimize government functions

- Often governments try to do too many things.
- It is not government's job to provide goods and services. It should facilitate their production and distribution and ensure competitiveness, efficiency and non-exploitation of customers.
- Government should not be looked upon to provide direct employment. It should ensure a vibrant economy in which people are gainfully engaged.

Minimize government expenditure

- Whatever functions the government must perform, must be performed in the most efficient way, thereby reducing the cost of governance to a minimum.
- Methods of governance should be regularly reviewed, debated in public, and benchmarked with other countries and states to ensure that they are most effective and efficient.

Taxation

- There should be a single authority in each country which can levy taxes. No one else should be allowed to collect tax from any one. However, governments should be allowed to sell specific goods and services, which the citizens should be free to buy, or not to buy.
- The taxes collected by the taxation authority should be distributed among country, state and local governments as per a pre-defined agreed formula.
- The distribution of revenue from taxes should consider both the needs of governments and their contribution to revenue.
- The needs should be determined by estimating the cost of functions the governments are expected to provide.
- It will be citizens' right to get the services for which money is provided by the tax authority.
- The tax structure should be simplified. There should be only two forms of taxes. Excise for all goods and services produced in the country, and Custom for all goods and services brought in a country from outside.
- Sales tax, octroi, income tax, etc. should be abolished.
- Collection of excise and custom should be made effective by allocating more

resources which would become available because of abolition of other taxes. In addition, the penalty for tax evasion should be very heavy, and corruption should be severely dealt with.

- It may be argued that income tax is applicable to only affluent sections of population. But, the same effect can be achieved by levying more excise on items which are consumed by these sections.

Norm-based governance

- People have started thinking that what the government does for them is charity. As a result, while some people get too much, others don't get even the basic minimum.
- This tendency is clearly visible. Constituencies of VIPs, e.g. prime minister, railway minister, etc. get generous allocation, which suddenly dries up if the concerned minister no longer holds office.
- This tendency is often justified by saying that at least somewhere something is getting done. This argument shows how little we have come to expect from our governments.
- In order to ensure that justice is done to all, we must define the functions of government, the levels in each function, and the entitlement criteria.
- For example we may say that all villages with population between 100 and 1000 will be linked with brick road, while those with a population of more than 1000, will be linked with tar road.
- Such norms will ensure fairness to all.
- Along with norms, the mechanism to redress grievances arising from not following the norms should be specified. In case of deliberate victimization, those responsible should be punished.

Government as service provider

- Where the government provides service, e.g. water, health care, education, roads, etc. it should be paid by the government treasury to the concerned government department for quantity and quality of service provided. This mechanism should replace the current mechanism of budgetary allocation.
- Government departments should be run as business. Their units should earn revenue, pay bills, and make profit or loss. The employees of each individual unit should be rewarded based on the financial performance of the unit.
- Citizens should be treated as customers and given bills for the service provided, showing the amount payable by them and the subsidies.
- Where possible, the quantity and quality of service should be certified by the individual customers. Where it is not possible, it should be certified by customer bodies.
- If private parties offer to provide service at a cheaper rate, the job should be given to them.

Accountability

- Government functionaries seem to have all power but no accountability.
- For example, the encroachment department of a municipal corporation has powers to demolish an illegal building. But such powers are often exercised selectively to demolish some and leave others. The municipal corporation is not accountable to people as to why rules are being applied selectively.
- Lack of accountability breeds corruption.
- Whenever someone is given power, he should also be made accountable, preferably to the public.

- For example, if an illegal construction is found in the jurisdiction of an anti-encroachment department, its officers should be punished.

Citizens role in governance

- Governance can be much better and easier if citizens are involved in it.
- Schemes to involve citizens in governance should clearly specify how the citizens are going to contribute.
- Citizens can contribute by providing information, monitoring situations and taking action.
- The schemes involving citizens' role should be planned keeping their convenience in mind and should utilize their contribution in a most effective way.
- For example, 'Each one teach one' is not a viable and effective method; but asking a citizen to teach for two hours in a week is both convenient to the citizen and also effective in spreading education.
- Citizens should be able to see the effect of their contribution.
- One way of involving citizens would be to have a well publicised telephone number, which citizens can use to report situations such as street lights being kept on in daytime, engine of a parked bus running, leakage in a water pipe, etc. The person manning such a telephone should contact the concerned officer, who in turn should remedy the situation. Only when citizens see their involvement resulting in action, they would participate more and more.
- Another way to involve citizens would be to assign them a small neighbourhood, which they will look after to ensure its cleanliness and orderliness. If someone digs up a road in their area, they will ensure that it is mended. They will also ensure that conservancy staff keeps their area clean. There can be many ways in which citizens can help.

Innovation

- Innovation can greatly help in good governance. Chronic problems faced by government can be solved by innovative methods.
- For example, a municipal corporation should never award a contract merely for building roads. It should always be a contract to build and maintain roads. Then the contractor will do a good job in building the road, as he will have to spend less on its maintenance. This will benefit everyone.

Political system

- In many countries, political system is corrupt because politics is not an economically viable profession.
- Every profession, except politics, offers a regular income.
- It is futile to argue that MLAs and MPs are paid a salary. These are the highest levels to which people reach in politics. The corruptionalisation is completed much before such levels are reached.
- We cannot expect to have politicians for free. If we do, we pay through our nose.
- Unless politics can attract young men and women and provide them a descent secure career, it is futile to expect politicians to be honest.
- Many countries have administrative or civil services. They should also create a political service in which young men and women should be recruited in an open competition. This service should conduct competitive examinations on the lines of the administrative or civil services.
- Those qualifying in the competitive examination should be trained and given

pay and perks at par with the administrative or civil services.

- Those selected for political service, should be barred from taking up any other job, or doing any business.
- They should not be given any regular work. They should do political or social work of their choice.
- Their work should be monitored by Judiciary to ensure that they do adequate amount of work. If the quantum of their work is found inadequate, they must be withdrawn from political service and assigned administrative work. If they are found to be corrupt, their services should be terminated.
- They will contest election like any other person, and if they get elected, they will be entitled to only one salary, either of the service or of the elected office.
- Only if we can attract young students, and allow them to make an honest career in politics, can we hope to end corruption some day.

Education

- The objective of the education system is not clearly defined.
- People claim that education system has failed without even defining what education is expected to achieve.
- The objective of primary and secondary education should be to impart skills in languages and mathematics, and to create general awareness and scientific temperament.
- The objective of higher level education should be to impart skills and knowledge which a person will need in his career.
- The availability of different courses should be based on the manpower needs of a country. Consequently, in a country like India a large number of students should be educated in agriculture, horticulture, fishery, cattle rearing, etc.

- Education should not be fashionable; it should be need based and add value. It should also be easy to obtain, preferably without sacrificing the earning capacity of students.

Judiciary

- The effectiveness of judiciary determines how civilized a society is.
- The objective of judiciary is not merely to hear cases and pronounce judgement, but also to create confidence in people that if they are wronged, judiciary will help remedy the problem. It should also create the impression that no one can do wrong and get away with it.
- From the above point of view, judiciary in many countries has failed miserably.
- Failure of judiciary is the primary reason of corruption in society.
- Judiciary must work out and implement a strategy to achieve the above objectives. Judicial management should be a part of judiciary.
- Judiciary must get its workload studied to see what part of it can be eliminated by improving the rules governing those situations. For example, Judiciary handles a large number of cases related to motor vehicle accident compensation. If rules are framed to determine this compensation based on relevant factors like age, earning capacity, number of dependants, etc. insurance companies will be able to settle most of the cases, and the number of such cases going to court will drastically reduce.
- Judiciary should work on cases in a time bound manner. It should fix time norms for different types of cases and endeavour to finish a case in the allotted time.
- Judiciary can work in a time bound manner only if it has a reasonable number of cases in hearing. Therefore, new cases should go in a queue from which they should be taken for hearing.

The cases may not be taken for hearing on a first-come first-served basis, but based on some guidelines which take into account the importance and urgency of a case.

- Judiciary must augment its capacity to meet the workload. The major resource that the judiciary requires is manpower. It is ironic that even in countries with excess manpower, this function is poorly performed due to lack of resources.
- Judiciary may take help of retired citizens to augment its capacity.
- Judiciary should review its policies to ensure that they are concomitant with speedy and effective justice.

E-Governance

- Information Technology (IT) is having a major impact on governance. Many country and state governments are changing their business processes to take advantage of the benefits that IT offers. However, if we have to get the most efficient e-governance at minimum cost, we need to do two things: commonize business processes and develop soft IT infrastructure.

Commonize business processes

- At present, the same business process gets computerized by different agencies in different ways. This creates islands of information which cannot talk to each other.
- A case in point is the computerization of RTO (Regional Transport Office) operations in India. Initially, different RTOs created their systems independently, and now it is proposed to scrap all those systems and replace them with a common central system. Needless to say the expenditure in independent systems could have been avoided.

Develop soft IT infrastructure

- We are aware of the importance of IT infrastructure in the development of IT. However, we usually think only of hardware infrastructure. It is high time we start thinking of soft IT infrastructure as well, and understand its importance in the development of IT. Let me explain.
- Any computerization project requires creation of master data, e.g. citizens, business entities, real estate properties, etc. At present each system creates its own master data. In India, a citizen has one id for income tax department, another for his driving licence, and yet another for his bank. He also has an id in each of the hospitals he visits, and so on. Obviously, these systems cannot talk to each other. If each person in the world were to be given a unique person id, that id would get used by all these systems, instead of trying to create their own. This not only would save development effort but also would enable diverse systems to talk to each other.
- It is not only the persons we need to identify uniquely but also every legal entity such as businesses, each piece of land and real estate, etc. The list is endless and so are the benefits of creating such unique identities.
- Wherever possible, we should look for natural attributes in giving id to an entity. For example, we can give a number to land and real estate based on its longitude, latitude and altitude. Similarly, we can codify the primary relation between two persons as Father (F), Mother (M), Brother (B), Sister (C), Husband (H), Wife (W), Son (S) and Daughter (D). All other relations can be derived by combining these primary relations.

- It is important that standards for master data creation and codification are discussed and agreed in international bodies such as International Standards Organization. If this is not done, the world will have to incur additional cost later either in changing the systems, or in building interfaces.
- The benefits of unique identification are enormous. If each person is given a unique numeric id, we can store a telephone number and an e-mail id against him. For calling a person, you would make the call on his person id with a prefix, say 1. The prefix will indicate to the telephone system that the following number is a person id which has to be converted into telephone number. If the person's telephone number changes, only the link needs to be changed. The callers will still call the same number. Similarly, a person can be contacted on the same e-mail id, even if he changes his service provider.
- E-governance should not be creating islands of computer systems. We must have a clear vision, strategy and master plan. We must understand what to do and what not to do, if we are not to waste our precious time and resources.

Pledge your time (samay daan)

- We citizens only criticize. We do nothing concrete.
- Things are not going to change if we expect others to change them. They will change if we act to change them.
- Those who want to change the world for better should pledge 1% of their time for society. This works out to less than 15 minutes a day and less than two hours a week.
- They can spend this time to pursue the cause of their choice. They can join an NGO, or form local groups to discuss and debate what can be done.
- Even if they just meet once a week to discuss what can be done, ideas will emerge and things will begin to happen.
- Their own efforts will shape their actions and organizations.
- The key thing is commitment and doing; not idle criticism.
- Register your time pledge (samay daan) with World Integration and Improvement Initiative (agrawal.prem@gmail.com)

City without Traffic Lights

Are you fed up with traffic lights? Traffic lights at every junction. Stop, start. Stop, start. Stop, start. Do you sometimes wish that the roads of your city were like expressway. Where your car would compete with the wind and you would reach your destination in minutes.

Fortunately, this is possible. In order to use this plan, the main roads of the city need to be like a grid, as shown in Figure 1.

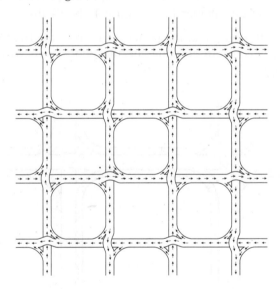

Figure 1

All roads will be one-way. When one road meets another at an intersection, there are two possibilities; you may either continue on your road, or you may turn on the other road in the direction of the traffic on that road. This is shown in Figure 2.

If you turn on the other road, there is no problem. But if you continue on your road, you will run into the traffic going straight on the other road. This is solved by a flyover or grade separator. Traffic on one road will go above the flyover, and the traffic on the other

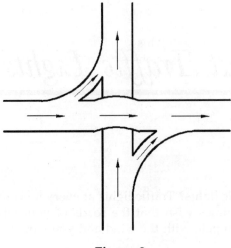

Figure 2

road will go under the flyover. This will ensure smooth flow of traffic without traffic light. This will be done on all intersections. Figure 1 shows this arrangement.

Sounds like a good idea. But how will the pedestrians cross the road? If the traffic moves at a fast speed, it will become impossible for the pedestrians to cross the road. The solution to this is in Figure 3.

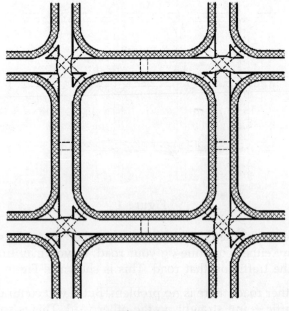

Figure 3

There will be a ring road for pedestrians and cyclists in each sector (the area bounded by main roads on all four sides). This pedestrian ring road will be connected to the pedestrian ring roads of adjoining sectors through subways. Thus, no pedestrian or cyclist will ever come on the main roads, allowing the vehicles to move freely on the main roads. Pedestrian roads will not be one-way. Pedestrians and cyclists will move on the pedestrian roads in both directions.

But how will a person take public transport, e.g. bus or taxi? This is explained in Figure 4.

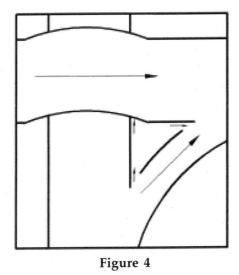

Figure 4

At each intersection, there are two triangular areas. Buses and taxis will go inside these triangular areas. There they will drop and pickup the passengers and come out of the triangle on the road they wish to take. These triangular areas will be connected to the pedestrian roads through subways.

Figure 5 shows the vehicle ring roads inside the sectors. This ring road will be connected to all the four main roads as well as to the internal roads of the sector. These roads will be two-way.

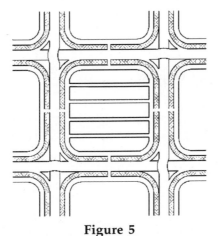

Figure 5

Figure 6 shows how the vehicles will move from one sector to another sector. Draw a horizontal and a vertical line from the source sector to the destination sector. You can do this in two ways. You can take either of these two ways to travel to your destination. You come out of the source sector taking the exit according to your travel path, move to the destination sector and enter it.

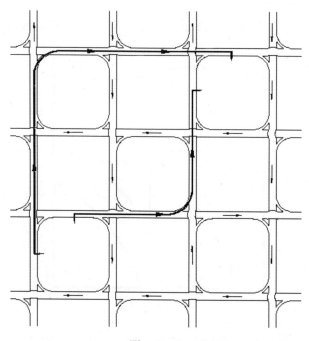

Figure 6

The main roads will be fenced on both sides so that no one can enter or exit them except through designated entry and exit roads. No pedestrian or cyclist will enter these roads. The vehicles will enter these roads, move to their destination and exit. Vehicles will neither stop on the main roads, nor be parked on it. Public transport will not stop on the main roads. There will be no shops or vendors on the main roads. Main roads will be like expressways. Enter, Move, Exit. No stoppage.

For further information, contact

P K Agrawal
L/A-4/303, Ajmera Housing Complex,
Pimpri, Pune 411018
E-mail: agrawal.prem@gmail.com
Phone: +91(20)27462635
Mobile: +919822847682

INDEX
(641–654)